EXCEPTIONAL CHILDREN

THE CENTURY PSYCHOLOGY SERIES

Richard M. Elliott, Editor

Kenneth MacCorquodale, Assistant Editor

EXCEPTIONAL CHILDREN

by

FLORENCE L. GOODENOUGH

University of Minnesota

with the assistance of

LOIS M. RYNKIEWICZ

New York

APPLETON-CENTURY-CROFTS, INC.

FOREWORD

FOR MANY YEARS I have felt that the major difficulty faced by the child who differs markedly from others of his age and sex is not so much the *fact* of difference as it is the *feeling* of difference for which the objective facts are but partially responsible. Equally and in many cases more important for the child's general adjustment and happiness is the manner in which others react to his exceptional characteristics. Too much admiration and praise may cause the bright child to regard himself as so superior to his mates that he looks upon them with covert or openly expressed scorn. He withdraws from their companionship as they from his. Thus his brilliance becomes more and more closely confined to the narrow range of abstract intelligence; it does not extend into the areas of social and emotional behavior. He does not become more tactful, more sympathetic, more self-controlled, or even more honest and trustworthy. Yet under other conditions, his superior ability might have been brought to bear upon all these and other desirable areas of conduct as well as upon academic matters.

In like manner, those who are defective in mind or body may be handicapped as much by their *attitude* toward their defect as by the defect itself. These attitudes are to a great extent determined by the behavior of those about them. Everyone, whether he is normal or defective, wishes to participate in the activities of others; he longs to be one of the crowd. Defective children have certain inescapable limitations, but most of them have further limitations imposed by their lack of confidence in their own ability to do things. Too much help, too much thoughtless sympathy forge chains for the handicapped child from which it is not easy for him to escape. Just as the social development of the intellectually superior child may be handicapped by a feeling that he is superior to others, so that of the defective child may be handicapped by the belief that he is inferior to his mates. In both cases there is a tendency for this feeling to become generalized, to extend far beyond the area of actual deviation.

Overcoming this feeling of difference thus becomes the first and most important task of those who deal with the problems of exceptional children, no matter what the nature of their deviation from the normal standard may be. Few, if any, are so exceptional that they are not on a par with others in some respects. The exceptional child must be taught to keep his resemblances in mind, to forget his differences, and to take an active part in the life and activities of his mates. Few defects are so severe that they must necessarily overshadow the entire life of those who suffer from them; nor does superiority remove the need for normal human relationships.

Rarely is it possible for us to control or modify the manner in which a child departs from the average, the degree to which he differs, or the age at which his exceptional characteristics first become manifest. Only one aspect of his developing personality lies within our control. We can see to it that the child's evaluation of and attitude toward himself do not extend in undesirable directions further than may be necessitated by the overt circumstances. As the intellectually gifted child becomes inevitably aware of his own superiority to others of his age he should, at the same time, be led to feel that superior mentality entails greater responsibility and that in itself it is of small consequence unless it is brought to bear upon personality and conduct as well as upon the acquisition of schoolroom knowledge. He must be helped to utilize his superior mentality by applying it to as many worthwhile fields as possible. The mentally defective child, on the other hand, should be led to restrict the effects of his intellectual limitations, as far as this is possible, within the range necessitated by the circumstances under which he must live. More than others, he must be guided by the judgment of others; he must live and learn by rote. But with wise guidance he can develop a pleasing personality, and if his deficiency is not too gross, he can acquire habits of conduct that are socially acceptable and pleasing.

The child who is physically disabled in some way must also be helped to restrict his loss to the area in which it occurs. Too much sympathy, which leads to self-pity, is of all things to be avoided. Emphasis should always be upon the child's abilities, not upon his handicap, and there should be liberal praise for all accomplishments. The physically handicapped child may excel in character and personality, and he may acquire much knowledge and skill within the limits set by his actual handicap.

The foregoing brief outline indicates the general theme of this volume. In it we have attempted to provide college students, teachers, parents, and others with a better idea of the nature and needs of children who differ so markedly from the generality that some special provision for their education and training is essential or at least highly desirable.

This book is the work of two persons. It was partially completed some years ago, at which time failing vision made it impossible for me to continue with it unaided. In this emergency I turned to my niece, Mrs. Lois M. Rynkiewicz, who, although a chemist, has always evinced much interest in psychology, particularly in the areas of child development and behavior. Mrs. Rynkiewicz is not only responsible, in the main, for writing Part V but has also rendered aid in editing and polishing the entire manuscript and has been completely responsible for the proofreading.

F. L. G.

CONTENTS

ILLUSTRATIONS

TABLES

PART I

General

Introduction

1

WHO IS EXCEPTIONAL?

ACCORDING TO Webster's dictionary, the word "exceptional" means "rare" or "unusual." In psychology, however, we require a more precise definition. We ask: In what respects does this person who we consider exceptional differ from his mates? Are these differences likely to be an advantage or a handicap to himself and to society? To what extent can they be modified by medical or surgical treatment or through education and training?

The statistician asks further questions. Is the difference under consideration a matter of *degree* or of *kind*? In other words, is this person regarded as exceptional because he ranks so far above or below the average of his age and sex in respect to a trait that all possess in some degree, or because he shows some characteristic or has had some kind of experience not shared by the generality? Are we dealing with a *continuous* or with a *discrete* type of function? [1] How accurately can the needed facts be determined? What conditions are most likely to give rise to erroneous diagnoses or to incorrect measurements? By what means can these conditions be minimized or avoided?

Finally, no matter what the other facts may be, we must know

---

[1] A *continuous* function is one, such as time or weight, that is theoretically capable of infinitely fine subdivision. A *discrete* function is represented by a single object, event, or *category*. In the case under consideration, the latter includes such classifications as those who have had scarlet fever and those who have not; children reared in the homes of their own parents as opposed to those brought up in institutions or foster homes, etc.

the character and limits of the group with which the individual in question is to be compared. The old saying, "In a company of the blind the one-eyed man is king" is sound psychology. A single Negro child in a school where all the other children are whites is certainly exceptional in that particular setting, but if placed in a school of colored children he would merely be one of the crowd. Before we can identify the exceptional we must know what is usual, not only within the population as a whole but within the particular group in which the subject in question chances to be placed.

Children differ in *pattern* of mental organization as well as in the degree or the type of traits which they exhibit. The bright child who seems completely unable to learn to read in spite of good vision and special training, the low-grade imbecile who can reproduce any simple melody once heard on the piano, the person with a phenomenal memory for numbers who is lacking in other gifts, and many others whose exceptional characteristics have to do with unusual *combinations* of abilities and disabilities rather than with traits that are rare when considered separately are well known to psychologists. Study of such cases has led to the formulation of many important hypotheses which will be considered in later sections of this book.

Four general classes of exceptional individuals may thus be distinguished. The first group is made up of those who display a remarkable degree of excellence or an equally noticeable deficiency in respect to some characteristic that all possess to a greater or less extent, such as intelligence, health, leadership, or emotional poise. The second group includes persons whose unusual characteristics are matters of kind rather than of degree. For example, there are the persons who have lost a limb through accident, or the children of whom an occasional report appears in the literature who were reared under highly exceptional conditions.[2] The third group is made up of persons, not necessarily rare

---

[2] The rather apocryphal cases of children reared by wolves, of which excellent critical reviews have been published by Mandelbaum and others,

when the general population is considered, who nevertheless differ markedly from the group in which they chance to be placed. The Negro child in an otherwise white school has already been mentioned. In a class of very superior children the youngster of merely average mentality may appear very dull, or, conversely, he may be regarded as a prodigy if he is enrolled in a class where all the other children are extremely backward.[3] We cannot afford to ignore such cases, for childhood experience as a social or educational misfit may and frequently does inflict lasting damage upon the personality. Within limits, the adult may choose his own environment and select his own friends. The child is pretty much at the mercy of circumstance. Finally, there are the children who attract our attention because their *pattern* of mental organization is so very different from that which experience and scientific investigation have led us to expect. The child who is exceptionally apt at learning one school subject usually learns others with at least average facility. The dullard is likely to be backward all along the line. The rule that correlation rather than compensation holds good for most mental traits has been repeatedly substantiated, but in few if any instances is this correlation so high that exceptions to the rule do not sometimes occur. So we have the dull child who exhibits some unexpected talent and the bright child whose teachers are baffled by his inability to learn some skill that the majority find easy to master.

---

would unquestionably come under this heading if the authenticity of the reports could be established. Because of their rarity and the consequent amount of attention they receive, quintuplets and quadruplets should probably be included as well. Less unusual but still sufficiently exceptional to merit consideration are children reared in adoptive homes or in institutions for dependent children.

[3] Maller found that the *average* IQ's of fifth-grade children enrolled in 273 different health areas in New York City ranged from 74 to 118. Unfortunately, Maller does not state the variability of the individual groups within the separate areas, but unless the dispersion of IQ's was much greater than has usually been found for similar populations elsewhere, a child ranking at the average level in one of the extreme groups would be so far separated from his classmates if he were transferred to a school at the other extreme that it would be very difficult for a teacher to adapt her methods of instruction to meet the situation.

In summary, then, we shall consider here the following classes of exceptional children:

1. Those who stand at the extremes of some trait which all display to a greater or lesser degree.
2. Those who exhibit some outstanding peculiarity in which the majority do not share at all or, at most, only to a minimal degree. This group is made up chiefly of the physically handicapped.
3. Children who show very unusual combinations of mental traits.

Certain types of exceptional children will here be given only incidental mention. Among these are the juvenile delinquents and other children who, though otherwise normal, show marked difficulties of personality adjustment or who constitute serious behavior problems. Institutionally reared children and those in other socially unusual situations will also receive only slight consideration. Although they have been extensively treated in the literature, there seems to be little agreement in the findings. Presumably the uncontrolled variables are both numerous and difficult to pin down. Each of these groups would require a volume by itself. Here we shall consider them only in connection with other topics.

REFERENCES [4]

ANASTASI, Anne, and FOLEY, John P., *Differential Psychology: Individual and Group Differences in Behavior* (New York, The Macmillan Company, 1949).

BAKER, Harry J., *Introduction to Exceptional Children*, rev. ed. (New York, The Macmillan Company, 1953).

BIRCH, Jack W., "Patterns of Clinical Services for Exceptional Children," *Exceptional Children*, 19 (1953), 214-222.

DRENNEN, Genevieve, comp., *Is Your Child Exceptional ... different from other children in speech, hearing, vision, social, mental or in*

[4] Since 1933 the *Elementary School Journal* has published an annual series of briefly annotated bibliographies entitled "Selected References from the Literature on Exceptional Children." These references are classified into several main groups and cover most of the important books and articles dealing with exceptional children that have been published in the English language. The foreign language literature is less completely handled. For additional source material the bibliographies found in many of the references cited here may be consulted. Note also the *Journal of Exceptional Children*, which is the official publication of the International Council for Exceptional Children.

physical development (Springfield, Ill., Illinois Congress of Parents and Teachers and Division of Education for Exceptional Children, Office of Superintendent of Public Instruction, 1950).

GARRISON, Karl C., *The Psychology of Exceptional Children*, rev. ed. (New York, The Ronald Press Company, 1950).

GESELL, Arnold, *Exceptional Children and Public School Policy* (New Haven, Yale University Press, 1921).

HECK, A. O., *The Education of Exceptional Children* (New York, McGraw-Hill Book Company, 1940).

HODGES, Margaret B., ed., *Social Work Yearbook* (New York, Russell Sage Foundation, 1949).

HOLLINGWORTH, Leta S., TERMAN, Lewis M., and ODEN, Melita H., "The Significance of Deviates," *Thirty-ninth Yearbook of the National Society for the Study of Education* (Chicago, University of Chicago Press, 1940), Pt. 1.

INGRAM, Christine P., and KVARACEUS, William C., "Selected References from the Literature on Exceptional Children," *Elementary School Journal*, 52 (1952), 471-482.

JENKS, William F., ed., *Special Education of the Exceptional Child* (Washington, D. C., The Catholic University of America Press, 1953).

MALLER, J. B., "Vital Indices and Their Relation to Psychological and Social Factors," *Human Biology*, 5 (1933), 94-121.

MANDELBAUM, David G., "Wolf-child Histories from India," *Journal of Social Psychology*, 17 (1943), 25-44.

MARTENS, Elise H., "Some Highlights in 1947 Legislation for Exceptional Children and Youth," *Journal of Exceptional Children*, 14 (1948), 203-206, 224.

National Society for the Study of Education, *Forty-ninth Yearbook: The Education of Exceptional Children* (Chicago, University of Chicago Press, 1950), Pt. 2.

Newark, New Jersey, Board of Education, *Functions and Services of Special Education in the Newark Public Schools; A Handbook of Information on the Schools, Classes, and Services for Exceptional Children in the Department of Special Education, Newark, N.J.* (Newark, Board of Education, 1949).

REED, Homer B., "The Number of Exceptional Children in Kansas," *Transactions of the Kansas Academy of Sciences*, 49 (1946), 333-349.

SCHEIDEMANN, Norma V., *The Psychology of Exceptional Children* (Boston, Houghton Mifflin Company, 1937), 2 vols.

SEGERS, J. E., *Psychologie de l'enfant normal et anormal d'apres Dr. O. Decroly* (Brussels, R. Stoops, 1948).

TYLER, Leona E., *The Psychology of Human Differences,* 2d ed. (New York, Appleton-Century-Crofts, Inc., 1956).

Woods Schools Child Research Clinic, "The Exceptional Child in Infancy and Early Childhood," *Proceedings Conference Child Research Clinic of the Woods School* (1950).

Dimensions of the Personality 2

E. G. BORING, in *The Physical Dimensions of Consciousness,*
describes a system for the analysis and description of mental
phenomena that, in an analogous sense at least, provides a useful
framework into which the basic information required to describe
the characteristics of exceptional children can be fitted. In utilizing Boring's scheme for this purpose, some liberties will of necessity be taken. In his discussion of conscious phenomena, Boring
depends largely upon introspection, whereas most of the facts
with which we shall be concerned are derived from observation
and measurement by an outsider. Boring uses the term *quality* to
denote the first of his four dimensions, inasmuch as the sensations
derived through the various sense modalities, when introspectively
considered, seem to differ from each other in a qualitative rather
than in a quantitative way. Since we shall be concerned with variations in the more complex attributes of behavior as well as with
those having to do with sensory perception, we shall use the term
mode [1] rather than Boring's *quality* as a more accurate designation
of the first of the four dimensions to be considered.

THE FIRST DIMENSION: MODE

That people differ from each other in a wide variety of ways is
a truism. Many of these modes of variation have little significance
for the generality of people although it is true that they contrib-

[1] Warren defines *mode* as follows: Any general class of characteristics or
attributes of the data under consideration.

9

ute their share to the well-nigh infinitely great series of small differences that render each individual a unique personality. It is unlikely that the modes we have chosen for discussion in this book include all or even all the most important of those which, in their extreme forms, render the individual who manifests them exceptional. Some have been intentionally omitted, not because of failure to realize their importance, but because so little information of scientific worth is available concerning them. Much, for example, has been written about the neurotic child, the child who is emotionally unstable. But what of the child who stands at the opposite extreme of the scale of neuroticism? It is reasonable to suppose that there are children as far removed from the average in the non-neurotic as in the neurotic direction, but we are not even agreed about methods of identifying them, much less as to the kind of education and training best suited to insure their optimal development. Yet it may be just here that the difference between those who might and those who do achieve greatly is often to be found. This is certainly suggested by Terman's study of the relative accomplishments and behavior as young adults of his group of over 1500 subjects who, as children, showed very remarkable intellectual endowment. Although very few of the group had become actually neurotic or psychotic at the time of the follow-up, when the majority of them were in their thirties, all the available data indicate far better emotional poise and greater stability of behavior on the part of the highly successful than for those of mediocre accomplishment. Examination of their childhood records showed that this difference had been apparent from a very early age.

Although there has been a tremendous amount of study of practically all types of poorly adjusted children, almost no effort has been made to examine the background and developmental histories of those whose personal-social adjustment is exceptionally good, or even to determine in what such "goodness" consists. So obsessed have we been with avoiding the wrong that we have given little thought to ascertaining what is right and still less to methods of achieving it. Certainly more studies of the superior deviate, and particularly of those who excel along personal-social lines, are greatly to be desired.

There are, of course, areas in which only the handicapped are properly considered exceptional. Children who have lost a limb through accident, epileptic children, or those suffering from the aftereffects of *encephalitis lethargica* do not mark the extremes of normal distributions but are the victims of disasters that fortunately are rare. Although it is conceivable that opposite extremes may exist in the form of children who are remarkably resistant to such hazards, no one as yet has succeeded in identifying them.[2]

There are also areas or modes in which extreme deviations are known to exist, but these extremes hardly seem to be of enough importance to warrant independent study. The length of the eyelashes may contribute to feminine pulchritude, their absence may be a symptom of dermal or ocular disease, but although marked individual differences unquestionably exist in this and many other similar attributes both of structure and function, we have not thought them of sufficient consequence, at least when considered by themselves, to merit special discussion here. Still other forms of conduct or ability, although frequently discussed, may in reality be considered superficial rather than fundamental. R. B. Cattell's distinction between "source traits" and "surface traits" is pertinent in this connection.

We shall therefore confine our attention in this book to children who may be considered exceptional in respect to the following modes: both the upper and the lower extreme of intelligence; the physically handicapped; children who manifest marked special talents in some branch of the arts or sciences; those who show serious disturbances of speech or who, in spite of good general intelligence, find it extremely difficult to acquire some special edu-

[2] For example, the many studies of accident proneness have shown that some people, even those engaged in similar occupations and subject to the same external hazards, nevertheless suffer so many more injuries than others that the differences can hardly be attributed to chance. Similar differences have been found, even among young children. Nevertheless the vast majority of persons go through life without ever experiencing an accident that results in a lasting handicap. For this reason the selection of the least accident-prone is a far more difficult task than the selection of the most accident-prone.

cational skill, such as reading. As was previously noted, juvenile delinquency, although recognized as an extremely significant mode of child behavior, is so many faceted a topic that no comprehensive account of the work done in this field could be encompassed within the limits of this volume. Its discussion will therefore be left to others except for such references as are required in connection with other topics.

During recent years, considerable attention has been focussed upon the question of childhood psychosis. In 1941, Bradley set the pace for these investigations by his well-known work on schizophrenia in childhood; a recent number of *The Nervous Child* is devoted in its entirety to articles dealing with suspected cases of childhood psychosis of the manic-depressive type. Nevertheless, there is much disagreement both among psychiatrists and among psychologists concerning its nature and even with regard to the very existence of other psychoses in childhood. The interested reader is referred to the chapter by Benda in the 1954 revision of the *Manual of Child Psychology*, for an excellent discussion of this subject.

THE SECOND DIMENSION: INTENSITY

Whatever the mode of variation may be, differences in its degree or intensity are readily observed. Poliomyelitis may leave one child without observable damage, a second slightly crippled, a third able to walk only with the aid of braces and a crutch, a fourth helpless. John, age five, is as tall as the average child of six, but William, who is the same age, overtops the typical nine-year-old. Sarah, whose IQ is 85, manages to struggle along in the regular grades, though her marks are usually poor; but her sister Jane, whose IQ is 60, attends a special class for mentally retarded children, and Anna, a neighbor's child with an IQ of 25, has to be sent to an institution.

No matter what the asset or handicap may be, the determination of its level or intensity is basic to all further inquiry, although such information is not always easy to state in quantitative terms. A major aspect of the advancement of science has been the gradual shift from descriptive to numerical statements. Narrative is giving place to measurement. We also ask how exact such measurements are likely to be and by what means errors in measurement can be minimized. In what terms should the measures be expressed and what facts are necessary for their correct interpretation? All these and many other related points are statistical questions which fall outside the scope of this book, though a few of the more general or most frequently overlooked of these considerations will be given brief mention in Chapters 3 and 4.

THE THIRD DIMENSION: EXTENSITY

Not only do individuals differ with respect to the mode and the intensity of their deviations from the characteristics usual for the group to which they belong. They also differ in respect to the extent to which such deviations as they may show affect other aspects of their personality.

Some modes of behavior or ability appear to be highly specific, extending over only a very narrow range of the personality. Even extreme deviates do not necessarily differ greatly from the generality of people in fields outside the range of their specialized talent or defect. Not all gifted artists are unusual in other respects, popular belief to the contrary. One may be so lacking in musical sensitivity as to be practically tone deaf, although otherwise entirely normal. But intelligence is another matter. It is true that not all those of exceptional mental endowment attain positions of eminence. Not all have attractive personalities. Nevertheless the chances that a person of superior intelligence will also be found superior in other respects are greater than they would be if he were stupid. At the other intellectual extreme the situation is more definite. The individual whose intelligence is exceptionally high may occasionally show specialized deficiencies, but when intelligence is exceptionally low specialized talents are extremely rare.[3]

Not only do the various modes of ability and behavior differ

[3] See the discussion of *idiots savants* in Chapter 19.

with respect to their breadth, the extent to which they tend to involve the personality as a whole. People also differ in respect to the degree with which they succeed in confining the effect of their deficiencies or handicaps within a comparatively narrow range and extending their abilities into as many areas as possible. Some of the most striking examples of these differences are to be found among the physically handicapped. Of two persons equally severely crippled, one is largely or wholly self-supporting; the other makes no effort to find work that he can do but depends upon the kindness of relatives or upon charity. One is cheerful and jocular, interested in events and in people; the other is moody and introspective, constantly complaining of the hardships of his lot. Although the intensity of a given mode of deviation is in many cases beyond the control of the deviate and of those responsible for his care and upbringing, something, at least, can usually be accomplished in the way of modifying its extensity. Talents should be made to serve as wide an area of the personality as possible; defects should be confined within their own narrow range.

That every effort should be made to improve the actual status of the handicapped child goes without saying. The physically handicapped should be given the benefit of the best medical and surgical aid that is available; the mentally handicapped should have educational opportunities suited to their capacities and be trained in habits of industry and self-help. All this has been said many times, but the major aim in training the handicapped child, regardless of the nature of his defect, has not always been clearly grasped even by those engaged in the work. Apart from actual corrective measures, this aim can be phrased as follows: *The major objective in the training and education of inferior deviates of all classes, both mental and physical, is to reduce the extensity of the defect to the smallest possible range.* Just as the quarantine officer tries to confine an epidemic to the region in which it originated or as the physician who treats an infected wound is concerned with preventing the trouble from affecting the entire bodily system, so those who are responsible for the care and training of defective children should devote a major share of their attention to confining the defect to its own specialized area as far as this is possible. The child who is crippled in body need not be crippled in mind or personality; the mentally defective child can be docile, friendly, and helpful. The intercorrelations of abilities and conduct cannot always be eliminated completely, but they can be materially reduced if thought and attention are directed to that end.

In the case of the superior deviate, the aim should be the opposite of that which we have just discussed. Again, no matter whether the mode of superiority is physical or mental, the child who exhibits it should be helped to bring his talent to bear upon as many aspects of his personality as possible—he should *increase* its extensity. The training of talented children is often too highly specialized; it makes for eccentricity rather than for an all-round personality. Limitation of defect but extension of talent should be the goal in all cases, particularly in the case of exceptional children.

THE FOURTH DIMENSION: PROTENSITY

In every deviate condition, the time factor must be considered. How long has the condition existed? What was the subject's age at the time it originated? What can be inferred with respect to its most probable duration?

The importance of these questions needs little discussion. The child who becomes deafened at the age of ten is in a very different position from the one who has been deaf from birth. The speech habits of the former have become well established; he knows the usefulness of language and so is ready to begin lipreading without having to find out what it is all about. In all probability he has already learned to read and can bring this accomplishment to bear upon learning the new skill. The child who is congenitally deaf lacks these advantages. Not only must he learn oral speech by a slow and laborious process in which he is denied the advantage of hearing his own voice and thus confirming the correctness of the sounds he makes by comparison with those made by others; the very concept of oral communication is strange to him. Certainly in these cases the time factor—the *pro-tensity*—is of tremendous importance.

Time also enters in when questions of prognosis are involved. That which can be accomplished with relative ease at one age may become difficult at another, for growth proceeds inexorably and ceases when maturity is reached. When asked, Can this condition be helped? the answer is often, Yes, if treatment is begun early enough. Correction of a physical ailment or straightening out of a warped personality often depends upon the stage which the difficulty has already reached at the time.

A similar condition exists in the case of highly talented children. For the best results, training should be begun early, and this means that talent should be discovered early. The identification of young gifted children is a task that warrants more attention than it has thus far received.

MEASUREMENT AND CLASSIFICATION OF THE EXTREME DEVIATE

Each of the four dimensions of the personality discussed in this chapter presents its own problems of measurement. Although in many instances, particularly in cases of physical handicap, the *mode* may be self-evident, this is by no means invariably true. The child with defective hearing or vision who is erroneously thought to be feeble-minded, the exceptionally bright youngster who, because of boredom, gets into such mischief in school that he is regarded as a potential delinquent by his teachers, or the truly feeble-minded child who is thought to be too lazy to study are well known to every clinician. Even in the scientific literature of today, errors of classification are common. The child suffering from the athetoid type of cerebral birth palsy is no more like the child who has lost a limb in an automobile accident than the latter is like one who has been blinded, yet all types are frequently lumped together under the single heading of "crippled children." Two or more modes may coexist in the same child; in these cases one condition may obscure the discovery of the other.

The measurement of *intensity* is usually a problem for the expert in the field in question. Statistical questions are also involved, a few of which will be considered in Chapters 3 and 4.

From the statistical point of view, *extensity* is primarily a question of correlation and, particularly, of the intercorrelation of traits. But it is more than this. As usually considered, correlations have to do with groups, whereas extensity, as we have discussed it, is primarily an affair of the individual.

In the measurement of *protensity*, the chief questions center about the accuracy of report and upon the relationship between present condition and progress under various types of defined situations or methods of treatment.

No single person can possibly be an expert along all the lines necessary for the diagnosis and treatment of all classes of extreme deviates. Nevertheless, the fact remains that unless someone among those whom the child is likely to meet in the course of his everyday life has enough information regarding a wide variety of human differences and their modes of expression to lead to the formation of tentative opinions concerning him, the likelihood that the exceptional child will ever receive the type of expert guidance and treatment of which he stands in need is rather small. Parents and teachers, in particular, should have a broader knowledge of these matters than the majority of them possess. Psychologists and physicians alike should be better informed about those children who deviate from the average in areas outside their own specialized fields of knowledge. The physician should know enough psychology to realize when a child is in need of the kind of psychological help that he is not himself equipped to give; the psychologist should recognize the child who is in need of medical advice. Better co-operation among those who deal with him would do much to prevent the handicapped child from becoming a burden upon society and to enable the superior one to make the most of his unusual gifts.

REFERENCES

BENDA, Clemens E., "Psychopathology of Childhood" in *Manual of Child Psychology*, 2d. ed. (New York, John Wiley and Sons, Inc., 1954).

BLUMBERG, Marvin L., "The Psychodynamics of Child Behavior," *New York State Medical Journal*, 49 (1949), 542-545.

BORING, Edwin G., *The Physical Dimensions of Consciousness* (New York, Appleton-Century Crofts, Inc., 1933).

BRADLEY, Charles, *Schizophrenia in Childhood* (New York, The Macmillan Company, 1941).

CATTELL, Raymond B., *Description and Measurement of Personality* (Yonkers, N. Y., World Book Company, 1946).

FULLER, Elizabeth M., "Injury-prone Children," *American Journal of Orthopsychiatry*, 18 (1948), 708-723.

GOODENOUGH, Florence L., *Mental Testing: Its History, Principles, and Applications* (New York, Rinehart and Company, Inc., 1949).

TERMAN, Lewis M., and ODEN, Melita H., *Genetic Studies of Genius: The Gifted Child Grows Up* (Stanford, Cal., Stanford University Press, 1947), Vol. 4.

TILLMAN, W. A., and HOBBS, G. E., "The Accident-prone Automobile Driver: A Study of the Psychiatric and Social Background," *American Journal of Psychiatry*, 106 (1949), 321-331.

WARREN, Howard C., ed., *Dictionary of Psychology* (Boston, Houghton Mifflin Company, 1934).

Special Needs of Exceptional Children

3

INDIVIDUALIZED INSTRUCTION AND TRAINING

UNTIL COMPARATIVELY recent years, all children were expected to meet certain inflexible standards set by the school authorities. The child was to be fitted to the school, not the school to the child. It was found, however, that some children could not and did not conform to these standards. In some cases, physical defects made the usual type of classroom instruction obviously unsuitable. With the advent of mental testing, individual differences in the ability to learn were recognized as never before.

The modern educator pays lip service, at least, to the principle that the school should be fitted to the child, not the child to the school, but it has been tacitly assumed by many that the fundamental needs of all children are much the same. To some extent this is true. All children need food and shelter, love, and a feeling of security. But children differ, and as their divergence from the group average increases their need for specialized treatment increases in like ratio. Just as the diabetic child requires a special dietary regimen if his health is to be maintained at the highest level possible for him, so other children of unusual mental or physical make-up need a type of education and training that is specifically adapted to the requirements of their exceptional characteristics. The exceptional child must have exceptional treatment. His education must be individualized.

What is meant by individualized education? It is education that begins where the child is and proceeds according to a definite plan that takes account of his potentialities for the future. It permits progress by rapid or by slow stages according to his abilities. It seeks to discover and to develop his talents and to minimize the effect of his deficiencies. In short, it is education that is primarily concerned with obtaining the best possible results for each individual rather than aiming at the highest average for the group to which he belongs. The majority of children whose divergences from each other and from the group average are not marked are usually able to profit fairly well from the conventional methods of mass education, though it is unquestionably true that some individualization of instruction is desirable for all. But for those who diverge so markedly from the generality as to be classed as "exceptional" according to the definitions given in Chapter 1, the usual methods of classroom instruction are not likely to be wholly suitable. Neither the rate at which new material is presented nor the methods of teaching are likely to fit their needs. In the larger towns and cities the provision of suitable training for exceptional children is simplified to some extent by the establishment of special classes for those of a given type, but in the smaller communities this may not be feasible. More detailed discussion of these matters will be found in later sections of this book.

MAINTENANCE OF A FEELING OF SECURITY

Early in life the extreme deviate begins to realize that he is not quite like other children and that in certain respects he does not conform to the standards set for him. He becomes conscious of covert glances, of whispered remarks. At first these things are not understood. They are vaguely disturbing but have no specific reference. Before many years have passed, however, these inchoate feelings of "being different" take on a more definite form. The handicapped child sees other children engaging in activities in which he cannot share. The brilliant child who tries vainly to persuade his companions to join in the intellectual pursuits he finds so engrossing is likely to be openly designated "queer" and to find himself left out in the cold. Such experiences are as puzzling as they are discouraging to a sensitive child. He is unable to maintain a foothold in a world so alien. He feels insecure, self-conscious in the presence of others, uncertain of himself or of what is expected of him. The urge to *belong*, to be one of the group, is one of the most basic of all human desires, regardless of the abilities or inabilities of the individual. The child who becomes oversensitized to the fact that he is not entirely like the other children of his age finds it hard to satisfy this urge, no matter whether the deviation is positive or negative in sign.[1] The solution is easy to state but not

[1] A letter from a lad whose Stanford Binet IQ in childhood was close to 200 is a case in point. At the time of writing he was just completing his junior year in a college of very high academic standing. He was expecting shortly to be drafted into the armed services, a prospect that he faced with grim resignation and utter distaste. His major source of unhappiness and bewilderment, however, was his inability to find a place for himself in a world of people by whom he was not understood and whom he could not understand. Unlike many highly gifted youngsters he had never been able to create a world of his own into which he could retreat and there find quiet happiness. He loved reading, but books could not satisfy his desire for human companionship. He wanted—to quote his own pathetic phrase—"to get close to somebody" and wondered vaguely if marriage might provide a solution. (Apparently he had no specific marital plans).

His social isolation dated from his early years. It is not easy for a six-year-old whose favorite game is chess, whose reading ability is above the standard for the eighth grade, and whose reading interests run the gamut of a home library of several thousand volumes to take a strong interest in tick-tack-toe or in the adventures of the Little Red Hen. Moreover, in spite of repeated cautions, his teachers found it hard to resist the temptation to exhibit his accomplishments to visitors, a practice that by no means endeared him to his classmates. His social difficulties were increased by his motor awkwardness. He was never good at games. He was shorter than the average child of his age with a chubby body and short, pudgy arms and legs. On the playground his clumsy efforts at participation were received with derisive howls and he was soon excluded from the group.

In her book entitled *Children Who Test above 180 IQ*, Hollingworth took the position that so great a divergence from the abilities and interests typical of the generality is well-nigh incompatible with normal social adjustment. That during childhood and youth when the social environment is for the most part regulated by others, such adjustment is at least very difficult, is supported not only by the cases reported by her but by the majority of those described in the literature. It may well be, however, that after the school and college years have passed and the individual is free to choose his own friends from whatever sources he will, a more happy state of affairs may ensue. It is unfortunate that so few cases of this type have been followed beyond the age of late adolescence. Perhaps when Volume 5 of Terman's *Genetic Studies of Genius*, which is now in preparation, becomes available a more exact answer to this question may be possible.

always easy to accomplish. The exceptional child, no matter what his mode of divergence may be, should learn to take his differences in his stride, recognizing their existence but not regarding them as the major determining factors in his life. This can best be accomplished through preoccupation with matters outside himself. The child who has many engrossing outside interests will have little time to brood over his own difficulties.

Self-confidence, curiously enough, is rooted in forgetfulness of self. It is the antithesis of self-consciousness. The latter arises from a feeling of insecurity. The child is uncertain of other people's attitudes toward him and of his own ability to conform to their standards. As a result his attention is drawn away from the task in hand and becomes focused upon himself. The physically handicapped child is made more keenly aware of his defects and this feeling is likely to be projected upon other people who, he believes, are as conscious of his condition and hate it as much as he himself does. From this stage it is but a short step to the belief that *he* is hated or despised. The exceptional child regardless of class is particularly subject to the insecurity that comes from *awareness of being different.* This awareness leads to an exaggerated view of the attitude that other people take toward him. Small successes and failures become highly personalized affairs in which actual accomplishment is subordinate to the child's self-feeling. It is not, "I did that well (or poorly)," but "What will other people think of me? Did I do as well as they expected?"

The infant's security is vested in those who care for him. As he grows older and begins to gain some independence of movement his confidence is extended to the material objects in his environment. Little by little he learns the rules. This chair is stable, he can pull himself to a stand by it; that one rocks at a touch and cannot be depended on. If left to himself, however, he soon learns to master the rocking chair and finds it a far more interesting object than the dependable but stodgy armchair. But if an anxious mother, fearful of bumps, pulls him away with nervous warnings which, though he does not understand he nevertheless senses as having an unpleasant connotation, his new-found self-confidence is weakened. He no longer feels so sure that the world is a secure place to be explored at will. Of course, a single experience of this kind is not enough to overcome the baby's natural instinct to investigate his surroundings. No one who has witnessed the determined efforts of the little crawler to return to the point from which he has just been forcibly removed will question the last statement. But that parental fearfulness and anxieties are in time absorbed by the child, who thereby loses much of his sense of security and confidence in the world and in his own power to cope with it, is a matter of common observation as well as of scientific experimentation and record.

The child who is mentally or physically handicapped faces a type of insecurity that his more favorably endowed companions do not experience. Sooner or later he is brought to grips with the stern fact that many of the pleasures which others enjoy can never be his. Upon the manner in which he accepts his limitations much of his later happiness will depend. As was pointed out in the last chapter, the basic question is this: Does he recognize the inevitable bounds of his defect and having done so turn his attention to activities and interests outside this limited area and make for himself a useful and happy life, or does he allow his inabilities to loom so large in his mental vision as to obscure his abilities?

It is here that the overwhelming importance of early training in the life of the handicapped child is most evident. The crippled child, the blind, or the deaf quicken our pity to a point at which its overt expression seems almost inevitable. But the handicapped child does not need verbal sympathy which calls his attention even more forcibly than before to the fact that he is not like other children and thus tends to increase his handicap by stimulating self-pity. Self-confidence is increased by finding that he can do many things for himself. Too much waiting on prolongs the helplessness of infancy and interferes with the normal development of such abilities as the child may possess. The popular phrase, "killed by kindness," is more truthful than humorous in such cases.

The normal progress of the child's sense of security is from almost complete external to almost complete internal reference;

from dependence on others to reliance upon the self. For the child whose mind and body are normal this change is usually accomplished without too great difficulty, though it is true that some find it a rather serious problem. The handicapped child, however, finds his way barred by both physical and social obstacles. There is the inescapable fact that certain things are truly beyond his powers.[2] If his defect is conspicuous, he must learn to ignore the curious glances of strangers, the well-meant but still embarrassing questions and the sympathetic remarks of friends and relatives, and the thoughtless jests of other children. Often he must learn to bear pain without complaining.

These things are not easy but they must be accomplished if the child's personality is not to be crippled along with his body. To this end, parents and teachers should be constantly on the alert to protect the child from the kindness that cripples and to help him to find ways of utilizing his undamaged capacities as compensating mechanisms to minimize the effect of his defect. Complete security in his own right may be impossible for the severely handicapped child, but if he is given sufficient guidance and encouragement, he can as a rule pass much further along the road to independence and self-reliance than would otherwise be the case.[3]

---

[2] It is of course assumed that all known means of correction by medical and surgical treatment have been used.

[3] Helen Keller is a classical example of what may be accomplished under extreme conditions of sense deprivation, but there are many people of whom the world has never heard who likewise perform remarkable feats of compensation for a physical defect. A young woman of my acquaintance is an example. A few years after her marriage, an accident completely destroyed her vision. Little money was available for household help and such as could be obtained proved inefficient. In this emergency the woman decided that she would have to carry on by herself. She learned to find her way about the house, to make beds, sweep, and dust. Gradually she took on more complicated tasks. She learned to prepare vegetables, to cook and bake, to wash and iron. Both she and her husband had always wanted children and as her efficiency improved the woman decided that she could undertake the care of one. In the course of time a baby was born, to the great delight of both parents. Except that she was unable to prepare its formulas, since she could not see the measurements, the mother took practically all the care of the child, and few children of sighted mothers receive more scrupulous attention. This is but one instance of many that might be cited in which the determination

EARLY DIAGNOSIS AND TREATMENT

Many defects can be remedied wholly or in part if they are discovered early enough. Growth processes are inexorable with definite limitations of time and sequence. Attitudes and habits are more flexible, but they, too, become less plastic with the passage of time and the added practice that usually goes with it. That which may be accomplished early in life becomes more difficult and sometimes is impossible to achieve later on. The child who is denied early diagnosis and treatment is thus robbed of much of the happiness he might otherwise enjoy, and society is likewise deprived of the contribution that he was potentially capable of making.

The importance of early diagnosis and treatment of physical handicaps is self-evident, but the equal if not greater need for early identification of those who stand at the extremes of the intellectual distribution is less generally recognized. Yet it is they who constitute on the one hand the greatest hope for the betterment of social conditions and the advancement of scientific knowledge, and on the other hand one of society's heaviest burdens. That many inferior deviates can be taught to become useful citizens has been amply demonstrated. That most industrial concerns number among their employees some persons whose mentality, when tested, proves to be far below the standard thought by many to be essential for independent self-management has been repeatedly shown. These persons carry on simple routine tasks faithfully and dependably. But there are others of similar mentality of whom this cannot be said. They are careless both with respect to property and with respect to their own safety. They tire of their jobs and quit without notice. They demand constant attention and interfere with the work of others. Unquestionably not all such behavior can be attributed to lack of intelligence, for it is shown at all levels of intelligence, but it is more common

---

to lead a normal life has reduced the effect of what would otherwise have been a crippling handicap to the lowest possible terms.

among the backward. We should be going far beyond available evidence if we were to assume that suitable training begun at an early age is the sole factor necessary to bring all cases of a given level of intellectual backwardness to the degree of industrial usefulness and personal dependability that some display. But there is plenty of evidence that early training is important, even though it may not be the sole determining factor. Both the Gluecks and Merrill found it plays a considerable role in the prevention of recidivism in young delinquents. Practically all studies of memorizing and acquisition of skill have shown a marked relation between the amount of overlearning (that is, between the amount of practice after a perfect performance has been achieved) and retention. The child who acquires certain habits of behavior at an early age has a longer time to practice them than the one who does not acquire them until he is older. This is as true of good habits as it is of bad habits, and it applies equally to his attitudes, his beliefs, his outlook upon the world in relation to himself.

We have said before that exceptional children require exceptional training. The earlier this training is begun, the more effective it is likely to be. Early specialized training, however, implies early identification together with diagnostic studies of their abilities and deficiencies, their interests and aptitudes, their potentialities for the future. A complete account of the methods used in making such analyses would be far beyond the scope of this book, but a very brief overview of some of the more important procedures together with a few cautions regarding some of the common errors in diagnosis and in the interpretation of research findings will be presented in the next two chapters.

REFERENCES

BENDER, Lauretta, "Neuropsychiatric Contributions to the Mental Hygiene Problems of the Exceptional Child," *Mental Hygiene*, 26 (1942), 617-630.

BLANTON, Smiley, and BLANTON, Margaret G., *Child Guidance* (New York, Appleton-Century-Crofts, Inc., 1927).

CARRINGTON, Evelyn M., *The Exceptional Child: His Nature and His Needs* (Denton, Tex., Texas State College for Women, 1951), College Bulletin No. 394.

CRUICKSHANK, William M., and DOLPHIN, Jane E., "The Emotional Needs of Crippled and Non-crippled Children," *Journal of Exceptional Children*, 16 (1949), 33-38.

DUNLAP, Knight, *Habits: Their Making and Unmaking* (New York, Horace Liveright, 1932).

GLUECK, Sheldon, and GLUECK, Eleanor, *One Thousand Juvenile Delinquents: Their Treatment by Court and Clinic* (Cambridge, Mass., Harvard University Press, 1934).

HOLLINGWORTH, Leta S., *Children Who Test above 180 IQ (Stanford Binet): Origin and Development* (Yonkers, N. Y., World Book Company, 1942).

MERRILL, Maud A., *Problems of Child Delinquency* (Boston, Houghton Mifflin Company, 1947).

National Society for the Study of Education, *Forty-ninth Yearbook: The Education of Exceptional Children* (Chicago, University of Chicago Press, 1950), Pt. 2.

Methods of Classification and Measurement

4

AMONG CERTAIN types of exceptional children, particularly those with physical handicaps, the main facts are immediately apparent to the eye. Elaborate study is not required to see that a child has but one arm, that his face is disfigured by a purple birthmark, or that his hair, eyes, and skin are so lacking in pigmentation that he is classed as an albino. With only slight further acquaintance one may discover that he is deaf or blind or grossly mentally defective. The person with specialized training or experience will note other facts on the basis of unaided observation. He will see that this child is a mongolian, that one suffering from the athetoid type of cerebral birth palsy, that other a microcephalic. After somewhat longer acquaintance, even the layman will discover the child who stutters or who shows other marked forms of speech defect; he will identify some but not all of the hard of hearing and the less severe cases of mental defect. However, in his judgments of the relative mental level of the children with whom he is acquainted he is likely to be misled by such extraneous factors as physical size, personal attractiveness, and the like.

Although direct observation is often sufficient to permit gross classification, more exact information is needed before remedial measures can be intelligently applied or sound provision made for education and training. No special training is required to see that a child has lost a leg, but expert medical and surgical examination of the remaining nerves and muscles is necessary before a satisfactory artificial limb can be fitted. Likewise, successful training of a handicapped child demands thorough appraisal not only of his deficiency but of his abilities in general. Teachers must be able to utilize such an appraisal wisely in planning the training of each child under their care. Classification is only the first step. Education and training are still to be accomplished, and for success in these thorough diagnosis is needed.

So far we have been speaking of unsystematized and inexpert observation—the kind that involves nothing more than looking at a child and drawing certain rather obvious conclusions about him. Not all observation is of this kind, even when no other instrument than the unaided human eye is employed. The trained physician or psychologist notes many things that the layman overlooks; he draws conclusions from facts that to the ordinary person seem wholly trivial. The difference between expert and untrained observation is as great as that between the surgeon's scalpel and the stone axe of the savage; the two hardly belong in the same category. The expert knows what to look for; he dissects the complicated tissue of significant and nonsignificant behavior with the keen discrimination born of knowledge and experience. Lacking this training, the tyro sees everything and nothing. He cannot put his facts together to form meaningful patterns.

Not only does the trained expert observe behavior as it spontaneously occurs. He purposely sets the stage in such a way as to elicit the forms of behavior in which he is especially interested. When a series of situations has been carefully worked out with respect to procedure and timing so that the same methods are used by different examiners these are generally called *tests*. Most psychologists and most physicians also make use of incompletely standardized procedures for stimulating the kind of behavior they wish to observe.

A number of special methods for observing and recording behavior of a given type have been devised by psychologists and sociologists. There is the *time sampling method*, in which the unit is a measured short interval of time and the child's score is the percentage of a fairly large number of such time intervals during which the behavior in question was noted. Children are observed in rotation, as a rule only once a day. If a sufficiently large number of these short observations are made and recorded for each of a group of children, those who stand at the extremes are readily identified. *Episode sampling,* in which the actual number of occurrences of certain forms of behavior observed during measured but longer periods of time becomes the score for each child, has also been used. As with time sampling, the method lends itself well to the selection of extreme cases within a group if enough material is collected to lend stability to the data. The great difficulty with all methods of this kind is the question of standards that are valid for more than just the small local group observed. Because no attempt is made to control the situation, variations from one group to another are almost inevitable. Murphy, for example, found that instances of "unsympathetic behavior" were about six times as frequent in one of the two nursery schools she observed as in the other. She ascribed the difference to the general setting, to the *esprit de corps,* rather than to differences among the children. Others have obtained similar results for various forms of child behavior. The use of children's play groups, where the amount of adult supervision is reduced to a minimum, has been much advocated by some because of the so-called "naturalness" of the behavior displayed. But all behavior is "natural" for a given combination of internal and external conditions; the real problem is to know what those conditions are. If the interest centers about only a certain group of children, then such methods as time or episode sampling are useful; but the standards obtained for one such group cannot safely be used for another because of the many uncontrolled variables in the two situations. Moreover, all such procedures are time consuming and therefore costly, since when no attempt is made to direct the subject's behavior along the line of the observer's interest, a very large proportion of his activities will have no direct bearing upon the problem at hand.

RATING SCALES AND RANKING METHODS

Rating scales of various kinds have been extensively used in the study of the personal-social characteristics of extreme deviates already chosen by other methods. They are of only moderate usefulness for purposes of original classification because few persons have a sufficiently intimate acquaintance with all the members of a large population to enable them to appraise all with equal fairness. Limited experience makes for warped judgments in which some individuals are given too favorable, others too unfavorable estimates. Once the choice has been made, however, ratings take on potentially greater value, since only those persons who have had long and close acquaintance with the persons chosen need take part in the ratings. Like direct observations, rating scales have many variations in form. Sometimes they consist only of a graded series of roughly quantitative categories in which the rater has no guide beyond his own subjective concepts of the terms used, as in the following example:

Do you consider the subject's health to be:
    Very superior   somewhat superior   about average   poor
very poor?
(Underline the correct answer.)

Sometimes the terms are defined more precisely, and the rater indicates his judgment by means of a cross on a line below the definitions. This arrangement permits him to make intermediate judgments if he desires to do so, since he is not required to place the cross exactly on the points of intersection but may locate it wherever he chooses. An example is given on p. 32.

Composite rating scales in which an attempt is made to analyze a broad category into more specific aspects of behavior or structure have also been rather widely used. The point of view here is in many respects comparable to that of most mental and educational tests. It assumes that such characteristics as health, emotional poise, or practical judgment are manifested in a wide variety of ways, and that some of these are likely to be overlooked when an attempt is made to judge the trait as a whole. It is further assumed that the various types of behavior included are additive when each is weighted in accordance with its independent contribution to the total.

HEALTH *

Extraordinarily good health; almost never sick; vigorous	Decidedly superior health	Rather superior health	Average for age	Rather weakly or sickly	Decidedly weakly or sickly	Extremely weakly and sickly; extreme lack of vigor

* Reprinted from Lewis M. Terman, *et al.*, *Genetic Studies of Genius*, Vol. 1, p. 524, with the permission of the author and of the publishers, Stanford University Press. Copyright, 1925, by the Board of Trustees of Leland Stanford Junior University.

The procedure is this: On the basis of observation and practical experience a tentative list of the components judged to be most fundamental for the trait in question is drawn up. As a rule, this list represents the combined judgments of a number of presumably competent persons. A graded series of scales for rating each of these components is then devised and tried out with a sufficiently large number of subjects to permit statistical analysis. On the basis of the statistical findings the scale is revised, often more than once, until it has been perfected to a point at which different raters agree fairly closely in their ratings of the same subjects. One of the most elaborate scales of this type is the Haggerty-Olson-Wickman scale for predicting problem behavior in school children. This scale is by no means new but is still in fairly wide use. Scales of this type commonly yield more stable results and permit standardization in terms of a larger and more representative population than those in which only a single rating is used to determine individual standing. They are accordingly better suited to the selection and description of extreme deviates.

Ranking differs from rating in that it merely involves arranging certain persons or things in serial order according to some specified criterion. By implication, it may mean only the selection of extreme cases. This is its chief application in the study of exceptional children. Teachers may be asked to name a specified number of children (usually, not more than three) whom they consider to be the brightest, the most stupid, or the most musically gifted in their respective classes. Because these children are usually more conspicuous than the generality by the very reason of their divergence from it, the dependability of such judgments is likely to be greater than are attempts to make valid distinctions among the rank and file. When funds do not permit the actual examination of all, judgments with respect to extreme cases are much used as easy, simple screening devices. More exact methods can then be used with the groups chosen in this way when making the final selection of cases for study.

ANTHROPOMETRIC MEASUREMENTS

It has been tacitly assumed by many psychologists that because measures of the external dimensions of the human body are made in physical units such as length or weight, they are of necessity very exact because of the high level of precision to which the instruments used for them have been brought. They fail to take account of the fact that no matter how exact the calibration of an instrument may be, when it is applied to the squirming body of a young child with its masses of soft tissue, its flexible joints, and varying stances, the results obtained are likely to be far less accurate than those the instrument is capable of yielding when used in the measurement of inert material.

Some anthropometric measures can be made with much greater accuracy than others. Assuming a good stadiometer, a well-balanced scale for weighing, and a capable technician skilled in the management of children, both standing height and weight can be measured with a high degree of accuracy. Measurements of sitting height show greater variability from trial to trial than do measurements of standing height, and the former vary both in respect to mean height and to the experimental error of measurement according to the position in which the child is placed for measuring the sitting height. Four different postures have been used. Some anthropometrists prefer one, others another. Some place the child on a chair with legs extended straight before him on a long seat, buttocks pressed firmly against the vertical back rest; others have him flex the knees and draw up the feet; others prefer to have the legs hanging free; still others use a chair of adjustable height and have the child plant his feet squarely on the floor. Boyd has shown that the first of these methods has the smallest experimental error, but she also points out that the experimental error inherent in measuring the growing body of a young child is at best decidedly greater than many have believed it to be. In general it may be said that anthropometric errors are greatest when a variable amount of compression of soft tissues is involved or when the measurement involves the location of bony points beneath soft flesh.

However, as far as the selection of children regarded as having exceptional physique is concerned, none of these errors is likely to be great enough to occasion serious disagreement among observers. But in the study of the physique of children chosen on some other basis, and particularly when different measurements are combined by means of formulas designed to yield indices of body build, the possible accumulation of errors in the various measures used must be taken into account. It can sometimes be sufficient to make the index valueless.

PHYSIOLOGICAL MEASUREMENTS

It is highly unfortunate that the majority of physicians do not give adequate consideration to the extent and practical significance of the experimental error inherent in the physiological measurements reported by the biological laboratories they employ. Some data on the dependability of the chemical, microscopical, and other measures used as aids in the diagnosis of disease are available in the literature, but this material is likely to be overlooked by physicians who are inclined to regard the laboratory findings as exact measurements. More precise demonstration of the amount of variation in the reports of different technicians analyzing the same specimen of blood or urine under routine laboratory conditions and without knowledge of the fact that their work is under inspection is much needed. Equally important is it that acquaintance with these facts be disseminated more widely among physicians who make use of such measurements in diagnosis and among the research workers in many fields who utilize them in the formulation and testing of scientific hypotheses. Too often differences arising from experimental error are accepted as significant.

PSYCHOLOGICAL TESTS OF ABILITIES AND OF PERSONAL-SOCIAL CHARACTERISTICS

Although some attempts at mental measurement were made as early as the 1880's and the mental test was christened by Cattell in 1890, more than two decades elapsed before the infant science threw off its swaddling clothes and began to speak for itself. Since then its voice has been loud and its virility amazing. The number of more or less well standardized tests that have been put on the market runs into the thousands; the number of allegedly different abilities and personality characteristics they are presumed to measure is certainly well in excess of a hundred. The literature describing these tests and the results obtained by their use is so voluminous that even the most rapid and industrious reader can scarcely keep abreast of it.

Almost from the beginning, however, the makers of psychological tests have been at pains to provide some information with respect to the magnitude of the experimental error of measurement or, to speak more precisely, of the extent to which the test results may be expected to vary from trial to trial because of circumstantial factors not easy to control. However, more serious difficulty arises from the uncertain meaning of these tests. Just what is meant by intelligence, by aggressiveness, by emotional stability? Is salesmanship so simple and undifferentiated an ability that the same person can sell cigars or scientific instruments with

equal facility and success? Are mental qualities for the most part
inborn or are they determined by experience and training? Are
geniuses born or made?

The proposal has sometimes been made that just as we define
weight in terms of the reading on a properly standardized scale,
so we may best define mental characteristics in terms of the results
obtained by standard tests designed to measure those qualities.
The difficulty here lies in the multiplicity of tests designed for the
same purpose and the lack of general agreement as to which
should be taken as the standard. As a matter of fact we are not
yet in a position to make such a choice. Improvements in methods
of test construction are constantly being made; it would be an
obvious mistake to stultify such improvements by the adoption of
definitive standards at this time, even if it were possible to obtain
general agreement on such standards.

There is another course along which some progress is being
made. In place of using test results to define a trait we may adopt
the practice of regarding the test as a type of performance in its
own right, as a form of behavior from which certain conclusions
may be drawn with a determinable level of confidence. One would
speak, then, not of children with exceptionally high intelligence
but of those whose scores on the _____ test are equalled or exceeded by only one child out of a hundred, a thousand, and so
on. A further advantage of the operational type of definition is
the readiness with which the population to which the child is
compared can be defined. Much confused thinking has resulted
from the use of such vaguely defined terms as the "general population." What peoples are covered by this term? Does it include
all the inhabitants of the globe, savage as well as civilized? If not,
what are its limits? When standing is referred to performance on
a particular test in reference to that of a specified population
group we know what is meant and can draw conclusions in terms
of ascertained facts. When, on the contrary, we speak of traits
that are variously defined by different people and compare an
individual with a population of unknown composition we stand
on very shaky ground.

MEASURES OF THE ENVIRONMENT

A child's environment has many structural elements. There are the home, the school, the neighborhood, perhaps church and Sunday school, summer camp, and more or less prolonged visits at the homes of relatives. Each of these physical units varies along many axes that are both physical and psychological in character. Families differ in size and composition and in their interpersonal relationships. Homes differ in size, in the attractiveness of their furnishings, and in their relative provisions for the comfort of the adults and the happiness and well-being of the children. Neighbors and neighborhoods differ, as do the relations of the home and family to the neighborhood setting. Schools and teachers differ almost as much as do homes and families. So it is with other aspects of the child's environment. The futility of attempting to include more than a small fraction of these varying factors within the limits of a single test or questionnaire is apparent; fortunately the problem is simplified to some extent by the fact that some factors are so related that it is possible to draw tentative inferences about the one from measuring the other.

The relationship of the exceptional child to his environment may be approached from either of two opposed angles. We may ask, "What is the effect of a given type of exceptional environment upon the children reared under its influence?" Conversely, we may begin with a group of children known to be exceptional in some way and examine the characteristics of the environments under which they were reared. In the first instance the selection of the environment is likely to be made on a descriptive rather than on a quantitative basis, and the major error lies in the tacit assumption that all environments of this type are so similar that sufficient information is provided by the mere name. Actually, orphanages, reformatories, institutions for the physically handicapped, and the like differ almost as much, one from another, as do homes and neighborhoods. The other method of approach by means of studying the environments of children known to be exceptional is handicapped by the lack of really dependable

methods of appraising environment. A number of scales have
been devised for studying various aspects of the home, family,
and neighborhood, but each is limited in scope, none have well
established norms, and, in most cases, the extent of the error of
measurement is unknown. References to a few of the more promising of these scales will be found at the end of this chapter.

COMMENTS

Technical devices for the measurement of human characteristics
are of many kinds. There are anthropometric devices for the
measurement of bodily size and for that of the separate parts and
organs of the body as well. There are chemical and microscopic
devices for more precise study of the body fluids and tissues, and
electronic and photographic methods of appraising body movements and functions. The variety and number of psychological,
educational, and sociological tests and measures have increased
so greatly during the past forty years that the task of selecting
the most nearly valid out of so many that are questionable becomes a serious one for the clinician.

No matter what the field of interest may be, all who are concerned with the study of children should bear in mind the fact
that no measuring device, no report, no judgment or opinion is
invariably dependable, though some are more likely to be accurate
than others. And unless the probable extent of the error of measurement is known, errors of interpretation are bound to occur.

Errors of measurement are of two kinds, known to statisticians
as *constant errors* because they are more likely to take one direction than the other and as *variable errors* that are equally likely
to take an upward or a downward direction. In the following
chapter a few of the problems resulting from errors of measurement in the study of exceptional children will be briefly
considered.

REFERENCES

ACKERLEY, L. A., OJEMANN, R. H., NEIL, B., and GRANT, E., "A Study of the Transferable Elements in Interviews with Parents," *Journal of Experimental Education*, 5 (1936), 137-174.

ANDERSON, John E., "The Limitations of Infant and Preschool Tests in the Measurement of Intelligence," *Journal of Psychology*, 8 (1939), 351-379.

ARRINGTON, Ruth E., "Time-sampling Studies of Child Behavior," *Psychological Monographs*, Vol. 51 (1939), No. 2.

BELL, John E., *Projective Techniques: A Dynamic Approach to the Study of Personality* (New York, Longmans, Green and Co., 1948).

BINET, Alfred, "Nouvelles recherches sur la mesure du niveau intellectuel chez les enfants d'école," *L'Année psychologique*, 17 (1911), 145-201.

————, and SIMON, Th., "Le Développement de intelligence chez les enfants," *L'Année psychologique*, 14 (1908), 1-94.

BOYD, Edith, "The Experimental Error Inherent in Measuring the Growing Human Body," *American Journal of Physical Anthropology*, 13 (1929), 389-432.

BRADWAY, Katherine P., "IQ Constancy on the Revised Stanford-Binet from the Preschool to the Junior High School Level," *Journal of Genetic Psychology*, 65 (1944), 197-217.

BUROS, Oscar K., *The Nineteen Thirty-eight Mental Measurements Yearbook* (New Brunswick, N. J., Rutgers University Press, 1939).

————, *The Nineteen Forty Mental Measurements Yearbook* (New Brunswick, N. J., Rutgers University Press, 1941).

————, *The Third Mental Measurements Yearbook* (New Brunswick, N. J., Rutgers University Press, 1949).

BURT, Cyril, *Mental and Scholastic Tests* (London, P. S. King and Son, 1921).

CATTELL, James McKeen, "Mental Tests and Measurements," *Mind*, 15 (1890), 373-381.

CATTELL, Raymond B., *Description and Measurement of Personality* (Yonkers, N. Y., World Book Company, 1946).

CHAMPNEY, Horace, "The Measurement of Parent Behavior," *Child Development*, 12 (1941), 131-166.

FREEMAN, Frank N., *Mental Tests*, rev. ed. (Boston, Houghton Mifflin Company, 1939).

GOODENOUGH, Florence L., *Mental Testing: Its History, Principles, and Applications* (New York, Rinehart and Company, Inc., 1949).

GOODENOUGH, Florence L., "Review of 'Measuring Intelligence,' " *Psychological Bulletin*, 34 (1937), 605-609.

——, and ANDERSON, John E., *Experimental Child Study* (New York, The Century Co., 1931).

HAGGERTY, M. E., OLSON, Willard C., and WICKMAN, E. K., *The Haggerty-Olson-Wickman Behavior Rating Schedules* (Yonkers, N. Y., World Book Company, 1930).

HILDRETH, Gertrude, *A Bibliography of Mental Tests and Rating Scales*, 2d ed. (New York, The Psychological Corporation, 1939); *Supplement* (1945).

KAPLAN, Oscar J., ed., *An Encyclopedia of Vocational Guidance* (New York, Philosophical Library, 1948), 2 vols.

KUDER, G. F., *Preference Record: Form BB.*, rev. ed. (Chicago, Science Research Associates, 1942).

LEAHY, Alice M., *The Measurement of Urban Home Environment: Validation and Standardization of the Minnesota Home Status Index*, University of Minnesota Institute of Child Welfare Monograph Series (Minneapolis, University of Minnesota Press, 1936), No. 11.

MCNEMAR, Quinn, *The Revision of the Stanford Binet Scale* (Boston, Houghton Mifflin Company, 1942).

MALLER, John B., "Vital Indices and Their Relation to Psychological and Social Factors," *Human Biology*, 5 (1933), 94-121.

MURPHY, Lois Barclay, *Social Behavior and Child Personality: An Exploratory Study of Some Roots of Sympathy* (New York, Columbia University Press, 1937).

MURSELL, James L., *Psychological Testing* (New York, Longmans, Green and Company, 1947).

OLSON, Willard C., *Problem Tendencies in Children* (Minneapolis, University of Minnesota Press, 1930).

PEARSON, Karl, *The Grammar of Science* (London, Contemporary Science Series, 1892).

ROSS, C. C., *Measurement in Today's Schools* (New York, Prentice-Hall, Inc., 1941).

SOUTH, E. B., *An Index of Periodical Literature on Testing: 1921-1936* (New York, The Psychological Corporation, 1937).

STREET, Roy F., "IQ Changes of Exceptional Children," *Journal of Consulting Psychology*, 6 (1942), 243-246.

STRONG, E. K., *Vocational Interest Blanks: Revised Form* (Stanford, Cal., Stanford University Press, 1938).

TERMAN, Lewis M., *et al.*, *Genetic Studies of Genius: Mental and Physical Traits of a Thousand Gifted Children* (Stanford, Cal., Stanford University Press, 1925), Vol. 1.

TERMAN, Lewis M., and MERRILL, Maud, *Measuring Intelligence: A Guide to the Administration of the New Revised Stanford-Binet Tests of Intelligence* (Boston, Houghton Mifflin Company, 1937).

THURSTONE, L. L., *Multiple Factor Analysis: A Development and Expansion of the Vectors of Mind,* 2d ed. (Chicago, University of Chicago Press, 1947).

VERNON, Philip E., *The Measurement of Abilities* (London, University of London Press, 1940).

WHIPPLE, G. M., *Manual of Mental and Physical Tests,* rev. ed. (Baltimore, Warwick and York, 1919 and 1921), 2 vols.

Further Problems of Classification

5

THE EXPERIMENTAL ERROR OF MEASUREMENT

IN THE physical sciences, precision of measurement is well-nigh unbelievable. There are scales so delicate that they can determine the weight of a pencil dot on a sheet of paper; chronometers that measure the passage of a hundred thousandth of a second of time. But in the biological and social sciences measuring devices are far less accurate. Not only are these devices relatively crude and inexact, but the living subjects with whom they are used are more complex in organization and less stable in their reactions than is the kind of material with which the chemist or the physicist usually deals. These facts greatly increase the difficulty of measurement and add to the likelihood of error.

That no measuring instrument thus far devised is free from the likelihood of error has repeatedly been stressed. It follows that in any individual measurement the result is made up of two components, the first of which represents the individual's true standing, the second, the experimental error of measurement. The relative proportions of the two will vary according to the general accuracy of the measuring instrument. Some scales are far more dependable than others. But the proportion of true score and error will also differ from one measurement to another when the same scale is used and even with repeated measurements of the same subject. It therefore becomes the task of the examiner to ascertain the nature and sources of errors in measurement with much care and to make the best possible estimate of the probable direction and amount of the measurement error in each individual case studied. True, this will be an estimate only and, like all estimates of its kind, will sometimes be wrong. But it is well for all of us to keep the matter of the experimental error involved in all mental and social measurements very constantly in mind, especially when dealing with children who, as a result of exceptional standing on some measure of this kind, may receive exceptional treatment. If this treatment is called for they should not be denied it, but if the deviation from the average measurement is due chiefly to an unusually large error component, such treatment may be not only unnecessary but highly unwise.[1]

Inasmuch as the experimental error may be either positive or negative in sign, it may either raise or lower the apparent value of the measurement. This means that the actual amount of probable variation or, more precisely speaking, the total range within which variation in scores has a stated probability of occurring will be double that of the experimental error as this is usually reported. If, for example, it is stated that 50 per cent of the subjects will not change their score by more than three units on the scale used, then the chances are even that a retest of a subject whose original score was 28 will fall somewhere between 25 and 31. But there is an equal probability that the divergence may be greater than this. If errors are distributed according to the normal curve, there is rather more than one chance in ten that a second measurement may turn out to be as low as 22 and an equal likelihood that it may be as high as 34. There is slightly more than one chance in fifty that it may be as low as 19 and one chance in fifty that it may run to 37 or more. A single measurement is thus not a

---

[1] In a personal letter to me, one of my former students who is now a research psychologist of some note described a survey of an institution for the feeble-minded in one of the western states. Among the inmates a disturbingly large number of children and adolescents whose mentality was normal or even superior were located. These children had been sent to the institution on the basis of single tests administered by a person with but a small amount of training, or, in a few instances, at the advice of teachers or other persons who found them difficult to handle. The institution may be well adapted to the needs of those for whom it was designed, but it is certainly not a suitable place for the training of those of normal or superior intelligence.

fixed or absolute value but an approximation that is likely to vary within certain definable limits of probability. A child who is regarded as exceptional because he stands at one or the other extreme of such a distribution of fallible scores may be quite as unusual as he seems or even more so. But the chances are against it, as we shall see in the following section.

THE PROBABLE DIRECTION OF THE ERROR OF MEASUREMENT: THE PRINCIPLE OF REGRESSION

If the errors of measurement are normally distributed when all the members of a given population are considered, they will also be normally distributed for those whose scores fall at the mid-point of the group.[2] But if one selects only the small group of cases whose scores fall at or near one of the extremes, that is, those whose scores are either exceptionally high or exceptionally low, the distribution of errors will no longer be normal but will be skewed. The reason for this is readily understood if it is remembered that the measurement actually obtained for any individual case is made up in part of true score [3] and in part of error and that the relative proportions of these two components are unknown. The selection must therefore be made, not on the basis of the unknown true scores but according to the fallible combination of true score and error. Unusually large positive errors will increase the obtained scores above their true value; unusually large negative errors will bring about a corresponding decrease. Thus when one *selects* children on the basis of exceptionally high or low standing on a continuous distribution of scores, one automatically selects an undue proportion of those whose errors of measurement have taken the direction indicated by the nature of the selection. This means that on the average,

[2] Assuming that the distribution of scores is also normal or approximately normal.

[3] The statistical definition of a *true score* is the average of an infinite number of comparable scores. Since no individual can be measured an infinite number of times under comparable conditions, a statistical approximation to the true score is all that can be had.

though not in every case, the true standing of individuals making very high scores on any fallible measure will usually be somewhat lower than the obtained scores; and the true scores of those with very low standing are likely to be somewhat higher than the actual measurement would indicate.

The tendency for the scores earned by the same subjects on the second of two related measurements to fall somewhat nearer the population mean than did those on the first measure was noted by Sir Francis Galton in 1886 in connection with a study of the resemblance between fathers and sons in stature. He found that although tall fathers tend to have tall sons and short fathers to have short sons, the sons differed less from the typical height of males than their fathers did.[4] To this tendency for the scores on a second or dependent measure to fall somewhat nearer the population mean than the corresponding scores on the first or independent measure, Galton gave the name of *regression toward the mean.*

Regression is the result of imperfect agreement between measures. The disparity may exist in the true scores as well as in the errors of measurement, as in all probability was the case with Galton's comparison of the heights of father and son. But it is bound to appear in the dependent [5] variable whenever the two measures are not perfectly correlated.

[4] In a sense, Galton's case is somewhat different from that which we have been discussing, since it deals with independent measures of two different groups of subjects, whereas we have been considering the errors involved in measuring the same subjects more than once. Actually, however, the mathematical argument is the same. We discover errors of measurement only by comparing (that is, by correlating) the results obtained when the measurement is repeated, and the mathematical principles involved in correlation are the same, regardless of the subjects used in obtaining the measures. The interpretation of the results may differ, as in this case it does, since Galton's findings have to do primarily with genetics, and the errors of measurement that undoubtedly existed would serve only to cause the relationship to appear lower than was actually the case.

[5] The independent variable is the series of scores used in starting the investigation. Galton, for example, began by selecting fathers who were either very tall or very short and comparing their heights with the heights of their sons. The distribution of fathers' heights is thus the independent variable, that of the sons is the dependent variable. Had he preferred to do so, he might have reversed the process, beginning with very tall and very short sons and

In the study of exceptional children, the factor of regression has two important implications. First, a group of children selected because of their unusually high scores on some test or scale are, on the average, likely to be not quite so remarkable as their test scores would indicate. It may be well to state once more that this is a rule that holds good for the average of the group but not necessarily for all its individual members. In the second place, it is quite to be expected that when a group of extreme deviates with respect to some imperfectly measured attribute is retested, their scores on the second test will be found to have shifted in the direction of the population mean. A similar regressive effect will appear if the second measure is of some other attribute whose correlation with the first is positive but less than perfect.

Although statisticians have been familiar with this principle for well over half a century, many persons still find it hard to grasp. Rarely does a year pass without some ardent experimenter "discovering" that bright children seem to grow less bright upon retest and that stupid ones usually improve their standing, or that the most able pupils as judged by their intelligence tests do not "work up to their ability" as judged by their performance on educational tests. Both results can usually be explained most simply in terms of regression.

THE ESTIMATION OF TRUE SCORES

Although the true score of an individual cannot be determined with assurance from his score on a fallible scale, it is possible to make an estimate of this score which is likely to be nearer the truth than the original score. The method of arriving at this estimate and its application to certain problems of child education

---

then examining the corresponding measures of the fathers, in which case the sons' measurements would have constituted the independent variable, and the regressive effect would have appeared in the distribution of fathers' heights. A group of children selected on the basis of unusually high scores on an intelligence test will ordinarily make better than average scores on an arithmetic test; but their arithmetic scores will not be as high as their intellectual standing because of the lack of perfect correlation between the abilities involved and because of the experimental error inherent in each of the tests.

have been described by Kelley on pp. 408-424 of the reference given at the end of this chapter. It is interesting to note that the true standing [6] of an individual can be estimated with less error than that of his standing on a second fallible test of the same kind. This is, of course, as it should be, inasmuch as the true standing, though unknown, is a fixed quantity at the time of measurement while the second test, like the first one, is subject to errors of measurement.

THE EFFECT OF SEMANTIC DIFFERENCES UPON THE SELECTION OF EXTREME DEVIATES

Personal opinion based upon more or less casual observation is notoriously subject to error. Semantic differences play an important part here; the same words mean very different things to different people. Such terms as *anxiety, parental rejection, depression, aggressiveness, seclusiveness,* and a host of others much used in the psychological literature are by no means so objective as many suppose. The use of "objective tests" for the measurement of such characteristics by no means objectifies the *terms* as they are employed by the majority of people. As a matter of fact, some of these tests bear little more than an arbitrary relation to the name chosen for them. Nevertheless, there is always a tendency to identify a measuring device with the trait it is presumed to measure. We speak of a child's intelligence when all that is really known is his score on a test designed to measure that function. Or we accept the classifications made by some alleged expert as indubitably "right" even in the face of other evidence which indicates that they are almost certainly wrong.

All this is to some extent inevitable in the present state of our knowledge. We communicate by means of language that was not immanent in man's original nature or structure but has grown and developed with his experience and has consequently taken on different forms as his experiences have differed. We are likely to think of a given form of language—English, Spanish, Italian—as

[6] See the definition of a true score, p. 44, n. 3.

being the same for all users, but even this is true only to a limited extent. Every man has his own language, his own set of word meanings and word associations that are as peculiarly his own as are his facial expressions or the lines of his palm. Failure to recognize these individual differences in word meaning is the basis of much misunderstanding in the field of mental and social measurement. Even when it comes to the selection of extreme cases, such as those with which we are here concerned, semantic differences often lead to disagreement and confused thinking. The differences in meaning are both quantitative and qualitative. The same bit of behavior is considered by one authority to be an indication of anxiety; by another, seclusiveness; by a third, as depression. That which the one looks upon as an extreme degree of a given condition, a second considers moderate or even slight. The methods of factorial analysis can go far toward resolving semantic difficulties of both types.

THE HALO EFFECT

All of us are inclined to allow our personal attitudes toward certain individuals or institutions to affect our interpretations of their abilities and behavior. We overlook the faults of our friends; we make much of the mistakes of our enemies. The knowledge that certain things are true leads us to expect that other things usually, though not invariably, associated with them will likewise be true, and so we read into our observations much that is not there. Moreover, in our dealings with those about whom we have previously formed some decided opinion, our own behavior is likely to be modified in ways of which we are quite unaware. The teacher who knows that Peter is unusually good at spelling glances hastily through his paper and marks a number of partially illegible words "correct," but Alfred, whose previous record has been poor, rarely gets the benefit of any doubt. The psychometrist who ascertains that on former testings Mary has earned a very high IQ urges her in every possible way to make her very best effort and interprets questionable or borderline responses in the most favorable light permitted by the manual of instructions. Ellen, on the other hand, whose record has previously been low, receives but little urging; her "I don't know's" are accepted at their face value, and somewhat more rigid standards are likely to be applied in scoring her responses.[7]

THE EFFECT OF CONTRAST

Almost everyone has noticed the effect of contrasting conditions upon the appearance of objects. When viewed against different backgrounds, colors change in apparent brightness and hue. Sunshine seems brighter after a long period of rain. During a sudden January thaw the air may seem to us almost like that of summer, though the thermometer tells a different story.

Contrast and halo are closely related; they are like the two sides of the same coin. Both are important factors in the lives of exceptional children. The halo that the teacher constructs for the unusually gifted child leads her to see in him favorable traits that he does not possess, but the time may come when his failure to live up to the high standard she has set for him may bring the obverse type of reaction into play. Now she is no longer impressed by his unusual gifts but by the *contrast* between her own unwarranted view of the universality of those gifts and some action that is not in harmony with this opinion. When expectation runs high, disappointment is more keen and this disappointment may be, and often is, vented upon its unwitting source.

Contrast also plays a part in family and neighborhood relations. The child who is noticeably different from his brothers and sisters or from his playmates is bound to receive different treatment, and

[7] Every testing laboratory should have an ironclad rule that no member of the staff may look up a child's previous record before giving a retest or conducting an interview. This rule is particularly important when experiments designed to test the relative efficiency of various modes of diagnosis or treatment are in progress. There is little doubt that many procedures owe much of the usefulness imputed to them to just such unconscious bias on the part of those who devised them. There is also little doubt that many of the reported discrepancies in the results obtained by different investigators may be traced to a similar factor.

however well meant it may be, the sense of being different that it is likely to arouse in the child as he grows older is rarely welcome and may be a source of acute disturbance. "Mother, am I a queer child?" tearfully inquired a brilliant ten-year-old after overhearing the tactless remark of a neighbor who had been amazed and puzzled by the child's use of some unusual word encountered in her reading. Jealousies between families with respect to the relative accomplishments of children are too common to require elaboration.

In the classification and description of exceptional children both halo and contrast must be considered. Reports may be rendered untrustworthy from either cause, even in the case of presumably objective tests and measurements. Not only do these factors constitute problems for the investigator. Their repercussion upon the exceptional child, regardless of the nature of the characteristic that renders him unusual, may be trying indeed, and in some cases the effects may be serious.

The points that we have mentioned by no means include all the difficulties that obstruct the study of unusual children. There are many technical problems of measurement and of the statistical handling of data that it has not seemed appropriate even to mention in a book of this type. The medical, physiological, and chemical aspects are specialized matters for the understanding of which a long and arduous training is required. Finally, a word of caution is needed. The investigator who locates a child who appears exceptional, regardless of the nature of his unusual qualities, must never lose sight of the fact that he is dealing with a human being in a real world. Children are sensitive, and the realization that they are being singled out in some special way may, if due care is not taken, have most unfavorable effects both upon the child himself and on his relationships with those around him. This type of effect, in the case of a presumably favorable deviation, has been observed with some, though by no means all, of the children selected for participation in radio and television quiz shows. It has also been seen when parents, having learned of a child's high standing on one test or another, have unwisely discussed the matter with friends and relations. Parents also are sensitive, and in giving them the facts concerning severe handicaps in their children, judgment, sympathy, and patience are required if severe emotional shock is to be avoided.

REFERENCES

DUDYCHA, G. J., "A Note on the 'Halo Effect' in Ratings," *Journal of Social Psychology*, 15 (1942), 331-333.

FLEMMING, Edwin G., "The 'Halo' Around Personality," *Teachers College Record*, 43 (1942), 564-569.

GARRETT, Henry E., *Statistics in Psychology and Education*, 3d ed. (New York, Longmans, Green and Company, 1947).

GILINSKY, Alberta A., "The Influence of the Procedure of Judging on the Halo Effect," *American Psychologist*, 2 (1947), 309-310.

GOODENOUGH, Florence L., *Mental Testing: Its History, Principles, and Applications* (New York, Rinehart and Company, Inc., 1949); see especially Pt. 2.

———, "Semantic Choice and Personality Structures," *Science*, 104 (1946), 451-456.

GUILFORD, J. P., *Psychometric Methods* (New York, McGraw-Hill Book Company, 1936).

HORROCKS, John E., and NAGY, George, "The Relationship Between the Ability to Make a Diagnosis and to Select Appropriate Remedial Procedures," *Journal of General Psychology*, 38 (1948), 139-146.

KELLEY, Truman L., *Fundamentals of Statistics* (Cambridge, Mass., Harvard University Press, 1947).

PETERS, Charles C., and VAN VOORHIS, Walter R., *Statistical Procedures and Their Mathematical Bases* (New York, McGraw-Hill Book Company, 1940).

RICHARDS, Thomas W., and ELLINGTON, W., "Objectivity in the Evaluation of Personality," *Journal of Experimental Education*, 10 (1942), 228-237.

WOODWORTH, Robert S., *Heredity and Environment: A Critical Survey of Recently Published Material on Twins and Foster Children* (New York, Social Science Research Council, 1941), Bulletin No. 47.

PART II

Superior Deviates

Fundamental Concepts 6

As WE SHALL use the term, superior deviates are those who stand at the upper or more desirable extreme with respect to some characteristic in which all share to a greater or less degree. The basis of classification is therefore quantitative, at least in a rough sense, and the subjects belong to the first of the four groups mentioned in Chapter 1.

THE CORRELATION BETWEEN GENERAL INTELLIGENCE AND SPECIAL TALENT

In her study of the childhood of three hundred men of recognized genius, Cox requested a number of presumably competent experts to make an estimate of the IQ each would probably have obtained had he been tested in childhood. The estimates were based upon an examination of the available biographical data which had previously been assembled by Cox. Regardless of the field in which they later attained renown, all were judged to have ranked above average in intelligence, though within each professional group some were placed higher than others, and differences also appeared in the mean standing of the various occupational classes.[1]

The extent to which knowledge of their later achievement may

[1] In terms of mean estimated IQ, the philosophers stood highest; the military leaders lowest.

55

have affected the selection of the material recorded in the biographies used by the judges in making their estimates is, of course, unknown. It is, however, quite possible that some degree of halo may have affected both the data and the interpretations placed upon it by the judges. It is natural enough for the writer of a biography to look for consistencies rather than inconsistencies in the material he chooses to report, except, perhaps, in those instances in which the incongruities are so striking that they lend color and vivacity to the story. Nevertheless, even though Cox's material may have been somewhat biased, it is unlikely that any exaggeration from this source was great enough to counterbalance the tendency to underestimate ability arising from the paucity of information with respect to the childhood of many of the subjects. Even if Cox's estimate that the true mean IQ of these famous men was in excess of 160,[2] with very few falling below 140, may be a slight exaggeration of the facts, there can be no reasonable doubt that all showed very unusual ability at an early age. Many completed college while still in their teens, and the recorded episodes of childhood sayings and doings are far in advance of those usual for children of corresponding ages.

Although a high level of general intellectual ability can be inferred from the biographical data with reasonable certainty, it would frequently be hard to predict from these records in what field the individual would later win renown. As a matter of fact, it seems likely that many of them might have been equally successful in any one of several types of work, had circumstances been different or had their interests followed a different pattern of development. Benvenuto Cellini,[3] for example, was not only a famous goldsmith and sculptor; the vigor and force of his autobiography, which remains one of the great literary classics of all time, is evidence of his skill as a writer. His scientific and mechanical ability is shown by the many sketches and drawings of me-

[2] In the population at large the mean IQ is assumed to be 100. Approximately one person in two hundred will reach or exceed an IQ of 140; fewer than one in a thousand will attain the level of 160 or higher.

[3] Cellini is not included in Cox's list.

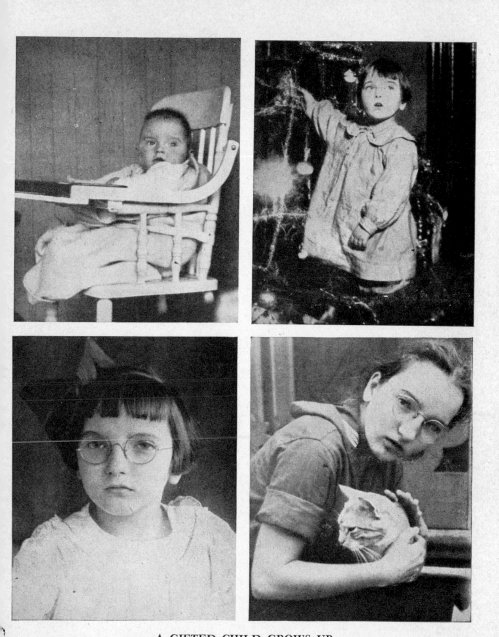

A GIFTED CHILD GROWS UP

These pictures show the subject (who is described on pp. 133-134) at the ages of 9 months, 3 years, 8 years, and 16 years.

chanical contrivances, unknown in the sixteenth century which foreshadow the inventions of a later period. He was also a brilliant soldier, and there is evidence that he might have become an important statesman if his fiery temper had not continually got him into trouble.

The celebrated astronomer, Johann Kepler, throughout his childhood and youth was interested mainly in religion and theology. Even after his first training in astronomy during his undergraduate years in college he showed no particular aptitude for it,[4] nor did it especially appeal to him. Theology and philosophy continued to be his absorbing interests. Had circumstances permitted he might have become one of the great divines. But he was financially dependent upon his own efforts for his support, and when, after taking his master's degree, he was offered the astronomical lectureship at the University of Gratz he "reluctantly" accepted it. Conscientiously the young man of twenty-two set to work to master the subject matter in his required field and was rewarded by finding that it soon compelled his interest even more strongly than had his theological studies of an earlier date.

More closely related to his later fame are the early interests of the poet, Thomas Moore, who stated that the one real love of his childhood and youth was music. He played the piano and had a good singing voice; yet he became a poet and not a musician.

One can multiply such instances almost indefinitely. Moreover, those of us who have followed the development of highly intelligent children over a period of years can hardly fail to be impressed by the scope of their interests and abilities, by the readiness with which they take up one hobby after another, and by the almost phenomenal speed at which specialized skills, not formerly noticeable, spring into being. There is no question that the great majority of highly intelligent children are potentially capable of success along more than one line and that the popular notion of the one-sidedness of genius is based upon the occasional exception rather than the general rule.

[4] See Cox, *Genetic Studies of Genius*, Vol. 2, pp. 475-477.

SPECIALIZATION OF INTEREST OR SPECIAL TALENT?

The belief that each person has his own special niche for which he is fitted by nature and that in no other line of endeavor is he likely to achieve more than a very mediocre degree of success was the keynote of vocational guidance programs a quarter of a century ago. More recent years have witnessed a change in emphasis. Instead of administering a long series of tests designed to measure each of a variety of special talents, modern psychologists are more likely to rely upon the combination of a test of general intelligence and an interest test. By the use of a multiple key, the interest test is scored in such a way as to indicate the degree of interest shown in each of a number of vocational fields.[5] One important reason for the shift is the greater consistency of the results. A second reason lies in the fact that the modern method is more economical of time and funds. Regardless of these points, however, a tacit feeling seems to have grown up among psychologists that if one is intellectually capable of securing the necessary training, the pattern of his interests provides a useful and perhaps a sufficient indication of the type of work which he is suited to do. The extent to which these specialized patterns of interest are the result of external conditioning alone is unknown. It is possible that they arise as the outward expression of inherent talent of an unusual order; in other words, that the measurement of interest and the measurement of talent are basically the same. Certainly interest is not likely to persist without some degree of success and this presupposes at least a modicum of special talent along the line in

[5] Such tests do not depend merely upon the subject's stated preference for certain types of work. It has been found that those who are successfully engaged in a given occupation usually show fairly similar patterns of interest in a wide variety of things—types of reading, of recreation, hobbies, and classes of people chosen as friends—and that these interests differ considerably from one occupational group to another. It is reasoned that when the interests of a young person who has not yet chosen his vocation are found to show a close resemblance to one of these occupational patterns while differing from most of the others, it is usually safe to advise him that he will probably find this a congenial type of work, assuming always that his measured intelligence appears sufficient to enable him to secure the requisite training.

question. The question is: Given the requisite level of general intelligence and as much, but no more talent in the special field as is possessed by the average person, is interest aroused through external circumstances sufficient to bring about outstanding success?

When, in the fall of 1921, Professor Lewis M. Terman of Stanford University began his now famous study of the development of intellectually gifted children, an initial attempt was made to locate subjects who, regardless of their intellectual capacity, showed exceptional talent in one or more of the following areas: music, art, or mechanical ingenuity and inventiveness. However, after a short period of trial this aspect of the project was discontinued for the following reasons. First, because such devices for measuring these talents as were then available [6] were so lacking in validity as to necessitate dependence upon the judgment of teachers and others who presumably have expert knowledge of the child's ability. These judgments, however, typically show much disagreement between judges (variable errors) as well as constant errors resulting from the general tendency to permit such factors as personal attractiveness, effort, docility, and the like to influence the judgments. Unreliability of selection was thus the first and chief reason for abandoning the attempt to locate children of unusual talent independently of those of extraordinary intellectual gifts.

The second reason for giving up this part of the project is more pertinent to the present discussion. It was found that almost without exception, children who showed unquestionable talent, particularly in music or mechanical inventiveness, also qualified for the group on the basis of general intelligence (Stanford Binet IQ 140 or higher). Most of these children would have been located in any case by the regular procedures of the study, hence the time spent in looking for special talent was largely wasted effort.

The progress made by the child of high intellectual gifts in almost any field in which his interest is keen is so remarkable that it becomes difficult indeed to say to what extent a separate and

---

[6] Even today, although some advances have been made in the past thirty years, the measurement of talent in these fields remains for the most part an unsolved problem.

distinct talent has influenced the picture. What is measured is always achievement; aptitude or talent is never measured directly but is inferred from accomplishment. But as we have seen, the inference of a one-to-one relationship between the two may be hazardous. One of the most striking things that was noticed among the California group of gifted children was their extraordinary facility for acquiring new skills and knowledge of a specialized kind within a relatively short length of time. Although this may possibly be ascribed to the sudden emergence of a special talent which previously had remained latent, there were many instances in which the occurrence of some event that awakened a strong interest on the part of the child seemed to be the major factor. Granting the necessary sensory and motor mechanisms,[7] it seems likely that child intelligence is largely polymorphous in its potentialities, though it may not be wholly so. This hypothesis is strongly suggested both by Cox's study of the childhood of famous men and by the Stanford study of gifted children.

THE STRENGTH OF INTEREST

Interests have a quantitative as well as a qualitative aspect. They vary along each of the four dimensions described in Chapter 2; a fact that indicates how closely they are bound in with the personality as a whole. They vary in mode, that is, in the objects and objectives to which they are attached. They vary in extensity, in the scope of the field which they cover. Michelangelo was almost equally renowned in painting, sculpture, and architecture; his interests extended over practically the entire field of art. Picasso's interest was confined to the development of a particular school of painting, though it is true that in his later years he endeavored with some success to adapt his art theories to stage

[7] The blind child is unlikely to become a painter or the deaf child a musician. There are many bodily conditions that may hamper a child's chances of success in certain fields, even though they may not preclude it. Conversely, robust health and a superior physique are assets in any line of endeavor, though of more consequence in some areas than in others.

design. Interests also differ in protensity, in the age at which they first appear and the length of time they endure. And they differ greatly in intensity.

It is a common misconception to think that interest as such is a fixed quantity and that, consequently, a greater amount of interest in one area is of necessity accompanied by a smaller amount elsewhere. This is true only to the extent that activity is time-limited, so that one can rarely be intently engaged in two or more activities simultaneously. But the total output of interest—if we may use such a term—is by no means equal for all. Some children seem generally apathetic. They rarely show intense interest in anything. Others are keen and alert, almost regardless of the field that engages their attention at the moment. Both the intensity and the type of interests vary with the level of intelligence. Not only does the bright child differ from the backward one in respect to the kind of activities that most strongly appeal to him but in general he shows more zest, is more keenly absorbed in what he does, is more definitely oriented toward a goal.

Putting all the evidence together it appears that the relation between specialized interest and special talent is probably circular rather than a one-way affair. The child who, as we say, has a natural bent for something is for that very reason likely to find it easier and more interesting than the one who is lacking in such talent. He therefore practices it more earnestly and in greater amount. However, a high level of achievement can also be attained by persons of ordinary talent but outstanding intelligence when their interest is so awakened that they are incited to apply their general ability to the specific field.

THE INTERCORRELATIONS OF TALENT IN THE INTELLECTUALLY GIFTED

That many, if not most, children of superior intelligence are potentially capable of success in more than one line of endeavor seems reasonably certain. It is, of course, true that there are overlapping elements in many occupational fields which make for correlation in the ability to deal with them. The relations between mathematics and engineering, between painting and sculpture, or between history and political science are obvious. Actually, there are few if any occupational fields that do not have some elements in common. Whether or not the parable of the ten talents remains applicable after allowance for this overlapping of elements has been made is not entirely certain, but the available evidence suggests that it does.[8] Over and above the relationship necessitated by the existence of common elements in the subject matter and techniques of the various occupations there seems to be greater than chance probability that the child who shows aptitude for one will also show some talent, at least, for others. Three factors, all of which have been mentioned before, appear to account for this. These are: (1) intelligence, (2) intensity of interest, and (3) zest in living and doing. The intellectually brilliant child is usually the zestful child, and he is also the talented child. In the majority of cases his talents are multiple rather than single.

REFERENCES

American Association for Gifted Children, *The Gifted Child*, ed. Paul Witty (Boston, D. C. Heath and Company, 1951).

BAUMGARTEN, Franziska, *Wunderkinder; psychologische Untersuchungen* (Leipzig, Barth, 1930).

BENTLEY, John E., *Superior Children* (New York, W. W. Norton and Company, Inc., 1937).

BERRY, Charles S., "The Gifted Child—a Future Leader," *National Parent-Teacher*, 38 (1944), 27-29.

CARMICHAEL, Leonard, "The Psychology of Genius," *Phi Kappa Phi Journal* (1934), pp. 149-164.

CARROLL, Herbert A., *Genius in the Making* (New York, McGraw-Hill Book Company, 1940).

CATTELL, J. McKeen, "The Origin and Distribution of Scientific Men," *Science*, 66 (1927), 513-516.

---

[8] "For unto every one that hath shall be given, and he shall have abundance, and from him that hath not shall be taken away even that which he hath" (Matt. 25:29).

Cox, Catharine Morris, *Genetic Studies of Genius: The Early Mental Traits of Three Hundred Geniuses* (Stanford, Cal., Stanford University Press, 1926), Vol. 2.

Cutts, Norma E., and Moseley, Nicholas, *Bright Children: A Guide for Parents* (New York, G. P. Putnam's Sons, 1953).

Delacroix, Henri, "L'Invention et le génie," in *Nouveau Traite de psychologie*, ed. G. Dumas (Paris, Alcan, 1939), Vol. 6, Bk. 4.

Dunlap, James M., "Testing the Tops," *Journal of Exceptional Children*, 11 (1945), 142-146.

Galton, Francis, *Hereditary Genius* (London, The Macmillan Company, 1869 and 1914).

Goddard, Henry H., "The Gifted Child," *Journal of Educational Psychology*, 6 (1933), 54-61.

Henry, Theodore S., "Annotated Bibliography on Gifted Children and Their Education," *Twenty-third Yearbook of the National Society for the Study of Education* (Chicago, University of Chicago Press, 1924), Pt. 1, pp. 389-413.

Hirsch, Nathaniel D. M., *Genius and Creative Intelligence* (Cambridge, Mass., Sci-Art Publishing Company, 1931).

Hollingworth, Leta S., *Gifted Children: Their Nature and Nurture* (New York, The Macmillan Company, 1929).

———, "What We Know about the Early Selection and Training of Leaders," *Teachers College Record*, 40 (1939), 575-592.

———, Terman, Lewis M., and Oden, Melita, "The Significance of Deviates: III. Superior deviates," *Thirty-ninth Yearbook of the National Society for the Study of Education* (Chicago, University of Chicago Press, 1940), Pt. 1, pp. 55-63.

Jenkins, Martin D., "The Upper Limit of Intelligence among American Negroes," *Scientific Monthly*, 66 (1948), 399-401.

Kretschmer, Ernst, *The Psychology of Men of Genius* (New York, Harcourt, Brace and Company, 1931).

Parkyn, G. W., *Children of High Intelligence: A New Zealand Study* (London, Oxford University Press, 1948).

Sanchez-Jiminez, Julian, "El Niño bien dotado y los problemas que implica: su asistencia especial" (The Mentally Gifted Child and the Problems He Implies: Special Assistance), *Revista de psicología y pedagogía aplicadas, Valencia*, 3 (1952), 263-291.

Schorn, Maria, "Psychologie des frühbegabten Kindes," *Zeitschrift für Psychologie und Physiologie der Sinnesorgane*, 105 (1928), 302-316.

Storm, Grace E., "The Gifted Child," *Elementary School Journal*, 49 (1948), 6-8.

STREET, Roy F., "The Mentally Superior Child," *Journal of Exceptional Children*, 3 (1937), 83-86.

TERMAN, Lewis M., *et al.*, *Genetic Studies of Genius: Mental and Physical Traits of a Thousand Gifted Children* (Stanford, Cal., Stanford University Press, 1925), Vol. 1.

———, "Psychological Approaches to the Study of Genius," *Science*, 92 (1940), 293-301.

———, and ODEN, Melita H., *Genetic Studies of Genius: The Gifted Child Grows Up* (Stanford, Cal., Stanford University Press, 1947), Vol. 4.

WITTY, Paul A., "Contributions to the IQ Controversy from the Study of Gifted Children," *School and Society*, 51 (1940), 503-508.

———, "Thirty Years of Research upon Gifted Children," *Understanding the Child*, 17 (1948), 35-40.

———, "The Gifted Child: Facts and Fallacies," *National Parent-Teacher*, 42 (1948), 4-7.

WOODS, Elizabeth L., "The Mentally Gifted," *Review of Educational Research*, 14 (1944), 224-230.

ZORBAUGH, Harvey W., ed., "Gifted and Talented Children," *Journal of Educational Sociology*, 10 (1936), 65-128.

The Exceptionally Intelligent Child: I. General Characteristics

7

INASMUCH AS intellectual ability is a continuous trait with no sharply defined levels or stages but varying in its manifestations by imperceptible degrees from idiocy to genius, the division of children into intellectual classes or groups on the basis of some accepted criterion is of necessity an arbitrary procedure. The number of classes and the lines of separation are determined at will by the experimenter. Moreover, the term *exceptional* has no exact quantitative meaning. One must always ask how unusual or how exceptional a given case may be. Thus the designation of a child as "exceptionally intelligent" is in large part a matter of definition. Before such an expression can be interpreted, certain facts must be known. We must know the criterion used to determine the level of intelligence. If it is a judgment, we should know something about the competence of the judge. If a test has been used, we should have sufficient information to make a fair estimate of its accuracy. In either case, we should know the minimum level of ability required for including a child in a group designated as exceptionally bright.

There are various ways of expressing this. The most direct method is in terms of frequency or rareness. For example, "not more than one child in a thousand of his age stands as high on the ____ test as he." Or a teacher may report, "in my twenty years of teaching experience, I have never before known so brilliant a child." The first statement is in some ways easier to interpret, since the experimental error of the test in question is known or can be ascertained and the consequent likelihood that the child's relative position would be altered upon re-examination may be determined. The experimental error inherent in the judgments of any individual teacher is rarely known. However, such judgments often have the merit of a broader view of intelligence than is likely to be given by any test not requiring more than an hour for its administration.

The widespread popularity of the intelligence quotient has lent to that measure a kind of pseudo-objectivity of meaning for those who have had extensive experience with its use. The clinical psychologist, the school supervisor, as well as many teachers, have grown to have a fairly exact idea of what may be expected from the child with an IQ of 120 or 140. Often, indeed, these concepts are much more precise than the facts warrant. Nevertheless, the use of the IQ for determining the limits of a group selected for study because of unusually high intelligence has much to recommend it, provided always that certain basic rules are kept in mind. An intelligence quotient is not the simple measure that many have supposed. Its valid use requires the fulfillment of a number of conditions.[1] If these conditions are not met its meaning becomes ambiguous. As a general rule, the use of the intelligence quotient should be confined to the Stanford Binet test for which it was originally designed. Its application to other tests with different content and distribution of scores can lead to much confusion.

Since the publication in 1925 of the first volume of *Genetic Studies of Genius,* the practice there adopted of confining the term *exceptionally intelligent* or *intellectually gifted* to children of IQ 140 or higher on the Stanford Binet [2] has been fairly widely

[1] For a discussion of these requirements see Florence L. Goodenough, *Mental Testing: Its History, Principles, and Applications* (New York, Rinehart and Company, Inc., 1949).

[2] This refers to the 1916 revision. The 1937 revision has a wider distribution of scores than has the 1916 test. Consequently, a higher IQ standard must be used if results are to be comparable to those obtained by Terman in the early 1920's. A minimum IQ of at least 145 on either Form L or Form M of the 1937 revision must be obtained if the group is to be comparable in ability to that studied by Terman.

adopted. Unless otherwise specified, it is the criterion which we shall use here. Children of this level of ability occur on the average only about once among two hundred cases when large and representative groups made up of all levels of society are considered.

The question of incidence, however, is of chief interest when comparing more homogeneous groups of known composition. Repeatedly it has been shown that children whose fathers belong to the learned professions not only rank much higher on standard intelligence tests than the generality, but the proportion of the intellectually gifted found among such groups greatly exceeds that which is typical of the population as a whole. From 5 to 10 per cent of such a group will reach the level designated by Terman as intellectually gifted. In contrast, scarcely one in a thousand among the children of day laborers attains so high a rank. Maller,[3] for example, found that the mean IQ's of fifth-grade children in different sections of New York City ranged from 74 to 118. This certainly means that the percentages of highly superior children would also vary greatly from one district to another, although Maller's report does not include these figures. Miles has summarized the data on the proportions of children testing at 140 or higher reported in a number of studies. Her figures vary from a little over 1 per cent to slightly above 13 per cent for populations of small or moderate size which were for the most part above the average in social status. In the course of the field work during the search for gifted children in the Stanford investigation the difference between schools in the proportion of children reaching the required level of 140 IQ on the Stanford Binet was noticeable. There were many schools in the poorer districts where no cases were located in spite of careful search, although in schools in other districts as many as 5 per cent were found. Taking all the investigations together, there seems no reasonable doubt that the

[3] This study is of special significance because it is one of the few in which approximately all the children in a large population were actually tested. Maller's study included all the fifth-grade children in the New York City school system who were present on the day the tests were given.

children of parents who have attained positions of responsibility and financial security average higher in intelligence and that more of them reach the top levels on standard tests of intelligence than do the children whose parents are of mediocre or inferior attainment.

The question of sex differences in intelligence has been debated for decades, not always with scientific detachment. The geniuses of history are for the most part male; the number of women who have merited such a designation is small. There are a number of possible explanations for this fact, however, and it is unquestionably true that as the labors of childbearing and homemaking have been lightened, a greater number of women have won positions of recognized importance in almost every line of endeavor. Few, however, have reached the topmost ranks.

Why? It has long been known that during the preschool years girls show a slight advantage over boys. On the average they walk and talk at an earlier age, their vocabularies are larger, and they rank a little higher on most standardized tests of intelligence. During the elementary school period also the girls continue to hold their own as far as averages are concerned. It was therefore a surprise to all concerned when the Stanford survey showed that the ratio of boys to girls among the preschool and elementary school children who qualified for the group was 121 to 100. In the high school group the ratio was even higher—212 boys to 100 girls.

Various hypotheses were proposed to account for these findings. Among them the most probable seemed to be the possibility of greater variability on the part of the boys. Even though the averages of two groups may be identical, if the abilities of one group spread over a wider range than do those of the other group, more cases will occur at the extremes. That this condition might exist in the case of sex differences in intelligence had been suggested before. The preponderance of males not only among those who have achieved renown but also in institutions for the feebleminded, obviously points to such a possibility. Each of these facts has been plausibly explained on the basis of economic factors and social conditions which, offering greater opportunity to the male, also demand more from him. The difficulty of securing a group in which biased selection could be absolutely ruled out proved for some time a major stumbling block in the way of securing incontrovertible evidence with respect to the relative variability of the sexes. It remained for a Scottish woman, Professor Agnes Macmeeken, to provide the needed data. During 1935-1937, Professor Macmeeken performed the well-nigh incredible task of locating all except one of the living children born in Scotland on four specified days of the year 1926. All the children, 874 in number, were given the 1916 revision of the Stanford Binet scale together with a series of performance tests. Macmeeken's study is unique. No other investigation has ever been made in which all the members of a large and representative group of subjects have been given an individual Stanford Binet. Maller's study, which was previously mentioned, was based upon two group tests, with the average of the two taken as the score for each child. Furthermore, no attempt was made to locate and test the absentees, who may well have constituted a different intellectual selection from those who took the test. Maller presents no figures on sex variability, but Macmeeken reports a standard deviation of 15.9 for the boys' IQ and of 15.2 for that of the girls. The difference seems small but the fact that it is based upon a complete population group lends it a significance that one based upon a sample does not possess. And even so small a difference is sufficient to account for a marked disparity in the proportions at the extremes. Terman has calculated that even if no allowance is made for the small difference in the mean IQ's found by Macmeeken (100.5 for the boys and 99.7 for the girls), the difference in the standard deviations alone would mean that at the 140+ level, the ratio of boys to girls would be 134 boys to 100 girls. If the difference in the means is also taken into account, the ratio would be 158 to 100. The greater male variability found by Macmeeken is lent further support by an earlier Scottish study in which nearly all the children born in Scotland during the year 1921, some 27,000 in number, were involved. From these, a random sample of 500 boys and

500 girls were given the Stanford Binet. The standard deviation of the IQ's was 17 for the boys and 16 for the girls.

McNemar has reported the means and standard deviations of the IQ's obtained for the standardization group of the 1937 revision of the Stanford Binet. However the number of cases at each age is too small to lend much stability to the figures, particularly in view of the well-known fact that variability on this test is not the same at all ages. In 10 of the 18 age groups for which separate figures are given, the variability of the boys exceeds that of the girls; but the fluctuations from age to age are so great that little importance can be attached to this figure. In general, students of sex differences have concerned themselves with means rather than variability, and few have realized the importance of bias in making up their samples.

The evidence thus points to a greater incidence of males than females at both extremes of the distribution of intelligence, but as yet it cannot be regarded as conclusive. However, if greater variability of males should be established by further data it would help to explain a number of known facts, such as the greater number of males who attain fame as well as the excess number whom it is necessary to place in institutions for the feeble-minded. Social factors, it is true, play a part in both instances. Nevertheless, if it is true that a sex difference in intellectual variability exists, this would constitute an inescapable fact making for a somewhat greater incidence of males at both the upper and the lower extremes of the distribution of intelligence.[4]

The question of racial or nationality differences in intellectual endowment is another that has evoked much heated discussion among those who have studied the matter. It is certainly true that in the United States both American Negroes and the children of immigrants from South Europe and the Spanish American countries not only earn lower scores, on the average, than do American whites of native parents, but the incidence of very high IQ's

---

[4] Assuming, of course, that the distribution is symmetrical in form, as most investigations have found it to be.

among these groups is notably smaller than that of the generality, although occasional sporadic cases are found among all. As far as the South Europeans are concerned, it seems likely that selective immigration of the least successful members of the community is largely responsible for the low standing of their children who were born in the United States. "One does not gather grapes from thorns nor figs from thistles" runs the proverb. Many of the great men of history have come from the very countries whose present representatives in America rank well toward the bottom of the distribution of intelligence. But tests given in their own countries to those who remained at home often tell a different story. Tyler has summarized the evidence on this point very well, and those who are interested will do well to read her report.

The Jewish groups almost invariably rank high, wherever they are found, and the incidence of the exceptionally able is also well above the average. In the Stanford study more than 10 per cent of the entire group were of Jewish ancestry, whereas the estimated proportion of Jews in the cities covered by the survey was only about 5 per cent at that time.

Place of residence is also a factor affecting the incidence of the exceptionally bright. The more able persons tend to migrate from the rural districts to the cities, where opportunities for business and professional success are greater. The more progressive states, where educational, health, and occupational facilities are above the average, also attract many of the best members of the less progressive communities. This process of selective migration tends to increase the geographical differences in the distribution of superior mental ability.

For all these reasons the question of the incidence of gifted children or adults must always be phrased in specific rather than general terms. It must refer to a particular population, defined as exactly as possible with respect to ethnic, cultural, economic, and geographical factors and probably with respect to sex. Only when these facts are known can the incidence of gifted children or adults take on real meaning.

THE STANFORD UNIVERSITY STUDY

From the beginning of his professional career, the major interest of Professor Lewis M. Terman of Stanford University has centered about the child of unusual intellectual ability. His Ph.D. thesis, written at Clark University in 1905, had to do with the comparative performances of one group of bright and another of stupid boys of the same age on a series of mental and motor tasks. From then on, his interest in the exceptionally bright child increased. At the outset he was handicapped by the want of a dependable measuring instrument, but after the standardization of his own 1916 revision of the Binet-Simon scales, this lack was fairly well supplied. Even before the publication of this new scale, he had begun to collect records of children whose performance had been unusually high, and after work on the scale had been completed, he set out to locate as many high-testing children as he could find. By 1921 he had secured more or less systematic records of over one hundred children whose IQ's on this scale were 140 or higher. At this time, his efforts were rewarded by the receipt of a grant from the Commonwealth Fund to enable him to carry on his studies more extensively. Financial limitations, however, forced him to confine the investigation to the larger cities of California. Testing programs were organized in San Francisco, Los Angeles, and the three Bay Cities—Oakland, Alameda, and Berkeley. By the use of a screening process involving teachers' judgments, standing on group tests, progress through the grades, and an abbreviated form of the Stanford Binet, an attempt was made to locate all or nearly all of the exceptionally bright children in these cities. The children selected by the various screening methods were given a complete Stanford Binet test and those who reached a level of 140 IQ or higher were included in the group finally chosen for study. In all, almost 700 cases were located in this way, but these were elementary school children only.[5]

Through the co-operation of high school principals in various parts of the state, a second group, consisting of about 350 high

[5] A few children of preschool age were also included.

school children whose standing on a group test of intelligence was remarkably high, was located. And, as it became known that the study was being made, psychologists from all over the country began to send reports of exceptionally bright children whom they had tested. This added more than 350 further cases which, together with the hundred-odd cases in Terman's files at the time the main study was begun, made up a total list of well over 1500 names. Co-operation from parents and teachers was for the most part excellent. By means of frequent correspondence and a series of first-hand follow-up studies, contact has been maintained with an amazingly high percentage of the group up to the present writing, some thirty years after the original grant was received. Few indeed are the investigations that have been continued over so long a period.

Both because of the large number of subjects and the amount of information secured for each and, particularly, because of the long-time nature of the study, the Stanford investigation provides our main source of information about the intellectually gifted child. Other studies have been made, but as a rule the subjects have been few in number and in many of them the criterion for selecting the cases has been less rigid or has been poorly chosen. For these reasons, the greater part of the material in this chapter will be based upon the Stanford investigation.

PHYSICAL CHARACTERISTICS OF INTELLECTUALLY GIFTED CHILDREN

Until Terman's study proved its falsity, the prevailing concept of the intellectually brilliant child was that of a puny, underdeveloped weakling, "all brains and no body." That such children exist is, of course, true; but they are by no means typical. The average gifted child in the Stanford group was found to be significantly taller and heavier than the standards for American-born children in general or even than those obtained for other California children. As a rule they had broad shoulders and hips, strong muscles, and well-developed lungs. The generally advanced size of the children dates from the time of birth. The mean birth weight was approximately three quarters of a pound above the average for the population as a whole.

Both with respect to general health and in health habits, such as diet and usual amount of sleep, the gifted children showed some superiority over those of the control groups with whom they were compared. These facts, of course, must be considered in reference to the superior intelligence and educational background of their parents. Whether or not their superior physical care can account for their better physical condition is unknown.

Almost eight hundred children were given complete medical examinations by one or the other of two competent physicians. Both found the general condition of the majority of the children to be distinctly above average. Tests of auditory acuity showed about 1 per cent to have decidedly defective hearing and about 10 per cent to have hearing slightly below average. None was deaf. It is impossible to make a definite comparison of these figures with those for the population as a whole (see Chapters 24 and 25) because of differing standards and varying thoroughness of examination, but such evidence as is available indicates a lower percentage of children with hearing loss among the gifted than among the population as a whole. Better home care is probably the main determining factor here.

Vision of the gifted group seems to have been at least average, though the lack of really dependable figures for the general school population during the corresponding period renders comparison difficult. About 8 per cent of the subjects had vision no better than 10/30, according to the Snellen charts; most of these cases had been adequately corrected by glasses. Only three cases of very marked visual defect (10/100 or less without corrective lenses) were found. All wore glasses which gave at least partial correction.

The medical examinations were exhaustive, covering practically every aspect of child health. Although a few mildly abnormal cases and an occasional instance of serious physical defect were found under almost every heading, the physicians were agreed that, on the whole, the health and physical development of the children was superior to the average and that such evidences of home care as cleanliness, diet, and hours of sleep were far better than are generally found. Both physicians commented on the mental alertness of the children, their speed of comprehension, and their lack of self-consciousness in following instructions.

These results are quite in accordance with the findings of other persons who have studied smaller groups of gifted children. As will be seen, the majority of intellectually brilliant children come from homes of relatively high cultural and educational status where standards of child care are much superior to those of the average home. It may be that these factors are entirely responsible for the superior physical health and vigor of the intellectually superior children reported by practically all who have investigated the matter. This hypothesis could readily be tested by comparing the physical status of children of superior and those of average or inferior intelligence who come from homes of similar educational and cultural status, if possible, those from the same home. As far as I am aware this has never been done. Such a study would be an important contribution to our understanding of superior deviates, for if it were to appear that the variance between the two intelligence groups is greater than can reasonably be ascribed to chance, the assumption that the intellectually superior deviate is made of better stuff throughout than is his less able brother would receive some justification.

SCHOOL ACHIEVEMENT OF THE INTELLECTUALLY SUPERIOR CHILD

The majority of bright children find school learning easy. In fact, so easy are their lessons likely to be that time hangs heavy on their hands and they are forced to all kinds of expedients in order to occupy themselves. Of the Stanford group, almost half had learned to read before entering school, but fewer than 10 per cent entered in a grade higher than the first. This means that from the moment of school entrance the academic work of the classroom offered little or no challenge to their ability, and in order to keep out of trouble many were forced to undesirable habits of idleness and day-dreaming. Extra promotions, averaging a little more than a half-grade per child, were given, but neither advanced initial placement nor later extra promotion can hold the answer for the child whose intellectual capacity and educational acquirements are so far in advance of his years. Placement in a class of comparable ability would mean that he would be hopelessly outclassed in physical size and motor ability, as well as in many of his play interests and social activities. In view of the great educational retardation of these gifted children [6] it is surprising to find so few of them really maladjusted in school. According to their parents, only 1 per cent had a strong dislike for school, though an additional 4 per cent had only a slight liking or were indifferent toward it. The teachers reported only half as many gifted as control children who displayed an undesirable attitude toward school.

All children in the elementary school grades were given the Stanford Achievement Test which provides an excellent measure of the child's knowledge of the subjects taught in the elementary school. From this test educational quotients, similar in derivation to the intelligence quotient, were derived, both for the separate subjects and the total. All the children stood high on these tests, and in many instances their performance was far above that indicated by the grade markings given by the teachers. There is evidence that the majority of these children get much of their education out of school hours, through reading, conversation with adults, and close observation of the world around them. This is indicated by their own and their parents' reports of their interests and of the way they spend their leisure time and, perhaps most

---

[6] Terman states: "In general the average gifted child has mastered the subject matter of instruction to a point 40 per cent above his chronological age though he has been held back to a grade location only 14 per cent above the norm for his chronological age." Reprinted from Lewis M. Terman, *et al.*, *Genetic Studies of Genius*, Vol. 1, p. 306, with the permission of the author and of the publishers, Stanford University Press. Copyright 1925 by the Board of Trustees of Leland Stanford Junior University.

objectively, by their standing on a test of general information where their scores exceeded those made by others of their age to an even greater extent than those earned on tests of general intelligence.

Although the typical gifted child is superior to the average along practically all lines of accomplishment, he has his specialties and, in some cases, his deficiencies as well. None of the 1500 children showed absolutely even development along all lines of accomplishment; indeed, it is doubtful whether such a child exists regardless of his level of ability.

THE INTERESTS AND ACTIVITIES OF GIFTED CHILDREN

The expressed interests of the gifted children tended to cluster about the more abstract school subjects rather than those making chief demand upon rote memory or manual skill. Their performance on the educational tests and the school marks given by their teachers followed the same pattern. Penmanship as it was then taught was positively disliked by a rather large proportion of Terman's group. Sewing, cooking, and manual training also stood low on the list, but such subjects as literature, dramatics, and general science were likely to be rated high.

Practically all the children were strongly interested in reading. A two-months record of books read which was kept both by the gifted children and by a control group of similar age chosen at random from the same schools showed that the average gifted child of seven years read more books during that time than did the average child in the control group before the age of fifteen. Moreover the books read tended to be of better quality; they included more informational literature, biographies, and the like.

The play preferences of the children were expressed in terms of liking or disliking each of a designated list of ninety games and activities. On the basis of the ratings given by a control group of corresponding age a maturity index was assigned to each of these activities. It was found that the gifted children, on the whole, pre-

ferred games and activities that are more likely to be favored by
children somewhat older than themselves. They also showed a
rather definite preference for quiet games requiring reasoning and
judgment and were slightly less interested in competitive sports
than were the members of the control group of corresponding age.
The fact that slightly more than half the subjects in Terman's
group were the youngest in their classes may have some bearing
on the point last mentioned, for it is obviously not easy for a young
and small boy to compete physically with those so much older and
stronger than himself.[7] As is true of most children, sex differences
in play preferences were shown in the records of the gifted children. These differences followed much the same pattern as that
found for children in general. In spite of his typically younger age,
the gifted child's companionship was sought by his classmates to
about the same extent as that of the other children.

THE PERSONAL-SOCIAL TRAITS OF THE GIFTED CHILD

That the child of superior intelligence has a better understanding of the rules of society, that he is more likely to know just what
is expected of him in a given situation and to see the advantages
of doing it goes without saying. In other words, intelligence may
be applied to conduct as well as to school learning. Moreover, the
type of home training received by the majority of bright children
is likely to be conducive to the formation of good social habits
and acceptable conduct.

On the other hand, the bright child, as we shall see in a later
chapter, faces many problems that his less able classmate rarely
meets. And when, as sometimes happens, he is driven by a sense
of injustice or of social isolation to a form of behavior that is
undesirable, he may be more fertile in devising ways of torment-
ing his enemies or more satisfied by solitary occupations than are
the majority of children. The number of very brilliant children

---

[7] It is true that the gifted children were on the average large for their age
but this superiority in size and strength was frequently not sufficient to make
up for the greater age disparity.

who come into active contact with the law is small; as a rule, they find some other way of obtaining revenge when revenge seems called for, or they substitute other types of activities for those that are denied them. Both the Gluecks and Merrill found fewer than the average number of high-testing children among their groups of juvenile delinquents, though Merrill reports a larger percentage than was found in the earlier study. As she correctly points out, apprehended juvenile delinquents (court cases) generally represent an unfavorable social selection, since the more influential parents can often procure favors for their children or propose methods of handling them other than those provided by the courts.[8] Since no records are usually available for these cases, the extent of the selective effect is unknown but that it exists is highly probable.

As a class, the gifted children were reported to be modest rather than conceited in their demeanor. They realize how much they do not know, and, at the same time, their school success is sufficiently marked to leave no feeling of need for overcompensation.[9] Exceptions to this rule exist, however, particularly among those children whose parents have unwisely boasted of their exceptional gifts or exploited them in public.

In the Stanford study, teachers were asked to rate both the gifted children and a control group of corresponding age and sex on each of twenty-five carefully defined traits having to do with abilities, personality, and conduct. The parents of the gifted children also rated them on the same list of traits. Ratings given by parents and teachers showed fairly close agreement, particularly with respect to the characteristics on which the gifted showed greatest divergence from the average. According to the teachers'

[8] Such as placement in private boarding schools where the supervision is fairly strict, treatment by psychiatrists or clinical psychologists, etc.

[9] A few of the earlier writers who based their conclusions on the study of a small number of selected cases ascribed the remarkable educational achievements of the gifted child, as well as his exceptional interest in reading, to overcompensation for feelings of physical inferiority. Although her statistical method of demonstration is of questionable validity, Hollingworth has nevertheless offered convincing evidence that this theory does not hold good for the typical child of high intelligence.

ratings, the greatest difference between the gifted and the control group was shown in the group of traits regarded as primarily intellectual in character, such as reasoning, judgment, memory, and the like. Volitional traits ranked next in degree of superiority of gifted over control subjects, followed in order by emotional, physical, and social characteristics. The only one of the twenty-five traits in which the control children were given a higher rating than the gifted was mechanical ingenuity, and the difference here was so small as to be undependable. It may be remarked that genuine mechanical ability is a trait that the ordinary classroom teacher is not likely to have much opportunity to observe.

The findings of the Stanford study have, in general, been duplicated in other investigations when the number of subjects has been reasonably large and the method of selection free from bias. Although individual exceptions exist, children who are superior in intellect have, on the average, proved to be superior in practically all other desirable characteristics as well. References to a number of these studies will be found at the end of the chapter.

Some question arises, however, with respect to those rare children whose intellectual superiority is so great that congenial companionships are hard for them to find. Hollingworth has described twelve such cases and others have been reported in the literature. We shall reserve further discussion of this topic for a later chapter.

SOME TYPICAL CASES

Herbert is the second in a family of five children. His father is a well-known lawyer, his mother, who married after completing two years of college, has published several short stories. Although the other four children are all of superior intelligence, no one of them is quite as remarkable as Herbert.

I first became acquainted with Herbert just after his third birthday. He was then a chubby little youngster whose "square" head and blond coloring clearly betrayed his Swedish ancestry. He was not shy and willingly left his mother to come to the testing room with me "to see my toys."

On the 1916 revision of the Stanford Binet at the age of 37 months he earned a mental age rating of five years, four months, which gave him an IQ of 173. His superior ability was evinced in the quality of his responses, as well as in the numerical result of the test as a whole. His definitions of words were remarkable for their precision and detail. For example, "A chair is a piece of furniture. Some of them are rocking chairs and some are big chairs and some are not very big that you use to sit on at the dinner table." "A tiger is a wild animal they keep in a big cage in the zoo; he has black marks that go like this" (making vertical strokes in the air to illustrate his meaning).

Herbert's abounding energy and physical vitality enabled him to hold his own with neighboring children a year or more older than himself. His father was an ardent spectator at most competitive games and sports, and this interest was early adopted by his small son who knew the rules of football and basketball almost as soon as he could talk. His interest in games and sports undoubtedly enabled him to make friends among children whose intellectual and academic accomplishments were far below his own.

Annual tests both with the Stanford and with various nonlanguage scales yielded results very similar to that obtained at the first sitting. None of the various IQ's obtained fell below 140; nearly all were above 160.

Herbert entered kindergarten at five but did not care for it. He thought the activities silly. But he did have a good time on the playground before and after school with the older boys. In the elementary school he got on better, for he was given two extra promotions of a half year each early in the primary grades which put him in the company of the older boys with whom he had been accustomed to playing. But a new difficulty soon developed. Like most brilliant youngsters he was a rapid and inveterate reader. He spent much time poring over such sources of information as encyclopedias, dictionaries, atlases, road maps and timetables. He listened avidly to the conversation of his father's guests, who were, for the most part, persons of ability and distinction. All this so increased his store of information that he began to catch the other children and sometimes even the teacher in erroneous statements to which he was not slow in calling attention. His mental alertness frequently made him so impatient with the more sluggish intellectual processes of his classmates that he would interject answers to the teacher's questions regardless of the person to whom they were put. These habits were irritating to teacher and students alike and Herbert's popularity was considerably reduced as a consequence. However his unfailing good humor, his friendliness, and keen interest in sports [10] kept him a member of the group, though not a highly favored one.

From the time he entered junior high school, Herbert voluntarily began the practice of carrying more than the usual number of courses. Since this apparently had no unfavorable effect upon his health, which was always excellent, and since his academic standing continued to be among the highest in his class, no objection was raised. He completed the senior high school course at fifteen and received his bachelor's degree from one of the leading universities in the country a few months after his seventeenth birthday.[11]

The following fall he was offered a graduate scholarship at another university which he accepted. Before the end of his first quarter of graduate work came Pearl Harbor. He finished the quarter with a brilliant record, resigned his scholarship, and applied at once for admittance to an officers' training camp, which he entered on his eighteenth birthday. He remained in active service throughout the war, spending most of his time overseas. While home on a furlough he married a girl whom he had known and loved since high school days. The marriage has proved a very happy one in every way. After his discharge from the services at the close of the war, Herbert, together with his wife, took up his residence again at the university where his graduate work had

[10] Because he was so much younger than the others in his class, Herbert was never a member of any regular athletic team, either in high school or college. But he was an active participant in playground sports of all kinds and a regular and highly enthusiastic attendant at the games.

[11] This was accomplished in part through attendance at summer sessions; in part by carrying additional credits as he had done in high school.

been begun. He received his M.A., with a major in physics and a minor in mathematics, at the close of the year and was offered a part-time instructorship which would enable him to continue his work toward the doctorate. By this time the bumptiousness that had marked his earlier years had pretty well disappeared; he had developed a quiet and unassuming personality combining social poise with a modest demeanor that won the immediate liking and respect of students and colleagues alike. In spite of the delay in his education caused by the war, he received his Ph.D. at the age of twenty-six and was at once offered an assistant professorship at a good salary in one of the oldest and best-known universities in the country. This position he has filled with much success. He now has four children, is making payments on the attractive home in which they live, and seems to be well embarked upon a happy and useful professional career.

Herbert affords a nice illustration of the kind of meteoric educational progress likely to be made by those children of remarkably high intelligence whose ability to learn and zeal for learning are not damped by lack of opportunity. The case also illustrates the kind of difficulties that may arise when mental ability and school progress run so far in advance of social maturity and the insight that comes with age and experience. The interruption of Herbert's education by the war was probably a good thing, quite apart from the undoubted value of the military discipline and the stabilizing effect of a happy marriage.

Although the hazards of rapid school promotion of intellectually gifted children should not be disregarded, school acceleration does not inevitably result in social maladjustment even of a temporary nature. In the Stanford group there were many cases whose rate of school progress had been even greater than Herbert's, but who nevertheless maintained a high level of popularity and even of leadership. Several of these have been described by Burks, Jensen, and Terman in Volume 3 of the *Genetic Studies of Genius*. For example, there is Donald [12] (IQ 157), who at the age of fourteen was not only making a straight "A" record in the third year of

[12] See *Genetic Studies of Genius*, Vol. 3, pp. 257-259.

high school but was also an active participant in school sports, a sergeant in the R.O.T.C. (a year later he was made a captain), and a recognized leader in most school activities. He was a voracious reader, and showed rather marked literary talent. His range of interests and hobbies was extensive. He had made a number of interesting and valuable collections, including approximately a thousand lead soldiers which he used to study battle formations and military tactics. He had a keen sense of humor, was easy and friendly in his social relations, and almost universally popular.

Dora, who is designated by Burks, Jensen, and Terman as "a typically normal gifted child" is another example. When first seen, she was doing outstanding school work in the fifth grade, though she had not yet reached her ninth birthday. Her Stanford Binet IQ at this time was 168. Six years later, at the age of fourteen, she was in the third year of high school and still getting exceptionally high grades. She was elected president of her high school class during her freshman year and held a number of other class offices. Although one of her teachers reported that she was sometimes inclined to be overcritical of the mistakes made by her less gifted classmates and to enjoy the defeat of a rival, this does not seem to have had a serious effect upon her popularity.

SUMMARY

Although it is true that bright children differ from each other in so many and in such diverse ways that characteristics common to all or even to the majority may at first seem hard to discover, certain trends have nevertheless appeared so generally in all studies in which objective methods of selection and measurement have been employed that in spite of occasional exceptions, we are warranted in regarding them as typical. Of these, perhaps the most nearly universal is interest and zest in the acquisition of knowledge and information and the ability to organize facts in such a way as to lead to logical generalizations. This seems to be the essence of the "abstract thinking" which Terman considers the essential element in determining the level of intelligence. Closely allied to this power of abstract reasoning and judgment is facility in the use of symbols. Since language is the great symbolic process, it is not surprising to find that bright children are almost invariably facile in the use of words. Their vocabularies are commonly much larger than those of the average child and they are more sensitive to small differences in word meaning. It is not unusual to find highly intelligent children playing with words much as they do with toys. Some time ago I chanced to overhear a very brilliant little four-year-old talking to her doll which she had set in a small chair before her. "Now listen, Peggy," she commanded. "I'm going to teach you all the washing words. We *bathe* in the tub and we *shampoo* our hair. We *launder* the clothes and we *scrub* the floor. We *wash* the dishes—and we wash our faces too, and our hands. And," she frowned in concentration for a moment, "we dust and sweep and clean too, but that's different. No," she announced with decision, "those are not *washing* words."

Most bright children master the subjects of the school curriculum with ease, and more than half of them pass through the grades in fewer than the allotted number of years. A large percentage learn to read at least simple stories before entering school, and this with little or no help.

There is a well-authenticated record of a little girl who, shortly after her fourth birthday, was asked what she would like to have for Christmas. The child thought a moment and then replied, "A copy of Longfellow's poems and a small bag of peanuts." The day after Christmas she, in company with her parents, traveled by train from New York to Pittsburgh. The little girl spent the day very happily poring over her treasured copy of Longfellow, which, to her parents' amazement, she was able to read with but slight help. Just how early this accomplishment had been learned is uncertain. From babyhood, books had been her favorite toys. She played with them for hours and at a very early age would turn the familiar pages of *Peter Rabbit, Little Black Sambo,* and other childish classics, "reading" the stories from memory. Her *Hiawatha Primer* was an early delight; it was probably this that first aroused her interest in Longfellow. A Philadelphia doctor who cared for her during an attack of whooping cough still refers to her in tones of awed disbelief as "that child who was reading the *Idylls of the King* at the age of six!"

Not only do most intellectually gifted children learn to read with amazing ease, but the amount and quality of their reading runs far in advance of that of the average child of corresponding age. Reading is the most favored of all recreations for the great majority of these youngsters. Although active play is enjoyed by most of them, games involving some degree of thought and reasoning are likely to be preferred. Puzzles are popular with many; such games as checkers, dominoes, and chess are also enjoyed. Collecting is a fairly common hobby, and the collections made are likely to have more educational and scientific value than those made by the generality of children.

By far the greater proportion of highly intelligent children come from homes of superior educational and cultural level. Many men and women of national and even international renown are numbered among their relatives. Although this undoubtedly makes for superior home care and training and also provides better opportunity and incentives for learning, it is questionable whether these advantages can account for more than a relatively small percentage of the differences between the behavior and interests of highly gifted children and those of average capacity. The number of exceptions is too great. There are brilliant children whose parents are poor and uneducated. There are others who remain stupid in spite of every advantage that wealth can provide.

On the average, gifted children are slightly taller and heavier than the majority, and they are likely to be in better health. As a rule they are popular with other children and are more often leaders than followers. For the most part they are happy and well balanced emotionally, alert and present-minded. Nevertheless, the great difference in abilities and interests that separates them from their mates, as well as the petty jealousies sometimes aroused by their superior school records and ease of learning, not infrequently create difficulties of a kind that children of more ordinary talent are unlikely to encounter. Some of the special problems of the intellectually gifted child will be considered in the following chapter.

REFERENCES

BAKER, Harry J., *Characteristic Differences in Bright and Dull Pupils* (Bloomington, Ill., Public School Publishing Company, 1927).

BALDWIN, Bird T., "Methods of Selecting Superior or Gifted Children," *Twenty-third Yearbook of the National Society for the Study of Education* (Chicago, University of Chicago Press, 1924), Pt. 1.

BERKHAN, Oswald, "Das Wunderkind, Christian Heinrich Heineken," *Zeitschrift für Kinderforschung,* 15 (1910), 225-229.

BLAIR, Glenn Myers, *Mentally Superior and Inferior Children in the Junior and Senior High School: A Comparative Study of Their Backgrounds, Interests, and Ambitions,* Contributions to Education Series (New York, Teachers College Bureau of Publications, 1938), No. 768.

BROWN, Andrew W., *The Unevenness of Abilities of Bright and Dull Children,* Contributions to Education Series (New York, Teachers College Bureau of Publications, 1926), No. 220.

BURKS, Barbara S., JENSEN, Dortha W., and TERMAN, Lewis M., *Genetic Studies of Genius: The Promise of Youth* (Stanford, Cal., Stanford University Press, 1930), Vol. 3.

CARMICHAEL, Leonard, ed., *Manual of Child Psychology* (New York, John Wiley and Sons, 1946).

CARROLL, Herbert A., *Generalization of Bright and Dull Children* (*A Comparative Study with Special Reference to Spelling*), Contributions to Education Series (New York, Teachers College Bureau of Publications, 1930).

———, "Intellectually Gifted Children," *Teachers College Record,* 42 (1941), 212-227.

COBB, Margaret V., and HOLLINGWORTH, Leta S., "The Regression of Siblings of Children Who Test at or above 135 IQ (Stanford Binet)," *Journal of Educational Psychology,* 16 (1925), 1-7.

———, and TAYLOR, Grace A., "Stanford Achievement Tests with a Group of Gifted Children," *Twenty-third Yearbook of the National Society for the Study of Education* (Chicago, University of Chicago Press, 1924), Pt. 1.

COX, Catharine M., *Genetic Studies of Genius: The Early Mental Traits of Three Hundred Geniuses* (Stanford, Cal., Stanford University Press, 1926), Vol. 2.

COY, Genevieve L., "The Daily Programs of Fifty Gifted Children," *Journal of Genetic Psychology,* 37 (1930), 123-138.

DAVIDSON, Helen H., *Personality and Economic Background: A Study of Highly Intelligent Children* (New York, King's Crown Press, 1943).

DEARBORN, Walter F., and CATTELL, Psyche, "The Intelligence and Achievement of Private School Pupils," *Journal of Educational Psychology,* 21 (1930), 197-211.

FREEMAN, Frank N., "The Treatment of the Gifted Child in the Light of Scientific Evidence," *Elementary School Journal,* 24 (1924), 652-681.

HAGGERTY, Melvin E., and NASH, Harry B., "Mental Capacity of Children and Paternal Occupation," *Journal of Educational Psychology,* 15 (1924), 559-572.

HARMS, Ernest, ed., *Handbook of Child Guidance* (New York, Child Care Publications, 1947).

HAWK, Sara S., "Visual and Auditory Factors in a Group of Gifted Children," *Psychological Bulletin,* 42 (1945), 538 (Abstract).

HILDRETH, Gertrude, "Characteristics of Young Gifted Children," *Journal of Genetic Psychology,* 53 (1938), 287-311.

———, "The Educational Achievement of Gifted Children," *Child Development,* 9 (1938), 365-371.

HIRT, Zoe I., "A Gifted Child," *Training School Bulletin,* 19 (1922), 49-54.

HOLLINGWORTH, Leta S., "Musical Sensitivity of Children Who Test above 135 IQ (Stanford Binet)," *Journal of Educational Psychology,* 17 (1926), 95-109.

———, "The Comparative Beauty of the Faces of Highly Intelligent Adolescents," *Journal of Genetic Psychology,* 47 (1935), 268-281.

———, "The Development of Personality in Highly Intelligent Children," *Yearbook of the National Society of Elementary School Principals,* 15 (1936), 272-281.

———, and COBB, Margaret V., "Children Clustering at 165 IQ and Children Clustering at 146 IQ Compared for Three Years in Achievement," *Twenty-seventh Yearbook of the National Society for the Study of Education* (Chicago, University of Chicago Press, 1928), Pt. 2, pp. 3-33.

———, and GRAY, Howard A., "Juvenile Achievement As Related to Size," *Teachers College Record,* 32 (1930), 236-244.

———, and MONAHAN, Jane E., "Tapping Rate of Children Who Test above 135 IQ (Stanford Binet)," *Journal of Educational Psychology,* 17 (1926), 505-518.

JENKINS, Martin D., "A Socio-psychological Study of Negro Children of Superior Intelligence," *Journal of Negro Education*, 5 (1936), 175-190.

———, "Case Studies of Negro Children of Binet IQ 160 and above," *Journal of Negro Education*, 12 (1943), 159-166.

JONES, Anna M., "An Analytical Study of One Hundred and Twenty Superior Children," *Psychological Clinic*, 16 (1925), 19-76.

LAZAR, Mary, *Reading Interests, Activities, and Opportunites of Bright, Average, and Dull Children*, Contributions to Education Series (New York, Teachers College Bureau of Publications, 1935), No. 707.

LEWIS, W. Drayton, *A Study of Superior Children in the Elementary School*, George Peabody College Contributions to Education Series (Nashville, Tenn., George Peabody College Press, 1940), No. 266.

———, "Some Characteristics of Very Superior Children," *Journal of Genetic Psychology*, 62 (1943), 301-309.

LINCOLN, Edward A., "The Stanford Binet IQ Changes of Superior Children," *School and Society*, 41 (1935), 519-520.

MACMEEKEN, Agnes A., *The Intelligence of a Representative Group of Scottish Children* (London, University of London Press, 1939).

MCNEMAR, Quinn, and TERMAN, Lewis M., "Sex Differences in Variational Tendency," *Genetic Psychology Monographs*, 18 (1936), 1-65.

MENSH, Ivan Norman, "Rorschach Study of the Gifted Child," *Journal of Exceptional Children*, 17 (1950), 8-14.

MILES, Catharine Cox, and WOLFE, Lillian S., "Childhood Physical and Mental Health Records of Historical Geniuses," *Psychological Monographs (Dodge Commemorative Number)*, 47 (1936), 390-400.

MONAHAN, Jane E., and HOLLINGWORTH, Leta S., "Neuromuscular Capacity of Children Who Test above 135 IQ (Stanford Binet)," *Journal of Educational Psychology*, 18 (1927), 88-96.

NEMZEK, Claude L., "Constancy of the IQ's of Gifted Children," *Journal of Educational Psychology*, 23 (1932), 607-610.

ROOT, William T., "A Socio-psychological Study of Fifty-three Supernormal Children," *Psychological Monographs*, 29 (1921), 1-134.

Scottish Council for Research in Education, *The Intelligence of Scottish Children* (London, University of London Press, 1933).

TERMAN, Lewis M., *et al.*, *Genetic Studies of Genius: Mental and Physical Traits of a Thousand Gifted Children* (Stanford, Cal., Stanford University Press, 1925), Vol. 1.

———, and BURKS, Barbara S., "The Gifted Child," in *A Handbook of Child Psychology*, ed. Carl Murchison, 2d ed. (Worcester, Mass., Clark University Press, 1933).

TERMAN, Lewis M., and DeVoss, James C., "The Educational Achievements of Gifted Children," *Twenty-third Yearbook of the National Society for the Study of Education* (Chicago, University of Chicago Press, 1924), Pt. 1.

THEMAN, Viola, and WITTY, Paul A., "Case Studies and Genetic Records of Two Gifted Negroes," *Journal of Psychology*, 15 (1943), 165-181.

THORNDIKE, Robert L., "Performance of Gifted Children on Tests of Developmental Age," *Journal of Psychology*, 9 (1940), 337-343.

————, "Problems in the Identification, Description and Development of the Gifted," *Teachers College Record*, 42 (1941), 402-406.

TROW, William C., "Who Are the Gifted?" *Educational Digest*, 7 (1941), 17-20.

TYLER, Leona, *The Psychology of Human Differences*, 2d ed. (New York, Appleton-Century-Crofts, Inc., 1956). See especially, ch. 15.

VAN WAGENEN, Marvin J., "A Comparison of the Mental Ability and School Achievement of the Bright and Dull Pupils in the Sixth Grade of a Large School System," *Journal of Educational Psychology*, 16 (1925), 186-192.

WADDLE, Charles F., "Case Studies of Gifted Children," *Twenty-third Yearbook of the National Society for the Study of Education* (Chicago, University of Chicago Press, 1924), Pt. 1.

WHITE, Ralph K., "The Versatility of Genius," *Journal of Social Psychology*, 2 (1931), 460-489.

WILKINS, Walter L., "High School Achievement of Accelerated Pupils," *School Review*, 44 (1936), 268-273.

WITTY, Paul A., *A Study of One Hundred Gifted Children*, University of Kansas Bulletin of Education, 2, No. 7 (1930), 1-44.

————, "The Relative Frequency of Gifted Boys and Girls in the Secondary School," *Educational Administration and Supervision*, 20 (1934), 606-612.

————, "A Genetic Study of Fifty Gifted Children," *Thirty-ninth Yearbook of the National Society for the Study of Education* (Chicago, University of Chicago Press, 1940), Pt. 2.

————, and JENKINS, Martin D., "Intra-race Testing and Negro Intelligence," *Journal of Psychology*, 1 (1936), 179-192.

————, and LEHMAN, Harvey C., "Drive: A Neglected Trait in the Study of the Gifted," *Psychological Review*, 34 (1927), 364-376.

————, and LEHMAN, Harvey C., "A Study of the Reading and Reading Interests of Gifted Children," *Journal of Genetic Psychology*, 40 (1932), 473-485.

YATES, Dorothy H., "A Study of Some High School Seniors of Superior Intelligence," *Educational Research Monographs* (Bloomington, Ill., Public School Publishing Company, 1922), No. 2.

YERKES, Robert M., "Psychological Testing in the United States Army," *Memoirs of the National Academy of Sciences* (Washington, D.C., 1921), Vol. 15.

The Personal Adjustment and Social Relations of Highly Intelligent Children

8

> Great wits to madness sure are near allied
> And thin partitions do their bounds divide.
>
> John Dryden

EVEN BEFORE the seventeenth century the belief in a close association between genius and insanity was widespread, and in spite of ample evidence of its falsity, the idea has persisted to the present day.

That some great men have fallen victims to mental disease is unquestionably true. That the very fact of their genius has brought these cases into prominence is likewise undeniable. The man of mediocre ability who is known only to a small circle of friends and relatives may become mentally deranged without attracting much attention. But when a similar disaster befalls one whose achievements in science, art, or the public welfare have made him widely known, the contrast between his former brilliance and his later condition is so striking that it can hardly escape notice. In the minds of many people the mental imbalance of such men as Poe or Van Gogh is inextricably interwoven with their fame, but the mental stability of Goethe, Michelangelo, Justice Holmes, and numerous others who not only made notable contributions to world progress during their youth and early maturity but retained their mental vigor and enthusiasm to a ripe old age [1] is taken for granted and so overlooked. The attention-getting value of contrast

---

[1] Dryden himself was a notable exception to the rule he laid down, for he remained in good mental health to the time of his death at the age of sixty-nine.

is nowhere better exemplified than in the persistent belief that genius is allied to insanity.

FACTORS AFFECTING THE SOCIAL LIFE OF THE GIFTED CHILD

1. Disparity Between Chronological Age and Mental Age

The disparity between the chronological age and the mental age of the highly gifted child may and sometimes does introduce special difficulties in his relations with his companions. Mental age, it must be remembered, is merely a convenient way of designating the level of difficulty of the tasks that the subject in question is able to perform. This level is given concrete meaning by reference to the average performance of children of a given chronological age, just as the sizes of children's clothing are indicated in terms of the average age at which they fit. Every mother knows that her child may require a larger or a smaller size than his age would indicate; she knows also that in many cases the child who is much larger or smaller than others of his age is likely also to differ from them in bodily proportions, so that the standard garments may require some alterations.

In like manner, the child whose chronological and mental ages diverge greatly from each other is likely to differ from the average child in pattern as well as in degree of mental ability. In some respects, his interests and ways of behavior resemble those of children of his chronological age; in others, they are more like those of children of his mental age; and in still other ways, they tend to be unique. In those matters that depend primarily upon physical size [2] or upon life experience his interests are likely to resemble those of children of his chronological age more closely than they resemble those of children of his mental age. In respect to his reading interests and to games and other occupations that call for thinking and planning, for imagination and dramatic abil-

[2] Although gifted children average somewhat above the generality in respect to height and weight, in neither respect are they likely to approach the average measurement of those of their mental age.

ity the reverse is true. Finally, his mental alertness and fertility
of ideas often provide him with forms of recreation that are unlike those which the child of average intelligence is likely to
devise at any age. These unusual forms of play sometimes make
the child a leader among his companions to whom he communicates them. In some cases they become satisfying forms of solitary
recreation. In any case they are frequently overlooked in studies
of the social life of the bright child, who may thus be greatly
misjudged as far as his social behavior is concerned. Robert, one
of the children in the Stanford group, is an example.

Robert was eleven years old at the time he was first located
and was then in the eighth grade. His Stanford Binet IQ was 165.
He was extremely nearsighted, and even the best corrective lenses
that could be had did not make it possible for him to participate
safely in the competitive outdoor sports upon which the playground director insisted. He therefore spent his playtime when at
school in reading. Although his poor vision was recognized by his
teachers, he was nevertheless regarded as very nonsocial. They
pointed out that he *liked* to read, that he did not apparently consider his inability to participate in the playground sports a serious
deprivation. "He wouldn't take part in them if he could" was the
consensus of opinion. But when the field worker visited Robert's
home she was almost knocked off her feet by a bevy of young
knights in shining tin-can armor who, mounted on bicycles and
armed with wooden lances, were just starting out on a crusade.
The idea had been Robert's; the armor was constructed from
flattened tin cans cut into shape with tin snips and fastened
together by means of a small hand riveter. The design was reasonably authentic; it had been carefully worked out by Robert
from the pictures in medieval histories. In out-of-school hours, his
workshop in a disused garage and his back yard were the constant
gathering places for the boys of the neighborhood. His lack of
social participation at school [3] was more than made up for by the

[3] When questioned, Robert's teachers admitted that he was not actually
unpopular. "The boys like him well enough; he simply doesn't have much of
anything to do with them" was the verdict. Apparently none of them was
in any way acquainted with the home situation.

active social life that he led at home. Although cases so extreme as this are not often found, it is unquestionably true that gifted children often develop somewhat unusual forms of play which may cause them to be seriously underrated when the usual methods of measuring social activities are employed. Because they are so much younger and smaller than the other children of their mental age they are necessarily excluded from many of the games and sports in which the latter take part, even though they may not be hampered, as Robert was, by any specialized physical handicap. On the other hand, their intellectual maturity makes the kind of amusements preferred by the majority of children of similar chronological age seem trivial and childish. In this dilemma they are forced into one of two alternatives. They may discover forms of recreation in which their small size does not constitute a handicap and persuade other children to participate in them, or they may learn to find satisfaction in pursuits that do not demand the co-operation of others.

That the majority of unusually bright children also develop superior habits of social behavior has been demonstrated by a number of studies, most clearly by the Stanford investigation, where teachers were asked to rate each gifted child and a control child of the same age and sex on each of a series of intellectual, social, and personality traits. Each trait was named and carefully defined. The social traits were designated as follows: fondness for large groups, leadership, popularity with other children, sensitiveness to approval or disapproval, freedom from vanity and egotism. On each of these traits more than half of the gifted children were rated as high or higher than the average child in the control group. Others who have studied smaller groups of very bright children have obtained similar results. The popular opinion that the brilliant child spends all or most of his time in reading and other solitary activities is not borne out by objective study of the facts.

The remarkable intellectual achievements of these children, however, serve to call attention to those cases who do not succeed in overcoming the social difficulties brought about by the disparate levels of development of their minds and their bodies. Because they are physically unable to participate on an equal basis in the games and sports of children of their own mental level and are bored by the amusements of those of their own chronological age, a good many exceptionally bright children adopt the second of the two alternatives mentioned in a preceding paragraph. They turn to solitary activities where they find a quiet happiness of their own. Just how serious this withdrawal from social contacts may be is not easy to say. Certainly to the extent that it shuts the child out from the world of human affairs, it makes for a one-sided type of development and tends to prevent him from utilizing his intellectual gifts in the service of others. Nevertheless, the fact remains that many, if not most, of the intellectual pursuits of adult life are carried out in the seclusion of a laboratory or study where the presence of others is usually unnecessary and may be a distraction. Perhaps we have placed too much stress upon the desirability of mere gregariousness. We may have confused social adjustment with social dependence, forgetting that the child or the adult who has no resources for enjoyment within himself but must always turn to others for entertainment presents quite as serious a problem of social adjustment as the one who spends too much time in solitude.

Paradoxically enough, the typical gifted child seems to spend more time both in solitary and in social activities than does the one of average intelligence. The explanation is to be found in the comparative amount of time spent without definite occupation, in just sitting around or waiting for something to happen. The bright child can always find enjoyment for his spare minutes within the pages of a book, but his less able fellow stands helplessly about, complaining of his boredom.

2. *Disparity between Chronological Age and Educational Achievement*

More than half of the children in the Stanford group were the youngest in their school classes. Nevertheless, their grade retardation, as measured by the disparity between the grade level indicated by their standing on tests of educational skills and knowledge and the actual grade placement, was very great. The average child in the group had already mastered the work of two or three grades in advance of that in which he was placed. Terman has put the matter very succinctly by saying that although the average gifted child had attained an educational standing 40 per cent in advance of his age, he had been held back to a grade placement only 14 per cent above his age. This, too, is quite in accordance with the findings of others who have investigated the matter.

The question of the optimum grade placement of the highly intelligent child is a difficult one to answer. Rarely is it possible to take up the gap between his educational achievements and the requirements of the school curriculum by means of extra promotion alone. Some of the methods that have been adopted to deal with the problem will be considered in a later chapter. Here we shall note only the special difficulties of social and personal adjustment brought about by the situation commonly prevailing.

The child for whom the established work of his school class entails little or nothing that he does not already know may respond to the situation in any one of a number of ways. He may become a kind of exhibitionist, insisting on showing off his superior knowledge and assuming a scornful attitude toward those whose accomplishments do not equal his own. He may retreat into daydreaming or surreptitious reading. He may become a leader in schoolroom mischief. Or he may become an active participant in classroom work by bringing in supplementary information or giving help to those who are having difficulty but without assuming an attitude of offensive superiority. This, of course, is the end to be sought; whether or not it will be attained depends largely upon the insight and skill of the teacher.

The fact that a large percentage of highly intelligent children are given one or more extra promotions lessens but does not compensate for the difference between their educational attainment and grade placement. Not only does it place them with companions who are older and stronger than themselves but it often makes them the subject of thoughtless remarks from the other children or from visitors. "Aren't you going to get a cradle for that little baby boy?" facetiously inquired a twelve-year-old when a rather small boy of nine was admitted to his sixth-grade class. "Why do they all *look* at me so?" wailed a sensitive little girl just turned eight after a delegation from a women's club had paid a visit to the fifth-grade class in which she was enrolled. Repeated experiences of this kind may render the child indifferent to them, but they are more likely to increase self-consciousness to a point where it expresses itself in retreat or in the more aggressive forms of conceit and attempts to attract attention by "showing off." The child who demands attention in undesirable ways is usually the child who has had too much of it. It is easy for the brilliant child to be made conspicuous, and this fact constitutes one of the most serious hazards in his personal and social adjustment.

THE SOCIAL EXPLOITATION OF BRIGHT CHILDREN

In her *Little Red Horses,* G. B. Stern has given an exceptionally sympathetic account of the emotional upheaval experienced by her heroine, a brilliant and sensitive child of seven [4] whose literary talents were at first unwisely exploited by the devoted maiden aunts who had undertaken to care for her after the death of her mother and then ruthlessly suppressed by her father and her paternal grandmother after they had forcibly removed her from what they rightly considered the unwholesome influence of her early guardians. Both the aunts and the grandmother were motivated by the best possible impulses; they loved the little girl and desired to give her the best possible upbringing. But the aunts were fast turning her into a little puppet who expected constant admiration and flattery; [5] and the grandmother's strict discipline succeeded only in making the child bitterly unhappy.

[4] This character is, of course, purely fictional, but the author's description of the responses of a child to conflicting and incomprehensible adult standards is remarkably true to life.

[5] Not all children respond to social exploitation by demanding more and more of it. Some become increasingly shy and self-conscious, a few painfully so. One brilliant five-year-old of my acquaintance who was frequently called upon by her parents to dance and sing before guests developed a habit of falling into a profound sleep from which she could not easily be aroused

In addition to the social exploitation of gifted children as a means of gratifying the vanity of parents and sometimes of teachers, the possibility of financial gain may enter the picture. Hollywood would be even more overrun with child actors than it is if no restrictions were placed upon the cupidity of parents who dream of easy wealth from this source. Radio and television have added to the possibilities. Most successful child actors are superior in intelligence.[6] At a later age, pulchritude alone may be a sufficient asset for screen success, a pleasant voice and an infectious laugh may serve for the soap opera stars, and a combination of the two for the television actors. But the successful child actor must also possess a mentality that will enable him to understand and follow directions quickly and accurately and the imagination to grasp the meaning of the part he is to play and thus to make his impersonation lifelike and convincing. The stupid child cannot do this. It is the brilliant youngsters who are likely to be exploited for financial gain, and in many cases the experience is far from beneficial. Only occasionally does it contribute to later vocational success; often the effect upon the child's personality is definitely harmful.

The number of exceptionally gifted children who are exploited as a means of adding to the family income, however, is very small in proportion to the number who suffer from excessive admiration and thoughtless boasting on the part of parents and sometimes of teachers. This may easily lead to a kind of innocent exhibitionism on the part of the child who overhears their remarks and realizes

---

whenever a car drew up before the house. Only in this way could she escape the hated ordeal. Eventually the situation became so serious that clinical advice was sought. The parents were warned against further exploitation of the child's talents and the little girl herself was repeatedly assured that no further exhibitions would be required. Only after some months of treatment and continued assurance that she would not again be called upon for entertainment did the child's sleep habits become normal.

[6] The writer was personally responsible for testing the children in the Hollywood district at the time of the Stanford investigation. Practically all of the leading child movie stars of that period were included in the testing program, as well as most of the important understudies and extras. Practically all these children tested high; a number of them high enough to be included in the Stanford group.

that his sayings and doings are of more than ordinary interest to them. The popular belief that bright children are usually conceited is due largely to unwise behavior on the part of adults which has led these children to exaggerate their proper position in the social group and to feel that they merit more than their fair share of the limelight. Obviously, this does not make them popular with other children.

JEALOUSY AS A SOCIAL PROBLEM FOR THE GIFTED CHILD

Even when parents are modest and every effort is made to avoid publicity, the attainments of the child whose intellectual level is such that not more than three or four out of a thousand will equal him in ability are usually sufficiently outstanding to attract attention. Not infrequently this becomes a source of jealousy on the part of neighbors whose children are not remarkable for intellectual endowment. Usually the jealousy is covert and not likely to be recognized by those who experience it, but it manifests itself in all sorts of subtle ways. The conduct of the gifted child is closely scrutinized, and small misdeeds or errors of judgment are noted with satisfaction. "Albert may be the smartest boy in school," says Mr. Smith, "but I'd be ashamed to own a kid that couldn't throw a baseball any straighter than he can." The fact that Albert is considered one of the best players in school is conveniently ignored by Mr. Smith who prefers to base his judgment on a single wild throw which he chanced to observe when passing the playground.

Although children are less likely than their parents to exhibit jealousy of the superior attainments of their friends, this attitude may constitute an added source of difficulty for the brilliant child whose social relationships are faulty. The following episode, which was recently reported to me, illustrates the manner in which the jealousy induced by a particular situation may crystallize an existing unfavorable attitude into overtly spiteful behavior.

Martin is a very brilliant high school boy but he has never been popular. All his leisure time goes to his books and to a few solitary hobbies; his only friends are two or three elderly adults. When grades were given out at the end of the term, Martin received only A's and A+'s. No other student in his class approached his high standing. A few evenings later a number of his classmates called at his home. To his mother who answered the bell they explained that they were having difficulty with one of their assignments and had come to ask Martin's help. But when the boy appeared, they formed a circle about him, chanting a rude doggerel

> He got an A in Algebra
> (A stands for Ass)
> He got an A in Latin, too
> (A stands for Ass)
> Nothing but A's for Martin
> Aint he an Angel child!
> Ah-a-a-a-a-a-a-a-ah!

With a long drawn-out howl of derision they rushed out of the door and down the street, shouting with glee at their crude jest, leaving Martin flushed and bewildered and his parents hurt and angry.

Whether the attainments of the bright child excite jealousy, emulation, or admiration depends upon the complicated organization of traits that make up the child's personality and upon the society in which he functions. Superior accomplishments are an asset to the leader, and so long as he maintains his position of leadership, any feeling of jealousy among his followers is likely to remain covert. But the reins of authority are brittle and may snap if the leader makes too open a display of his superior accomplishments or is impatient with those whose ability is less than his own. The step from admiration to jealousy is short and quickly taken, as many a bright child has learned to his cost.

That jealousy is likely to be associated with the social exploitation of gifted children is easy to understand. Particularly when such exploitation leads to behavior on the part of the gifted child that his companions regard as indicative of conceit or of "showing off" unpleasant results are likely to occur. Although exceptional gifts by no means necessitate the spiteful forms of behavior that arise from jealousy on the part of a child's companions or their parents, it is unquestionably true that such gifts provide a basis for these reactions. It is therefore of the utmost importance that parents of brilliant children recognize this danger and guard against it by the cultivation of a modest attitude on their own parts as well as on that of their children.

CHILDREN OF EXTRAORDINARY INTELLECTUAL ABILITY: STANFORD BINET IQ 180 OR ABOVE

Children with authentic test records as high as 180 IQ are rare. Just how frequently they occur in an unselected population of American school children is unknown. Estimates from various surveys have varied greatly. In the Stanford group [7] there were 15 children who ranked at this level out of a total of approximately 160,000 canvassed. As Hollingworth has pointed out, the proportion of one child in a little more than 10,000 is almost certainly a larger figure than would be found for an unselected population drawn from the country as a whole. The greater concentration of superior intelligence in the large cities as compared to the small towns and rural districts is well known. The chance inclusion of a few excess cases in so small a total would change the proportions very markedly; in other words, the experimental error of the proportion found so far out at the extreme point of a distribution is very large. Estimates from other sources have varied considerably; some place the most probable frequency as low as one child in a million.[8] In spite of differences in the precise figures, all investigators are agreed that such children are rarely encountered.

Hollingworth, who made an extensive and careful study of these remarkable children, was convinced that their divergence from others of their age is so great that the likelihood of their

[7] Only the main experimental group examined by the regular field workers in 1921-1922 is included in the figures given above.

[8] See Hollingworth, *Children above 180 IQ*, pp. 23-25.

establishing satisfactory social relations with other children is small. Almost without exception, the twelve cases whom she studied directly, as well as the nineteen others of whom she was able to find reports in the literature, spent most of their time in solitary activities, since they were rarely able to find companions who could share their interests. Reading occupied the greatest part of their leisure time; play of a dramatic or imaginative nature with or without the use of toys was also common. Several had invented imaginary companions or imaginary countries which served to some extent as a compensatory mechanism, taking the place of the real playmates whom they lacked. The difficulties of adjustment likely to be experienced by children whose abilities and the intererests resulting from them differ so greatly from those of the generality are so great that Hollingworth was led to suggest the concept that:

there is a certain restricted portion of the total range of intelligence which is most favorable to the development of successful and well-rounded personality in the world as it now exists. This limited range appears to be somewhere between 125 and 155 IQ. Children and adolescents in this area are enough more intelligent than the average to win the confidence of large numbers of their fellows, which brings about leadership, and to manage their own lives with superior efficiency. Moreover, there are enough of them to afford mutual esteem and understanding. But those of 170 IQ and beyond are too intelligent to be understood by the general run of persons with whom they make contact. They are too infrequent to find many congenial companions. They have to contend with loneliness and with personal isolation from their contemporaries throughout the period of immaturity. To what extent these patterns become permanently fixed, we cannot yet say.

There is thus an "optimum" intelligence, from the viewpoint of personal happiness and adjustment to society, which is well below the maximum. The exploration of this concept should yield truths of value for education, and for social science as well. The few children who test at the very top of the juvenile population have a unique value for society. On them depends in large measure the advancement of learning. If they fail of personal happiness and human contact, their work for society as a whole may be impaired or lost.[9]

[9] *Ibid.*, pp. 264-265.

No one who has had first-hand association with one or more children who reach a Stanford Binet level of 180 or higher can fail to realize the social and educational difficulties they present. The following brief account of one such child, personally known to me, will serve as an example.

I first became acquainted with Arthur shortly after his fifth birthday when his parents came to consult me about his education and training. At that time Arthur was attending the kindergarten connected with the State Teachers' College in the small town where he lived, but he found little there to interest him. He was a courteous little fellow who took part in the games and listened politely to the teachers' stories but he was bored and puzzled by their triviality. He had learned to read at a very early age [10] and was by this time browsing freely in his father's large library. It is therefore not surprising that he found the kindergarten stories uninteresting and the games "babyish."

On the 1916 revision of the Stanford Binet he earned an IQ of 186. A year later he was given the 1937 revision on which he reached an even 200.[11] At the age of five his standing on the reading tests of the Stanford Achievement Scale was at the eighth-grade level; in arithmetic reasoning it was above the fifth grade standard. He could do little with the arithmetic computation since he had had no instruction whatever and did not know the meaning of the signs $(+, -,$ etc.$)$.

According to his parents' report, Arthur was a healthy, full-term infant of a placid temperament. Physically he is inclined to be

---

[10] The exact age at which he began to read is uncertain. Books were always favorite playthings, and the association between favorite stories and their printed symbols was made so easily and gradually that no one was aware of the process until after it had been accomplished. All that his parents could say was that at the age of five he had been reading for his own pleasure for at least two years. Similar stories are told of many other very brilliant children. In the Stanford study, almost half of the children in the main experimental group are said to have learned to read before entering school and twenty are reported as reading before the age of four. How well they read is, of course, unknown.

[11] As had been noted elsewhere, the standard deviation of IQ's on the 1937 revision is slightly greater than that on the 1916 revision. The two figures thus correspond very closely as far as their rarity is concerned.

clumsy. His poor motor control as a child was primarily due to lack of practice, although his short, heavy body and stubby fingers undoubtedly contributed to his difficulty.

As Arthur grew older his educational problems increased. Obviously no ordinary schoolroom can provide much intellectual stimulation for a five-year-old who reads and comprehends material suitable for the eighth school grade. It was hoped, however, that the school would succeed in providing him with the social contacts that he needed and that it might also help him to overcome the motor awkwardness and arouse an interest in normal play. To this end his parents were also advised to furnish the home yard with playground equipment calling for large muscle activities—a swing, parallel bars, a slide, and the like—and to encourage the children of the neighborhood to come there to play. For a time these measures seemed effective. Other children were readily enticed to visit the yard, where, with the pride of ownership, Arthur displayed his new possessions and endeavored to demonstrate their use. But his ineptness soon caused him to be pushed aside. For the most part he was relegated to a position as onlooker.

Arthur was enrolled in the second grade of a small private school at the age of six.[12] Although his interest in active play continued to be slight, he nevertheless participated to some extent in the games and activities of the other children both at school and in the home yard. But here, as previously, the circular reaction so often noted by psychologists and educators became manifest. Physically he inclined rather markedly toward Kretschmer's "pyknic" type, with a heavy body and short arms and legs. Although the handicap thereby produced was slight and could have been overcome by practice, it did make the acquisition of motor skills somewhat more difficult for him than for those of a more slender build. Moreover, his superior intelligence made him become aware of his relative lack of motor success at an age when

---

[12] The choice of grade was based upon the fact that the teacher of this class had taken a number of university courses in child psychology and had manifested considerable insight with respect to child behavior.

most children are untroubled by such comparisons. Thus his original handicap was increased through self-consciousness and awareness of failure.

During his first years in school, a certain amount of social experience was obtained by Arthur through helping his classmates with their lessons. But the contrast between their abilities and his own was so great that mutual understanding was not easy. In spite of the teachers' efforts, the social gap between him and his contemporaries constantly widened. At the age of eight he was sent to a summer camp. This experience proved decidedly unsatisfactory; he did not enjoy the activities and took as little part in them as possible.

Meantime, in school he was forming habits of idleness. His social isolation and tendency to physical lethargy prevented him from becoming an active behavior problem but the classroom activities provided little or nothing in the way of intellectual occupation or stimulation. When he was twelve he was sent to a private preparatory school of high academic standing. Here, for the first time, he met genuine scholastic competition. Although he made few friends during this period, he was not unpopular, and the intellectual challenge he encountered gave him a sense of companionship that he had not experienced before.

At last hearing, Arthur was a junior in one of the large eastern universities and was making a satisfactory but not an outstanding academic record. He had few friends and took no part in the college activities. He was admittedly unhappy, dissatisfied with himself and with his accomplishments, and very lonely. What the future may hold for this lad of extraordinary mental endowment is uncertain.

Arthur's history raises a number of important questions. Certainly it tends to support Hollingworth's contention that a child can be too intelligent for satisfactory social and emotional adjustment. Nevertheless while admitting the difficulties that such extreme departure from the typical pattern of development displayed by children in general necessarily entails, we must still ask whether or not these difficulties are insurmountable. Arthur had the advantages that come from a cultured home and parents who were eager to provide him with the best possible opportunities. Psychological and psychiatric advice was given, and as far as possible this advice was followed. Yet the outcome thus far has been tragically unhappy. Where was the mistake made?

Only conjecture is possible at this time. One thing, however, seems apparent. The persistent efforts, well meant though they were, to urge upon the child a pattern of interests and of behavior that differed so greatly from his inherent propensities were almost certainly unwise. Unquestionably the methods adopted were ineffective. Perhaps we have been too strongly dominated by the concept of a "well-rounded personality"; almost certainly we have been inclined to insist upon a stereotyped pattern as the only possible example of a well-adjusted person. We have sung the praises of the extrovert, found virtue in gregariousness, but have overlooked the desirability of being able to find resources for enjoyment within oneself. This does not mean that social relationships are unimportant. But too much emphasis upon social contacts, particularly for children with many intellectual interests, can defeat its own object. Often more will be accomplished if less is attempted.

One cannot help but wonder what would have happened in Arthur's case if no attempt had been made to place him in school. A private tutor for an hour or two daily could have maintained his intellectual interests at a high pitch and helped him to gain many skills that would have been of much value to him. After school hours and on Saturdays he would have been free for play, and it is possible that after a day spent largely in intellectual work he would have felt inclined for relaxation and companionship. Certainly the procedure actually followed, although it meant that a larger proportion of his time was passed in the company of other children, did not result in the establishment of any really functional social relationships.

The loss to society of even a single case of such rare potentiality is incalculable; the failure of the methods used with Arthur, as well as those described for the children studied by Hollingworth, should cause us to reconsider our concept of what, for these cases, is the most desirable pattern of behavior and to ascertain feasible methods of bringing this behavior about. Until more has been ascertained with respect to this question, too much insistence upon conformity to a preconceived mode of personal-social attitudes and behavior would appear to be a questionable practice.

THE PERSONAL-SOCIAL REACTIONS OF THE TYPICAL BRIGHT CHILD: EXPERIMENTAL FINDINGS

That the child of very superior intelligence encounters many difficulties in the course of his personal-social development that the average child is likely to escape is an undeniable fact. It is also true, however, that the greater number of these children possess certain assets with which to surmount these difficulties. As a rule, though not invariably, their parents are also above average in mentality. This should and generally does mean that their early training is more intelligently planned and carried out than is that of the average child. As a rule, too, they have more material advantages. Their parents may not be wealthy but fewer of them are very poor, and the income they have is likely to be used to better advantage. All this means that the typical gifted child starts life with some advantages in the way of social prestige.

Moreover, intelligence may be applied to the acquisition of social skills and to gaining insight into one's own attitudes and behavior, as well as to learning to read or to memorizing the multiplication table. The bright child is more fertile in ideas than is his less gifted neighbor. He thinks of new games, makes up stories and plays, devises better ways of doing things. He has a larger vocabulary and expresses himself more clearly and forcibly than others of his age; he is more quick-witted and alert in argument. If once accepted as a leader, these characteristics make it easier for him to maintain his position.

In 1919, Terman reported the results obtained by having both teachers and parents rate each child in a group of 41 very bright children on a number of personal-social characteristics. On each of the 20 traits studied, the ratings given by the teachers were above the theoretically defined average and, in most cases, somewhat higher than those given by parents. Just how superior the ratings were is not known, since there was no control group and, as is now well known, most people are reluctant to use the lower half of a rating scale unless the inferiority of the subject in question is rather marked. A similar list of 25 traits was used in the large-scale Stanford investigation carried out in 1921-1922. Again, both parents and teachers rated the gifted subjects, and ratings were also secured from teachers for a control group of children of an age and sex distribution similar to that of the gifted subjects. In this case, although the theoretical average was set at 7.00, with a possible range from 1 (highest) to 13 (lowest), in only three instances was the mean rating given by the teachers to the control group as low as the theoretical mean of 7.00. The actual means for this group ranged from 5.31 (control girls, cheerfulness) to 7.69 (control girls, mechanical ingenuity). But the mean ratings of the gifted children by their teachers were almost without exception higher than the corresponding means for the control group of similar age and sex. Many of the differences were large and reasonably consistent from child to child. Considering only the teachers' ratings, 81 per cent of the gifted boys and 82 per cent of the gifted girls equaled or exceeded the control groups of the same sex in self-confidence; in will power and perseverance the corresponding figures were 83 and 86 per cent respectively; in truthfulness, 72 and 70 per cent. In popularity the difference less consistently favored the gifted children, with only 53 per cent of the boys and 59 per cent of the girls equaling or exceeding the median rating of the control group; in fondness for large groups the boys were considered to be slightly inferior and the girls slightly superior to the control children. When all the traits were combined, 70 per cent of the gifted boys and 72 per cent of the gifted girls had a total rating equal to or exceeding that of the control group. Contrary to Terman's earlier findings, which were based on much smaller numbers, the ratings given by the parents of the gifted children averaged slightly higher than those given by teachers, though the differences were for the most part small.

No objective tests of personal-social characteristics have ever been devised equal in dependability to the best test of intelligence or of achievement in the ordinary subjects of the school curriculum, and those available in the early 1920's when Terman's main study was begun were less valid than some that have been developed more recently. However, a large number of the best tests that were then available, together with others devised especially for the survey, were given to the gifted children in Terman's group and to control groups of corresponding age and sex. These tests were intended to measure such characteristics as truthfulness, honesty, self-confidence, emotional stability, and the like. Tests of play interests were scored in such a way as to indicate both the degree of interest in play and the maturity and masculinity of the expressed interests. A test of the free-association type devised by Wyman, the details of which were described in Volume 1 of the *Genetic Studies of Genius* was scored in such a way as to provide measures of three types of interest; intellectual interests, social interests, and interest in activity. All of these tests yielded fairly high self-correlations, but the lack of dependable criteria rendered it very difficult to ascertain the extent to which they could be depended upon to measure the actual traits indicated by the names assigned to the tests.[13] Taking the results at their face value, it was found that the gifted subjects were more honest, more truthful, had fewer emotional disturbances, were much more mature in their play interests, and displayed much stronger intellectual and social interests than the control subjects of corresponding age and sex. With respect to their activity interests (defined as interest in *doing*, rather than merely thinking or talking about the act in question or in just watching others do it),

[13] A further difficulty in the way of establishing valid criteria for use in standardizing tests of nonintellectual characteristics is the lack of agreement among authorities as to the meaning of terms. Although it is true that semantic difficulties of this kind also exist in such areas as intelligence or school achievement, conceptual variability from person to person is much less marked than it is with respect to such traits as introversion, emotional stability, or social interests.

the gifted children ranked equally as high as the control group but not materially superior to it. The play interests of the gifted boys were slightly more "masculine" than those of the control boys, and those of the gifted girls did not differ materially from those of the control girls in this respect.[14] All in all, to the extent that the tests used really do measure the characteristics they purport to measure, the gifted subjects of the Stanford investigation exceeded the unselected children who served as controls in practically all the personal-social traits that were studied.

No other study of superior children approaches the Stanford investigation in respect to the number and representativeness of the selection within the population canvassed,[15] the amount of information secured for each child, and the care taken in securing and analyzing the facts. A good many smaller studies have been made, and these, on the whole, tend to confirm the findings of the Stanford study. Hollingworth and Rust gave the Bernreuter Inventory to 50 adolescents who in childhood had earned Stanford Binet IQ's ranging from 135 to 190 and to an equal number of unselected college students. The scores of the gifted adolescents averaged significantly lower in neurotic tendencies and in submission and significantly higher in self-sufficiency than those of the college students. McElwee found that children who had received one or more double promotions were given higher ratings by their teachers in practically all the desirable mental, physical, and emotional characteristics of a list compiled by her, and that those who had failed of promotion one or more times were usually ranked higher on the undesirable traits. One hundred children equally divided as to sex were included in each group. Intelligence tests

[14] For the method of deriving the maturity and masculinity indices, the reader should consult *Genetic Studies of Genius,* Vol. 1, ch. 14.

[15] This population included the five largest cities in California. There is reason to believe that relatively few of the elementary school children in those cities who were capable of reaching the standard set (Stanford Binet IQ of 140 or higher) were missed in the survey, but there is, of course, no assumption that the population of these cities is representative of the elementary school population in the entire country. As Hollingworth has pointed out, the frequency of such children found in this survey is probably considerably higher than would have been found had all the children of corresponding age in the country as a whole been canvassed.

were not given, but it is fair to suppose that the accelerated children were for the most part of superior mentality. Lewis and McGhee compared the interests of children earning the highest 10 per cent of scores on the Kuhlmann-Anderson Group Intelligence Test with those of the children whose scores comprised the lowest 10 per cent. Four hundred and fifty-five schools were canvassed. The bright children had many more interests and hobbies than the backward ones. However, a slight and unreliable superiority of the latter with respect to social activities, clubs, and sports was reported. It was concluded that the schools are not doing enough to socialize the bright child.

Witty and Lehman, using the Lehman Play Quiz with 50 children of an IQ of 140 or above, each of whom was matched for age, sex, and environment with a control child of average mentality, found that although the gifted children were equally as versatile in their play interests as the controls, they tended to avoid certain of the most vigorous and competitive forms of sport, such as boxing, and had a slightly lower index of social participation.[16] As in practically all other investigations, the gifted spent much more time in reading and in activities in which reading is involved than did the control group. Other studies have agreed in finding that when representative groups of intellectually gifted children are compared with the generality of similar age and sex, the gifted children are found to be superior in most nonintellectual traits as well as in those dependent chiefly upon abstract intelligence; they have a wider range of interests and hobbies and are superior in character traits. With the possible exception of a small number of the children at the extreme upper end of the intelligence distribution, they rank at least as high as the average child in most social traits and are above the average in leadership. The experimental evidence thus lends little support to the popular idea that exceptionally bright children are likely to be "queer" or that they are emotionally unstable.

[16] The index of social participation was obtained by dividing the total number of activities in which the child claimed to have participated during the past week in company with one or more other children by the total number of activities in which he took part.

Although the majority of gifted children thus appear to be happy, well adjusted, and at least as popular as the average, this cannot be said of all the children at any intellectual level. And when a child of very superior intelligence fails to realize his potentialities, the loss to society is far greater than it would be if those potentialities had been less. For this reason, particular interest attaches to children who do poorly in school in spite of high standing on intelligence tests or to those whose social or emotional adjustment is unsatisfactory. Many attempts have been made to study such cases with a view to finding the causes of their difficulties and developing methods of correcting them. Some of these investigations take the form of case reports; others have looked for consistent trends within larger groups. No attempt will be made here to review all of these investigations, since examination of the findings shows that the factors which handicap the adjustment of the gifted child are not, in most cases, greatly different from those that disturb the lives and interfere with the happiness of children in general. Such differences as appear are due chiefly to the keener perceptiveness of bright children, their greater awareness of, and sensitivity to, the behavior and attitudes of others, and to the special difficulties resulting from the differences between them and other children, some of which were discussed in the early part of this chapter.

With respect to scholastic standing, we may dismiss at once a large body of well-meant but invalid studies in which the so-called Accomplishment Ratio (EQ/IQ) or one of its many variants has been used. The errors inherent in this method have been pointed out so often [17] that it is unnecessary to do more than repeat the statement that regression due to errors of measurement will inevitably penalize the bright child and give an unfair advantage to the backward one when this method of comparison is used. The conclusion frequently drawn by these investigators that "bright

[17] See especially, Florence L. Goodenough, *Mental Testing: Its History, Principles and Applications* (New York, Rinehart and Company, 1949), p. 254.

children do not work up to their ability" [18] is unwarranted since it is based upon spurious statistical reasoning.

A study by Lewis illustrates the fact that the conditions accompanying inferior educational performances of gifted children do not differ greatly from those generally found. From a group of 4529 elementary school children who constituted the top 10 per cent of a school population of over 45,000 to whom the Kuhlmann-Anderson Group Test of Intelligence had been administered, two groups were chosen for study. The first group, known as the educationally accelerated group, was made up of those whose educational ages, derived from a composite of the 11 tests making up the Unit Scales of Attainment, were a year or more in advance of their mental ages. The second, designated as the educationally retarded group, consisted of those whose educational ages were a year or more below their mental ages. Ratings on a number of personality traits were secured from the teachers, together with a certain amount of information on the home and family. The following are examples of the traits on which the accelerated group surpassed the retarded group to an extent great enough to be statistically reliable: originality, self-reliance, ambition, honesty, desire to investigate, persistence, politeness, neatness. With respect to the following traits, the differences were likewise statistically reliable but took the opposite direction: inattentiveness, slovenliness, laziness, a "quitter," a whisperer, lack of interest. Other differences, less reliably established, followed the same general pattern. Various ratings on parental attitudes and on other factors in the home background also favored the accelerated group. It seems unlikely that these findings are significantly different from what would be found for any two groups of comparable intelligence who show similar differences in educational accomplishment. Laziness, lack of interest in school, or poor home conditions are handicaps to learning; industry, neatness, and strong

[18] What is meant, of course, is that bright children, *selected on the basis of high IQ's*, do not achieve as high scholastic standing as *unselected* children of corresponding mental age. Exactly what "working up to one's ability" would mean in a more abstract or general sense it is impossible to say.

desire to achieve make for superior school performance at any intellectual level. Conklin, whose subjects were 65 elementary school children with IQ's of 140 or higher who were failing in two or more subjects, and a control group of children of similar ages and IQ's whose work was satisfactory, obtained results that were, on the whole, similar to those found by Lewis, though the differences between the groups were less marked. Laycock compared teachers' ratings of matched groups of children of superior and inferior intelligence on a list of 102 social and emotional characteristics, and he himself made similar ratings of each on the basis of personal interviews with the parents. On 88 of the traits the superior group received more favorable average ratings by the teachers than did the inferior group. Most of these differences were statistically reliable. Ratings derived from reports by the parents showed smaller differences between the groups, but the differences for the most part took the same direction as those from the teachers' ratings.

A number of studies based on individual children or on small groups of children referred to a behavior clinic have purported to show the special difficulties surrounding the child of high intelligence. In many instances, however, the authors of these studies have failed to realize that coincidence does not necessarily mean causation and that the fact that these children were brought to the clinic because of some behavior difficulty means that they cannot be considered representative examples of their intellectual level, whether that level be low or high. Thom and Newell, for example, examined the later adjustment of 43 children of superior intelligence who had been studied at a behavior clinic at a date averaging eleven years before the follow-up. Twenty-one cases were judged to be making a superior adjustment; the remaining 22 were rated average or inferior in adjustment. The proportion making a superior adjustment seems astonishingly high, since these cases were selected on the basis of early difficulties. The lack of any control group also makes evaluation of this study difficult. Although the article is entitled, "Hazards of the High IQ," the factors contributing to the relative lack of success among the second group do not appear to be closely related to the level of intelligence. The authors report poor home conditions, financial insecurity in some cases amounting to financial distress, inconsistent management by the parents during the early years, and far more family discord in the home backgrounds of the unsuccessful group than among those whose later adjustment was good. Examination of the several brief case histories reported reveals only one in which high intelligence appears to have been a material factor in the child's problems. This child had been a "quiz kid" on a local radio program. He refused to give any attention to his formal school work but devoted all his study time to getting the kind of incidental information likely to be called for in the radio sessions. He failed of promotion several times and eventually had to be sent to a private school to make up his work. In this case, the high IQ was presumably a factor in enabling him to get on the radio program in the first place, but it does not account for his being kept there when it was obviously having such undesirable results.

The conclusion that may be drawn from this and other studies of the same type is that certain environmental conditions are unfavorable for the optimum development of any child, whether he is bright or dull. In some instances, however, the child of very superior intelligence may be more seriously disturbed by matters involving his own or his family's reputation than is the one who is intellectually less capable of understanding the implications of such conditions. The following case, personally known to me, is an example.

The S____ family consisted of four boys. The mother, a college graduate said to have been of very superior intelligence, died eight years after her marriage. The boys, ranging in age from two to seven years, were placed in an orphanage where they remained for approximately four years. The father then remarried. The second wife was a kindly woman who insisted upon providing the boys with a home. The boys became very fond of their stepmother. But with the passage of time, Mr. S____ became increasingly intemperate and abusive toward his wife and children.

I first became acquainted with the family when I was requested by

authorities of the school which the boys were attending to examine
B_____, the second in age of the four boys, whom I shall designate as
A_____, B_____, C_____, and D_____, A_____ being the oldest and D_____
the youngest. The reasons for requesting the examination were twofold:
first, to see whether he would profit by an extra promotion, and, second,
in order that I might, if possible, ascertain the cause for the marked
change in his behavior over the preceding months. Formerly a cheerful,
alert, active youngster, popular with his classmates and at the top of his
class, he had become depressed, silent, inattentive in class and no longer
took part in playground activities. His teachers had questioned him
about the cause of his evident unhappiness and anxiety without success.

B_____ proved to be a handsome lad, tall for his 12 years but somewhat pale with deeply shadowed dark eyes. He seemed rather appre-
hensive on first coming to the testing room but soon became interested
in the tasks set him and responded to them freely. However, he immediately veered away from all attempts to direct the conversation into
more personal channels and gave only very brief and evasive replies to
questions about his home and family.

On the Stanford Binet he earned an IQ of 145; on standard tests of
school achievement his performance ranged from one to five grades
above that in which he was enrolled.

A call at the home and talk with the stepmother revealed the following story. The father's behavior had become a neighborhood scandal.
He had openly brought loose women to the home, was drinking heavily
much of the time, and was noisy, profane, and abusive. A few months
previously he had been brought into court on a charge of violating the
Mann Act but had been acquitted on his claim that the woman from a
neighboring state had been engaged to help him in his office. A small
room had been partitioned off the office for her occupancy. In spite of
his claim of a purely business relationship, the woman had by now
become obviously pregnant.

According to the stepmother's report, the father's rages were usually
directed against B_____ and C_____, particularly the latter, who, at this
time, was just recovering from an attack of pneumonia brought on
apparently by two nights' exposure to a heavy rain when, although
already suffering from a severe cold, he had run away from home after
a beating by his father. Mrs. S_____ had then decided to leave her husband as soon as C_____ became a little stronger. She pleaded urgently
that something be done for the boys, particularly for B_____ and C_____.
"The other two," she stated, "seem to get along with their father better.
They generally manage to keep out of his way when he gets mad, and
they don't care so much about what people say. They joke with him

sometimes, and they even seem to look up to him in some ways. The other day A—— said to me, "My dad can lick anybody on this block, drunk or sober.' And D—— grinned and said, 'Or anybody in this town, I guess, or maybe the whole world.' It's queer, but those two really seem to think a lot of their father."

The stepmother's reports were verified by other responsible persons. It seemed apparent that steps should be taken to place the children in a more suitable environment. At the request of the Children's Welfare Society, intelligence tests were given to the other three boys. The following IQ's were established: A——, 94; C——, 142; D——, 87.

DISCUSSION

In spite of popular opinion to the contrary, the typical child of high intellectual gifts is by no means eccentric, unpopular, or "one-sided." Such children exist, it is true, but they are exceptional rather than typical of the top centile of intellectual ability. With the possible exception of the rare child whose average rate of mental development has been almost twice as rapid as that of the generality of children of his age and for whom social problems are correspondingly extreme, the majority of exceptionally bright children reach successful solutions of social as well as academic problems. Regardless of whether the criterion is the judgment of teachers or other presumably competent observers or the child's standing on the various tests designed to measure personal-social characteristics, children whose Stanford Binet IQ's fall at or above the 140 level have been found to excel the average of their age and sex with respect to most traits having to do with social or emotional characteristics.

However, as we have said, exceptions occur. In the first place, bright children are not immune to the unfortunate conditions of home and family life from which some children suffer, regardless of their level of intelligence. Some of them come from homes that have been broken by divorce which may have been preceded by a long period of family bickering and quarreling. Some have been embarrassed by poverty and the consequent lack of many things which their mates enjoy. Some feel ignored by their parents;

others have to contend with parental boasting and personal exploitation.

These are difficulties encountered by children at all levels of ability. If they oppress the bright child more severely than those of lesser ability—as some of them are likely to do—it is because of his greater awareness of their implications for himself and others. The situation in the S____ family is a neat example of this. The two boys of highly superior intelligence were painfully aware of the neighborhood gossip; they felt it as a reflection upon their own standing in the community, as well as upon that of their father. They felt disgraced and humiliated. But the two brothers of rather less than average intelligence were little if at all distressed by it.

Because the world is so largely made up of persons whose mental ability is near the midpoint of the population as a whole, its social customs and systems of education and training are suited to this large group of mentally average individuals. But neither the schools nor the ways of society are so well adapted to the smaller group of extreme deviates. In the preceding sections we have indicated a few of the special difficulties that are likely to beset the lives of children of highly superior intelligence. The fact that the great majority of these children succeed in surmounting these difficulties, as Terman and others have so clearly demonstrated to be the case, affords remarkable proof of the *extensity* of intelligence, of the degree to which this aspect of the mental life can overflow into other channels, thus rendering the typical child or adult of highly superior mental ability better adjusted in his personal-social relationships than the generality of people. This, however, is not always the case. As is true at all levels of ability, there may be difficulties too great for the individual to master. It is likely, too, that among the gifted, as well as among those of less ability, there are cases whose inherent stability of temperament is so weak that only an exceptionally favorable environment could prevent a breakdown. That such cases are actually less common among the mentally superior than among the population as a whole has previously been implied. Further evidence along the same line will be presented in Chapter 10.

REFERENCES

BERMAN, Abraham, and KLEIN, Abraham, "A Personality Study of Maladjusted Pupils of Superior Mentality," *High Points*, 24 (1942), 57-63.

BURKS, Barbara Stoddard, JENSEN, Dortha Williams, and TERMAN, Lewis M., *Genetic Studies of Genius: The Promise of Youth* (Stanford University, Cal., Stanford University Press, 1930), Vol. 3.

COHLER, Milton J., "Scholastic Status of Achievers and Non-achievers of Superior Intelligence," *Journal of Educational Psychology*, 32 (1941), 603-610.

CONKLIN, Agnes M., *Failure of Highly Intelligent Pupils: A Study of Their Behavior by Means of the Control Group*, Contributions to Education Series (New York, Teachers College Bureau of Publications, 1940), No. 792.

DAVIDSON, Helen H., *Personality and Economic Background: A Study of Highly Intelligent Children* (New York, King's Crown Press, 1943).

DAVIS, Helen, "Personal and Social Characteristics of Gifted Children," *Twenty-third Yearbook of the National Society for the Study of Education* (Chicago, University of Chicago Press, 1924), Pt. 1.

GARRISON, Charlotte G., BURKE, Agnes, and HOLLINGWORTH, Leta S., "The Psychology of a Prodigious Child," *Journal of Applied Psychology*, 1 (1917), 101-110.

GOLDBERG, Samuel, "A Clinical Study of K., IQ 196," *Journal of Applied Psychology*, 18 (1934), 550-560.

HENRY, Theodore S., "Classroom Problems in the Education of Gifted Children," *Nineteenth Yearbook of the National Society for the Study of Education* (Chicago, University of Chicago Press, 1920), Pt. 2.

HOLLINGWORTH, Leta S., "The Child of Very Superior Intelligence as a Special Problem in Social Adjustment," *Mental Hygiene*, 15 (1931), 3-16.

————, *Children above 180 IQ, Stanford Binet* (Yonkers, N. Y., World Book Company, 1942).

————, and RUST, Meta M., "Application of the Bernreuter Inventory of Personality to Highly Intelligent Adolescents," *Journal of Psychology*, 4 (1937), 297-293.

LAYCOCK, Samuel R., "Adjustment of Superior and Inferior School Children," *Journal of Social Psychology*, 4 (1933), 353-366.

LEWIS, W. Drayton, *A Study of Superior Children in the Elementary School*, George Peabody College Contributions to Education Series (Nashville, Tenn., George Peabody College Press, 1940), No. 266.

———, "A Comparative Study of the Personalities, Interests, and Home Backgrounds of Gifted Children of Superior and Inferior Educational Attainment," *Journal of Genetic Psychology*, 59 (1941), 207-218.

———, and McGEHEE, William, "A Comparison of the Interests of Mentally Superior and Retarded Children," *School and Society*, 52 (1940), 597-600.

McELWEE, Edna W., "A Comparison of the Personality Traits of 300 Accelerated, Normal and Retarded Children," *Journal of Educational Research*, 26 (1932), 31-34.

———, "Seymour: A Boy with 192 IQ," *Journal of Juvenile Research*, 18 (1934), 28-35.

MARGOLIES, Abraham, "A Portrait of George Miles—Problem Child," *High Points*, 28 (1946), 25-30.

MARTENS, Elise H., *Gifted Children: Teachers' Problems with Gifted Children* (Washington, D. C.: U.S. Department of the Interior, Office of Education, 1933), Pamphlet No. 41 (II); rev. ed. (1940).

MATEER, Florence, "Clinical Problems of Bright Children," *Journal of Educational Sociology*, 10 (1936), 91-99.

MUSSELMAN, John W., "Factors Associated with the Achievement of High School Pupils of Superior Intelligence," *Journal of Experimental Education*, 11 (1942), 53-68.

MYERS, Garry C., "The Social Problem of the Gifted Child," *Journal of Exceptional Children*, 2 (1935), 39-43.

NEVELL, E. Mildred, "Brilliant Children with Special Reference to Their Particular Difficulties," *British Journal of Educational Psychology*, 7 (1937), 247-257.

REGENSBURG, Jeanette, "Studies of Success and Failure in Supernormal Children," *Archives of Psychology* (1931), No. 129.

RIGG, Melvin G., "A Superior Child Who Would Not Talk," *Child Development*, 9 (1938), 361-362.

SCHOTT, Emmett L., "Superior Intelligence in Patients with Nervous and Mental Illnesses," *Journal of Abnormal and Social Psychology*, 26 (1931), 94-101.

———, "School Adjustment of Some Mentally Superior Patients in a Psychiatric Clinic," *Psychological Clinic*, 21 (1932), 202-207.

STERN, Gladys B., *Little Red Horses* (London, Heinemann and Company, 1932).

STRANG, Ruth, "Mental Hygiene of Gifted Children," in *The Gifted Child*, ed. Paul A. Witty, prepared under the auspices of the American Association for Gifted Children (Boston, D. C. Heath and Company, 1951), ch. 7.

TERMAN, Lewis M. *et al.*, *Genetic Studies of Genius: Mental and Physical Traits of a Thousand Gifted Children* (Stanford, Cal., Stanford University Press, 1925), Vol. 1.

THOM, Douglas A., and NEWELL, Nancy, "Hazards of the High IQ," *Mental Hygiene*, 29 (1945), 61-77.

THORNDIKE, Robert L., "Performance of Gifted Children on Tests of Developmental Age," *Journal of Psychology*, 9 (1940), 337-343.

VAN ALSTYNE, Dorothy, "A Study of Ten Gifted Children Whose School Progress Was Unsatisfactory," *Journal of Educational Research*, 8 (1923), 122-135.

WARNER, M. L., "Eugene, A Brilliant Boy Who Failed in School," *Psychological Clinic*, 19 (1930), 143-165.

WHITE, Ralph K., "Note on the Psychopathology of Genius," *Journal of Social Psychology*, 1 (1930), 311-315.

WILKINS, Walter L., "The School Adjustment of Accelerated Pupils," *School Review*, 44 (1936), 445-455.

WITTY, Paul A., *A Study of One Hundred Gifted Children*, University of Kansas Bulletin of Education, 2, No. 7 (1930), 1-44.

———, "Exploitation of the Child of High Intelligence Quotient," *Educational Methods*, 15 (1936), 298-304.

———, "The Gifted Child: Facts and Fallacies," *National Parent-Teacher*, 42 (1948), 4-7.

———, and JENKINS, Martin D., "The Case of 'B'—a Gifted Negro Girl," *Journal of Social Psychology*, 6 (1935), 117-124.

———, and LEHMAN, Harvey C., "The Play Behavior of Fifty Gifted Children," *Journal of Educational Psychology*, 18 (1927), 259-265.

———, and LEHMAN, Harvey C., "Nervous Instability and Genius: Some Conflicting Opinions," *Journal of Abnormal Psychology*, 24 (1930), 486-497.

The Education of Exceptionally $\quad$ 9
Intelligent Children

THE AIMS OF EDUCATION

THE WORD education is derived from the Latin words *ex* and *duco*, meaning to lead or to draw out. Properly speaking, therefore, education is a process of bringing the latent gifts inherent in the child's endowment to full development, not of putting in something that was not already there. To perform this task wisely and well it is necessary to ascertain what the abilities and potentialities of each child are, to learn what conditions are best suited to insure their optimal development, and to find means of providing these conditions. Although our methods of accomplishing these ends are as yet inept and bungling, we shall nevertheless approach the goal more closely if we keep our purposes clearly in mind. We wish to foster in each child those traits that will lead to the utmost satisfaction and happiness for himself and enable him to be of the greatest possible service to humanity.

In this process of bringing out the best of which each child is capable, the acquisition of skills and knowledge should be regarded as means to an end, rather than as an end in itself. Our major concern is with the growth of character; with the development of attitudes that will enable the child to make the most profitable use of such abilities as he may possess and such knowledge as he may acquire. Knowledge and skills are important, it is true. One of the great mistakes of many educational leaders of the present day lies in overlooking the fact that every child is born into a civilization that has resulted from many centuries of blind striving on the part of his predecessors in the course of which an elaborate pattern of living has been developed. Into the short space of time that lies between infancy and maturity, the work of many generations of his ancestors must be compressed. To do this without the aid of the tools that have been devised for the construction and operation of the machine that we call civilization would be impossible, for the only alternative would be to repeat the long and painful process of experimentation and invention that has gone into its building. Neither can the child take time to develop his own tools; the most that he can do is to effect slight improvements in those already forged or to make some feeble beginnings in a new and hitherto untried direction. Thus each new generation builds upon the work of generations past. Each one must take the world as he finds it, learn, as best he can, to understand it in the hope of bringing about such changes as seem to him good. In the absence of understanding, neither social reform nor material advancement is likely to occur.

An important aim of education is thus to help the child to understand the world in which he must live, to learn the use of its tools, to become familiar with its social customs, and to know something of the principles by which human behavior is governed. Such understanding is the key to a happy and successful adjustment. The maladjusted child is a puzzled child, a child who has come into conflict with society because of unwitting blunders and who, in consequence, has gradually built up a feeling of resentment, insecurity, and uncertainty that leads some to an unhappy retreat, others to rebellion.

The child whose intellectual endowment is exceptionally high is both at an advantage and at a disadvantage in this process of learning to adjust to the world into which he is born. His superior intelligence makes understanding of rules and principles easier; but at the same time it renders him more sensitive to inconsistencies, social injustices, and other unfortunate conditions that his less well-endowed companions overlook. Often his perception of these conditions outruns his understanding of their causes, with the result that his reactions to them are ill-chosen and likely in their turn to be misunderstood by others.

A major fault in most educational systems of the past was the narrowness of the concepts upon which they were based. Education, in the eyes of most of our forefathers, consisted in the imparting of knowledge and training in skills. The usefulness of the knowledge or the aptitude of the child for the skills he was required to learn were but little considered. Now the pendulum has swung in the opposite direction. The modern educator is preoccupied with finding media for "self-expression" on the part of the child; he considers that the fleeting interests and desires of the moment provide a sufficient guide to the content of the child's education. He is likely to forget that interests do not arise in a vacuum but are the products of experience. The quality of this experience, its potency in arousing the child's wish to gain more of it, is dependent not only upon the child's general capacity and special propensities but also upon external factors which are subject to our control. The child is not born with ready-made understanding of the culture to which he must conform. The adult who has acquired some knowledge of its rules and principles must help him to gain this understanding.

The child of high intelligence will usually find little difficulty in mastering certain of the tools that have been devised for the maintenance of modern civilization. The three R's are acquired with ease, and the informational subjects such as history and science need but slight external incentive for their acquisition. One of the most characteristic traits of the gifted child is his intellectual curiosity, his desire to know. Given adequate opportunity and a minimum amount of assistance, most children of very superior intelligence will master the ordinary subjects of the school curriculum with ease and celerity.

But culture is social as well as academic. No amount of book knowledge can compensate for failure to comprehend the social rules by which society is governed. And it is just here that the gifted child is likely to be handicapped. Although his capacity for acquiring social skills may be very high, in too many instances both adequate opportunity for doing so and suitable external incentives are largely or wholly lacking. The brilliant child who can so readily outdo his companions in the formal work of the classroom, and who finds in reading a satisfaction that the more childish occupations of his associates do not provide turns to the things in which he can win success. Because practice counts for as much in the field of social relationships as elsewhere, lack of practice means failure to develop skill, and thus the child falls further and further behind his mates.

This is by no means true of all gifted children, or even of the majority, but it does point the need for special attention to the field of social behavior and the development of desirable social attitudes in the education and training of children of superior intellectual gifts. If these children are to make the greatest contribution to social welfare and social progress that they are potentially capable of making, it is of the utmost importance that their social development keep pace with their intellectual development, that they be as skillful in dealing with people as in the handling of verbal symbols and abstract concepts.

In the special classes for gifted children (known as the Major Work Classes) in the city of Cleveland, Ohio, specific educational aims as they apply particularly to the education of gifted children have been explicitly stated as follows: [1]

1. Increasing the range of knowledge and skills of the students
2. Developing alertness
3. Developing initiative and creative power
4. Developing an attitude of critical thinking
5. Developing power to work *independently* to plan and to execute and to judge
6. Developing increased ability to *share* in undertakings
7. Developing leadership

The Cleveland plan very explicitly states that children are to be kept at the grade level corresponding to their chronological age;

[1] Quoted from Merle R. Sumption, Dorothy Norris, and Lewis M. Terman, "Special Education for the Gifted Child," *Forty-ninth Yearbook of the National Society for the Study of Education* (Chicago, University of Chicago Press, 1950), Pt. 2, ch. 14.

that the program for these children is to be entirely one of enrichment with no acceleration. The present writer is inclined to think that the saving in time which results from a reasonable amount of acceleration along with enrichment is valuable and for the majority of gifted children does not involve much risk of social maladjustment, provided always that this acceleration is not too great. Practically all studies have shown that the typical gifted child prefers companions a year or more older than himself and that his recreational and intellectual interests are likely to be somewhat more mature than those of other children of corresponding age. A further aim in the education of the gifted child which is perhaps implied but not explicitly mentioned in the foregoing list is the encouragement of interests that are similar to those of the generality along with those in which many are not intellectually able to share. Interest in athletics, social dancing, bridge, and similar recreations will do much to bridge the gap that sometimes separates the person of superior intelligence from his mates.

THE SPECIAL NEEDS OF THE INTELLECTUALLY SUPERIOR CHILD

Every child, no matter what his intellectual status may be, needs food and shelter, love, and feeling of security. At any given age level the bright child has advanced further along the road leading to independent action than have his companions whose intelligence is at a lower stage of development. Too often, however, parents and teachers fail to realize his capacity for self-government. Traditional customs of child management, together with the habits formed when the children were younger, combine to make it very difficult for those in charge of gifted youngsters to appreciate either their ability or their desire to direct their own affairs.

As a rule, bright children are socially perceptive. The child who attempts to avoid unpleasant social situations by running away from them succeeds only in building up barriers between himself and others which he finds increasingly hard to pass of his own volition but which afford him little protection against the intrusions of the outside world. The oversensitive child needs sympathetic understanding; he also needs help in learning to understand others and in developing an attitude of tolerance that will enable him to accept the world as he finds it.

One of the most characteristic traits of the gifted child is his intellectual curiosity. He *needs* to learn and to know. So compelling is this urge for knowledge that those who have little opportunity to acquire it will often go to extreme lengths to satisfy their craving. The biographies of great men are full of accounts of the deprivations to which they voluntarily subjected themselves in order to gain the scholarly ends which to them were more important than sensory gratification. The only thing that little *C.S.*____[2] took with him when he ran away from home was a small dictionary that he had contrived to buy with the pennies he had painfully scraped together and hoarded against the grasping fingers of his father and brothers. To this dictionary he clung throughout all the vicissitudes of his troubled boyhood. It went with him to reform school and was still his most treasured possession when he was released and sent to a boarding home. This intense desire for knowledge was noted as early as 1919 by Terman in *The Intelligence of School Children*. As was previously stated, when the main Stanford investigation of gifted children was undertaken, it was found that the mean information quotient of the elementary school children who composed the main experimental group was actually slightly higher than the mean intelligence quotient of the same children.

In summary, then, we may note that although the basic needs of the gifted child are similar to those of children in general, the typical child of superior intelligence attains the ability to direct his own affairs at an earlier age than do children whose mentality is less well developed. This gives rise to a greater urge for independent action, for freedom from unnecessary restraint. Because of his relative lack of life experience, wise parental guidance is needed in order that the leading strings may be loosened without too disastrous mistakes on the part of the young child. Neverthe-

[2] Described in Ch. 8, pp. 116-118.

less, the chances are that the bright child will be permitted too little, rather than too much freedom of action. All of us are inclined to place too much faith in vicarious learning. We expect children to profit from our experience, rather than by their own. One of the most fundamental rights of childhood is the right of a child to make his own mistakes and win success by his own efforts. Even more than children in general, the bright child needs freedom, for the reason that he is better able to profit by it.

The brilliant child needs congenial friends. Because his interests are likely to be so different from those of most other children of his own age, some help may be required in order to bring him into contact with a suitable number of other children whose abilities do not differ too greatly from his own. In addition, as Sumption has shown, some relationship with the generality of children should be maintained if a truly well-rounded personality is to be developed. For this reason the segregation of brilliant children in special schools becomes a questionable practice, since neither in the classroom nor on the playground are they given sufficient opportunity to learn what the rank and file of children are like. More will be said about this in a later section.

Finally, the bright child needs plenty of intellectual nourishment. He needs direct contact with a variety of adult activities and an ample supply of interesting and meaty reading material. Visits to factories, museums, art galleries and the like are of great value if integrated with the child's level of understanding and interests; but these should not be forced. Even the bright child may suffer from mental indigestion.

These are the major ways in which the needs of the gifted child differ from those of children in general. They are differences of degree and not differences of kind. All children need independence, usually more than they are granted. All need friendship and all need intellectual stimulation. Greater attention to these matters is required in the case of the exceptionally bright child, either because he is better able to profit by them or because circumstances beyond his control make them especially difficult for him to attain.

EDUCATING THE GIFTED CHILD: THE ROLE OF THE HOME

"Happiness first, all else follows" is the oft-repeated motto of the Vineland Training School for mentally defective children. It may well be taken as the guiding principle in the training of children of every level of intelligence. Perhaps it applies most strongly to the training of the gifted child, for if he is happy, if his attitudes and behavior are such as to make for his continued happiness, other matters are likely to take care of themselves.

The gifted child, even more than others, reflects the emotional states of those about him. He is keenly sensitive to parental discord; he grieves with his parents' grief and rejoices in their joy long before he is able to understand why he does so. If this social perceptiveness is not blunted, it may become one of the child's greatest assets as he grows older, since it is the foundation of tact and social understanding. But if the child is too often hurt, scar tissue may develop as a protection against further wounding. He withdraws into a world of his own, a world that is rarely very happy but that at least is a less painful one than the world of reality. But in this escape from immediate pain, he fails to gain the social experience that would fit him for a happy and useful life later on. One of the most important aspects of the home training of the gifted child lies in the maintenance of his natural responsiveness to the moods of others.

The importance of allowing the gifted child to assume a degree of responsibility that is in accordance with his mental age rather than with his chronological age can hardly be overemphasized. While still a small child, he should begin to have the decisive voice in managing his own allowance, which, as he grows a little older, will be made to cover minor articles of clothing. Later on, he should help to plan the family budget. In doing so, he will gain much useful information from looking up the relative merits of different makes of major household appliances, such as washing machines or refrigerators, when these are to be bought, and will have an active voice in the selection of a new car. The practical knowledge acquired in this way does much to offset the tendency to bookishness that so often acts as a barrier between the child and his mates.

More than half of the gifted children in the Stanford study learned to read before starting school. Fondness for reading is an almost universal trait among children of high intelligence, and some guidance in the choice of reading material is desirable. Parents can do much to help children in the use of reference material and to stimulate their interest in the exact use of words, the location of places, the use of maps, the names of birds, trees, and flowers, the habits of animals, and the movements of the stars. Every bright child should have his own library card as soon as he is able to make use of it.

The happy and congenial family usually has many friends. The child belonging to such a family is inclined, as a rule, to conform to the family pattern. Yet this is not invariably the case. It sometimes happens that parents with many social obligations and activities become absorbed in their own affairs to an extent that leads them to overlook the child's need for companionship on his own level. They entertain adults and are themselves entertained, but they are too busy to arrange a party for the children for whom their chief concern is that they shall stay out of the living room and dining room lest they disarrange the furniture. Fortunately these cases are rare. As a rule, the socially gifted parent provides suitable social activities for his children.

One further point should perhaps be mentioned; its importance has already been stressed in Chapter 8. Nothing is more disastrous for the child's social relationships than egotism, the conscious assumption of superiority. It is fruitless to tell the child who excels all the other children in his class that he is no more able than they or that his ability is of no consequence. Only a very stupid child would be deceived by such a statement. Instead, he can be brought to see that his greater ability entails greater responsibilities both toward himself and toward his companions, that a higher level of accomplishment will be expected from him than from those who find it harder to learn. Moreover, he must see that although book knowledge is important, it is not enough.

The ability to understand the other person's point of view and to see himself as others see him is equally essential, as is the habit of finding greater satisfaction in helping those who need and desire assistance than in competition too easily won. If the bright child can be brought to see and accept these ideas, there is little danger that he will make himself disliked through boasting or other displays of egotism. The kind of attitudes that a child develops toward himself and toward others is largely in the hands of the parents. No other aspect of the home training of the gifted child is of greater importance.

SCHOOL PROVISIONS FOR THE GIFTED CHILD

For more than a quarter of a century educators have recognized the need for special provisions for the education and training of intellectually gifted children. So keenly was the problem felt that in 1924 the National Society for the Study of Education devoted Part I of its annual series of yearbooks to this topic. More than thirty of the leading educational experts of the country contributed to this volume. An annotated bibliography of 453 titles attests to the widespread interest in the education of gifted children which was felt even at that early date.

Methods of dealing with the gifted school child may be grouped under a number of headings as follows:

1. *Laissez-faire* method. Children remain in the regular grades appropriate to their ages with only such attention to their intellectual needs as the individual teacher may provide.

2. Accelerated rate of progress through the grades by means of extra promotions but without change or enrichment of the regular curriculum.

3. Some enrichment of curriculum while children remain in regular classes. This may be accomplished by supervised reading or the working out of special projects or by dismissing the child from the class for certain periods of the day in order that he may receive special instruction in languages, music, etc.

4. Segregation of the most able children into special classes where they are given specialized instruction. There are many variants of this plan.

5. Segregation of the gifted into special schools, either public or private. This plan usually means both an enriched curriculum and some degree of accelerated progress.

The *laissez-faire* method has little to recommend it, except, perhaps, when classes are small and the teachers specially trained in the art of individual instruction and in arranging co-operative projects that make use of the special abilities of each child.

Double promotions for bright children have been more generally used than any other method of providing for their ability. Repeated studies have shown that children of high intellectual gifts who enter high school or college one or more years earlier than the generality are usually not academically handicapped but maintain a high scholastic standing in spite of their youth. Provided their acceleration is not too great they may also be well adjusted socially. But the child who enters college at the age of thirteen or fourteen years, even though he may be able to handle the work of his courses easily and with distinction, rarely gets much fun out of his college life. Much, of course, depends on his physical and psychological development; but even if he is advanced in physique as well as in mentality, too great a discrepancy between his chronological age and that of his fellows is almost certain to prove a handicap in his social relationships. His fellow students consider him something of a freak; they do not invite him to their parties or include him when a double date is being arranged. Inevitably he misses much of that for which college life usually stands.

As was indicated under point 3, a resourceful teacher or school principal can contrive some enrichment of program for the gifted children under his supervision without segregating them into special classes. One such child of my acquaintance, whose IQ was 180 but who attended a school where the enrollment was too small to warrant the establishment of a special class for gifted children, was permitted to join the high school class in beginning French while she was still in the fifth grade, by being excused from her regular class at that time. She continued with the high school class in French for the three years during which that subject was offered, then began German. Throughout this time she was having violin lessons and doing a very large amount of reading on a wide variety of subjects. Horseback riding, swimming, and tennis were her favorite sports; she was an active and enthusiastic Girl Scout and frequently went on overnight hikes with one or more friends, sleeping out of doors or staying at youth hostels. All this kept her busy and happy in spite of the fact that her grade placement, which was only one year in advance of the standard for her chronological age was far below the level of her mental capacity. Her case illustrates what can be done for the exceptionally bright child when school and parents are able and willing to collaborate in carrying out a program of enriched instruction on a purely individual basis.

When the majority of the subjects in Terman's group had reached the age of thirty or over, they were asked to state, first, whether or not they had been accelerated in school and, second, whether they regarded this acceleration as an advantage or a disadvantage. Unfortunately, the question was so worded that many of the subjects evidently misunderstood it. In general, however, their responses, taken in conjunction with other evidence as to their present characteristics seemed to indicate that although very rapid progress through the grades, which places the child with others much older than himself, frequently makes for social maladjustment *at the time*, this handicap is in most cases overcome in later years. Terman and Oden are of the opinion that the dangers of acceleration have been greatly exaggerated. There is an obvious advantage in being able to start on one's professional career at as early an age as possible, provided always that one's training has been as thorough as though it had been received at the normal rate.

Broad rather than minimal knowledge of the various subjects, as well as the addition of other subjects not included in the regular curriculum, is more readily achieved when the children of very superior intelligence are placed in special classes where their progress is not hampered by the slow rate of learning and the amount of repetition required by the majority. By the provision of

an enriched curriculum at the same general level as that of the
ordinary grades, the children can be provided with plenty of
intellectual stimulation without losing place with others of their
age. Moreover, the fact that their classmates are of about the same
intellectual caliber as themselves makes for an intellectual challenge to the individual child that is absent when he is able to excel
the other children in the regular grades with little or no effort.
Too easy success as a child is a poor preparation for the competitive life that each must live as an adult when he moves into a
group at his own intellectual level.

The advantages of the special class for exceptionally bright children may be summarized as follows: it simplifies the problem of
providing an enriched curriculum for these children, including the
addition of subjects, such as one or more foreign languages, not
included in the regular course of study. Also, it makes possible a
reasonable amount of acceleration without the disadvantages inherent in skipping grades, which always involves the possible
omission of essential skills or types of information. The competition with others whose intellectual capacity is similar to their own
provides a challenge to effort that is valuable training for adult
life, since it makes for habits of industry and efficient work rather
than the laziness and time-wasting that almost inevitably ensue
when success can be attained without effort. Finally, when children of similar mental ability are brought together, they are more
likely to find congenial companions and thus are able to live a
more normal and happy social life than would otherwise be possible. The gifted child is frequently a lonely child. His social
development and his intellectual development are likely to be
facilitated by placing him with others whose interests are more
nearly like his own.

The segregation of gifted children into special classes is, however, not devoid of hazards which the schools should keep in mind
when planning for such classes. First, there is the danger that
these classes may become the object of a special type of jealous
reaction on the part of other children and their parents. The children enrolled in them are sneeringly referred to as "smarty-pants,"

"brainies," and "world-wonders." Watchful eyes are upon them to note their every mistake. On the playground they are shunned and laughed at.

This, of course, is neither a necessary nor a usual state of affairs, but it is all too likely to occur when, as sometimes happens, the special classes are made the subject of newspaper publicity or when in some other way too great attention is called to them within the school or community. As one means of preventing these unfortunate attitudes, the special classes should be given some nondefinitive title. In Cleveland, Ohio, where the first class of this type in the United States was organized in 1921, they are known as Major Work Classes. Elsewhere, they have been called Opportunity Classes, Individual Progress Classes, etc.

The attitude of the children in the special classes also calls for some attention. Feelings of superiority and of egotism may easily be evoked if unwise methods are used for selecting the cases or for dealing with the children and their parents. The maintenance of a casual attitude toward these children with emphasis on what is still to be learned rather than their present accomplishments is highly important. Bright children should be taught to look to the future rather than to the past, to be made aware of the great body of knowledge that lies beyond them. Study of the lives of the great men of history is valuable, not only for the information thus afforded but also for the effect upon the development of the personal characteristics of the children.

The city of Cleveland was not only the first to establish special classes for superior children; it has continued to be among the foremost in providing these facilities and in carrying out research to determine their effectiveness. One of the most elaborate and carefully controlled of these investigations, the results of which were published in 1941, was made by Sumption. By examination of the school records, Sumption was able to locate a fairly large number of subjects then approximately twenty-one years of age who had attended the Major Work Classes for varying lengths of time as well as others of equal test intelligence who, for various reasons, had remained in the regular grades. From these lists three groups of sixty-five children each, matched with respect to sex, age, intelligence, and general social status as children, were chosen. Group A (the control group) was made up of children who, though of equal test intelligence, had never attended the special classes. Group B was made up of children who had attended these classes not longer than four years; and Group C, of those enrolled for more than four years. All the members of each group had previously agreed to fill out a questionnaire having to do with their personal histories, attitudes, and the like. Their school records, including records of achievement in the various subjects, were also compared.

Sumption does not indicate the reliability of the differences found, which, in most cases, were small but tended to favor Group C, which had the longest period of attendance in the special classes. An exception to this rule was noted with respect to interest in athletics, where the control group exceeded both of the special-class groups. A further weakness of the special-class children was their relative lack of expressed interest in the welfare of others, together with a too narrow acquaintance with the activities and interests of other children. This finding underlines one of the most serious hazards of the special class—the likelihood that such segregation may remove the children too far from the interests and activities of the majority and in so doing may lessen their chances of later service to humanity. Sumption is of the opinion that more effective integration of the work of the children in the special classes with that of the school as a whole and closer association on the playground would be highly desirable.

Other studies have for the most part confirmed Sumption's findings with respect to the superior academic accomplishments of gifted children who have been given the advantages of an enriched curriculum. It is unfortunate that in spite of the great amount of theoretical discussion as to the relative advantages of enrichment and acceleration as methods of providing for the superior intellectual advancement of these children, there have been few carefully controlled experiments in which these procedures have been compared directly with each other. That both methods are on the whole to be preferred to the *laissez-faire* method has been amply demonstrated. Terman and Oden, in comparing the later development of the children in the Stanford group some twenty years after the original selection of these cases, chose the 150 boys who, according to the joint opinions of several judges, were the most successful in their early adult lives, and the 150 who were least successful. The first group completed both elementary school and high school at an earlier age than the second, the difference averaging approximately a year. But at the time the study was begun, the special class for gifted children was almost unknown, so that a comparison between this method and that of grade skipping is not available.

Of the three methods of providing for the needs of the gifted child in school—accelerated progress through the grades; segregation in special classes; and a combination of the two together with project work, field trips, early training in the use of a foreign language, etc.—the writer is inclined to favor the last. It must be admitted, however, that objective information with respect to the comparative advantages of these methods is for the most part wanting. More research in this area is urgently needed.

THE GIFTED CHILD IN THE COMMUNITY

That the public attitude toward the gifted child is likely to be less sympathetic and understanding than it should be has been pointed out before. Community education with respect to the potentialities of these children, their characteristics, and their needs is definitely called for. Above all, people should be brought to understand why the gifted child often finds it difficult to make friends, even though he craves friendship. Much can be done to relieve the situation through intelligent community action.

Help for the gifted child who is financially unable to continue his education beyond the legal requirements is another objective of community education. Many women's clubs, churches, fraternal organizations, and similar groups maintain scholarships for deserving students, but the number and usual cash value of available scholarships is insufficient to care for all the able students who are in need of financial aid. Goetsch has shown that although more than 90 per cent of the intellectually superior students whose families were in the upper-income brackets attended college, fewer than 20 per cent of equally able students from the lower-income brackets did so. Obviously here is a great waste of human material which every effort should be made to correct.

The assignment of scholarships by local organizations is not always as well planned as it might be. Local favoritism, either on the part of the school authorities or of the leading members of the organization conferring the grant may be the chief determining factor. Competitive examinations have their faults, but they are at least objective and so are equally fair to all applicants. The common practice of requiring favorable reports with respect to personality characteristics should be exercised with caution, for in many instances it may rule out the very students who are most in need of help.

Nothing will be said here about the community provisions for child welfare, of which all children, regardless of their intellectual status, stand in need. These include playgrounds, health clinics, library facilities, etc. (The practice of rigidly confining all children to the use of the books in the children's room of the public libraries is to be deprecated. Certainly the establishment of such rooms is of great advantage to children in general, but the gifted child needs free access to such books as strike his fancy. These will often be surprisingly mature.) Much has been done to awaken the public conscience to these general requirements of child well-being, but the many services that the community can perform to aid the most promising members of the child population have not been fully realized. Many of these children stand in urgent need of the kind of help that an intelligent public can give them.

REFERENCES

ADAMS, Fay, and BROWN, Walker, *Teaching the Bright Pupil* (New York, Henry Holt and Company, Inc., 1930).

ALPERN, Hymen, "Educating the Superior Student in the High Schools of New York City," *Journal of Educational Sociology,* 13 (1939), 112-119.

ATKINS, Herbert A., "The Gifted Child and His Teachers," *Mental Hygiene,* 13 (1929), 719-739.

BRIGGS, Leslie J., "Intensive Classes for Superior Students," *Journal of Educational Psychology,* 38 (1947), 207-215.

BRUNER, H. B., "Some Issues and Problems Raised by the Conference on Education for the Gifted," *Teachers College Record,* 42 (1941), 432-460.

BURNSIDE, Lenoir H., "An Experimental Program in the Education of the Intellectually Gifted Adolescent," *School Review,* 50 (1942), 274-285.

———, "Psychological Guidance of Gifted Children," *Journal of Consulting Psychology,* 6 (1942), 223-228.

CALSON, Edith F., "Project for Gifted Children: A Psychological Evaluation," *American Journal of Orthopsychiatry,* 15 (1945), 648-661.

———, "Problems in Educating the Highly Endowed," *Journal of Exceptional Children,* 13 (1947), 201-220.

———, and WILES, Marion E., "Special Education for Gifted Children," *Journal of Exceptional Children,* 10 (1943), 73-77.

COY, Genevieve L., *The Interests, Abilities, and Achievements of a Special Class for Gifted Children,* Contributions to Education Series (New York, Teachers College Bureau of Publications, 1923), No. 131.

DANIELSON, Cora L., "A Study of the Effect of a Definite Course of Reading in General Literature upon the Achievement in Content Subjects with Children of Superior Mental Ability," *Journal of Educational Psychology,* 20 (1929), 610-621.

DRANSFIELD, J. Edgar., *Administration of Enrichment to Superior Children in the Typical Classroom,* Contributions to Education Series (New York, Teachers College Bureau of Publications, 1933), No. 568.

Educational Policies Commission of the National Education Association and the American Association of School Administrators, *Education of the Gifted* (Washington, D. C., National Education Association, 1950).

ENGLE, Thelburn L., "Achievements of Pupils Who Have Had Double Promotions in Elementary School," *Elementary School Journal*, 36 (1935), 185-189.

———, "A Study of the Effects of School Acceleration upon the Personality and Social Adjustment of High School and University Students," *Journal of Educational Psychology*, 29 (1938), 523-539.

EVANS, N. Dean, "New England Provides for the Exceptionally Intelligent Child in the Secondary School," *Journal of Exceptional Children*, 17 (1950), 40-43, 63.

GODDARD, Henry H., *School Training for Gifted Children* (Yonkers, N. Y., World Book Company, 1928).

GOETSCH, Helen B., *Parental Income and College Opportunities*, Contributions to Education Series (New York, Teachers College Bureau of Publications, 1940), No. 795.

GRAY, Howard A., and HOLLINGWORTH, Leta S., "The Achievement of Gifted Children Enrolled and Not Enrolled in Special Opportunity Classes," *Journal of Educational Research*, 24 (1931), 255-261.

GRAY, William S., "Education of the Gifted Child with Special Reference to Reading," *Elementary School Journal*, 42 (1942), 736-744.

GREENBERG, Benjamin B., "The Education of the Intellectually Gifted," *Journal of Exceptional Children*, 5 (1939), 101-109.

HILDRETH, Gertrude Howell, *Educating Gifted Children at Hunter College Elementary School* (New York, Harper and Brothers, 1952).

HOLLINGWORTH, Leta S., "An Enrichment Curriculum for Rapid Learners at Public School 500: Speyer School," *Teachers College Record*, 39 (1938), 296-306.

———, "Problems of Relationship Between Elementary and Secondary Schools in the Case of Highly Intelligent Pupils," *Journal of Educational Sociology*, 13 (1939), 90-102.

HORN, Ernest, "The Curriculum for the Gifted; Some Principles and an Illustration," *Twenty-third Yearbook of the National Society for the Study of Education* (Chicago, University of Chicago Press, 1924), Pt. 1, pp. 73-84.

JENSEN, Dortha Williams, "The Gifted Child: I. Educational Concepts and Practices," *Journal of Educational Research*, 15 (1927), 34-45.

———, "The Gifted Child: II. Present School Provision for the Gifted Child," *Journal of Educational Research*, 15 (1927), 126-133.

———, "The Gifted Child: III. Present Practices in Special Schools for the Gifted," *Journal of Educational Research*, 15 (1927), 198-206.

JONES, Vernon A., and McCALL, William A., "Application of Two Techniques in Evaluating Some Policies of Dealing with Bright Children," *Teachers College Record*, 27 (1926), 826-835.

KYTE, George C., "Two Types of Experimental Programs in the Education of Gifted Children," *Yearbook: National Education Association, Department of Elementary School Principals*, 3 (1924), 395-430.

LAMSON, Edna E., "To What Extent Are Intelligence Quotients Increased by Children Who Participate in a Rich, Vital, School Curriculum?" *Journal of Educational Psychology*, 29 (1938), 67-70.

LOOMIS, Grace I., *The Education of the Gifted Child; with Implications for School Practice*, Curriculum Bulletin (Eugene, University of Oregon, 1951), No. 97.

MARTENS, Elise H., *Curriculum Adjustments for Gifted Children* (Washington, D.C., U.S. Department of the Interior, Office of Education, 1946), Bulletin No. 1.

————, *Statistics of Special Schools and Classes for Exceptional Children: Biennial Survey of Education in the United States* (Washington, D. C., United States Government Printing Office, 1950).

NEWLAND, T. Ernst, "The Education of Exceptional Children: The Mentally Gifted," *Review of Educational Research*, 11 (1941), 277-287.

OSBURN, W. J., and ROHAN, B. J., *Enriching the Curriculum for Gifted Children: A Book of Guidance for Educational Administrators and Classroom Teachers* (New York, The Macmillan Company, 1931).

PEACHMAN, Marguerite C., "Attitudes: Their Significance in Education for the Gifted," *Journal of Educational Psychology*, 33 (1942), 83-98.

PRESSEY, Sidney L., "Efficiency Engineering in the Educational Emergency," *School and Society*, 65 (1947), 425-428.

SHEIFELE, Marian, *The Gifted Child in the Regular Classroom* (New York, Teachers College Bureau of Publications, 1953).

STEDMAN, Lulu M., *Education of Gifted Children* (Yonkers, N. Y., World Book Company, 1924).

SUMPTION, Merle R., *Three Hundred Gifted Children: A Follow-up Study of the Results of Special Education of Superior Children* (Yonkers, N. Y., World Book Company, 1941).

————, NORRIS, Dorothy, and TERMAN, Lewis M., "Special Education for the Gifted Child," *Forty-ninth Yearbook of the National Society for the Study of Education* (Chicago, University of Chicago Press, 1950), Pt. 2, ch. 14.

TERMAN, Lewis M., "The Gifted Student and His Academic Environment," *School and Society*, 49 (1939), 65-73.

THEMAN, Viola, and WITTY, Paul A., "A Follow-up Study of the Educational Attainment of Gifted Negroes," *Journal of Educational Psychology,* 34 (1943), 35-47.

THOMPSON, Nellie Z., "Education of the Gifted in Various Countries," *Journal of Exceptional Children,* 15, Pt. 1 (1949), 193-198 and 224; Pt. 2 (1949), 239-243 and 254-256.

THORNDIKE, Edward L., "How May We Improve the Selection, Training, and Life Work of Leaders?" *Teachers College Record,* 40 (1939), 598-605.

WASHBURNE, Carleton W., "The Attainments of Gifted Children under Individual Instruction," *Twenty-third Yearbook of the National Society for the Study of Education* (Chicago, University of Chicago Press, 1924), Pt. 1.

WHIPPLE, Guy M., "Some Features of the Education of Gifted Children," *School and Society,* 12 (1920), 175-179.

———, "School Provision for Gifted Children in the United States," *Proceedings of the National Conference of Social Work* (1923), pp. 399-404.

WOODS, Elizabeth L., "Personality Traits of Children of Superior Intelligence in Special Classes and in Regular Classes," *Third Yearbook of the Psychological and Educational Research Division: Los Angeles Public Schools,* No. 185 (1929), pp. 102-109.

ZORBAUGH, Harvey W., "How May the Community Utilize Its Gifted Children?" *Mental Hygiene,* 24 (1940), 1-16.

The Adult Achievements of   10
Gifted Children

ALTHOUGH SOME intrinsic interest attaches to the study of children whose intellectual achievements rank far above those of others of their age, these studies would lose much of their significance if it should be found that early achievement of a high order has no predictive value. Its significance is greatly changed if the gifted child is the victim of some unwholesome condition that makes for precocious ripening but, like the worm at the core of an apple, makes at the same time for early decay without arriving at complete and unblemished maturity. Considered from the standpoint of its relation to adult achievement, high intellectual ability in childhood might be any one of the following: (1) a sign of probable high accomplishment in adult life, (2) an evanescent phenomenon with no predictive value, or (3) an unwholesome precocious ripening which is likely to result in mental disease or early death. Which of the three possibilities is usually the correct one can only be ascertained by objective study of actual cases. It should be noted at this point that whatever may be the probabilities for the majority, some examples of each possibility are likely to be found. The Stanford investigation has done much to provide us with data on this question.

The studies of Galton and others on the inheritance of genius suggest some continuity of ability from childhood to maturity in the individual. Early in the history of intelligence testing it was found that during childhood Stanford Binet IQ's remain relatively constant over a period of several years. This demonstrated that superior ability once manifested is not soon lost. But when the

Stanford investigation was begun, insufficient time had elapsed since the development of objective measures of intelligence to show conclusively whether or not superior childhood ability as measured by tests would carry over into adult life.

One of the earliest well-substantiated reports of extraordinary accomplishment in early childhood is that of Christian Heinrich Heincken, born in 1721. By the age of four he could speak and read German, Latin, and French. He had an extensive knowledge of Bible stories, of European history and geography, and of natural science. At this age he was taken before the king of Denmark who presented him with a diamond studded order which he at once recognized as the Order of the Elephant, commenting in French, "The jewels are precious but the life of the king is far more precious." He was never in robust health, and this probably accounts for his death at the age of four years and four months. However, there were many who regarded it as confirmation of the popular belief that gifted children die young.

Karl Witte gave a public demonstration of his ability to read Greek, Latin, French, Italian, and German at the age of seven years and ten months. At the age of nine he entered the University of Leipzig and at fourteen received the degree of Ph.D. He became a full professor of jurisprudence at the University of Breslau at twenty-three. He continued an active and important career as teacher and writer up to his death at the ripe age of eighty-three. Here is a clear instance of exceptional mental ability in childhood that continued without marked change throughout the course of a long and highly successful life.

Following the example of Terman who, largely on the basis of a letter written at the age of four, had estimated the childhood IQ of Sir Francis Galton as not far from 200, Cox assembled the available data with respect to the childhood abilities of approximately three hundred historical geniuses. This material was then presented to several persons who had had considerable experience in mental testing. They estimated the childhood IQ of each subject.

In many cases the available data on the childhood of these men were too few to warrant anything more than a very tentative estimate. Since in the absence of all knowledge as to the mental ability of an individual the best possible estimate of his IQ would fall at 100, there was a definite tendency on the part of the raters to assign lower ratings to those cases for whom the information as to childhood characteristics was relatively small. In the belief that these estimates were spuriously low because of incomplete data Cox devised and applied a correction which is fully described in the original publication. Its effect was to increase the final estimates of the IQ's all along the line, but more for those given the lower than for those assigned the higher ratings. After correction, the mean of the ratings was above 160, with a fair number reaching or exceeding 180.

The possible halo effect of knowledge of the later achievements of the subjects both upon the selection of the facts which the biographers recorded and upon the raters who made the estimates has perhaps received less consideration than it merits. All the raters knew the identities and later accomplishments of the subjects. Although they were instructed to disregard this knowledge, it would undoubtedly have been better if they had not had it before them when making their ratings. It might also have been desirable if a number of similar histories of persons whose adult careers were undistinguished had been included, and also histories of children whose Stanford Binet IQ's had been measured.

For these and other reasons, a forward, rather than a backward approach is much more satisfactory; a study that begins with gifted children and follows their careers to maturity. The Stanford investigation is such a study. Since the original investigation in 1921-1922, Terman has maintained continual contact with the subjects by means of letters and mailed questionnaires. Additional field studies were made in 1927-1928, 1940, and 1952. In 1947, Terman and Oden reported the findings of the 1940 followup and those of a questionnaire mailed in 1945. At this writing, evaluation of the 1952 follow-up is in progress. The response of the subjects and that of their parents and teachers and, in the last two surveys, of their spouses has been extraordinary. In 1945,

95.3 per cent of the 1467 survivors of the original group of 1528 subjects were still actively co-operating in the study. No other comparable group of subjects, regardless of their intellectual or social level, has ever been followed for so long a time or studied so intensively from so many angles.

At the time of the 1945 study, the average age of the subjects was approximately thirty-five years. Although few of them would have reached the peak of their earning power or professional achievement, the majority had embarked upon their life careers and were beginning, at least, to demonstrate what they were capable of doing.

In 1940, the 954 subjects who were accessible to the field-workers were given an intelligence test especially designed to reach the higher levels of ability. Their mean score on this test was approximately 2.3 standard deviations higher than that made by the average adult. In other words, only about one adult in a hundred would rank as high as the average member of the gifted group. The proportion of the group who had entered or completed college was approximately eight times as great as for their contemporaries in the general population of California. About 30 per cent of those who had completed college graduated with honors. The mean age at graduation was more than a year below that of the general average.

Almost half of the men [1] were engaged in one or another of the learned professions (doctor, lawyer, etc.) by 1945. Only about 4 per cent were following such occupations as truck driving, factory work, clerking in stores, and the like, although more than half of the general population is so engaged.

Incomes varied greatly, in part because the ages of the subjects were at a point where some of them would be fairly well established, others just starting on their professional careers. The earned incomes reported by the employed men for the calendar year 1944 averaged $4,700, with 13 per cent reporting earned incomes for

[1] Only the men are considered, because so many of the women were married and fully occupied with their families.

that year of $10,000 or more. These figures are far above those reported for employed males in the United States as a whole.

In spite of their relative youth, the group had an impressive record of scholarly attainments. They had published more than 30 books and approximately 1500 articles in scientific and literary journals, and had taken out more than 100 patents for various types of scientific inventions. Many of the men and a number of the women earned outstanding honors and recognition in the course of their war services.

In 1922 the children were found to be somewhat superior to the generality in physique and in general health. Funds were not available for the repetition of the medical examinations in 1940, but the subjects reported their own height and weight and rated themselves with respect to general health. Almost 90 per cent claimed to be in good or very good health, and their reported heights were also higher than those of the general population, and even above those of the average of college graduates.

With the exception of the records of actual mental breakdown involving at least temporary residence in a mental hospital,[2] the data on mental health and adjustment are necessarily rather subjective. They are based upon a combination of reports by the subjects, their spouses, and their parents, having to do with such matters as happiness and contentment, number and seriousness of personal problems, worries, and the like. Putting all the facts together, Terman and Oden rated the subjects on a five-point scale, ranging from satisfactory adjustment to serious maladjustment with psychosis. Of the entire group, approximately 80 per cent were considered to have a satisfactory adjustment in 1940, with a slight drop to about 79 per cent in 1945, which may perhaps be attributed to the increased stresses and strains of the war years or may arise from the greater responsibilities likely to be incurred between the ages of thirty and thirty-five. Only for the mental hospital cases are adequate control figures available. In 1940, fewer

---

[2] The data on this point were carefully checked from information given by parents and spouses and by investigations made by the fieldworkers. They are believed to be complete and accurate.

than 1 per cent had developed psychoses severe enough to require hospitalization; by 1945, the percentage had risen to slightly more than 1 per cent. Both figures are slightly lower than those reported by Pollock for the general population of corresponding age.

By 1945, around 84 per cent of the group had married. This figure is much higher than has generally been reported for college graduates of corresponding age. About 15 per cent of these marriages had ended in divorce or separation. The mean number of children born to those who had been married five years or longer was 1.52. Inasmuch as many of the families may be regarded as complete at the time of the 1950-1951 survey, the question as to whether these highly intelligent persons are reproducing at a rate sufficiently high to maintain the stock will be tentatively answered when those data are published. Obviously this question has great import for society.

From the foregoing brief summary it will be noted that although the average performance of the group was far above that achieved by the generality of corresponding age, success was not equally distributed among them; nor were all equally happy in their personal lives and social relations. The question immediately arises: Had present knowledge been available in 1922, could we then have predicted which members of the group were likely and which unlikely to become well-adjusted, happy, and successful adults?

In an attempt to answer this question, three psychologists made independent examinations of the records of all male subjects who had reached the age of twenty-five or over at the time of the 1940 follow-up. From the 730 cases who met the age and sex requirements, they selected the 150 who were judged to have met the demands of early maturity most adequately (Group A) and the 150 at the other extreme (Group C).[3]

The groups so chosen were first compared on the basis of childhood IQ. The difference, although favoring the more successful group (A), was small (IQ 155 *vs.* IQ 150), with considerable over-

[3] The instructions given the judges were necessarily general rather than specific. Nevertheless, there was surprisingly little disagreement among them in their classification. All cases in which there was not complete agreement were discussed, and the final classification was made by majority vote.

lapping between the groups. Ages at the time the ratings were made were very similar (between thirty and thirty-one for both groups). In education and occupational status, however, the contrast between the groups was striking. More than 90 per cent of the A's but only 37 per cent of the C's graduated from college. Of the former, about 76 per cent completed one or more years of graduate study, but only 15 per cent of the latter did so. More than 68 per cent of the A's but only a little more than 9 per cent of the C's were engaged in one or another of the learned professions in 1940. An additional 31 per cent of the A's and 7 per cent of the C's were in semiprofessional and managerial positions. None of the A's and only 6 of the C's was unemployed, but more than half of the C's were engaged in semiskilled trades or clerical work or minor business positions.

Examination of the childhood records revealed fairly consistent lower ratings for Group C in respect to most traits having to do with personal-social adjustment. These differences, at first small, tended to increase with advancing age. By the time college age had been reached, the separation between the groups had become very marked. In Group A, more than 50 per cent of the fathers, as well as over 60 per cent of the brothers and sisters, were college graduates, and an additional 18 per cent of the latter had completed from one to three years of college work. The corresponding figures for Group C are much lower. Only a little more than 15 per cent of the fathers and fewer than 30 per cent of the siblings had graduated from college, and a little more than 15 per cent of the latter had finished from one to three years of college work. The A subjects unquestionably had the better start in life. The majority of them came from homes in which education was a tradition.

That the family attitude toward higher education had something to do with the superior educational achievement of Group A is strongly suggested by the figures just given. It is doubtful, however, whether the differences can be wholly accounted for in this way. Even in childhood the A subjects were rated much higher than the C's on a group of four volitional traits as judged by both parents and teachers. The traits included were the follow-ing: *prudence and forethought, self-confidence, will power and perseverance,* and *desire to excel.* In the 1928 follow-up, when most of the subjects were in high school or college, ratings were again secured for the two traits last named, and, again, the rat-ings given by parents and teachers to the *A* subjects were reliably higher than those assigned to the *C* subjects.[4] In 1940, the subjects themselves, their wives, and their parents made ratings on the fol-lowing traits: *perseverance, integration toward goals,* and *absence of inferiority feelings.* On each of these traits Group *A* was reliably superior to Group *C*.

It would thus seem that a major factor—perhaps the chief factor—accounting for the differences in adult achievement of subjects who as children manifested a remarkable degree of intellectual superiority is to be found in their willingness to persevere in the face of difficulties, in their ability to foresee a goal and to hold steadily to their course without serious distraction or loss of con-fidence in their ability to realize their aims. Examination of the biographical data in Cox's study offers strong confirmatory evi-dence that the motivation or drive which enables the individual to maintain his efforts to achieve his purposes[5] in spite of circum-stances that daunt his weaker associates was a factor of outstand-ing importance in the attainments of these great men.

The *A* and *C* groups were at no time reliably differentiated in physical health. Many popular beliefs with respect to the impor-tance of size of family, birth order, age of parents, and the like were in no way substantiated by this study. In 1921-1922, there was little difference between the groups with respect to evidences

[4] On a composite of the four traits rated by parents and teachers in 1921-1922, the critical ratio of the difference between the *A* and the *C* groups was 3.95; on the two traits rated in 1928 the critical ratio was 5.93.

[5] This does not necessarily mean that the ends for which the subject strives undergo no shifts between childhood and maturity. Repeatedly it has been observed that the interests of gifted children frequently go through a series of phases. But while the interest lasts, it is intense and not readily dis-turbed by external difficulties. The changes occurring from time to time rep-resent a series of experiments with life rather than the lack of purposiveness and the easy discouragement so characteristic of the less successful members of society.

of personal maladjustment; but in 1928, many more such symptoms had appeared among the members of Group *C* than among those of Group *A*, and these differences had increased still further by 1940. A similar pattern appeared with respect to signs of social maladjustment. The marriage rate of the *C* men was lower than that of the *A* men, but the divorce rate among the married was more than twice as high. Scores on the Terman Test of Marital Happiness were higher for the *A* than for the *C* men, and those made by the wives of the *A* men were very much higher than those made by the wives of the *C* men.

Occupational maladjustment was also far more evident among Group *C* men than within Group *A*. Changes of jobs without improvement of status or earnings had occurred much more often, and there had been more periods of unemployment. More than three times as many members of Group *C* as of Group *A* reported that they had merely drifted into their present jobs and would prefer work of some other type. Further evidence of vocational maladjustment was afforded by the Strong Test of Occupational Interests, on which 23 per cent of the *C*'s but only 5 per cent of the *A*'s earned ratings below *B* for the occupation in which they were engaged. In this connection it was noteworthy that the *A* men rated high on many more occupations than did the *C* men. This suggests greater flexibility of temperament and a wider range of interests and hobbies.

The fieldworkers' ratings placed the members of Group *A* far above those of Group *C* in *appearance, attractiveness, poise, alertness, curiosity,* and *originality,* and somewhat higher in *speech* and *friendliness.*

The importance of this long-time study of the careers and characteristics of so large a group of individuals who as children showed remarkable intellectual ability can hardly be overestimated. No other study ever made has been continued over so long an age span. Few have been so searching with respect to the amount and kind of information secured. The study has answered in part a number of the questions that were posed earlier in this chapter. It now seems quite clear that the child who shows remarkable intelligence rarely, if ever, drops to the mental level of the average person in adult life, but that intelligence alone is insufficient to guarantee achievement commensurate with capacity to achieve. Along with abstract ability of the kind measured by present-day intelligence tests, there must be the drive to excel, a certain zest in living and doing, a purposeful attitude that enables its possessor to integrate his purposes toward an end that is at least dimly foreseen and to persevere in his efforts to reach his goals in spite of difficulties. Important, also, is the subject's self-confidence and freedom from feelings of inferiority, as shown in his superior poise, more fluent speech, a more attractive manner, and greater friendliness.

Unanswered as yet are a number of questions. Given at least an average level of intelligence, to what extent can the drive to excel compensate for lack of the exceptional mental ability possessed by the Stanford group? Terman has shown that a fairly large number of this group when in their thirties were accomplishing little more than the average person of similar age. Are there also a fair number of persons whose childhood abilities were in no way outstanding but who, through superior drive and good social attitudes, arrive at exceptional success in adult life? How do abstract intelligence and the personal-social traits which Terman's comparison of the A and C groups has shown to be so important rank with respect to the attainment of success in maturity? Perhaps a high degree of both is required for extraordinary attainment. But it might be enlightening to look up some of the children who were tested and found wanting when the 1921-1922 survey for the selection of the gifted group was made, to ascertain how their later careers compare with those included in the study. Or, since to do this would be difficult, further study of the accomplishments of the brothers of the gifted subjects would be desirable, especially since the level of education and occupation achieved by the fathers was shown to be so important a factor in differentiating between the groups. Many of the siblings were also tested in 1921-

1922,[6] and since not all showed unusually high ability, at least a small control group is thus still available.

The popular idea that the brilliant child is doomed to early death or to early mental deterioration or disease has been definitely contradicted by Terman's findings. Whether the greater incidence of mental maladjustment in Group C as compared to Group A is a cause or an effect of their lower degree of success in life cannot be determined from the evidence now available. It would be of the utmost importance to know how many of these poor achievers might have been brought to a more complete realization of their potential gifts by more adequate guidance during childhood and youth.[7] Nevertheless, the total picture provides an unequivocally affirmative answer to the question: Has the brilliant child a better than average chance for success in life?

REFERENCES

ADAMS, F. J., "College Degrees and Elementary School Intelligence Quotients," *Journal of Educational Psychology*, 31 (1940), 360-368.

ANDERSON, John E., "The Limitations of Infant and Preschool Tests in the Measurement of Intelligence," *Journal of Psychology*, 8 (1939), 351-379.

BURKS, Barbara S., JENSEN, Dortha Williams, and TERMAN, Lewis M., *Genetic Studies of Genius: The Promise of Youth* (Stanford, Cal., Stanford University Press, 1930), Vol. 3.

CATTELL, J. McKeen, "The Origin and Distribution of Scientific Men," *Science*, 66 (1927), 513-516.

COX, Catharine M., *Genetic Studies of Genius: The Early Mental Traits of Three Hundred Geniuses* (Stanford, Cal., Stanford University Press, 1926), Vol. 2.

[6] At least two of the fieldworkers made an attempt to test all the siblings of school age and most of the preschool siblings aged three or older. Lack of time made it impossible to do this in all cases, but it was accomplished for nearly all the subjects in the Los Angeles region.

[7] It may perhaps be well to point out that nothing was done to alter the lives of these children apart from the possible psychological effect that frequent testing and the ultimate knowledge of their high standing may have had on some of them. To have interfered in any way with the lives of these children would have destroyed the value of the study, for no one could have said whether superior ability or superior guidance was responsible for the generally superior accomplishments of the group as a whole.

GOETSCH, Helen B., *Parental Income and College Opportunities*, Contributions to Education Series (New York, Teachers College Bureau of Publications, 1940), No. 795.

HOLLINGWORTH, Leta S., "The Subsequent History of E," *Journal of Applied Psychology*, 6 (1922), 205-210.

———, "The Subsequent History of E: Ten Years after the Original Report," *Journal of Applied Psychology*, 11 (1927), 385-390.

———, "Do Intellectually Gifted Children Grow Toward Mediocrity in Stature?" *Journal of Genetic Psychology*, 37 (1930), 345-360.

LAMSON, Edna E., *A Study of Young Gifted Children in Senior High School*, Contributions to Education Series (New York, Teachers College Bureau of Publications, 1930), No. 424.

———, "High School Achievement of 56 Gifted Children," *Journal of Genetic Psychology*, 47 (1935), 233-239.

LORGE, Irving, and HOLLINGWORTH, Leta S., "Adult Status of Highly Intelligent Children," *Journal of Genetic Psychology*, 49 (1936), 215-226.

RIGG, Melvin C., "A Follow-up Study of 16 Superior Students," *School and Society*, 48 (1938), 411-412.

STRONG, Edward K., *Vocational Interests of Men and Women* (Stanford, Cal., Stanford University Press, 1943).

TERMAN, Lewis M., *Psychological Factors in Marital Happiness* (New York, McGraw-Hill Book Company, 1938).

———, "Suggestions for Follow-up Studies of Intellectually Gifted Children," *Journal of Educational Sociology*, 13 (1939), 82-89.

———, and ODEN, Melita H., *Genetic Studies of Genius: The Gifted Child Grows Up* (Stanford, Cal., Stanford University Press, 1947), Vol. 4.

WITTY, Paul A., and THEMAN, Viola, "A Follow-up Study of the Educational Attainment of Gifted Negroes," *Journal of Educational Psychology*, 34 (1943), 35-47.

ZEIGEL, William H., "Achievement of High School Honor Students in the University of Missouri," *School and Society*, 25 (1927), 82-84.

Manifestations of Special   11
Talents in Childhood

DISTINCTION BETWEEN GENERAL AND SPECIALIZED ABILITY

THE DISTINCTION between general and specialized ability is one of *extensity*, using the term in the sense in which it was defined in Chapter 2. General ability, as the name implies, underlies all, or nearly all, functions of the human mind and to some extent sets limits to all lines of attainment. Specialized abilities, or, as they are often called, special talents, have a much narrower extent. The gifted musician may find it well-nigh impossible to grasp anything beyond the most elementary principles of mechanics; the talented writer may have no head for mathematics. The portrait painter may be blind to the beauties of great literature; Euclid may have seen beauty bare in his geometrical theorems, but whether or not he found it also in the great paintings and sculpture of his time, history does not tell us.

As a matter of fact, exceptional intelligence and some form of special talent are far more likely to be found together than separately. This raises an interesting question: Have we special talents or highly developed special interests leading to excessive amounts of very intensive practice within some specialized field and a consequent high development of skill? The latter explanation is frequently given to account for the remarkable performances of the so-called *idiots savants*. Cox has shown that even those individuals who won great fame in some narrow field of endeavor were usually possessed of very high general intelligence as well. Many of the world's famous men have given evidence that, under different

156

circumstances, equal success might have been attained along one or more lines quite different from that in which they actually won renown. Benvenuto Cellini is equally celebrated for his art work and for his memoirs, but he also left behind him many drawings and descriptions of mechanical contrivances which foreshadow those actually developed many years later. Examination of the lives of famous men suggests strongly that the parable of the talents holds good in the modern, as well as in the earlier, sense of the word.

It is true, of course, that great achievement along some lines, such as singing or dramatic work, is impossible in the absence of the requisite type of development of the vocal apparatus. Most lines of excellence, however, appear to be little, if at all, dependent upon physical characteristics. Not all great men have been strong and healthy in body. Neither Milton's blindness nor Beethoven's deafness was sufficient to stop the flow of their productivity. Each composed his greatest masterpiece after having been stricken by a sensory disaster so great that ordinary men would have been overwhelmed by it. Francis Parkman, the historian, won lasting fame despite ill health which during much of his life rendered it impossible for him to read or write for more than very brief periods daily. The outstanding importance of drive, of the will to achieve and the courage that no obstacle can daunt which, as we have indicated elsewhere, seems to be the major differentiating factor between those who achieve greatly and those who permit their talents to rust is nowhere better exemplified than in the accomplishments of such men.

SPECIAL TALENTS IN CHILDHOOD

As Thorndike has so admirably shown, the effect of a successful performance is to expedite the learning process. And since success is pleasant, the act is likely to be repeated. Thus it happens that given either an original predisposition in the form of an aptitude or well-planned early instruction, there is likely to be far more practice in the particular skill involved than occurs in the absence of these conditions. Moreover, the child who shows some talent along a particular line is more likely to receive instruction and encouragement in that area than is the one who does not. Talent thus has a circular effect, since the satisfaction that comes with rapid progress is intensified by the admiration of others, and, in many cases, the talented child is given the advantage of additional instruction along the line of his specialized ability.

Particularly in the case of intellectually gifted children, it is easy to confuse interest with talent. Gifted children typically have many interests, and it is not unusual for some external circumstance, such as intense admiration for some talented person, to arouse in the child a tremendous zeal to emulate the achievement of his ideal. Toward this end he strives with both diligence and enthusiasm which often bring results that lead parents and teachers to look upon him as highly talented and perhaps to make extensive plans for his future career in that field. Many a parent has felt bitter disappointment when the child for whom they had such hopes later shifts his interest to some other field. They fail to realize that childhood and youth are times of experimentation and that superior intelligence enables a child to progress further with his experiments in any given field than the average child. Such experiments are not necessarily indicative of the field which will eventually be chosen for his life work. Often they represent nothing more than special interests grafted upon average talent which his exceptional intellectual gifts enable him to develop far beyond the level that is reached by the majority of children.

The study of special talent is thus complicated by the number of variables that are involved which are not always easy to separate. Of these, the most important appear to be (1) interest with resultant excess amounts of practice; (2) amount and quality of special training, including association with adults who have been successful in the field in question; (3) general intelligence of a high order; (4) special talent in the sense of a greater innate aptitude for that field than for others of equal difficulty.

The best method of determining the relative importance of the four factors would be by means of a long-time study of the development of talented children similar to Terman's study of intellectually gifted children. Such a study is made extremely difficult by the present absence of dependable ready-made tests by which talented children may be identified. This throws the experimenter back upon a consensus of expert judgments for the identification of his subjects. Such judgments are not only relatively undependable but they have the further disadvantage of being unobtainable until the talent has matured to a point at which a fair degree of skill has been attained; and such maturation may not take place in the absence of opportunities that are not equally available to all. In spite of these difficulties, however, the only hope of untangling the present confusion with respect to the origin and nature of special talents seems to lie in the developmental approach. Much time and thought is being expended upon efforts to develop measures of special aptitudes and to predict the fields in which a given individual is most likely to win success. It may be significant that those who have approached this problem from the standpoint of vocational *interests* as displayed in adolescence or early maturity have been more successful than those who have attempted to measure *talent* apart from interest.

Research by the methods of factor analysis has resulted in the identification of a number of factors which, in varying combinations, can account for the intercorrelations in a matrix, usually made up of the various part-scores in a group test designed to measure some specified general characteristic, such as intelligence, personal-social adjustment, and the like. Once these factors have been isolated, it becomes possible, at least in theory, to devise other tests that are "purer" measures of the factors that make up the ability and that when properly weighted and combined provide a better measure of the trait as a whole than was given by the original test. In a sense, these "primary abilities," as they are called, may be looked upon as special talents, although most of those who have been working in the field have regarded them rather as components of some more general trait. But since children, even at an early age, show fairly marked differences with respect to their standing on the various components making up a total, one of the major difficulties previously mentioned in the study of the identification of talented children is obviated, at least within certain limited areas, by these tests. Thurstone, who has gone furthest both in the theory of factor analysis and in its practical applications, has devised a test of primary intellectual abilities suitable for use with children of five and six years.[1] This test identifies five underlying components, which we may perhaps call "talents." Test results for these components when combined make up a serviceable measure of general intelligence, but separate standards are also available. Some years ago, Thurstone also worked out similar measures of primary intellectual abilities suitable for junior and senior high school students. An unanswered but highly significant question is this: To what extent do the special intellectual abilities shown in early childhood as measured by the Thurstone test persist over a term of years? And, furthermore, do either the special intellectual abilities indicated by the childhood tests or those shown later, after adolescence has been reached, have useful predictive value with respect to the vocational areas in which a given subject is most likely to achieve success?

Perhaps the most convincing evidence for the existence of innate talent which manifests itself under conditions that provide only the minimal opportunity for it to show itself and which shows remarkably rapid development under suitable training is provided by the childhood history of great musicians and by the occasional authentic cases of children who, at a very early age and with little or no instruction, become fairly accomplished performers on some musical instrument to which they chance to have access. True, the majority of these children never carry their accomplishment beyond the amateur level. Others become teachers of music, organists in small churches, and the like. But even though they never achieve wide renown, they still rank above the average of their fellows in musical ability. It is probably because of the many early instances of musical aptitude, as well as the large number of vocational outlets for musicians of varying degrees of talent and

[1] In collaboration with his wife, Thelma G. Thurstone.

competence, that so many attempts have been made to measure musical talent in childhood.

EARLY EVIDENCES OF MUSICAL TALENT

The first attempts to measure musical aptitude were based upon the assumption that musical ability is a complex of many relatively simple abilities, such as a well-developed sense of rhythm, the ability to distinguish between small differences in pitch, a feeling for harmony as opposed to dissonance, and so on. The first person to develop a well-standardized series of tests based on this concept was Carl Seashore of the University of Iowa, who standardized a series of five phonograph records designed to measure respectively sense of pitch, intensity or loudness, time, consonance, and musical memory. Each record began with relatively marked contrasts for which the judgments were easy and proceeded to smaller differences requiring finer discriminations.

The Seashore measures aroused great interest which has continued. Many investigations were made to ascertain the extent to which scores on these measures were correlated with the judgments of competent musical instructors as to the musical aptitudes of their students and their progress under instruction. The net result was to show that the tests were fairly useful in selecting cases who were so lacking in musical aptitude that special training was likely to be wasted effort, but they were of little value in identifying the musically gifted. Real musical genius, although it unquestionably requires the kind of musical sensitivity that is to some extent measured by the Seashore tests, is a far more complex gift than the Seashore tests or others (such as the more recent Kwalwasser-Dykema tests) constructed on the same basic principles can identify. Also available are a number of tests of musical appreciation and musical information, as well as various tests of musical knowledge designed primarily to measure progress under instruction, which, it may be noted, is a good practical means of testing of musical aptitude, although differences in the quality of the instruction, including the ability of the instructor to arouse and maintain the student's interest, are a confusing factor here.

All in all, it must be admitted that, so far, attempts to select children with high musical aptitude in advance of the manifestation of such ability in terms of actual performance have met with only mediocre success. But some children, even at a very early age and with only a moderate amount of instruction, become musicians whose accomplishments attract widespread attention. Some of these children, of whom Mozart and, in modern times, Yehudi Menuhin are examples, continue their musical careers into adult life and become artists whose fame is world-wide; others find the ladder of mature achievement too arduous for them to climb and are content to rest on the laurels gained in childhood. Some shift to other interests. Of the eleven great musical geniuses studied by Cox, ten were well embarked upon their musical careers long before they were past their teens. The musical precocity of Mozart is well known; his earliest published compositions (Op. 1, 2, and 3), were completed at the age of five years. From then on, the child continued to compose, and his skill as a musical performer soon attracted attention in many places. At thirteen, he was made Grand Ducal Concertmaster; at fourteen, his first Italian opera was produced with marked success. The list of his achievements while still a child is so extraordinary that if it were not a matter of record it could hardly be believed.

Beethoven's first public concert was given when he was seven; his first musical composition appeared when he was ten. Mendelssohn began the study of music at seven and gave his first concert at nine; his first opera was composed and performed in public before he was fifteen. Weber is said to have had a passion for music from babyhood; his first composition appeared when he was eleven. Bach was taught by his father to play the violin while still a young child; the exact date of his first compositions is unknown except that they were done while he was still at a tender age.

That musical talent seems to run in families is well-known. An outstanding example is the Bach family, whose founder, Veit Bach, a baker by trade, was an amateur musician who played the guitar and sang. From him there came a long train of descendants, among whom were counted an amazing number of musicians. Biographical dictionaries of musicians list no fewer than 57, of whom well over 20 may be considered eminent.[2] The grandfather of Ludwig van Beethoven was a brilliant musician; his father, also talented, failed to achieve fame because of his intemperate habits, but he was a tenor singer in the Elector's Chapel at Cologne. Weber's father was a well-known musician, and he had a number of other musical relatives. Mozart's father was a professional musician who gave him his first instruction. This list might be extended almost indefinitely.

The exceptionally early age at which genuine musical talent is usually shown through outstanding musical achievement mitigates to some extent the unfortunate lack of really useful diagnostic tests for the early identification of musical aptitude. The opportunities available to most children of the present day are probably adequate to permit real talent to show itself for what it is. Progress under special training provides further check upon the accuracy of the diagnosis. Once the musically gifted child has been identified, provision for his musical education should be co-ordinated with the arrangements for his general education. The fact that most children who show pronounced musical talent at an early age are intellectually gifted as well [3] simplifies the educational problem to some extent.

However, it is not only the potential musical geniuses who profit by musical training in childhood. Even a moderate degree of musical talent, if it is cultivated, can become an important social asset to the one who possesses it. The adolescent who can sit down at the piano and lead the crowd in singing its favorite songs, who can pinch-hit at dances when one of the musicians fails to appear, and who is available as an entertainer at amateur concerts, has a talent whose ramifications extend far into the structure of his life

[2] See the account of the Bach family in Francis Galton, *Hereditary Genius: An Inquiry into Its Laws and Consequences* (New York, D. Appleton and Company, 1870).

[3] The mean of the estimated IQ's of the eleven musical geniuses studied by Cox was 130.5. In the opinion of the present writer this is far too low.

activities. It is a mistake to think that only those with truly exceptional musical talent require musical training in this age of mechanized music. There are many with more moderate gifts which, if properly developed, may become important aids to their social adjustment and personal happiness.

CHILDREN WITH ART TALENT

During recent years, the drawings and paintings of children have been the subject of an unusual amount of psychological study. A review by Goodenough and Harris lists 330 references selected from a much larger number dealing with this topic. In spite of the widespread interest in the subject—which is manifested not only by the number of psychological investigations but also by the establishment of children's art classes, arrangements by art museums for specially conducted tours for school children, or for exhibitions of art in the schools—the identification of talented children is still for the most part a matter of subjective judgment. In the case of music, there is a practical criterion of *difficulty of performance*, which, if met at an early age, may properly be regarded as an indication of talent, though not necessarily of real genius. The child who at the age of six can play the *Apassionata* in a manner that brings tears of delight to the eyes of his hearers is certainly as far in advance of the average child of his age in the field of music as is intellectually the one who, at a corresponding age, earns a mental age of ten or eleven years on the Stanford Binet. Although the problem is complicated by differences in training, it is questionable whether training alone, in the absence of special talent, could accomplish such a result. But drawing and painting are different. Standards of excellence differ, and there is no such clear-cut indication of the level of achievement in terms of difficulty of performance as exists in the case of music. Most children like to draw and paint, and most will occasionally achieve results that impress the sophisticated adult as showing signs of real artistry. The tests that must be applied here are the following: Are these occasional successes merely sporadic, resulting as much from chance as from talent, or are they the result of definite effort toward a given end? Does the child himself distinguish between his successful and his unsuccessful attempts at portrayal of his ideas and continue his efforts until he achieves his purposes?

As Goodenough and Harris have pointed out, the great obstacle in the way of studying artistic talent in childhood is the lack of an adequate criterion for evaluating art products. In the absence of such a criterion, we turn once more to the evidence provided by the childhood histories of men whose later artistic achievements leave no reasonable doubt as to their talent.

Cox lists 13 artists whom history has placed in the rank of the great geniuses of all time. Practically all are said to have shown great interest in drawing and painting from early childhood, but there are few, if any, examples of early accomplishment that are at all comparable to those recorded for the young musicians. Either art talent has a slower rate of maturation than musical talent or we have not yet learned to identify its early stages. Canova, whose father was a stone-cutter, is said to have carved two little shrines in marble at the age of eight years, but none of the other 12 is reported as having done anything thought worthy of preservation before the middle or late teens. A number of them, however, showed sufficient interest and talent to cause them to be apprenticed to artists.

A number of attempts have been made to devise methods of classifying the rank and file of children with respect to art talent. The methods most often used may be divided into two general classes: (1) product scales and (2) tests of art appreciation and judgment. In the first of these, specimens of the child's art work are compared as to merit with a series of standard samples to which numerical values have been assigned. The earliest of these scales was developed by Thorndike in 1913. A number of more recent applications of the method have since been devised. In the second method, the child is asked to differentiate between good and poor examples of artistic design. The McAdory Art Test, which utilizes pictures of everyday objects, and the Meier Art

Test, which is based upon line drawings of famous paintings in which an exact copy is to be compared with another modified in such a way as to violate some well-established rule of art composition, are examples. The many studies in which the art of children and adults has been used as an aid to uncovering emotional disturbances of various kinds will not be discussed here. The interested reader will find them dealt with in the article by Goodenough and Harris which is cited in the references at the end of this chapter.

Goodenough has shown that the drawings of children furnish a useful index to their intellectual level. Drawings are scored on the basis of a system of points shown to be definitely related to intelligence rather than to the artistic quality of the drawing. Most investigations, however, have agreed in finding only a slight relationship between art talent as such and general intelligence. The mean of the estimated IQ's of Cox's group of great artists was only 122.3. Talent in art seems to be a narrower gift, more nearly independent of other aspects of the personality than are most other special talents. Its extensity is relatively short. As a social asset for the individual its value is less than that of musical ability.

LITERARY TALENT AMONG CHILDREN

Early in life some children display a remarkable sensitivity to words and their meaning. They have a feeling for euphony and rhythm in language and often create small rhyming couplets or, as they grow older, verses and short poems that sometimes have a charming originality and freshness both in form and imagery. Nevertheless, these early literary efforts do not appear to be as significant for literary talent, as judged by the field later chosen by the subject for his life work, as for general intellectual ability. Terman and others have shown that the size of vocabulary is the best single index of intelligence that has so far been discovered. In the appendix to Volume 3 of *Genetic Studies of Genius*, Cox has given excerpts from the early writings of well over a hundred of her subjects. Only a few of these were done during childhood;

the great majority date from the time of middle or late adolescence. It is noteworthy that early attempts at writing poetry are by no means confined to those who later won fame as writers either of poetry or prose. The popular idea that most adolescents go through a period when they try their hands at composing poetry probably has some foundation in fact. The difference between the trite and sentimental verses composed by the lovesick boy or girl of mediocre intelligence and the often extravagant but nevertheless original and metrical stanzas that our great literary geniuses wrote in their early youth is sufficiently marked to be recognized by all who have a feeling for literary quality. Most adolescents try at some time to write; the majority soon grow to realize their lack of literary talent and give up the effort. The real geniuses learn to recognize and correct their early faults and persist in their efforts. A second difference that separates the genius from the mediocre is uniqueness of style. Those who possess little talent of their own are likely to try to imitate those whom they know to be great writers. The highly talented develop and perfect a style of their own, as purely individual as are the features of their faces. They are creators, not imitators. Even when the same metric form is used, no one who is familiar with the writings of one poet is likely to confuse them with those of another.

In mental extensity, however, literary talent probably ranks next to general intelligence, and during childhood and early adolescence the overlapping of the two is so great that they are hard to distinguish. Children whose early interests and abilities appear to run almost entirely along verbal lines not infrequently turn to some field of science later on and devote their literary talents to the writing of scientific books and papers. As a matter of fact, the ability to express oneself in clear and pleasing verbal terms is so great an asset for success in almost any line of endeavor that training in the use of good English in speech and writing is stressed above all other subjects in modern American education.

During her work on the 1927-1928 follow-up of the Stanford group, Jensen became much impressed with the literary performances of many of these brilliant children. On the basis of a series of descriptions ranging from *"the best work of the ten best writers in the English language,"* to which a statistical treatment of the ratings by a group of presumably competent judges assigned a value of 133, down to *"the average work of children below school age,"* which was given a value of 0, a scale of literary merit was constructed. From the Stanford group, together with a number of persons who later became eminent in literature, 42 individuals were selected by Jensen as showing exceptional ability as child writers. Of these, 14 were members of the California gifted group and 28 were chosen from those who later became eminent.

A total of 151 juvenile writings produced by these subjects were evaluated on this scale by each of seven judges. The ages of the authors varied from five to nineteen years. Of specimens written before the age of seventeen, slightly more than 11 per cent of those composed by the California children earned mean ratings of 85 or higher. Of those who eventually became eminent in some field of letters, approximately 13 per cent were rated at that level. The small difference is well within the limits of chance. I have attempted to compare the rate of improvement with age for those subjects who had a number of specimens written at different ages. There is a suggestion that the eminent authors showed more consistent and regular improvement than the children, whose ultimate field of endeavor was as yet unknown, but the data are insufficient to test the hypothesis.

A rather large number of methodological studies have been devoted to the derivation of scales for appraising some aspect of linguistic ability or language usage among the generality of children. Exceptionally high scores on these tests are frequently regarded as indicators of literary talent. Such measures include product scales for judging the quality of English compositions, tests of literary appreciation, of correct language usage, vocabulary tests, tests of literary information, interest tests, and various attempts to appraise the depth and quality of the subject's emotional reactions, the extent to which he is able to project himself into a situation and identify himself with the characters he is attempting to depict. The tests last named are still in the experimental stage.

As is true of other arts, the study of literary talent in childhood is hampered by the lack of suitable criteria. How much weight should be given to correctness of form, how much to richness and fluency of vocabulary, how much to sensitive imagery? Is it feasible to rate such matters separately or must the composition be judged as a whole? By what means can the investigator escape the bonds of tradition sufficiently to enable him to appreciate a new and original style at its true worth? How many specimens of the writings of a given subject are needed for a fair appraisal of the quality of his performance at any given stage of development? It is apparent from Jensen's data that a single specimen may be very misleading and that even the three or four that were secured from a few of her subjects within a limited period of time vary too greatly with respect to their estimated degree of excellence to warrant much confidence even in the average of the scores assigned to them.

The close relationship between intelligence and literary ability has been mentioned before. The mean of the estimated IQ's of the 95 writers in Cox's group falls just short of 140, a value that is exceeded only by the philosophers and the Revolutionary statesmen. I have yet to find a child showing marked ability in the writing of original prose or poetry whose intelligence as measured by standard tests was not also high. The converse, however, does not necessarily hold good, for some exceptionally bright children show little interest in writing but devote their talents to other fields.

EARLY MANIFESTATIONS OF SPECIAL TALENT IN SCIENCE, MATHEMATICS, OR MECHANICS

While still young, some children show unusual interest in numbers and quantities. Counting becomes a favorite occupation. They can tell you how many steps lead to the front doors of their homes, how many cookies there are on a certain plate, and the prices of sundry coveted toys at the ten-cent store. They are interested in the relationships of things about them; they note processes and the instruments by which these processes are carried out. All this seems to presage a specialized talent in some field of science. Nevertheless, the fact remains that objective methods for identifying genuine scientific talent during the years of childhood are for the most part wanting. One reason for this lies in the fact that children at this time are so occupied in acquiring a knowledge of the simpler tool subjects—reading, writing, and the elements of arithmetic—that such evidences of special scientific talent as they may show are likely to be overlooked. The vocational significance of a special proclivity for numbers and exceptionally high rank on arithmetic tests is unknown. There are a number of tests of mechanical aptitude that may be used as early as the fifth or sixth school grade, but none of these has been validated in terms of later achievement in such fields as engineering or the physical sciences.

It is not until the high school years that talent in science or mathematics becomes sufficiently distinct from general intelligence, on the one hand, and the results of circumstantial and temporary interests, on the other, to enable us to identify those so endowed with any reasonable certainty. This may be because we have not yet learned what the earlier signs are. It is also possible that such signs do not emerge above the general matrix until a certain level of familiarity with facts and tools has been gained. Whatever the reason may be, effective search for scientific talent is at present confined for the most part to the high schools and junior colleges.

The annual Science Talent Search conducted for the Westinghouse Scholarships is notable for two reasons: first, because it is directed by a group of competent psychologists who make use of objective tests of scientific knowledge and skills, high school records and ratings, and an essay on some scientific topic which is submitted by each contestant, and secondly, because it makes use of annual follow-up studies in which the later achievement of the successful contestants is compared with that of those who were not chosen. The search was begun in 1942, and the follow-up studies have been continued since that time. The results show very conclusively that the candidates chosen for scholarships more frequently enter and succeed in some scientific area than those who were unsuccessful in the contest, that they make higher records in college and are more likely to continue for graduate study. These findings are the more significant since the comparison is not made between the successful candidates and the generality of high school students but between the successful candidates and others who were believed sufficiently talented to warrant their entering the contest. As yet, insufficient time has elapsed to permit these young scientists to reach the peak of their professions, but within a few years it should be possible to determine which of the various types of measurements used was most useful in selecting those of really exceptional talent.

THE FUTURE STATESMAN

Both industrial leaders and the general public are highly conscious of the importance of making use of all available talent for engineering and the physical sciences. The social sciences, however, have lagged far behind the physical sciences with respect to both the identification and the provision of specialized training for those who will become the social and political leaders of the future. Yet few would deny that it is upon the behavior and attitudes of human beings, upon the relationships between man and man and between nation and nation that the destinies of mankind chiefly depend. Physicists may learn how to release and control atomic energy, but governments decide how it shall be used. Inequitable distribution of material goods, for which governments are largely if often indirectly responsible, has led to many a social upheaval. Conflicts between labor and management add vast sums to the cost of producing the goods and services that make life pleasant and easy. Racial and religious prejudices divide communities.

The cost of war is immeasurable. Suffering and grief cannot be valued in dollars and cents. Money paid out for the instruments of warfare becomes a matter of record, and the total thus expended is a staggering sum. But no one can know how great is the financial loss to the country resulting from diverting the efforts of millions of young men into destructive rather than productive channels. No one can know how greatly the world might have profited by the work of those who were killed or broken in the course of the struggle. Certainly, the expenditure of any amount of money upon the training of potential leaders who could work effectively in the direction of establishing world peace would be well worth while. Experience since the close of World War I strongly suggests that by the time middle or late maturity has been reached, unfriendly attitudes and prejudices are likely to have become so firmly established that genuine understanding and co-operation among the representatives of different nations is not easy to achieve. Yet no nation seems to have given really serious thought to the early selection and training of youths who show special talent for statesmanship. Granted that we do not now know what the signs of such talent may be, it would still be worth while to devote time, thought, and money to a vigorous effort to find out. Granted also that we are by no means certain as to the kind of training best suited to develop the statesman, we do know something of the methods by which this knowledge might be gained. If it is worth while to seek out and provide special training for those talented along lines of far less consequence for society, is it sensible to leave those with political talent to mature unrecognized, ignorant of themselves and untrained in the wise use of their abilities?

Whether talent for statesmanship is a specialized aptitude or a conjunction of a high level of general intelligence with other special talents and interests is not known. In either case it is certain that achievement in statescraft varies as greatly as in other lines of endeavor. Not all who enter the field succeed in reaching their goal. Not all who attain positions of political leadership are fitted for the duties that they assume. An attempt to identify those capable of becoming statesmen of the future, coupled with the provision of a carefully planned and directed course of training designed to provide a comprehensive understanding of world affairs, of peoples and their needs both at home and abroad, and to inculcate attitudes and habits of incorruptible honesty and trustworthiness, might lead to greater accomplishments for world progress and international harmony than we have yet seen.

The many studies that have been made of "leadership" among high school and college students fail to meet the requirements in at least three respects. They are based almost entirely upon leadership in the social and popular sense of the word; they are calculated to select the future club president or the local politician rather than the statesman; they do not point the way toward suitable training for those in the top rank. Finally, there are no follow-up studies which would point the way to improvement in the program.

REFERENCES

ALSCHULER, Rose H., and HATTWICK, LaBerta W., *Painting and Personality: A Study of Young Children* (Chicago, University of Chicago Press, 1947), 2 vols.

ANASTASI, Anne, and FOLEY, John P., Jr., "An Analysis of Spontaneous Drawings by Children of Different Cultures," *Journal of Applied Psychology*, 20 (1936), 689-726.

BAUMGARTEN, Franziska, "Supranormales Zeichnen eines Kindes," *Zeitschrift für Kinderpsychiatrie*, 2 (1936), 182-189.

BECK, O. W., *Self-development in Drawing as Interpreted by the Genius of Romano Dazzi and Other Children* (New York, G. P. Putnam's Sons, 1928).

BECKHAM, Albert S., "A Study of Social Background and Art Aptitude in Superior Negro Children," *Journal of Applied Psychology*, 26 (1942), 777-784.

CANE, Florence, "The Gifted Child in Art," *Journal of Educational Sociology*, 10 (1936), 67-73.

CARROLL, Herbert A., "A Preliminary Report on a Study of the Relationship Between Ability in Art and Certain Personality Traits," *School and Society*, 36 (1932), 285-288.

CATTELL, Raymond B., "Personality Traits Associated with Abilities: I. With Intelligence and Drawing Ability," *Educational and Psychological Measurement*, 5 (1945), 131-146.

EDGERTON, Harold A., and BRITT, Steuart Henderson, "The Science Talent Search," *Occupations*, 21 (1943), 177-180.

———, and BRITT, Steuart Henderson, "The Annual Science Talent Search for the Westinghouse Scholarships," *Transactions of the New York Academy of Sciences*, 11 (1949), 118-120.

FARNSWORTH, Paul R., "Ratings in Music, Art, and Abnormality in the First Four Grades," *Journal of Psychology*, 6 (1938), 89-94.

———, "Auditory Acuity and Musical Ability in the First Four Grades," *Journal of Psychology*, 6 (1938), 95-98.

FLEMING, Edward G., "Personality and Artistic Talent," *Journal of Educational Sociology*, 8 (1934), 27-38.

GOODENOUGH, Florence L., and HARRIS, Dale B., "Studies in the Psychology of Children's Drawings: II. 1928-1949," *Psychological Bulletin*, 47 (1950), 369-433.

HARTLAUB, G. F., *Der Genius im Kinder: Zeichnungen und Malversuche begabter Kinder* (Breslau, Hirt, 1930).

HOLLINGWORTH, Leta S., *Special Talents and Defects: Their Significance for Education* (New York, The Macmillan Company, 1923).

JENSEN, Dortha Williams, *The Evaluation of Literary Juvenilia* (Stanford, Cal., Stanford University Press, 1930).

LARK-HOROWITZ, Betty, BARNHART, E. N., and SILLS, Esther M., *Graphic Work-sample Diagnosis, an Analytic Method of Estimating Children's Drawing Ability* (Cleveland, Ohio, Cleveland Museum of Art, 1939).

LÖWENFELD, VIKTOR, *The Nature of Creative Activity* (Harcourt, Brace and Company, 1939).

———, *Creative and Mental Growth* (New York, The Macmillan Company, 1947).

MCADORY, Margaret, *The Construction and Validation of an Art Test*, Contributions to Education Series (New York, Teachers College Bureau of Publications, 1929), No. 383.

MEIER, Norman C., "Special Artistic Talent," *Psychological Bulletin*, 25 (1928), 265-271.

———, "Studies in the Psychology of Art," *Psychological Monographs*, 45 (1933), 1-188.

———, "Art Ability Without Instruction or Environmental Background: A Case Study of Loran Lockhart," *Psychological Monographs*, 48 (1936), 155-163.

———, "Factors in Artistic Aptitude: Final Summary of a Ten-year Study of a Special Ability," *Psychological Monographs*, 51 (1939), 140-158.

MEIER, Norman C., and SEASHORE, Carl E., *The Meier-Seashore Art Judgment Test* (1929); revised (1940), under the title *The Meier Art Test* (Iowa City, Iowa, Bureau of Educational Research and Services, 1940).

MERRY, Ruth C., "Art Talent and Racial Background," *Journal of Educational Research*, 32 (1938), 17-22.

RUSSELL, D. H., "Trends and Needs in the Study of Special Abilities and Disabilities," *Teachers College Record*, 42 (1940), 239-249.

SCHEERER, Martin, ROTHMANN, Eva, and GOLDSTEIN, Kurt, "A Case of 'Idiot Savant': An Experimental Study of Personality Organization," *Psychological Monographs*, 58, No. 4 (1945).

TERMAN, Lewis M., and CHASE, Jessie C., "A Preliminary Report on a Gifted Juvenile Actor," *Journal of Applied Psychology*, 5 (1921), 163-171.

ZILLIG, Maria, "Zur Psychologie des dichterischschaffenden Kindes," *Zeitschrift für Psychologie und Physiologie der Sinnesorgane*, 112 (1929), 302-324.

PART III

The Intellectually Inadequate

The Nature of Intellectual Inadequacy

12

INADEQUATE—FOR WHAT?

"Well, I decided not to go on for my Ph.D.," remarked one of the two young men sitting behind me in the bus. "I got my Master's," he continued, "but it took me more than two years after I'd finished college. My grades weren't any too hot either, though I sweated blood over the stuff. Anyway," he added in a more cheerful tone, "it's over now and I've got a good job."

"Don't blame you for quitting the profs," remarked the other. "I flunked out of medical school myself. Too stiff for me. So I just switched over to pharmacy."

"No," said Mrs. Ardley, flushing a little as she replied to her friend's question. "No, Louise isn't going to college. She—well, you know she never did learn as easily as Evelyn does. She had to repeat the sixth grade; and high school work was very hard for her. Oh yes," forestalling the next question, "she *graduated*. But she wasn't recommended for college, and when I talked to the principal about it, he told me very plainly that he thought it would be a great mistake for us to send her. She's thinking of taking a business course, typewriting, you know, so she can work in an office."

"And her age?" asked the school principal, with pen poised above the yellow registration card.

"Eight," admitted the mother, apologetically.

"She's never been to school? Why not?"

"Well ... she ... she's a little backward in some ways. I didn't think ..."

"What makes you think she is backward?" With an appraising glance born of long experience, the elderly principal turned his attention to the little girl who was clinging tightly to her mother's hand.

"She doesn't—she didn't talk very plainly. I could understand her all right but hardly anybody else could. But I've been working with her, and she does a good deal better now. And last year she still used to wet her clothes quite often, but that hardly ever happens any more. So I've been teaching her at home. She knows her colors, now, and quite a lot of her letters."

"Wed," announced the child proudly, pointing to a book on the principal's desk.

"No, darling," corrected the mother in some embarrassment, "that's a *blue* book. She just loves red," she explained, "so she calls everything red, even though she knows better."

The principal nodded but made no verbal comment. He stared at the yellow card before him for a moment and then said quietly, "Since Emily has never been to school before, I think we had better have our school psychologist see her. I'll call up and find when she is free."

An appointment was made. The day afterward the following report arrived at the principal's office.

"Emily Andrews. Age 8 years, 4 months. Stanford Binet mental age 4 years, 3 months, IQ 51. Marked articulatory defect together with slight stutter. On tests not requiring the use of language, her performance was slightly better than that on the Stanford, averaging about a five-year standard. Comprehension of pictures very poor; could only point to a few simple objects on request. None was named spontaneously.

Brief physical examination by Dr. Peters revealed no special defects. Vision and hearing apparently normal; nutrition good. Mother says child has always been well.

Tentative diagnosis: Mentally defective child of low-moron grade.

Recommendation: Enroll on trial basis in special class for young retarded children. Arrange for special training in speech correction. Retest after six months.

The great clinic was a scene of activity. Nurses hastened along the corridors, patients came and went. But in the book-lined office at the end of the short hallway opposite the reception desk there was tense silence. Sitting at his desk, Dr. Burton stared at the open folder lying before him. He had said what he must say; he knew too well the look on the faces of those who had listened to him.

The silence was broken by a hoarse, inarticulate shout. A boy of some ten years lurched forward, arms swinging loosely, his gait shambling and uncertain, saliva drooling from his open mouth. With fumbling hands he reached for the calendar on the doctor's desk, but his father stopped him.

"No, Dennis," he said in a voice that trembled a little in spite of his attempt to control it. "You stay here with me."

But the little episode had broken the spell. It was the mother who spoke first.

"But, Doctor," she gasped, "surely you don't mean—surely there's something—treatment of some kind—or even an operation! We aren't rich people but we'd gladly give our last cent . . ."

Dr. Burton shook his head. "That's just what I'm afraid of," he said, firmly. "So many people in your circumstances feel that way—it's natural that they should—and, unfortunately, there are charlatans who take advantage of it. I must be cruel if I am to be kind and so I repeat what I just said. Your little boy—just why it happened I do not know—is idiotic. He will never be much, if any, better than he is now. No one knows how to cure such cases. But there are schools and institutions where they can be cared for and taught the little that they are capable of learning by people who have special training and experience in dealing with children like him. I strongly urge you to send him to one of them. You should not give up your entire lives to caring for him and run the risk of ruining your marriage and losing the happiness that can still be yours. Yes," he repeated as the child's mother sobbed a protest, "yes, I mean just that. If this lad had died at birth you would have grieved but you would have recovered. You must look upon this in something of the same spirit."

"Better if he had," murmured the father bitterly.

"That we cannot know," replied the doctor sadly. "I wish I could encourage you to hope but I cannot. All I can do for you is to urge these things. First, do not keep on making the rounds from doctor to doctor as you have been doing. No one at present knows how to help you. But I promise that if any method should be discovered I will let you know at once. The next thing I urge is that you place him at once in a school where he can be cared for by those who know how. My assistant—" he pressed a button on his desk—"has a list of such schools and will help you to choose one. And finally," he smiled as he offered his hand, but his eyes were full of sympathy, "keep up your courage. Fill your lives with other matters. Don't allow yourselves to brood over what has happened. Let it sink into the past. Mrs. Meadows," he turned to introduce a quiet-faced woman who had entered the room in response to his summons, "will talk to you further about this. Goodby."

The cases described here illustrate the fact that few people, if any, are endowed with sufficient intellectual ability to meet any and all situations that life may offer. The two young men in the bus were, it is safe to say, distinctly above average mentality, yet each had found himself unequal to the requirements for the highest professional levels and had been forced to find a place where the intellectual demands were somewhat less strenuous. Although they were intellectually inadequate for the topmost ranks, the great bulk of human activities were still well within their power to achieve. Louise, who completed high school but was not recommended for college, has a more limited choice of careers before her. None of the professions are open to her, but it is quite likely that her tentative plan to become a typist will succeed. Failing that, there are a good many other occupations in the field of business and industry or household help into which she might fit, pending the marriage which is likely to take place later on.

The two younger children, Emily and Dennis, are far more limited in their potentialities. Dennis is not equal to the demands of any sort of independent life outside the shelter of an institution. The chances are that Emily, too, will need such protection as she grows older. However, she is only eight, and there is a bare possibility—though not a probability—that her retardation may be in part superficial rather than fundamental. This possibility was recognized by the psychologist who recommended a second examination after the lapse of a few months.

In any case, Emily is less completely inadequate for meeting the demands of ordinary life than Dennis. She is able to communicate by means of speech, although her vocabulary is small and her articulation poor. She can do a good many things for herself. She can feed herself, dress and undress with some help, wash her own hands and face, handle her toys with only occasional breakage. In spite of her eight years, however, she has not yet reached a stage of mental development at which she is likely to be able to keep up with an ordinary first-grade class, but whereas the public schools could not admit Dennis in any department, Emily is thought suitable for trial in a special class. How well she will get on there cannot immediately be foretold.

Intellectual inadequacy is thus seen to be a matter of *more or less* rather than *all or none*. All of us are inadequate in some way and to some degree. Only a few are so inadequate in mentality that they cannot learn to perform some useful occupation or, to use Tredgold's phrase, "conduct themselves and their own affairs with ordinary prudence." It is with this group that we shall be concerned in this section. Such persons are often called *mentally defective*, or *feeble-minded*. *Amentia* and *oligophrenia* are terms less often used. A more appropriate term has been suggested by Leo Kanner. He prefers to speak of this group as the *intellectually inadequate* since this at once raises the question, inadequate for what? For the extremely inferior deviates with whom we shall deal here, the question can be answered in very simple terms: Inadequate for self-support and self-direction in a world of normal people.

DEGREES OF INTELLECTUAL INADEQUACY

In modern usage the intellectually inadequate are divided into three groups: *idiots, imbeciles,* and *morons*. Idiots comprise those of the lowest intellectual level; roughly speaking, those whose IQ's do not exceed 25. Idiots of high level usually learn to walk and perhaps to say a few words; they can be given some training along the line of personal cleanliness, although accidents will continue to occur from time to time. Few learn to dress without help. Their perception and muscular control are insufficient for safe handling of any but sturdy objects. Those at the lowest levels are commonly known as vegetative idiots. Throughout life, they continue to be as helpless as a neonate.

Imbeciles comprise those whose IQ falls very roughly between 25 and 50. The lower levels can usually be taught the elements of self help; here their abilities end. Those of high grade can frequently be taught to perform simple household tasks. They learn to speak intelligibly, though their vocabulary is limited and their articulation nearly always poor.

Morons are those whose IQ is between 50 and 70. Their abilities range from those closely resembling the high grade imbecile to those whose deficiency is so slight that only continued observation or examination by mental test is likely to reveal it.

There is no sharp separation between these classes. In the final analysis, the assignment of a child to one or the other must depend upon the level of behavior at which he actually functions. Differences of personality, adjustment and training will frequently be highly important in determining this level. This is particularly the case for individuals whose IQ is near a borderline.

CASES AT THE BORDERLINE OF ADEQUACY

Since intellectual inadequacy is a quantitative rather than a qualitative expression, it is inevitable that questions of classification should sometimes arise. There is no sharp line of demarcation between what is sometimes called the "dull normal" group, who are able to get along reasonably well in jobs making little demand upon abstract intelligence, and the more seriously handicapped, who cannot get on at all without close supervision. The poorest of the former and the best of the latter may be intellectually indistinguishable, for circumstantial as well as fundamental differences may weight the balance in one direction or the other. Strong muscles and robust health may compensate to some extent for lack of intellectual acumen. When jobs are few and applicants many a higher level of ability is required in order to secure and hold a position than is the case in times of labor shortage. The distinguished lawyer whose son chances to have an IQ of 70 is likely to be reluctant to see him take a pick and shovel job in which he might succeed, but the day laborer has no objections.

There are few areas in the field of mental measurement about which there is so much confusion of thought as that of the distinction between the normal and the feeble-minded. Because Terman, in one of his earlier writings, suggested that *as a rule* an IQ of 70 may be considered the division point, enthusiastic mental testers were quick to proclaim the doctrine that here *is a rule* that may be applied blindly to all cases. Actually, of course, all that was meant by the original statement is that the chances were more than even that a child whose Stanford Binet IQ falls below 70 will prove to be intellectually inadequate in the sense in which we have used the term. This is a far cry from saying that *all* such cases should be so classified. In the first place, the experimental error of measurement, even on so carefully standardized a test as the Stanford Binet, is large enough to permit a considerable shift in standing on repeated measurement. This makes it impossible to use any arbitrarily fixed standard as a point of division between the normal and the subnormal. We can speak only in terms of probability. As the IQ increases, the probability that the child will be *intellectually* equal to meeting the ordinary demands of life also increases, though he may still fail for other than intellectual reasons. As the IQ lowers, the likelihood that he will be able to meet these requirements lessens. Experience has shown that Terman's estimate of IQ 70 as the approximate point at which the balance of probability shifts from favorable to unfavorable is not far off the mark. Nevertheless, there are an appreciable number of persons who rank distinctly below this level but who fill useful if humble places in the social structure. Others, whose measured intelligence is considerably above IQ 70, make such poor use of the abilities they possess that they can hardly be considered intellectually adequate.

There is, accordingly, a fairly wide range of *test intelligence* within which the distinction between the intellectually adequate and the intellectually inadequate may be difficult to make. In part, the difficulties arise from the experimental error of the test itself. An IQ obtained from a single test may differ by several points from that found when a retest is given, and even the average of two or three tests cannot always be depended upon as an indicator of the true intellectual level of the subject, especially when a source of error, such as extreme shyness or a marked language handicap, remains much the same from one examination to another. Doubtful cases of this kind are usually known as *borderline cases*. Such cases are found within a very wide range of IQ levels,[1] probably not shorter than that represented by IQ 50-90, although by no means are all the cases within this range of questionable mental competence. Most of those who rank near 90 have sufficient mental ability to get along under ordinary circumstances; few of those who test close to 50 are likely to do so. But it must not be forgotten that intelligence differs in quality as well as in degree. Its extensity differs somewhat from person to person among those in whom its intensity or absolute level is much the same. This fact, taken in conjunction with the imperfections inherent in even the best test, should render it obvious that no absolute level in terms of IQ can ever be set as the dividing line between those who are and those who are not intellectually adequate to meet the requirements of everyday life. There are, and presumably always will be, a fair number of borderline or questionable cases, particularly among younger children, for whom the decision must be deferred until events provide a more decisive answer.

The child of borderline intelligence presents one of the most challenging problems in the entire field of the education of retarded children. It now seems clear that some of these children who would otherwise remain charges upon society can be salvaged for a useful life. The earlier point of view that all those with IQ's below 70 were hopelessly "feeble-minded," fit only for permanent placement in an institution is no longer tenable. Even the institutions, in many cases, are changing their emphasis as far as the less seriously retarded among their inmates are concerned. Instead of confining their efforts to making these cases as useful around the institution as possible, attempts are being made to train as many as are able for life outside the institution. At the end of this training they are discharged, usually under some plan of supervision until it is clear that they can get along without further guidance. Some fail, it is true, but many succeed. In a number of states which contain more than one institution for the mentally retarded, subjects of relatively high IQ are separated

[1] Unless otherwise stated, the IQ obtained from the Stanford Binet test administered by a properly trained examiner is always to be understood.

from those of less promise and placed in special schools where vocational training is combined with training in self-government, the handling of money and the management of other personal affairs.

Whether in or out of institutions, the intellectually inadequate constitute a serious burden upon the normal members of the population. If for only a few of those who stand close to the borderline the extensity of their intellectual defect can be so reduced that they become contributors to society to however slight degree, the effort is well worth making.

THE CAUSES OF INTELLECTUAL INADEQUACY

There are many factors which may and sometimes do interfere with normal mental growth. Physical damage to the brain, such as occurs in cerebral birth palsy, may do so. Certain diseases, such as encephalitis, in which the brain is affected may leave lasting results. Deficient activity of the thyroid gland, if untreated, results in the condition known as *cretinism,* in which the body is malformed and the mental state little, if at all, above the idiot level. Other bodily conditions, some of which are operative before birth, others not until infancy or early childhood, may so work upon the nervous organization as to prevent the development of normal mental capacity.

We have seen in previous chapters that the majority of intellectually superior children come from intellectually superior families. By analogy, we might expect that those of inferior mentality would tend to come from families in which the average mental level is below the usual standard. Dozens of investigations have shown this to be the case. "One does not gather grapes from thorns or figs from thistles," say the Scriptures. Retarded children come from all ranks of society but by no means in equal proportions. Moreover, those who exhibit the physical signs of some organic defect or injury make up the great bulk of the inferior deviates in families of superior mental status. Such cases are unlikely to have a hereditary base.

That the majority of mentally defective children from defective stock should be made up of those who, although they are intellectually inadequate for unsupervised life in the outside world, are nevertheless able to learn to perform a good many useful activities is understandable. The very low-grade cases, the idiots and low-grade imbeciles, rarely produce offspring. Many of them are physically incapable of doing so, others are prevented by being kept in institutions or by the watchful care of guardians. But a large percentage of those who approach more closely to the normal standard without quite attaining it are neither placed in institutions nor given the guidance and supervision they need. In and out of wedlock they produce children, many of whom are of the same intellectual caliber as themselves. So it comes about that the very lowest of the intellectually inadequate group are almost if not quite as likely to come from superior as from inferior families,[2] although the majority of those less severely affected are likely to have been born of mentally inferior stock.

A word of caution is needed at this point. We can ascertain the nature of general antecedent factors in intellectual inadequacy by comparing the relative frequency of these conditions among groups of normal and seriously retarded cases. We must be wary, however, of placing interpretations upon these facts that are not directly given by the data. Practically all investigations have shown that among children reared by their own parents, there is usually a fairly close resemblance in the mental levels of parents and offspring. Not all are agreed, however, as to how this relationship has been brought about. Many believe it to be a result of biological inheritance, just as is the color of the eyes or the hair. Some, however, reject this view. They believe that parent-child resemblance in mentality is not a biological but a social phenomenon brought about by the kind of intellectual opportunity and stimulation provided by the different homes. A discussion of this controversy would be out of place here; the interested reader will

---

[2] In most such cases an injury to the brain was sustained, usually during birth, or some physiological defect is responsible wholly or in part for the mental condition. A comparatively small percentage are physically normal.

find a large share of the evidence on both sides in Parts 1 and 2 of the *Thirty-ninth Yearbook of the National Society for the Study of Education* and in an excellent critical review by Woodworth, both of which are cited among the references at the end of Chapter 14.

REFERENCES

BARR, Martin W., *Mental Defectives: Their History, Treatment, and Training* (Philadelphia, P. Blakiston's Son and Company, 1904).

BENDA, Clemens E., FARRELL, Malcolm J., and CHIPMAN, Catherine E., "The Inadequacy of Present-day Concepts of Mental Deficiency and Mental Illness in Child Psychiatry," *American Journal of Psychiatry*, 107 (1951), 721-729.

BICE, Harry V., "A Decade of Psychology," *American Journal of Mental Deficiency*, 53 (1948), 57-66.

CATTELL, Raymond B., "The Meaning of Clinical Psychology," *An Introduction to Clinical Psychology*, ed. L. A. Pennington and Irwin A. Berg (New York, The Ronald Press Company, 1948).

CRUICKSHANK, William M., "Arithmetic Ability of Mentally Retarded Children: Ability to Differentiate Extraneous Materials from Needed Arithmetical Facts," *Journal of Educational Research*, 42 (1948), 161-179.

———, "Arithmetic Ability of Mentally Retarded Children: II. Understanding Arithmetic Processes," *Journal of Educational Research*, 42 (1948), 279-288.

DOLL, Edgar A., "Borderline Diagnosis," *Proceedings of the American Association for the Study of the Feebleminded*, 32 (1927), 45-59.

———, "Idiot, Imbecile, Moron," *Journal of Applied Psychology*, 20 (1936), 427-437.

———, "The Nature of Mental Deficiency," *Psychological Review*, 47 (1940), 395-415.

———, "The Essentials of an Inclusive Concept of Mental Deficiency," *American Journal of Mental Deficiency*, 46 (1941), 214-219.

———, "The Feebleminded Child," in *A Manual of Child Psychology*, ed. Leonard Carmichael (New York, John Wiley and Sons, 1946), ch. 17.

———, "What Is a Moron?" *Journal of Abnormal and Social Psychology*, 43 (1948), 495-501.

ENGLE, T. L., and HAMLETT, Iona C., "Constancy of the I.Q. with Mentally Deficient Patients As Measured by the Time Appreciation Test," *American Journal of Mental Deficiency*, 56 (1952), 775-776.

GESELL, Arnold L., "Differential Diagnosis of Mental Deficiency in Infancy," *Nebraska State Medical Journal,* 32 (1947), 304-307.

GODDARD, Henry H., *Feeblemindedness: Its Causes and Consequences* (New York, The Macmillan Company, 1914).

———, "Feeblemindedness: A Question of Definition," *Proceedings of the Fifty-second Annual Session of the American Association for the Study of Feeblemindedness* (Atlantic City, N. J., 1928).

HACKBUSH, Florentine, and KLOPFER, Bruno, "The Contribution of Projective Techniques to the Understanding and Treatment of Children Psychometrically Diagnosed as Feebleminded: With Sample Case Histories," *American Journal of Mental Deficiency,* 51 (1946), 15-34.

KANNER, Leo, *Child Psychiatry* (Springfield, Ill., Charles C Thomas, 1935); rev. ed. (1948).

KINDER, Elaine F., "Feeblemindedness (Mental Deficiency)," in *Encyclopedia of Psychology,* ed. P. L. Harriman (New York, Philosophical Library, Inc., 1946).

MILLER, J. Charles, "Early Prognosis in Mental Defect," *American Journal of Mental Deficiency,* 51 (1946), 214-218.

New York City Welfare Council, *Report of the Committee on Mentally Defective Children under Five of the Welfare Council of New York City* (New York, Welfare Council, 1950).

PENROSE, Lionel S., *The Biology of Mental Defect* (New York, Grune and Stratton, Inc., 1949).

SCHEERER, Martin, ROTHMANN, Eva, and GOLDSTEIN, Kurt, "A Case of 'Idiot Savant': An Experimental Study of Personality Organization," *Psychological Monographs,* Vol. 58, No. 4 (1945).

SHERMAN, Mandel, "The Mental Defective," in *An Introduction to Clinical Psychology,* ed. L. A. Pennington and Irwin A. Berg (New York, The Ronald Press Company, 1948).

TREDGOLD, A. F., *A Textbook of Mental Deficiency (Amentia),* 7th ed. (Baltimore, William Wood and Company, 1947).

WHITNEY, E. Arthur, "A Pathetic Type—the Borderline Defective," *Journal of Child Psychiatry,* 2 (1951), 171-186.

YANNET, Herman, "The Progress of Medical Research in the Field of Mental Deficiency," *American Journal of Mental Deficiency,* 57 (1953), 447-452.

The Causes of Intellectual Inadequacy

13

TWO MAIN CLASSES OF MENTAL DEFECT

ON VISITING any large institution for the feeble-minded, the inexperienced person is likely to be impressed by the fact that so many of the inmates show no physical signs that anything is wrong with them. "But they *look* all right," he exclaims in surprise. In most cases, however, observation of their behavior and listening to their speech will reveal peculiarities that betray their lack of mental maturity, although when seen in repose they appear normal enough. But normal appearance is not characteristic of all. Physical defects are common, and in many cases these defects assume a pattern rarely seen among the mentally normal. Often this is apparent, even to the casual observer; in some cases only the trained clinician is likely to note the signs. A study of the child's personal history may be necessary to provide the essential clues.

The intellectually subnormal may thus be divided into two main classes: one in which the mental defect is characteristically accompanied by specific physical signs; and another in which no physical abnormality is apparent.[1] As our knowledge increases and more complete examinations are made it is likely that some of the cases originally placed in the second group will be found to belong in the first. In any case, it must not be thought that any

[1] The terms *exogenous* and *endogenous* are used by some authorities to designate the two conditions. However, there has been some confusion in the use of these terms, which, in any case, seem to imply a degree of etiological knowledge far in advance of that which we now possess.

intellectual state, whether superior or inferior, is without its foundation in the neurological structure of the organism, for mind and body are an indivisible whole. The division between the two groups is thus based upon the state of our knowledge. The assumption sometimes made that all or even most of the cases included in the second grouping can be traced to inherited differences in the germ plasm is not well founded. Better to acknowledge our ignorance and to designate the two groups simply as the *organic* cases, in which a physical cause is known or a group of characteristic physical symptoms justifies the belief that such a cause exists although its exact nature is unknown, and those *not known to be organic*. The latter group may be subdivided further into those in which the defective mentality is believed to be the result of an inherited defect in the germ plasm, and those for whom the cause is completely unknown. The first subgroup will include those cases with significantly more than the chance number of near relatives whose mentality is low; the second subgroup, those who are not known to have other similar cases in the family. Caution is necessary here because our knowledge of the laws of human heredity is small and the amount of information with respect to the family history of a given child is usually too scanty to warrant more than a very tentative classification.

ORGANIC CASES OF MENTAL DEFECT

1. The Cretin

The body contains a number of small but highly important ductless glands which discharge their products directly into the bloodstream and thus affect all parts of the organism and its functioning. Taken as a whole, these glands comprise what is known as the *endocrine system.* Although typically of small size, they are of utmost importance for normal growth and behavior. One of these glands, the *thyroid,* situated directly above the larynx, secretes a hormone that is essential for normal physical growth and functioning and for mental development as well. If this hormone is lacking or insufficient for the needs of the organism, a condition known as *cretinism* results. Cretinism may be divided into two classes. The first, *endemic cretinism,* is caused by the lack of certain essential nutritional elements, particularly iodine, in the food and drinking water.[2] Once its cause became known, endemic cretinism was for the most part abolished, since it was found possible to supply the missing elements through the drinking water and other items of the diet. The second, *congenital cretinism,* which can occur in all localities, is due to a defective thyroid gland that cannot make use of what is supplied it. In such cases it is useless to add iodine to the water or food, for the gland cannot convert it into the hormone which the body needs. It is possible, however, to supply the hormone derived from the thyroid gland of animals, and during recent years chemists have learned to make it in the laboratory. As Benda and others have shown, congenital cretinism, at least in its severe forms, can be recognized in the newborn by an experienced physician, and within the first few months of life, the signs become so striking that no unprejudiced observer, however untrained medically, would judge the baby to be normal. The defective gland may be genetically determined or the result of intrauterine factors or, in some cases, caused by birth injury or the early occurrence of certain infectious diseases, particularly measles. In somewhat milder cases, the weak or poorly developed thyroid may function well enough to fulfill the needs of the infant but may prove increasingly inadequate as the child develops. In such cases, the physical and mental signs of cretinism appear only after a longer or shorter period of normal development.

It should be noted, however, that true cretinism, whether congenital or endemic, always involves a defect in the thyroid gland. Even in the iodine-poor regions, the majority of persons do not become cretins. If the needed food elements are not artificially added, the thyroid is likely to enlarge, causing a goiter; or in some cases more effective use of such supply as is present maintains the individual in a healthy condition without enlargement of the thyroid. But minor weaknesses of the gland, which in a more for-

[2] Endemic means "peculiar to a certain locality."

tunate environment would still permit normal functioning, may bring about a state of cretinism if the supply of iodine is poor. Endemic cretinism thus differs from congenital cretinism in that the former is a joint product of thyroid weakness and an iodine-poor environment, whereas the latter is solely due to the glandular weakness.

The untreated cretin may be distinguished from other mentally defective cases by a host of bodily characteristics. His stature is short, his head is noticeably large. His hair is abundant and usually black in color. His nose is flat with depressed bridge and is remarkably flexible. The readiness with which its tip can be moved from side to side is a useful diagnostic sign. His thick skin forms pouches around the eyes which thus look like narrow horizontal slits, giving him a sleepy appearance. His ears are unusually large and, like the nose, are extremely flexible. His neck is short and broad with fatlike subcutaneous growths that often give the impression that a goiter is present; but as Benda points out, these growths are not thyroid tissue. His skin is thick, rough, and scaly. His arms are short, his hands broad, his fingers are clumsy and spatulate in form. His nails are thick and brittle. His legs are also short, frequently bowed, and his feet are broad.

Mentally the untreated cretin does not advance beyond the idiot or low-grade imbecile stage. If his physical needs are cared for he is usually docile and placid, content to sit all day in the sun amusing himself with some simple toy. The lack of the thyroid hormone makes him sluggish in mind and body.

Childhood myxedema, which is a mild form of cretinism marked particularly by dry and scale skin and by physical and mental lethargy, also yields to thyroid administration, as a rule more readily than the more profound condition.

2. The Mongoloid

Far more common than cretinism today is the condition known as *mongolism*. The name was applied because the persons so afflicted bear a certain superficial resemblance to the Mongolian race. Needless to say, this does not imply any biological or ethnic relationship. The resemblance is largely due to the fact that in the mongoloid imbecile the palpebral fissure in which the eyeball lies is unusually narrow and has a downward slope toward the depressed bridge of the broad flat nose, thus giving the eyes the peculiar slantwise appearance characteristic of the Mongolian race. In many cases this appearance is heightened by lax folds of skin that overlie the eyelid (the epicanthic folds) and make the eyes seem still more narrow. Further resemblance is brought about by the round flat face and brachycephalic skull, in which the typical occipital bulge is so greatly reduced that in many cases the line from the crown of the head to the shoulders is practically straight. The head is small in size, with all measurements significantly below the average for normal children.

The hand of the mongoloid child is as characteristic as its face and skull. Typically it is broad and short, with the thumb and little finger much shorter than the others which are often practically equal in length. The little finger is usually incurved and all the joints are readily flexed in any direction. The mongolian is usually very inept in the use of his hands, and it is difficult for him to perform even simple acts of manual skill. Abnormalities of structure such as polydactylism, webbed fingers or the absence of the second phalanx are more common among mongolians than among the general population. Palm prints also differ from what is usually found among the normal. Frequently there is but one major crease instead of the usual two, and a number of other peculiarities of the prints have been noted. Like the hands, the feet are broad and clumsy in appearance, and there is usually a wide separation between the great toe and the second toe.

The mouth is usually small and the lips thick. Mouth breathing is the rule, and the tongue may be habitually protruded. In many cases the tongue is marked by ridges and furrows due to enlargement of the papillae. This is a condition rarely found among other defectives or among the normal population. Dentition is usually delayed, and dental anomalies are common.

In physical build the mongolian is usually somewhat below the average of his age and sex in both height and weight. His arms and legs are short and his trunk is relatively large, giving him a stumpy appearance. His circulation is poor, and his breathing resembles the Cheyne-Stokes pattern, in which a series of short, shallow breaths is followed at intervals by a sudden long, deep inspiration as the need for aeration of the blood is gradually built up. The mongolian is particularly subject to respiratory diseases of all kinds.

Mongolians are generally short-lived. Many die in infancy, and very few reach middle age. Not only is their resistance to infections of all kinds poor, but they age rapidly. A mongoloid man of forty looks and acts like a man of eighty, content to drowse in the sun with no apparent thoughts or desires beyond his physical needs.

Around 5 per cent of the institutionalized population under the age of twenty are mongolians. Because of the high death rate in the early years this figure may underestimate the number born, many of whom die before institutional placement can be arranged. On the other hand, it is probable that no other type of mentally defective individual is so likely to be recognized and so apt to be placed in an institution. In the home, their appearance renders them conspicuous and often repulsive; they can be taught little and require much care. Parents are usually more reluctant to institutionalize a child who "looks bright" than one whose appearance as well as his behavior betrays his weakness of mind.

The majority of mongolians fall in the class of low-grade imbeciles. Some, however, never advance beyond the idiot level; a very few of the less profoundly affected may be classed as morons. The typical mongolian learns to walk and to say a few words, though both the speech and the walking are late in developing and clumsy in performance. Patient training will usually result in fair cleanliness of toilet habits, though occasional accidents are likely. He learns to feed himself, to dress and undress with some help if fastenings are simplified for his awkward fingers. A few mongolians learn to perform simple routine tasks.

In temperament the mongoloid child is usually placid unless disturbed, when he may become irritable. During childhood, mon-

A CRETIN, AGE 23

This girl was given thyroid treatment from an early age but did not respond well.

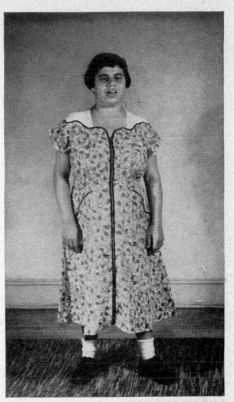

A TYPICAL MONGOLOID, AGE 12

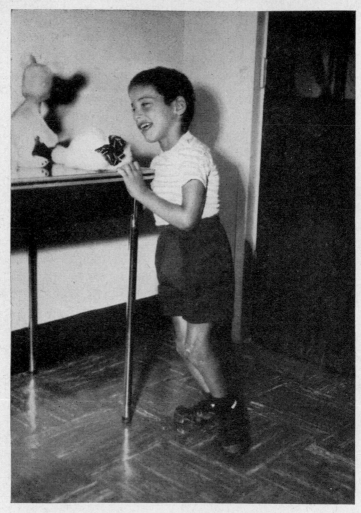

A MENTALLY DEFICIENT CEREBRAL PALSIED CHILD

MICROCEPHALY

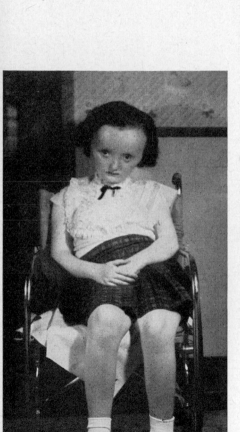

HYDROCEPHALY

A FAMILIAL MENTAL DEFECTIVE

Of eight children in this boy's family, four are mentally deficient, and four are classed as borderline or dull normal.

golians are active and superficially alert, running about restlessly and making clumsy attempts to join in the play of the other children. As age advances they become lethargic.

In no other type of mental defect is there such close general resemblance from one subject to another as is true of mongols. The superintendent of a large institution in which some thirty or more mongoloid patients were enrolled had a photograph taken of the entire group which he called "the mongolian family." Visitors unacquainted with the term who were shown the picture were invariably impressed by the remarkable "family" resemblance. When told that all were inmates of the institution they were horrified to think that so universally degenerate a family could exist! An experienced clinician is able to recognize and identify well over 90 per cent of mongoloid children and adults at first glance, and having done so, prognosis and advice follow as a direct result of the diagnosis. Formal examination is mainly for purposes of research; as a practical measure it is needed only in the relatively small number of borderline or doubtful cases.[3]

Although hundreds of scientific studies have been made, the cause of mongolism remains obscure. It seems fairly certain that some form of endocrine disorder is involved. Benda, who is one of the most active workers in the field at the present time, is of the opinion that mongolism starts as a deceleration of fetal growth (conceivably the result, for example, of a period of fetal anoxia) the direct result of which is congenital *pituitary* deficiency.[4]

There is general agreement as to the importance of certain maternal factors in the production of mongoloid children. For example, the proportion of mongolians born to mothers past the age of forty is considerably in advance of that found in the general

[3] Although few mongolians display all the characteristic physical signs of the condition, not all of which have been enumerated here, the general picture is in most cases unmistakable to the trained eye.

[4] The pituitary is a very small gland situated within a cavity in the brain, the *sella turcica*. It secretes a number hormones and seems to regulate the activity of many of the other glands, so that insufficient pituitary activity results in diminished function of the thyroid, the *gonads,* and others.

population. Brousseau compiled data for 584 institutionalized mongolians. She reports that more than 38 per cent of the mothers of these cases were forty or older at the time of the birth of the mongolian child. Among Terman's group of gifted children, fewer than 5 per cent of the mothers had reached that age. Yet not all mongolian children come from parents in the upper age brackets. Almost 4 per cent of Brousseau's cases were born to girls still in their teens. Thus although the advanced age of the mother may be a contributing factor, it is certainly not a necessary one. Moreover, when we recall that the total incidence of mongolians at birth is only about 3.4 per 1000 (Benda, 1949), it is apparent that the chances of giving birth to a mongoloid child are relatively small. Even for mothers of forty-five or older, the chance of bearing a normal child is about ten times as great as that of bearing a mongol (Benda, 1951).

The mongoloid child is, in many cases, the last that the mother bears. This is due in part to the age factor already mentioned; but even among younger women, the birth of a subsequent child is less frequent than would be expected. It has also been shown that poor maternal health—as evidenced by previous spontaneous abortion or by threatened abortion during the pregnancy which results in a mongoloid, or by the beginning of the menopause, or by other endocrine disturbances—is found much more often in pregnancies resulting in mongoloids than in those resulting in normal children. These facts, taken in conjunction, have led to the hypothesis that mongolism results from some condition or conditions of the mother that prevent normal development in the prenatal period. Such a condition might occur at any age but presumably would be more frequent in older women, though even then it would be exceptional.

Evidence suggesting an inherited defect is slight. Unlike many types of mental defect, mongolians occur with approximately equal frequency at all levels of the socioeconomic distribution. Instances of two or more mongoloid children in the same family occur about as often as would be expected on the basis of chance. A number of cases of mongolism in twins have also been reported.

The fact that in some instances both members of the pair are affected but in others one child is normal and the other is a mongol poses some interesting questions. Some authorities have regarded this as evidence for an inherited defect, upon the assumption that when both are mongols monozygotic twinship is involved, whereas among the dizygotic twins only one is likely to show the condition. This, however, might be equally well explained upon the hypothesis that if both twins are mongols, they are almost certain to be *classed* as monozygotic, whereas if only one is a mongol, the great difference in appearance will most certainly result in the classification of the pair as dizygotic. Benda (1949) has discussed this question at some length. He arrived at the conclusion that at least in the great majority of cases the physical condition of the mother during pregnancy, rather than biological inheritance, is responsible for the child's condition.

3. Cerebral Birth Palsy

As the name implies, cerebral birth palsy is the direct result of an injury to the brain during the birth process. The extent to which prenatal factors of various kinds may predispose to such injuries is a controversial matter, though it is known that premature infants, whose skulls are not yet completely calcified, are particularly liable to it. The results of the damage are manifested in many ways, which will be discussed in some detail in Chapter 26. Here we are concerned only with the effects upon the child's mentality.

Reports from different investigators vary considerably with respect to the proportion whose minds as well as bodies are damaged by the birth trauma.[5] The differences in the findings result

[5] It must be remembered in this connection that it is often difficult to say in any given case whether or not mental damage has occurred. A child whose mentality as observed and measured is well up to the average for his age or even somewhat superior to the average *might* have been much brighter had no injury occurred. The experienced clinical psychologist may note certain signs in the pattern of his test performance that suggest the possibility of some degree of specialized handicap. Goldstein and Scheerer state that marked difficulty in the performance of tests involving some abstract principle coupled with relatively good performance on concrete tests or those involving rote memory only is often suggestive of some form of brain damage. It is questionable, however, whether any of these signs is sufficiently exact to differen-

from the typical smallness of the samples, from selective factors arising from the particular sources of supply,[6] and from differences in the methods of examination and in the interpretation of the findings. Putting the figures from a number of sources together, however, it appears that at least one fourth of all recognized cases are so severely retarded mentally as to be unfit for any type of useful occupation, particularly when the accompanying physical handicaps are considered. An additional 10 per cent are of doubtful or borderline mentality. Considerably fewer than half are of average or superior ability. A few, however, even among those with extreme muscular inco-ordination or flaccid paralysis,[7] are mentally very brilliant and attain positions of eminence. Among these, Professor E. R. Carlson of the University of Chicago is a notable example.

4. *Other Forms of Brain Injury*

Although it is theoretically possible for mechanical injury to the mother during pregnancy to damage the brain of the developing fetus and cause mental deficiency, such cases, if they occur at all, are rare. The unborn child is well protected from such accidents by the enveloping amniotic fluid in which it is suspended and by the surrounding tissues of the mother's body. Miscarriage is the usual result of any accident severe enough to have lasting effect upon the fetus. Pressure from a too small or malformed amniotic sac has also been suggested as a possible cause in cases of defec-

---

tiate reliably between children of potentially superior ability in whom brain trauma has brought about a psychological deficit reducing them to the average level and normal children of average ability. More severe damage resulting in actual mental deficiency usually carries with it more positive signs, such as extreme inequality of performance on tests of different kinds, including marked "scatter" on the Stanford Binet.

[6] Private physicians or clinical psychologists draw their patients from a different social and economic class than do the free clinics. Surveys differ in thoroughness and therefore in the proportion of the less severely handicapped that they discover. Local and circumstantial factors affecting popular interest will cause parents to seek help of whose existence they were previously ignorant.

[7] See Chapter 26 for an account of the effect upon bodily structure and upon the mechanisms of movement and speech.

tive mental development, but the evidence for this is highly questionable. The hypothesis that such prenatal injury is responsible for some cases of mental defect is based in part on theory and to a lesser degree on observation. It is argued that inasmuch as the head is the widest and most resistant part of the body during prenatal life, it is therefore most liable to injury from blows or pressure.[8] On the empirical side, case-history material unquestionably shows a certain number of cases among the mentally defective in which a fall or other injury during gestation is reported by the mother as an explanation for the child's condition. Like the analogous reports of postnatal falls and injuries, most, if not all, of these reports must be taken with the proverbial grain of salt as far as their relation to the later mental status of the child is concerned. It is likely that most of the reported accidents really occurred, but their seriousness is likely to have been exaggerated in the mother's mind when the child's defect made itself evident. Unless the maternal injury was severe enough to leave physical as well as mental effects upon the unborn child, it is unlikely that it can provide an adequate explanation for mental deficiency, particularly when this deficiency appears as a developmental defect and is manifested only in terms of retarded mental growth.

Postnatal head injuries to the child himself are very frequently cited by parents and sometimes by the family physician as causes for the child's subsequent failure to make normal mental progress. "He fell down the steps and got a terrible bump," they report. Few children, however, escape such accidents. Unless the injury was severe enough to produce skull fracture or concussion with at least a brief period of unconsciousness, it is unlikely to have had lasting effect upon the child's mentality. Even in such cases, the effect may be only temporary shock, which may persist for some weeks or even a few months in the form of ocular disturbances, some disorientation with respect to time and place,

[8] Pressure from extremely tight clothing worn by the mother in an attempt to conceal her condition has been cited as a possible cause, but the evidence is shaky. So many exceptions, both positive and negative, are found that the occasional coincidence of the two conditions can best be attributed to chance.

lapses of memory, and the like. Nevertheless, complete recovery may ensue.[9]

That some cases of mental defect arising from injuries to the brain in infancy or early childhood [10] do occur is well known, but the number of such cases is much smaller than most untrained people suppose. Such cases are distinguished from other defectives both on the basis of the medical history of the accident and on the child's mental and physical characteristics as he develops. Unlike the birth-injured child, the one suffering from postnatal brain injury does not, as a rule, show either athetoid inco-ordination of movement or spastic paralysis.[11] His test performance is usually more irregular with greater "scatter" of successes and failures than that of the child without known organic basis for the defect, though this is by no means a dependable or invariable symptom. Typically, he is likely to be especially weak in the ability to organize facts on the basis of logical relationships, in reasoning for himself, or grasping reasons given by others. He thinks in concrete rather than in abstract terms. This is a point particularly emphasized by Goldstein (1939, 1941), and his collaborators.

The effect of incompatible blood groups in the parents upon the mentality of their children is a controversial issue. It is known that when a woman whose blood classification is Rh⁻ carries an

---

[9] In one such case, personally known to me, a child of ten received serious head injuries in a motor accident. Shortly before the accident the child had been given a Stanford Binet test and was found to have an IQ of 140. After recovery from the physical effects of the accident, she continued to show considerable mental disturbance. She was unable to fix her attention on any subject for more than a very short period; there were disturbances of memory and associations. A second mental test given about six weeks after the accident showed very irregular results with a total IQ in the low 70's. Some three months later, in connection with a suit against the driver, the court requested a third test. By this time, the mental as well as the physical symptoms had pretty well cleared up. The IQ on this testing was back at approximately its original level, the actual figure being 138. The case affords a striking example of the necessity for distinguishing between the temporary or "shock" effects of head injuries and the lasting effects of actual destruction of brain tissue.

[10] Exclusive of those resulting from injuries received during the birth process which are far more common. These were discussed in the preceding section.

[11] See Ch. 26.

Rh⁺ child or when a woman of blood group A or B carries a child of the incompatible groups, a condition known as *erythroblastosis fetalis* [12] may sometimes occur. A few authorities believe, at least in some cases, that the mentality of such children is damaged. Further evidence is needed on this subject.

5. Brain Damage Resulting from Disease

The only disease in which prenatal infection of the fetus by a diseased mother is known to be possible is syphilis. The tiny needle-shaped spirochete which gives rise to the diseased condition is so small that it is able to penetrate the placental barrier and so pass directly from mother to child. The usual result of prenatal syphilitic infection is death of the fetus, with subsequent miscarriage; but a small number of infants survive. Early diagnosis and treatment are essential and will save many from the later effects of infection; but some cases are not diagnosed and so escape treatment, and in others, the treatment is ineffectual or the condition may reappear some time after an apparent cure has been effected.

The physical signs of congenital syphilis are manifold. Both sight and hearing may be affected. The signs in the eyes are interstitial keratitis, in which small growths appear on the cornea; inflammation of the eyes, particularly of the choroid coat; and unequal size of the pupils. The teeth are likely to be irregular and notched at the edges (Hutchinson's teeth), the lips and nose are often marked by scars, and there are sometimes bosses on the skull. The general physique is likely to be poor, and anemia is common.

There is some disagreement as to the number of mentally defective whose condition may be traced to congenital syphilis. That it is responsible for many prenatal deaths is well known; that it is also responsible for many, if not most, cases of juvenile paresis (though some of these are due to direct infection in infancy or

[12] This is a condition characterized by extensive destruction of the red blood cells. The resulting anemia and jaundice are likely to cause death unless suitable blood transfusions can be administered.

childhood) is also well known. There is likewise little question that more children of low mentality show the physical signs of congenital syphilis than those of average or superior ability. Some, however, have argued that this means only that such children are usually the offspring of parents who are too unintelligent to guard against infection. Most authorities, however, agree with Benda (1940), who has stressed the extensive cerebral lesions caused by the disease in prenatal life and the consequent improbability that normal postnatal mental development can take place. Congenital syphilis thus seems to be the basis for some cases of mental deficiency; but the modern social-hygiene movement, which provides free treatment for those who are willing to take advantage of it, has undoubtedly reduced the number of affected parents, and the high prenatal and early postnatal death rate among the children of syphilitic mothers [13] brings the total number of syphilitic children who survive to a still smaller figure. Finally, most states require a premarital examination of both sexes for the presence of venereal disease, as well as a serological test of every woman as early in pregnancy as possible. These measures, combined with improved medical treatment, have reduced the importance of congenital syphilis as a cause of mental defect to a fraction of its value a generation ago.

There is no good evidence that infections other than syphilis can pass the placental barrier or that other maternal diseases frequently have any other effect than that of increasing the likelihood of miscarriage. Penrose (1949) accepts the view that some of the febrile diseases, especially *rubella* (German measles), occurring during the early months of pregnancy may be responsible for some cases of mental deficiency in the offspring; but this opinion is not widely accepted.

Of the diseases occurring during the postnatal life of the child himself, *epilepsy* and *encephalitis lethargica,* both of which will be considered at more length in a later section, are outstanding as factors that sometimes lead to mental deficiency, especially when

[13] Sterility is a frequent result of syphilis in both males and females. This reduces the number of children who might be affected.

occurring in the early years. Epileptic seizures, when of the severe or *grand mal* type and of frequent occurrence, generally leave in their wake a feeling of intense mental lethargy with temporary inability to concentrate the attention or to remember what occurs during this period. The effect gradually wears off unless further convulsions recur before the effect of the earlier ones have passed. Under such circumstances the patient gradually becomes confused, and mental deterioration, together with arrest of further mental growth, is likely to ensue. Epilepsy in childhood does not always, or even usually, result in intellectual retardation, but in the more severe cases it may do so.

Encephalitis lethargica (incorrectly known as "sleeping sickness") has a high mortality rate, particularly among children. Of the surviving cases, many show serious mental sequelae involving both abnormal behavior and intellectual retardation, usually of a very uneven character. This will be discussed further in Chapter 27.

Although a few authorities hold that such diseases as measles, scarlet fever, or whooping cough may be responsible for some cases of mental deficiency, as they are known to be for blindness, deafness, and other sensory defects, it is doubtful whether this is the case. That feeble-minded as well as normal children fall victims to these diseases is, of course, true, and it is natural enough for parents, searching for causes for their child's failure to make normal mental progress, to look upon the early illness as the source of his difficulties. Unbiased study of the relative number of subnormal cases among those who have and those who have not had these diseases, however, gives little reason for assuming a casual relationship.

6. Structural Brain Defects

In the *microcephalic* child the head does not attain normal size and the brain within it is correspondingly small and undeveloped. Some microcephalic skulls are almost unbelievably tiny, attaining at maturity a size no larger than that of the head of a normal newborn. The mentality of such cases varies with the degree of the structural defect along with other factors, such as inheritance. Not only size but shape of the head must be taken into account. No dependable standards for classifying the microcephalic child are available, but Tredgold, who also emphasizes the importance of head shape, considers that if the head measures less than 17 inches in its greatest circumference at maturity, the individual may be considered microcephalic and will, in most cases, be mentally defective. (Of course, this statement does not apply to the true midget.) Without citing the source, Penrose refers to a "clinical tradition" that if the skull in childhood measures less than 13 inches in circumference, idiocy is inevitable. Age is not specified, but inasmuch as the head has attained approximately 90 per cent of its adult size by the age of six years, age differences among school children are less important than they might at first seem, though some allowance should be made for this factor when young children are to be considered.

The typical microcephalic has a low, receding forehead with the cranial portion of the skull much reduced in size, although the face, particularly the lower part of it, retains comparatively normal proportions. This disproportion between the facial and the cranial parts of the head gives the subject a peculiar birdlike appearance, which caused Lombroso to give them the designation of "birdmen." The resemblance is often heightened by their habits of quick, restless movement and their generally small stature.

Neither the cause nor the cure of microcephaly is known. There is evidence that, in some cases at least, it may be a familial characteristic. Cases of two or more occurrences in the same family have been reported by several investigators, in one case (Hanhari, 1943, cited by Penrose, 1949) as many as ten interrelated subjects having been identified. The institution at Faribauld, Minn., contains a pair of identical twins of low-grade imbecile status who are rather remarkable examples of this type.

In appearance, the *hydrocephalic* subject is the opposite of the microcephalic, since the head is abnormally large rather than abnormally small. Hydrocephalus, as the name implies, is the direct result of an accumulation of fluid within the cranium, either in the cerebral ventricles (internal hydrocephalus) or surrounding the brain on the outside (external hydrocephalus) or both. Pressure from the fluid causes the skull to enlarge, often very greatly, and to become progressively thinner and more membranous. At the same time, the brain is reduced in size and develops many abnormalities of structure.

Porencephaly and *anencephaly* are abnormal conditions due to the failure of certain parts of the brain to develop. Their diagnosis usually depends upon post-mortem examination. In porencephaly, the part of the brain around the lower extremity of the Sylvian fissure does not develop, and a deep, funnel-shaped cavity is formed that communicates with the lateral ventricle, thus giving rise to the name which literally means a "hole in the brain." A few cases of anencephaly have been reported. As the name implies, these cases lack the entire cerebral hemispheres. Such cases are, of course, profound idiots and rarely survive the period of infancy.

Various other anomalies of the brain structure have been noted. They range from trifling malformations that are not incompatible with normal mental development to rare cases in which large masses of brain tissue are lacking or are represented only by small groups of rudimentary nerve cells.

Although gross abnormalities of brain structure, many of which are reflected in the size and shape of the head, are usually incompatible with normal mental development, it should be noted that the range of variation in skull contour and cranial capacity among normal individuals is very great. The weight of the brain shows only a low correlation with intelligence or achievement. Although the scientist who would avoid metaphysical explanations must take the position that all intellectual differences have a structural basis, the exact nature of the physical differences is in most cases unknown. For the most part, such differences are presumed to consist in variations in the finer details of nerve structure and organization of which as yet we know but little. Post-mortem study of the brains of institutionalized feeble-minded subjects has shown that on the average the cerebral hemispheres are somewhat subnormal in weight and the nerve cells tend to be of a more primitive type than those of normal individuals of corresponding age and sex. Individual differences, however, are marked, and, as a rule, such differences in brain structure as have been found are not characterized by observable alterations in the size or contour of the skull. Head measurements have not proved to be of much service in the identification or classification of the mentally subnormal, since it is only in very extreme cases that a significant relationship between intelligence and head form or size has been found to exist.

7. Inherited Constitutional Defects

In a few rare instances, mental deficiency is clearly part of an inherited syndrome. Among these is the condition known as *amaurotic family idiocy*, of which an excellent description has been given by Kanner. Since these children rarely survive beyond the age of three years, they are not often seen outside medical clinics.

Bodily malformations of practically all kinds, and particularly those known to be inherited (such as polydactylism), are much more common among the mentally defective than among the normal population. Such defects cannot be looked upon as causes of the mental retardation since they occur among the normal as well as among the subnormal, but their greater frequency among the latter suggests a common antecedent. Although there are plenty of mentally defective individuals whose bodies are well grown and vigorous, the general impression given by a visit to an institution for the mentally subnormal is that of physical as well as mental inferiority, of weakness rather than of strength, of stunted bodies, many of which show physical deformities. In spite of many exceptions to the rule, the positive though low correlation generally found between physique and intellect [14] shows up clearly at both the lower and the upper extremes of the intellectual distribution. In many cases, mental subnormality

[14] See Paterson, *Physique and Intellect*.

seems to be but one manifestation of a generally poor constitutional stock.

MENTAL DEFECT WITHOUT KNOWN ORGANIC BASIS

1. Familial Cases

A very large proportion, usually well over half, of institutionalized mentally defective cases whose deficiency is not due to any known organic cause have one or more relatives who are also mentally subnormal. As a rule, the homes from which these patients come are inferior with respect to both material advantages and intellectual and educational stimulation. Whether, as many believe, the generally poor home background from which so large a proportion of the mentally defective come is a major determinant of the mental backwardness of the children reared under these conditions or whether the poor homes merely reflect the poor mentality of the parents who established and have maintained them and who passed on their mental as well as their physical characteristics to their children is a question that we shall not attempt to answer here. The interested reader is referred to the *Yearbook of the National Society for the Study of Education* for 1928 and 1940 and to the critical review by Woodworth cited at the end of Chapter 14. Familial mental deficiency is an observed fact, whatever may be its basis. Furthermore, it is a fact with important social consequences.

2. Sporadic Cases, of Uncertain Origin

The majority of people know little of their family history beyond two or three generations. Even the few who can trace their ancestry back far beyond this usually know only the main line of descent. No sane biologist, finding an instance of some characteristic not previously observed in a breed of which so little is known, would be willing to assume that the trait had not appeared in former generations and was not inherited according to the usual laws. For this reason, it is hazardous to state that no cases of mental deficiency have occurred in the family of a given child. As is well known, a recessive trait may skip many generations between appearances. The possibility that a sporadic case of mental defect, occurring in a family which has no record of similar instances, is due to such a trait can rarely, if ever, be ruled out.

REFERENCES

ALDRICH, Cecelia G., and DOLL, Edgar A., "Comparative Intelligence of Idiots and Normal Infants," *Journal of Genetic Psychology*, 39 (1931), 227-237.

ALLAN, W., HERNDON, C. N., and DUDLEY, F. C., "Some Examples of the Inheritance of Mental Deficiency; Apparently Sex-linked Idiocy and Microcephaly," *American Journal of Mental Deficiency*, 48 (1944), 325-334.

ARAI, Seizaburo, "On the Retardation of Mental Development in Physically Backward Babies: First Report, on the Mentality of Nutritionally Disturbed Babies," *Tohoku Psychologica Folia*, 13 (1953), 75-84.

ARTHUR, Grace, "Some Factors Contributing to Errors in the Diagnosis of 'Feeblemindedness,'" *American Journal of Mental Deficiency*, 54 (1950), 495-501.

BARR, Martin W., *Mental Defectives: Their History, Treatment, and Training* (Philadelphia, P. Blakiston's Son and Company, 1904).

BEIDLEMAN, Barkley, "Mongolism," *American Journal of Mental Deficiency*, 50 (1945), 35-53.

BENDA, Clemens E., "The Central Nervous System in Mongolism," *American Journal of Mental Deficiency*, 45 (1940), 42-47.

———, *Mongolism and Cretinism*, 2d ed. (New York, Grune and Stratton, Inc., 1949).

———, "Empiric Risk Figures in Mongolism," *American Journal of Mental Deficiency*, 55 (1951), 539-545.

———, "What is Mongolism (Congenital Acromicria)? Pathogenesis and Experimental Treatment," *International Record of Medicine*, 165 (1952), 75-91.

BIXBY, E. M., "Further Biochemical Studies in Mongolism," *American Journal of Mental Deficiency*, 45 (1940), 201-206.

BJELKHAGEN, Ingemar, "A Case of Infantile Amaurotic Family Idiocy," *Acta Paediatrica, Stockholm*, 39 (1950), 445-451.

BOEHM, Alice E., and SARASON, Seymour B., "Does Wechsler's Formula Distinguish Intellectual Deterioration from Mental Deficiency?" *Journal of Abnormal and Social Psychology*, 42 (1947), 366-368.

BOLDT, Waldemar H., "Postnatal Cerebral Trauma as an Etiological Factor in Mental Deficiency," *American Journal of Mental Deficiency*, 55 (1951), 345-365.

BOOK, J. A., GRUBB, Rune, ENGLESON, G., and LARSON, C. A., "Rh Incompatibility and Mental Deficiency," *American Journal of Human Genetics*, 1 (1949), 66-78.

——, SCHUT, John W., and REED, S. C., "A Clinical and Genetical Study of Microcephaly," *American Journal of Mental Deficiency*, 57 (1953), 637-660.

BRADWAY, Katherine P., "Paternal Occupational Intelligence and Mental Deficiency," *Journal of Applied Psychology*, 19 (1936), 527-542.

BROUSSEAU, Kate, *Mongolism: A Study of the Physical and Mental Characteristics of Mongolian Imbeciles*, rev. H. G. Brainerd (Baltimore, The Williams and Wilkins Company, 1928).

BUCKLEW, John and HAFNER, A. J., "Organismic Versus Cerebral Location of Biological Defects in Feeble-mindedness," *Journal of Psychology*, 32 (1951), 69-78.

CAIN, Louise, "Exploration of Metabolic Patterns in Mentally Deficient Children," *University of Texas Publications*, No. 5109 (1951), pp. 198-205.

CENTERS, Richard, "Four Studies in Psychology and Social Status," *Psychological Bulletin*, 47 (1950), 263-271.

CHIPMAN, C. R., "The Constancy of the Intelligence Quotient in Mental Defectives," *Psychological Clinic*, 18 (1930), 103-111.

CUMMINS, Harold, and PLATOU, R. V., "Mongolism; An Objective Early Sign," *Southern Medical Journal of Birmingham*, 39 (1946), 926-928.

DAVENPORT, Charles B., "Causes of Retarded and Incomplete Development," *American Journal of Mental Deficiency*, 41 (1936), 208-214.

DOLL, Edgar A., "The Vineland Social Maturity Scale: Revised Edition," *Training School Bulletin*, 32 (1935), 1-7.

——, "Etiology of Mental Deficiency," *Training School Bulletin*, 41 (1944), 1-8.

——, "Practical Implications of the Endogenous-Exogenous Classification of Mental Defectives," *American Journal of Mental Deficiency*, 50 (1946), 503-511.

——, PHELPS, Winthrop M., and MELCHER, Ruth Taylor, *Mental Deficiency Due to Birth Injuries* (New York, The Macmillan Company, 1932).

DOLPHIN, Jane E., "Pathology of Concept Formation in Children with Cerebral Palsy," *American Journal of Mental Deficiency*, 56 (1951), 385-398.

ENGLER, Markus, *Mongolism* (*Peristatic Amentia*) (Baltimore, The Williams and Wilkins Company, 1949).

——, "A Comparative Study of the Causation of Mongolism, Peristatic Amentia, and Other Types of Mental Defect," *Journal of Mental Science,* 98 (1952), 316-325.

FALK, R., PENROSE, Lionel S., and CLARK, E. A., "The Search for Intellectual Deterioration among Epileptic Patients," *American Journal of Mental Deficiency,* 49 (1945), 469-471.

FISHER, R. A., "Correlation Between Relatives on the Supposition of Mendelian Inheritance," *Transactions of the Royal Society of Edinburgh,* Vol. 52 (1918).

GARTH, Thomas R., *Race Psychology* (New York, McGraw-Hill Book Company, 1931).

GAUGER, Adeline B., "Mental Deficiency in Cases of Organic Brain Damage," *Medical Woman's Journal,* 55 (1948), 37-40.

GLANVILLE, A. Douglas, "Deficiencies in Amplitude of Joint Movement Associated with Mental Deficiency," *Child Development,* 8 (1937), 129-138.

GODDARD, Henry H., *The Kallikak Family: A Study in the Heredity of Feeblemindedness* (New York, The Macmillan Company, 1912).

——, *Feeblemindedness: Its Causes and Consequences* (New York, The Macmillan Company, 1914).

GRONEMEYER, W. H., "Cretinism and Mongolism in the Same Family," *Journal of Pediatrics,* 36 (1950), 636-657.

HACH, Paul H., "Some Psychological Aspects of Organic Brain Damage," *Proceedings of the American Psychopathological Association,* 36 (1947), 149-162.

HARDY, William G., "The Relation Between Impaired Hearing and Pseudo-feeblemindedness," *The Nervous Child,* 7, No. 4 (October, 1948), 432-445.

HOLLINGWORTH, Leta S., *The Psychology of Subnormal Children* (New York, The Macmillan Company, 1920).

——, "Differential Action upon the Sexes of Forces That Tend to Segregate the Feebleminded," *Journal of Abnormal and Social Psychology,* 17 (1922), 35-37.

INGALLS, Theodore H., "Mongolism," *Scientific American,* 186, No. 2 (1952), 60-66.

ITARD, Jean-Marc-Gaspard, *The Wild Boy of Aveyron,* trans. George and Muriel Humphrey (New York, The Century Company, 1932).

JERVIS, George A., "Recent Progress in the Study of Mental Deficiency: Mongolism," *American Journal of Mental Deficiency,* 46 (1942), 467-481.

JOSEPHY, Herman, "Phenylpyruvic Oligophrenia," *Illinois Medical Journal*, 94 (1948), 107-111.

KANNER, Leo, "Feeblemindedness: Absolute, Relative and Apparent," *The Nervous Child*, 7 (1949), 366-397.

KENNEDY, Foster, "The Problem of Social Control of the Congenital Defective: Education, Sterilization, Euthanasia," *American Journal of Psychiatry*, 90 (1942), 13-16.

KREEZER, George, "The Relation of the Electroencephalogram to Intelligence Level in the Mongolian Type of Mental Deficiency: Series 2," *Psychological Bulletin*, 36 (1939), 511-512.

KUGELMASS, I. Newton, "Mental Deficiency of Hypopituitarism in Childhood," *New York State Journal of Medicine*, 52 (1952), 1655-1659.

LAWRENCE, Evelyn M., "An Investigation into the Relation Between Intelligence and Inheritance," *British Journal of Psychology: Monograph Supplement No. 16*, 5 (1932), 1-80.

LEVINSON, Abraham, "Pneumoencephalography in Mentally Deficient Children," *American Journal of Mental Deficiency*, 52 (1947), 1-8.

LEVY, Sol, and PERRY, H. A., "Pertussis as a Cause of Mental Deficiency," *American Journal of Mental Deficiency*, 52 (1948), 217-226.

MALLER, J. B., "Vital Indices and Their Relation to Psychological and Social Factors," *Human Biology*, 5 (1933), 94-121.

MAUTNER, Hans, "Congenital Heart Disease in the Feebleminded," *American Journal of Mental Deficiency*, 55 (1951), 546-556.

PANTIN, A. M., "Bloodgroups of Mental Defectives and Their Maternal Parents," *Nature*, 167 (London, 1951), 76-79.

PATERSON, Donald G., *Physique and Intellect* (New York, The Century Company, 1930).

PENROSE, Lionel S., "The Complex Determinants of Amentia," *Eugenics Record*, 26 (1934), 121-126.

——, *The Biology of Mental Defect* (New York, Grune and Stratton, Inc., 1949).

——, "Birth Injury as a Cause of Mental Defect: The Statistical Problem," *Journal of Mental Science*, 95 (1949), 373-379.

——, "The Incidence of Mongolism in the General Population," *Journal of Mental Science*, 95 (1949), 686-688.

PROBST, H., "Über psychische Folgen des Schädelbruches in Kindesalter: Auszug aus einer Dissertation von der Universität Zurich, 1949" (Psychical Sequelae of Skull Fracture During Childhood: From a Dissertation, University of Zurich, 1949), *Zeitschrift für Kinderpsychiatrie*, 15 (1949), 186-192.

ROBERTS, J. A. Fraser, "High Grade Mental Deficiency in Relation to Differential Fertility," *Journal of Mental Science,* 93 (1947), 289-302.

SCHEINFELD, Amram, *The New "You and Heredity"* (Philadelphia, J. B. Lippincott Company, 1950).

SCHOLL, Mary Louise, WHEELER, Warren E., and SNYDER, Laurence H., "Rh Antibodies in Mothers of Feebleminded Children," *Journal of Heredity,* 38 (1947), 253-256.

SNEDEKER, Doris M., "A Study of the Palmar Dermatoglyphics of Mongoloid Imbeciles," *Human Biology,* 20 (1948), 146-166.

TOWN, Clara Harrison, *Familial Feeblemindedness: A Study of One Hundred Forty-one Families* (Buffalo, Foster and Stewart Publishing Corporation, 1939).

TYLER, Leona E., *The Psychology of Human Differences,* 2d ed. (New York, Appleton-Century-Crofts, Inc., 1956).

WHEELER, L. R., "A Comparative Study of the Physical Growth of Dull Children," *Journal of Educational Research,* 20 (1929), 273-282.

WUNSCH, William L., "The First Complete Tabulation of the Rhode Island Mental Deficiency Register," *American Journal of Mental Deficiency,* 55 (1951), 293-312.

YANNET, Herman, "Mental Deficiency Due to Prenatally Determined Factors," *Pediatrics,* 5 (1950), 328-336.

YANNET, Herman, and LIEBERMAN, Rose, "Mother-child Incompatibility: A Relation of Secretor Status to Mental Deficiency," *American Journal of Diseases of Childhood,* 76 (1948), 176-183.

Attempts to Remedy
Mental Retardation

14

THE FIRST SCHOOLS

UP TO ABOUT the middle of the nineteenth century the belief was generally held that attempts to educate the feeble-minded, to teach them useful skills, or even to train them in habits of decency and cleanliness were for the most part wasted. It is true that only the lower grades of mental defect were recognized at this time. To these persons the term *idiot* was indiscriminately applied, and that idiots were uneducable was a well-nigh axiomatic belief. Even such men as Pinel, the friend of the insane, held little hope for those who were congenitally defective in mind. It was he who first examined the famous "wild boy of Aveyron" and advised Itard against undertaking his education and training on the grounds that it would be useless since the boy was an idiot. Had Itard accepted Pinel's diagnosis at this time, it is unlikely that he would have attempted to educate the child and an experiment of much importance to science would thus have been still-born. It was only when five years of patient effort had resulted in meager success that Itard, bitterly disappointed, was forced to admit that Pinel had been right and brought his experiment to a close.

Although Itard never succeeded in bringing his pupil to even a semblance of normality, however, he did succeed in training him in a number of the habits and customs of civilized life. The boy learned to wear clothes (he had been naked when first captured) and to dress and undress with a little help. He learned to use table implements instead of his fingers and teeth, to drink from a cup instead of putting his mouth down to the liquid as an animal does. And although he never learned to speak, he did learn to associate a number of printed words with their appropriate objects. All this was a great advance over his original condition and demonstrated beyond question that even so low grade a creature as this child can still acquire at least a few useful habits that will make him better fitted for life in a civilized world. Although Itard himself looked upon his experiment as a failure, it was not so regarded by others who had followed his work with interest and enthusiasm. The French Academy of Science warmly commended Itard for his work, pointing out that the results should be evaluated only in terms of the changes in the boy himself, not in terms of the standards expected of normal children.

During the first half of the nineteenth century a number of schools for feeble-minded children were established in various parts of Europe. Of these, by far the most important was that founded by Eduard Seguin, who had studied both with Itard and with Esquirol, the author of the first important book on mental defect. Although Esquirol had openly stated his belief that mental defect is incurable, Seguin seems never to have accepted this point of view. The school for feeble-minded children that he established in Paris was based upon the concept that mental defect is amenable to education, not, it is true, the same kind of education that is given to normal children in the regular schools but a special kind of education adapted to their needs. In proof of his theory he opened his school to visitors. Educational leaders from all parts of the world came to observe his methods. They were amazed to see, instead of the drooling, babbling, animal-like creatures they had anticipated, a group of clean, neatly dressed, well-behaved children, each quietly engaged in some engrossing occupation of his own. Some were fitting blocks into their proper recesses in boards; others were having lessons in speech; a few were learning to sew or knit. The surprised and delighted educators returned to report to their colleagues at home: "Incredible as it seems, in Paris idiots are being educated." [1] Little heed was paid at first to the very simple nature of the habits and skills that were learned. If so good a beginning could be made, why set bounds to the possibilities?

In 1848 Seguin came to America, where his influence upon the education and training of the mentally deficient was profound. He encouraged the establishment of schools in which his system of training was followed. His book, *Idiocy and Its Treatment by the Physiological Method*, was for years the standard reference. But the hopeful note there sounded was destined not to be fulfilled.

Inspired by the apparent success of Seguin's methods, the first schools were established. In the words of Dr. S. G. Howe of Massachussetts, their purpose was to transform "brutish men back into human shape" or, at least, to bring subnormal children closer to the normal standard of intelligence. But it was soon found that although under the influence of skillful and patient training these children could be taught many useful habits and simple skills, each nevertheless had his intellectual limits beyond which he could not go. Once more, it was shown that education can develop potential capacities in such a way as to render the individual more efficient but can add nothing to his original endowment. Long before the turn of the century, schools for the mentally deficient had ceased to hope to turn their inmates into normal individuals. Instead, they were trying to instill good personal habits and to train them in such simple arts and skills as would not only add to their usefulness about the institution but would, at the same time, increase their feeling of personal worth and responsibility.

THE NATURE-NURTURE CONTROVERSY

The belief that intellectual endowment, at least in a broad sense, is determined by the constitution of the organism and can-

---

[1] The term *idiot* at that time was applied to all recognizably feeble-minded persons.

not be materially changed by any system of education or training now known was rarely challenged during the first two decades of the present century. The work of Goddard at Vineland, which showed the marked tendency of feeble-mindedness to run in families, demonstrated beyond question that some constant factor was at work. Goddard and most of his contemporaries believed this factor to be heredity, a matter of poor family stock. The rise of intelligence testing during this period provided a more objective basis for the classification of individuals as to their intellectual level, even though imperfections in the scales first used caused many persons to be misjudged. Nevertheless, the fact that a constant standard was being used for all made it possible to examine the instrument and correct its errors. This could not be done so long as individual judgments were depended on. Such judgments have no constant referent but vary from judge to judge. When, in 1916, the Stanford Binet test was published and the IQ made its bow to the world, it was soon discovered that this measure tended to remain much the same for a given individual upon retest, even after a period of several years and in spite of quite radical changes in external circumstances. This "constancy of the IQ" was particularly noticeable in the case of low-testing individuals, though the mathematical reason for this observed fact was not pointed out until a number of years later.[2] All this tended to confirm the belief that although mentally defective subjects may acquire habits, skills, and knowledge up to the limits set by their original endowment, their fundamental capacity is not increased by education and training.

Not everyone, however, agreed with this point of view. No one has ever claimed that the IQ is absolutely constant. Terman himself was the first to point out that small fluctuations in its value are common and that large changes sometimes occur. Thus whether one accepts or rejects the statement that the IQ tends to remain constant depends upon the relative emphasis that is

[2] See the discussion of this point in Lewis M. Terman and Maud Merrill, *Measuring Intelligence: A Guide to the Administration of the New Revised Stanford Binet Tests of Intelligence* (Boston, Houghton Mifflin Company, 1937), pp. 44-47.

placed upon the large group for whom changes are small or upon the smaller group for whom such changes are of greater amount. Thus by the early 1920's, clinical psychologists and psychometricians found themselves divided into two camps: the "hereditarians" and the "environmentalists." The former looked upon intelligence as a characteristic of the family stock which might be used well or poorly, developed or allowed to lie dormant, but which could not be improved beyond the limits set by the original endowment. The mentally deficient might thus be taught many things, but if truly defective, they could not be made normal by any educational procedure. The "environmentalists" claimed that intelligence, at least among those who are physically normal and who show no signs of brain damage, is not inherent but is the product of experience and training. The first believed that intelligence makes education possible; the second that education gives rise to intelligence.

As far as the correction of mental defect is concerned, few of the studies based on environmental stimulation or educational training have reported much success. Skeels and Skodak, however, have made a series of studies on the later development of children placed in adoptive homes during infancy. They report that the mental growth of these children appeared to be entirely dependent upon the character of the adoptive home and was in no way related to the social, educational, or intellectual status of the true parents. Even the children of feeble-minded mothers, if placed in good homes in early infancy, were later found to be as bright as those whose parents belonged to the learned professions. In another study, Skeels and Dye found that when children originally classified as feeble-minded were placed in an institution under the care and tutelage of moron girls, their intelligence improved at so rapid a rate that many became normal within the short space of a few months. The mean gain in IQ for the entire group was considerably greater than that which the child-welfare experts of the University of Iowa were able to bring about through special nursery school education in an orphanage in Davenport, taking three years time for the task.

The investigation by Bernadine Schmidt would require little comment, were it not for the attention given to it in popular magazines and newspapers. Dr. Schmidt's claim of having brought practically all members of a large group of mentally deficient children, many of whom were of imbecile grade, to a normal level of intelligence, as indicated both by test scores and by the practical criteria of self-support and self-direction, has been severely criticized by a number of psychologists, notably Kirk and Goodenough, both of whom found such serious discrepancies in her reported figures as to discredit the entire study.[3]

Putting all the facts together, it thus seems highly questionable whether the mental status of defective children, who have reached an age at which their deficiency can be detected by means of standard intelligence tests or through observation by competent judges, can be materially improved by any method of education and training now known.[4] But it must not be forgotten that the rate of mental growth is extremely rapid during infancy and early childhood. It is wholly possible that after this period of rapid growth is over, attempts to improve the intelligence of the defective may be largely fruitless because they are begun too late. The time for mental growth may be too nearly over, the mental pattern fixed for good or ill. Had the training and mental stimulation been begun in infancy, the results might have been different. There are many who believe that the good intellectual caliber of children who have been adopted in infancy into homes of superior culture points to such a conclusion. However, most child-placing agencies hesitate to place children of questionable mental heritage

---

[3] Kirk undertook to check the findings at first hand by means of a visit to the Chicago schools in which the study had been carried on. In spite of Schmidt's refusal to co-operate with him he was able to check a number of her statements and to ascertain that many of her figures could not be correct. For the most part, however, Schmidt's data have never been reported in such form as to permit checking for accuracy. Such figures as she presents include many errors in simple arithmetic.

[4] Except for the organic cases, who can usually be recognized at a very early age by means of physical signs, and the idiots and low-grade imbeciles, whose defectiveness is also apparent at a comparatively early age, the great bulk of mentally deficient children cannot be diagnosed as such with any reasonable degree of certainty before the age of five or six years.

in adoptive homes before they have reached an age at which their mental status can be ascertained. Such agencies for the most part adhere to the rule of "fitting the child to the home," that is, of placing the most promising children in homes where opportunity is likely to be greatest and assigning those of average or somewhat inferior family stock to homes where less in the way of intellectual accomplishment will be expected from them. This practice obviously makes for correlation between the cultural status of the foster home and the intelligence of the child, quite apart from any direct effect of intellectual stimulation or home training.

Whether or not a physically normal child whose intellectual heritage appears poor can be made mentally normal by training and environmental stimulation begun in infancy is thus an unanswered question. When such training is delayed until the child has reached an age at which he can be definitely classified as mentally deficient, no method of education currently known is likely to make him into a normal child. It is possible, of course, that sufficiently early training would prevent the development of such a defect. Moreover, even though the intellectual status of the child is not increased, much can be accomplished in the way of establishing desirable habits and attitudes and of imparting skills and knowledge that fall within the framework of such ability as he may possess. Of this we shall have more to say in a later chapter.

MEDICAL AND SURGICAL ATTEMPTS TO REMEDY OR AMELIORATE MENTAL DEFICIENCY

Few types of mental defect are more conspicuous than the congenitally microcephalic cases with their tiny heads and dwarfed bodies. It was only natural that the early students of these cases should arrive at the hypothesis that the mental retardation was the result of the small size of the skull which did not allow sufficient space for the brain to grow properly. It was thought, therefore, that suturing the skull at several points in such a way as to permit the bones to spread apart and thus provide for more space within which the brain could develop might bring about some improvement in the mental condition. Many operations of this kind were performed, but the results were uniformly unsuccessful. It is now known that the small size of the skull is but one manifestation of a constitutional defectiveness which likewise involves a small and imperfectly developed brain and a correspondingly deficient mentality. Under these circumstances, an operation on the skull could have no effect upon the mentality.

Hydrocephalus (water on the brain), with the accompanying great bulging skull, is another condition which, it was once hoped, might be helped by surgical treatment. The surgical procedure was to tap the skull at one or more points and withdraw the fluid, hoping thereby to relieve the pressure upon the growing brain. This practice, too, proved generally ineffective, since it could not correct the brain damage that was the original cause of the trouble.

The most striking results of medical treatment in any class of mental defectives have been obtained from the administration of thyroid hormone to cretins, provided that this treatment is begun when the child is still young, with a major share of his mental growth still to be accomplished, and that the treatment is continued without intermission under competent medical supervision. Cretinism has been known since very early times, but the basic physiological and chemical knowledge of the condition dates from the second half of the nineteenth century. The discovery that cretinism is the inevitable result of lack of the hormone secreted by the thyroid gland at once suggested that if this lack could be supplied the trouble might be corrected. At first, the ground-up thyroid glands of animals were used,[5] and the effects were striking indeed as far as the physical symptoms were concerned. The dry, harsh skin became soft and moist; the hair took on luster, the pot-bellied, dwarfish body gradually assumed

---

[5] Later, it was found possible to produce a synthetic form of the hormone, which is now generally used since its strength can be more accurately determined and it is more readily made available for medical use.

normal proportions, the limbs became longer and straight. Tests of metabolic rate and of other physiological processes approached the normal level. Mentally, the child seemed more alert, showing greater responsiveness to people and to events. All this led to great hope for the transformation of the misshapen cretin idiot to an individual normal in mind and body.

These hopes, however, have been only partially fulfilled. As Benda has pointed out, thyroid is an essential element in mental growth, and its administration at an age when mental maturity is normally well advanced cannot make up for the growth period that has been lost. Moreover, its use does not cure cretinism in the sense that the treatment may be discontinued after a time. If the thyroid gland is deficient, its function must continuously be supplied artificially. Discontinuance of the treatment means that all improvement previously gained will be lost and the subject will again become a repulsive idiot.

The importance of early diagnosis and continuous treatment in cases of cretinism can hardly be overemphasized. Growth is time limited, and that which can be accomplished during its early stages becomes difficult or impossible as the process draws near its close. Although older children and adults can usually derive some benefit from the use of thyroid, complete physical and mental normality are scarcely to be hoped for in the cretin who remains untreated until the age of early childhood has passed. Nevertheless, even a small improvement is worth while in so serious and so repulsive a condition as that of the cretin to whom thyroid treatment has been denied. If early diagnosis is followed by systematic treatment under competent medical supervision, the thyroid deficiency can be fully compensated in almost all cases. Since the hormone dosage must be as large as can be tolerated and must be constantly increased to keep pace with the growth of the child, even a short period of neglect may result in serious damage. The body can tolerate a period of food starvation more easily and with less risk of permanent damage than a period of endocrine starvation.

The marked effect upon cretinism and childhood myxedema

resulting from thyroid treatment brought hope that glandular therapy might prove equally efficacious in other forms of mental and physical retardation. Endocrinology became the fad of the day. Interest in the subject was heightened by the discovery in 1922 by Collins of a practicable method of extracting and purifying insulin from animal pancreas material for use in diabetes mellitus. The hormone itself and something of its effect upon the utilization of sugar by the body had been known since 1880, but the early studies did not succeed in showing how the hormone could be prepared for clinical use. Now, once more, a condition that had formerly been for the most part obdurate to treatment was brought under medical control.

The effects of other glandular extracts were studied. Pituitary dysfunction was found to be present in some cases of mental and physical retardation, and treatment by pituitary extract was sometimes said to be beneficial; but the discovery that this gland secretes not one but several different hormones introduced difficulties. The discovery that the glands of internal secretion do not act singly but by a complicated system of checks and balances led some workers to advocate a polyglandular treatment for mental retardation, especially for cases of the mongoloid type. The period between 1920 and 1940 was marked by many claims for the efficacy of various types of endocrine treatment both for children showing intellectual retardation and for those manifesting personal-social maladjustment. Most of these investigations were untrustworthy because of the lack of adequate experimental control.

From time to time spectacular claims are made as to the favorable results obtained through various types of medical treatment of mongoloid children. The remarkable success of thyroid treatment in cretinism and of insulin in diabetes, together with the widespread belief that mongolism also is a deficiency condition, led to the hope that if this deficiency could be supplied, the mongoloid child also might be greatly benefited. Polyglandular treatment was most popular in the past, and many false hopes were aroused through the apparent success of certain formulas with small groups of mongoloid children. With disappointing regularity further study showed the apparent improvement to be fallacious. Glutamic acid has been tried, not only with mongolians but with other types of mentally defective and mentally disturbed cases. Although the findings have not been entirely uniform, some improvement in behavior and in test performance has been reported by a number of investigators. Changes, however, in most cases, have not been great, and much further investigation is needed before we can be sure of the facts. Recently, Benda has reported on a method which, although stated to be still in the experimental stage, appears to open new possibilities in the treatment of mongolism. The early glandular preparations were produced from mature animals; the radically new feature of this treatment consists in the use of pituitary extract derived from immature animals. (Thyroid extract is also used in the treatment.) No child has yet been treated from early infancy to maturity, but results thus far appear encouraging. Benda states that it cannot be expected to do more than ameliorate the condition; even a small gain would be well worth while. If future reports confirm the present results, we may reasonably hope that the way is clear to a more fully successful attack on the problem of mongolism.

During recent years, the use of glutamic acid as a means of improving the intellectual status of mentally retarded children has attracted much attention. References to a number of these studies will be found in the bibliography at the end of this chapter. The fact that glutamic is believed to be the only one of the amino acids that is oxydized by the brain gave rise to the hope that its administration in suitable dosage might have a stimulating effect upon brain function; in other words, that it might improve intelligence. Zimmerman and his associates, who have been among the most persistent workers in this field, report some improvement after six months' treatment, particularly among the mongoloid group. The changes found are not large, however, and, for the most part, are confined to the verbal type of intelligence test. Little or no improvement is shown on performance tests. These findings were not confirmed by Loeb and Tuddenham in a carefully controlled experiment in which two groups of subjects matched for age, sex, IQ, and type of mental defect were used. To one group glutamic acid was given; to the other a placebo. No effect of the glutamic-acid treatment could be ascertained at the end of the period of treatment. Studies of animal learning have also generally yielded negative results. Nevertheless, the number of favorable reports in the literature is sufficiently large to merit serious consideration. A number of workers have suggested that the observed effects may represent an improvement in personality rather than in mental functioning itself. Final judgment on this question must be deferred until a larger and more consistent body of evidence is available.

From all this, one inescapable conclusion emerges. If mental status is to be improved, treatment must be begun early, before the growth process has reached a stage at which mental progress is noticeably slowing up. The time is short—far shorter than most people realize—for 90 per cent of the growth of the brain has been accomplished by the age of six years, and there is evidence that half the child's ultimate mental stature is gained before the age of three. The child who, on arriving at school age, has already fallen so far behind his mates as to be classed as mentally defective may show improvement under the kind of therapeutic treatment that is adjusted to his particular needs, but it is unlikely that the loss will be completely made up. Time is inexorable. While the backward child is struggling to compensate for what he has lost, his more favored companions are already pushing on to new achievements. The importance of early diagnosis is self-evident.

REFERENCES

ALBERT, Kathryn, HOCH, Paul, and WAELSCH, Heinrich, "A Preliminary Report on the Effect of Glutamic Acid Administration in Mentally Retarded Children," *Journal of Nervous and Mental Disease,* 104 (1946), 263-274.

ANGUS, Leslie R., "Prefrontal Lobotomy as a Method of Therapy in a Special School," *American Journal of Mental Deficiency,* 53 (1949), 470-476.

ARBITMAN, Herman D., "The Present Status of Glutamic Acid Therapy for Mental Deficiency," *Training School Bulletin,* 48 (1952), 187-199.

BENDA, Clemens E., *Mongolism and Cretinism,* 2d rev. ed. (New York, Grune and Stratton, Inc., 1949).

———, "Research in Congenital Acromicria (Mongolism) and Its Treatment," *Quarterly Review of Pediatrics,* 8 (1953), 79-96.

DAYTON, N. A., *et al.,* "Mortality and Expectation of Life in Mental Deficiency in Massachusetts: Analysis of Fourteen Year Periods, 1917-1930," *New England Medical Journal,* 206 (1932), 566-570, 616-631.

DOLL, Edgar A., "Is Mental Deficiency Curable?" *American Journal of Mental Deficiency,* 51 (1947), 420-428.

———, PHELPS, Winthrop M., and MELCHER, Ruth Taylor, *Mental Deficiency Due to Birth Injuries* (New York, The Macmillan Company, 1932).

ESQUIROL, Jean-Ettienne Dominique, *Des Maladies mentales consi-derées sous les rapports medical, hygienique, et medico-legal* (Paris, J. B. Balliere, 1838).

GADSON, Eugene J., "Glutamic Acid and Mental Deficiency: A Review," *American Journal of Mental Deficiency,* 55 (1951), 521-527.

GOODENOUGH, Florence L., "Review of Bernadine Schmidt's 'Changes in Personal, Social, and Intellectual Behavior of Children Originally Classified as Feebleminded,'" *Journal of Abnormal and Social Psychology,* 44 (1949), 135-139.

HARNEY, Sister Maureen, *Some Psychological and Physical Character-istics of Retarded Girls Before and Following Treatment with Glutamic Acid* (Washington, D. C., Catholic University of America Press, 1950).

HOVEN, H., "L'Acide glutamique chez les deficients mentaux," *Acta Neurologica et Psychiatrica Belgica,* 51 (1951), 1-8.

KELLEY, Truman Lee, *The influence of Nurture upon Native Differences* (New York, The Macmillan Company, 1926).

KIRK, Samuel A., "An Evaluation of the Study of Bernadine G. Schmidt Entitled 'Changes in Personal, Social, and Intellectual Behavior of Children Originally Classified as Feebleminded,'" *Psychological Bulletin,* 45 (1949), 321-333.

KREEZER, George L., "Electric Potentials of the Brain in Certain Types of Mental Deficiency," *Archives of Neurology and Psychiatry, Chicago,* 36 (1936), 1206-1213.

LANDIS, Carney, and McCUNE, Donovan J., "The Amelioration of Amentia," *American Journal of Mental Deficiency,* 54 (1950), 473-475.

LEVINE, Edna S., "Can We Speed up the Slow Child?" *Volta Review,* 51 (1949), 260-270, 316-319.

LEVINSON, Abraham, "Medical Aspects of Mental Deficiency," *American Journal of Mental Deficiency,* 54 (1950), 476-483.

LOEB, Harold G., and TUDDENHAM, Read D., "Does Glutamic Acid Administration Influence Mental Function?" *Pediatrics,* 6 (1950), 72-77.

LURIE, L. A., "The Medical Concept of Feeblemindedness," *American Journal of Mental Deficiency,* 50 (1946), 512-515.

National Society for the Study of Education, *Twenty-seventh Yearbook* (Chicago, University of Chicago Press, 1928), Pt. 1: *Nature and Nurture, Their Effect upon Intelligence;* Pt. 2: *Their Effect upon Achievement.*

National Society for the Study of Education, *Thirty-ninth Yearbook* (Chicago, University of Chicago Press, 1940), Pt. 1: *Intelligence, Its Nature and Nurture;* Pt. 2: *Original Studies and Experiments.*

NISBET, John, "Family Environment and Intelligence," *Eugenics Review,* 45 (1953), 31-40.

PENROSE, Lionel S., *The Biology of Mental Defect* (New York, Grune and Stratton, Inc., 1949).

POSEY, H. Tharp, "The Electroencephalogram in Mental Deficiency," *American Journal of Mental Deficiency,* 55 (1951), 515-520.

SCHMIDT, Bernadine G., "Changes in Personal, Social, and Intellectual Behavior of Children Originally Classified as Feebleminded," *Psychological Monographs* (1946), 144 pp.

SEGUIN, Edward, *Idiocy and Its Treatment by the Physiological Method* (New York, Bureau of Publications, Teachers College, Columbia University, 1907). Reprinted from the original edition of 1866.

SKEELS, Harold M., and DYE, H. B., "A Study of the Effect of Differential Stimulation on Mentally Retarded Children," *Proceedings and Addresses, American Association on Mental Deficiency,* 44 (1939), 114-136.

SKEELS, Harold M., and HARMS, Irene, "Children with Inferior Social Histories: Their Mental Development in Adoptive Homes," *Journal of Genetic Psychology,* 72 (1948), 283-294.

SKODAK, Marie, "Children in Foster Homes," *University of Iowa Studies in Child Welfare,* 16, No. 1 (1938), 156 pp.

————, "Mental Growth of Adopted Children in the Same Family," *Journal of Genetic Psychology,* 77 (1950), 3-9.

SKODAK, Marie, and SKEELS, Harold M., "A Final Follow-up Study of 100 Adopted Children," *Journal of Genetic Psychology*, 75 (1949), 85-125.

STELLAR, Elliot, and McELROY, William D., "Does Glutamic Acid Have Any Effect on Learning?" *Science*, 108 (1948), 281-283.

WAELSCH, Heinrich, "A Biochemical Consideration of Mental Deficiency: The Role of Glutamic Acid," *American Journal of Mental Deficiency*, 52 (1948), 305-313.

WEIL-MALHERBE, Hans, "Studies of Brain Metabolism: Glutamic Acid in Brain," *Biochemical Journal*, 30 (1936), 665-675.

WILLIAMS, R. T., *Metabolism and Function in Nervous Tissue* (London, Cambridge University Press, 1952).

WOODWORTH, Robert S., *Heredity and Environment: A Critical Survey of Recently Published Material on Twins and Foster Children*, Council Bulletin (New York, Social Science Research, 1941), No. 17.

ZIMMERMAN, Frederick T., "The Glutamic Acid Treatment of Mental Retardation," *Quarterly Review of Psychiatry and Neurology*, 4 (1949), 263-269.

———, and BURGEMEISTER, Bessie B., "The Permanency of Glutamic Acid Treatment," *American Medical Association, Archives of Neurology and Psychiatry*, 65 (1951), 291-298.

———, BURGEMEISTER, Bessie B., and PUTNAM, Tracy, "A Group Study of the Effect of Glutamic Acid upon Mental Function in Children and Adults," *Psychosomatic Medicine*, 9 (1947), 175-183.

———, BURGEMEISTER, Bessie B., and PUTNAM, Tracy, "The Ceiling Effect of Glutamic Acid upon Intelligence in Children and Adolescents," *American Journal of Psychiatry*, 104 (1948), 593-598.

———, BURGEMEISTER, Bessie B., and PUTNAM, Tracy, "The Effect of Glutamic Acid upon the Mental and Physical Growth of Mongols," *American Journal of Psychiatry*, 105 (1949), 661-668.

The Feeble-minded Child in Home, School, and Community

15

THE FEEBLE-MINDED CHILD AT HOME

"Saturday will be your birthday," said Mrs. Evanson, smiling as she sprayed hot water over the dishes in the drainer. "Don't you think it would be nice to invite some of your friends for a little party on that day? They could come for lunch and then spend the afternoon. Would you like that?"

Meredith's dark head bent lower over the glass she was polishing and her voice was very low as she answered, "No, mother. I think it would be better just to have Grandmother Brown and Aunt Molly, I don't—I don't think I want a party."

The smile faded from Mrs. Evanson's face. "Why, Meredith—" she began, but before she could finish her question a whining cry came from the back door. "I'll see what he wants," she added hurriedly. But before she could reach the door, it burst open and a loutish boy of fourteen stumbled in, blubbering loudly as he held out a finger from which a few drops of blood were trickling. "B'ackie stratched me," he blubbered loudly, rubbing an already dirty face with a grimy fist.

"Oh, Paul, Paul, what a state you're in," said his mother reprovingly as she propelled the howling boy into an adjoining lavatory. When they emerged a few minutes later, Meredith had finished drying the dishes and was putting them away in the cupboard. She spent more than the usual time over this, sorting cups and plates and arranging the glasses in neat rows. When this was done she turned to the window, still keeping her face averted. "I think it's going to rain," she remarked.

But Mrs. Evanson was not to be put off so easily. "Why don't you want a party, Meredith?" she inquired soberly. "Is it because of Paul?"

Silent tears were rolling down Meredith's flushed cheeks as she nodded. For a moment, neither of them spoke. Then Meredith burst out, "Anne Morrison said to me the other day, 'Your brother's crazy

230

isn't he?' She said her mother thinks we ought to send him away—to—
to an asylum or some place I suppose. I heard some of the teachers
talking about it too; I don't know just what they were saying, but Miss
Torrey said, 'I feel so sorry for Meredith.' Then one of them saw me
and said, 'Sh-sh,' and they all looked at me. I wanted to—to hide some-
place. And Vera said to me once, 'I don't see how you can stand it to
have Paul around. He slobbers so.'" She stopped abruptly at the sight
of tears in her mother's eyes.

After a pause, Mrs. Evanson said quietly, "I've never talked to you
about this before, Meredith. But you are eleven years old now and I
think you can understand. Your father and I have wanted for a long
time to send Paul to a school for backward children—ever since the
public school refused to take him—but the private schools cost more
than we can afford. We would have to have him committed to one of
the state institutions. We do not like to do that but perhaps we must.
He is getting to be such a big boy, and I'm afraid he may get into
trouble if we try to keep him here. You know he ran away last week,
and the police had to bring him home. Perhaps, too, it's not fair to
you. . . . I know you don't like to bring your friends here any more."

The mother's self-control broke down and she burst into unrestrained
weeping. Meredith stood helplessly beside her, stroking her mother's
graying hair on which her own tears fell unavailingly. There was no
further discussion of the party.

This incident illustrates some of the problems that are likely to
develop when a conspicuously feeble-minded child is reared in a
home where there are other children of normal intelligence. But
it does not tell the whole story. Because of the amount of care and
the constant watching that Paul required, Mrs. Evanson had been
forced to give up practically all her own social activities. When
Paul was smaller, an occasional evening out with her husband
could be managed with the help of a "baby-sitter," but as he grew,
his physical size and strength made this no longer practicable.
The deprivation was hard for both parents, and their marital relations in consequence were becoming somewhat strained. Both
were aware of the criticisms of their neighbors to which Meredith
had referred. Most of all, the bitter grief over the hopeless future
of their first-born child for whom they had entertained such high
hopes was to both a constant pang.

For eleven-year-old Meredith the situation was even more

tragic. By temperament neat and tidy, her brother's slovenly habits—his "slobbering"—had become increasingly hard to bear as she grew older. Now at the dawn of adolescence, she sensed the repulsion felt by her friends and in some ill-defined way felt that this repulsion extended to herself and to the other members of her family. It was a *family* disgrace that had been visited upon them. The taint that had infected Paul had contaminated them all. At times she wondered if she, herself, was wholly like the other girls of her age. Small mistakes, minor errors of judgment, or such little mishaps as a spilled glass of milk began to assume tremendous importance to her. At night she lay sleepless, the same horrifying thought occurring and recurring in her mind: *Am I getting to be like Paul?* Shamed and self-conscious she recoiled from her friends, fearing ridicule behind their advances and suspecting repugnance when she was ignored.

Help came; let us hope that it was not too late. The growing change in Meredith's personality had been noted by her teachers, and a few days after the episode we have reported, the visiting teacher from her school called on her parents. Tactfully she raised the question as to the wisdom of keeping Paul at home, pointing out how hard the situation was becoming for Meredith and emphasizing her need for a normal home environment. Learning of the mother's dread of a state institution, she asked if the parents had ever visited the one to which Paul would probably be committed and urged that they do so. This was wise advice, for instead of the bestial atmosphere and desolation they had expected, they found an attractive group of cottages standing in well-kept grounds, each cottage under the charge of a pleasant-faced matron. They saw comfortable dormitories, attractive dining rooms, playgrounds and playrooms well equipped with toys and motor apparatus. They found the older children learning to do various kinds of useful work under the supervision of trained instructors; the younger ones in school where the work of each was adjusted to his capacity to learn. They visited the kitchens and tasted the simple, appetizing food that was being prepared. So changed was their impression that on the following day they made out the necessary application forms for Paul's admission to the institution. The unfortunate thing was that, as is true in most states, they found a long waiting list ahead of them. It might be years, they were told, before Paul's turn would come.

Many people, like the Evansons, have an erroneous impression of institutions for the feeble-minded or the mentally deranged. They think of them with horror as places where hundreds of gibbering unhappy souls are forced to subjection by means of straitjackets and other less harmless devices. They hear rumors of bad food, unsanitary conditions, and harsh treatment by ignorant attendants. Small wonder that they hesitate to send their children to such a place! Yet the fact remains that the ordinary modern home is not a suitable place in which to rear a feeble-minded child, especially one of imbecile or idiot level. The problems that the Evansons encountered are typical of those likely to be met by any family in which there are one or more normal children in addition to the one of defective mind. Even when there are no other children, it is questionable whether it is wise to divert so much of the mother's time and attention to the care of such a child because of the consequent interference with her personal life and social relationships which is likely to ensue. And although it is true that most state institutions are hampered by overcrowding and lack of funds, it is also true that most of them are carrying on surprisingly well in spite of such difficulties. Although it is not a state institution, the influence of the Vineland Training School continues to permeate many, if not most, of the publicly supported institutions for the feeble-minded throughout the country. Early in the present century, under the wise rule of E. R. Johnstone, its superintendent, and H. H. Goddard, director of research, the school's slogan, "Happiness first; all else follows," was drilled into the minds and hearts of the hundreds of "summer teachers" who there received their training and from there went out to exert their influence in both public institutions and private schools throughout the country. No one can estimate what the Vineland spirit has done to improve the treatment of the feeble-minded in American institutions. The Village of Happiness, as it

has sometimes been called, has served as a model for many others
of its kind, both public and private.

The growing tendency toward small rather than large dwelling
units, the increase in the number of apartment houses, housing
projects, and small bungalows, makes the problem of the feeble-
minded child in the home more difficult than it was in the days
when more space could be provided for his care. Even today, in
rural districts where houses are usually larger and plenty of outdoor space where he may roam with safety is available, the feeble-
minded child whose mentality is not of such a low level that he
cannot be trusted to look after himself is not always the problem
that he becomes in the city. There are many simple tasks about
the home and farm that the child of moron grade can learn to
perform; even the high-grade imbecile can be taught a few routine tasks. The extent to which the social life of the normal children
in the family is interfered with will depend largely upon the attitude of the community which, in rural districts where social intercourse involves all who reside in the neighborhood, is likely to
be more uniform than it is in the city where friendships are selective rather than localized. In some communities, the backward
child is accepted for what he is, or it may be that he is looked
upon in much the same spirit as he would be if he were physically
crippled, blind, or deaf. The other children, if there are any in the
family, do not feel ashamed of him unless his habits are such as
to make him physically repulsive. But in other cases, the small
community may adopt an attitude toward the feeble-minded child
and his family that renders it even harder for the normal siblings
than it would be if the social group were larger and less intimate.
There is gossip as to causes, for which parents are usually not held
blameless. As the child grows older and stronger, there is fear that
he may injure persons or property. "You can't tell what anybody
like that will do" is the concensus of opinion. Even the normal
children in the family may be regarded with suspicion. It is felt
that there must be "something wrong with the family" and that
none of its members therefore can be completely trusted.

The problem of the feeble-minded child in the home is thus a

many-angled one, but its major aspects are these: first, the effect
on the social life of the family and, especially, on that of the other
children; second, the physical, nervous, and emotional drain upon
the person or persons who must take the responsibility of looking
after him; and third, the well-being and happiness of the child
himself, who, in these circumstances, usually lacks companions
whose interests and pleasures are enough like his own to make
them congenial mates. I say nothing here of the grief and anxiety
of parents, who, little by little, are forced to the realization that
their child is not developing normally. Pearl Buck has given a
moving account of her own experience with her child, who is now
in Vineland. She has described the hope with which she greeted
the baby's arrival, her delight in its healthy infancy, and the terror
with which she rejected her first doubts as to its mentality. She
describes her almost frantic efforts at training and the meager
success with which these efforts were rewarded. She tells of the
renewed hopes with which she took the child from doctor to
doctor, from clinic to clinic, and of how, ultimately, she was forced
to accept the heartbreaking fact that her daughter would never
be normal. She tells, too, of the thoughtless, cruel comments of
others, and of the equally cruel kindness of doctors who advised
her not to give up hope, though they had no hope to offer. Finally,
she describes her reasons for feeling that the child must be placed
in a world of her own kind in which suitable and congenial companions and training of a kind adapted to her ability could be had,
inasmuch as the world of normal people was forever closed to
her. The story is a personal document that will bring the consola-
tion of a shared sorrow to other parents who must meet similar
problems.

So far we have spoken only of the obviously feeble-minded
child in the family where the other members are of normal intelligence. Two other conditions should be mentioned. There is the
case of the moron child whose backwardness may not be discovered until, on entering school, it is found that he cannot learn
as the other children of his age do. Such children may present no
physical signs of their defectiveness; they may be trained to neat-

ness in their personal habits and to conformity to the usual rules of child conduct. Their articulation is likely to be somewhat slovenly, and their vocabularies small; yet their linguistic retardation is generally not so marked as to render them conspicuous. In sustained conversation, however, their backwardness becomes apparent. In some ways, too, their very nearness to the normal level makes these children greater problems than those who are at once seen to be defective. It is less easy for people to accept their limitations. They feel that if the child would "only try a little harder," he could do as well as others. They fail to see that it is his backwardness that prevents him from "trying," for he is mentally incapable of seeing either why or how he should do so.

If his deficiencies are understood and accepted, however, and no more is expected from him than he is able to perform, the moron child may present no great problem in the home while he remains a child. Suitable companionship and educational training appropriate to his level of understanding are provided by the special classes for backward and mentally deficient children that are a part of the public school systems of most large cities. (More will be said about these classes in the following chapter.) But the feeble-minded child will not always be a child. In the course of time, he will become a feeble-minded adult, and of this future the parents must think and plan long before it arrives. Few indeed are those who can provide both for the financial security and the personal guardianship that these children of a larger growth will continue to need. But their future must be safeguarded. How?

Even if the need for institutional care seems less immediately pressing in these cases, the wise parent will see to it that when the child reaches an age at which the provisions made by the home and by the public school are no longer adequate transfer to the appropriate state institution will take place. Most states now separate the children of higher from those of lower mentality, with corresponding adjustments in care and training. But because of the long waiting lists that usually exist, application for the child's admittance must be made while he is still a child. This condition has one advantage; it gives the parents time to adjust to the coming separation and to realize its advantage as well as its necessity.

What of the feeble-minded family in which not merely one but all or most of the children are backward or definitely mentally defective and the parents are little, if at all, above that level? Here the home problems are many, but the family is rarely able to come to grips with them. Thus they become essentially problems that are thrust upon the community which must deal with them as best it can.

THE FEEBLE-MINDED CHILD AT SCHOOL

The difficulties that beset child and teacher alike when a feeble-minded child is enrolled in a class of normal children have been so frequently enumerated that it is unnecessary to repeat them here. To be sure the modern system of promoting all children annually on the basis of age, regardless of accomplishment, has pretty well abolished the condition found in many schools two or more decades ago when the primary grades were likely to include children of all ages from six to sixteen. But the more recent system, although it tends to keep the mentally defective child with those of his own chronological age, puts him for that very reason with those whose mental ages are so far in advance of his own that he can comprehend little or nothing of what is going on. The resultant behavior can easily be foreseen.

The establishment of special classes for backward children has partially solved this difficulty, but it has done so only in part. In the first place, these classes are rarely sufficient in number to take care of all the children who need the special training they provide. In the second place, the educational philosophy of these classes has not been well formulated, and teachers are often inadequately prepared for the work they are attempting to do—if, indeed, they know what that work is. Finally, few communities have provisions for the supervised out-of-school and postschool activities which many of these children need.

That the schools of today are doing far more and better work for the child of inadequate intellectual endowment than was done a quarter of a century ago there can be no doubt. But there are still many unsolved problems to which answers are not easy to find. Even in the special class, the defective child is not easy to teach, a fact that has long been recognized in the small number of pupils assigned to each teacher.

THE FEEBLE-MINDED CHILD IN THE COMMUNITY

Community problems, as they relate to mental deficiency, are of several kinds, depending upon the existing conditions. There are the more or less isolated cases for which community education is needed, both for the sake of the feeble-minded child and for the sake of his family. Many people have a superstitious dread of someone whom they regard as "not quite right;" a dread that is based in part upon the frequent lack of discrimination between the insane and the feeble-minded. They avoid him and those associated with him as well. The mentally defective child is thus cut off from social experience to an even greater extent than necessarily results from his inability to participate in many of the activities of normal children. This tends to increase his peculiarities, since they are not corrected by the give and take of ordinary child intercourse. Lack of companionship also leads to unpleasant personal habits, such as picking the nose until it becomes sore or, in some cases, overt masturbation. Such habits have a circular effect, for they cause the careful parent to warn her children against associating with the feeble-minded one, and so his isolation and loneliness are increased.

If the child's deficiency is not too great, if he is of moron rather than of imbecile level, he may feel this isolation the more keenly. Because he so often makes stupid blunders or is slow in learning a new game, he is likely to be excluded from much of the fun that the other children enjoy. Yet he *could* take part in it if some understanding adult were to point out his loneliness to the other children in the group, show them his need for friendliness, and persuade them to display a greater degree of patience and forbearance. As has been pointed out before, the difference between the moron of middle or high grade who, as an adult, contrives to be self-supporting and self-directing, after a simple fashion, and the one who requires permanent care and protection, is largely one of character and attitude, for which the seeds are sown in childhood. If children, as well as adults, are taught to realize that some special attention is required to see that X learns the rules of their games and is given a part in them, they, as well as the backward child, will profit by the experience. Even if the defective child is of too low a mental level to make this possible, children should learn to adopt a kindly attitude toward him, rather than one of fear or ridicule.

The community can do much to help the parents of a mentally defective child. By their attitude toward him and by means of such friendly counsel as they can offer without offense, they can make it clear that in their eyes the situation is an affliction but not a disgrace. They can help the parents to accept the hard but necessary fact that for the great majority of such children the protection and care that can be given only in an institution provide the only safe solution to their problem.

Since Seguin came to America in 1848 and since the active crusading work of Johnstone and Goddard and the many others who labored to bring the needs and problems of those whose minds do not develop normally before the public eye, much has been accomplished in the way of correcting the widespread misconceptions and overcoming the many superstitions that formerly prevailed with respect to this unfortunate group of people. Community education is still needed, but a beginning, at least, has been made.

REFERENCES

BIRCH, Jack W., and MATTHEWS, Jack, "The Hearing of Mental Defectives: Its Measurement and Characteristics," *American Journal of Mental Deficiency*, 55 (1951), 384-393.

BUCK, Pearl S., *The Child Who Never Grew* (New York, The John Day Company, 1950).

CUTTS, Richard A., and SLOAN, William, "Test Patterns of Adjusted Defectives on the Wechsler-Bellevue Test," *American Journal of Mental Deficiency*, 50 (1945), 98-101.

DAS GUPTA, J. C., "Social Adjustment of Mentally Deficient Children," *Indian Journal of Social Work*, 9 (1948), 105-111.

DAVIS, Parker, "Emotional Problems of the Retarded Child," *Training School Bulletin*, 48 (1951), 50-56.

DOLL, Edgar A., "Social Adjustment of the Mentally Subnormal," *Journal of Educational Research*, 28 (1934), 36-43.

——, "Social Adjustment of the Feebleminded under Extra-institutional Care," *Psychiatric Quarterly*, 11 (1937), 450-464.

——, "The Social Competence of Special Class Children," *Journal of Educational Research*, 31 (1937), 90-106.

——, "Foster Care for Mental Defectives," *Training School Bulletin*, 36 (1940), 193-205.

EELS, Kenneth, DAVIS, Allison, HAVIGHURST, Robert J., HERRICK, Virgil E., and TYLER, Ralph, *Intelligence and Cultural Differences: A Study of Cultural Learning and Problem Solving* (Chicago, University of Chicago Press, 1951).

FOX, Evelyn, "Community Schemes for the Social Control of Mental Defectives," paper read at the First International Congress for Mental Hygiene (Washington, D. C., May 8, 1930).

GEGENHEIMER, Ruth A., "A Quarter Century of Community Supervision of Mentally Deficient Patients," *American Journal of Mental Deficiency*, 53 (1948), 92-102.

GREBLER, Anne Marie, "Parental Attitudes toward Mentally Retarded Children," *American Journal of Mental Deficiency*, 56 (1952), 477-483.

GREENE, C. L., "A Study of Personal Adjustment in Mentally Retarded Girls," *American Journal of Mental Deficiency*, 49 (1945), 472-476.

HACKBUSH, Florentine, "The Legal Settlement of Mental Defectives," *American Journal of Mental Deficiency*, 51 (1947), 735-737.

HARMS, Ernest, "Sociology of the Mentally Disadvantaged Child," *School and Society*, 66 (1947), 305-307.

HEILMAN, Ann E., "Parental Adjustment to the Dull Handicapped Child," *American Journal of Mental Deficiency*, 54 (1950), 556-562.

HUNGERFORD, Richard H., "The Young Retardate Outside His Home Community," *American Journal of Mental Deficiency*, 51 (1947), 758-765.

JOHNSON, G. Orville, "A Study of the Social Position of Mentally-Handicapped Children in the Regular Grades," *American Journal of Mental Deficiency*, 55 (1950), 60-89.

KATZ, G. H., "Should the Child Be Sent to an Institution?" *The Nervous Child*, 5, No. 2 (April, 1946), 172-177.

LAYCOCK, S. R., "Helping Parents to Accept Their Exceptional Children," *Exceptional Children*, 18 (1952), 129-132.

MACDONALD, J., and GILBERT, C., "Social Adjustment of Hypothyroid Children," *Smith College Studies in Social Work*, 17 (1946), 1-31.

McKEON, Rebecca M., "Mentally Retarded Boys in War Time," *Mental Hygiene*, 30 (1946), 47-55.

MAGARET, Ann, and THOMPSON, Clara W., "Differential Test Responses of Normal, Superior, and Mentally Defective Subjects," *Journal of Abnormal and Social Psychology*, 45 (1950), 163-167.

MANGUS, A. R., "Effect of Mental and Educational Retardation on Personality Development of Children," *American Journal of Mental Deficiency*, 55 (1950), 208-212.

MICKELSON, Phyllis, "Minnesota's Guardianship Program As a Basis for Community Supervision," *American Journal of Mental Deficiency*, 56 (1951), 313-325.

SARASON, Seymour B., and SARASON, Esther K., "The Discriminatory Value of a Test Pattern in the High Grade Familial Defective," *Journal of Clinical Psychology*, 2 (1946), 38-49.

SCHLANGER, Bernard B., "Speech Examination of a Group of Institutionalized Mentally Handicapped Children," *Journal of Speech and Hearing Disorders*, 18 (1953), 339-349.

SCHUMACHER, H. C., "A Program for Dealing with Mental Deficiency in Children up to Six Years of Age," *American Journal of Mental Deficiency*, 51 (1946), 52-56.

SHEIMO, S. L., "Problems in Helping Parents of Mentally Defective and Handicapped Children," *American Journal of Mental Deficiency*, 56 (1951), 42-47.

STERN, Edith M., and CASTENDYCK, Elsa, *The Handicapped Child: A Guide for Parents* (New York, A. A. Wyn, Inc., 1950).

STICKLAND, C. A., "The Social Competence of the Feebleminded," *American Journal of Mental Deficiency*, 53 (1949), 504-515.

WARDELL, Winifred, "Case Work with Parents of Mentally Deficient Children," *American Journal of Mental Deficiency*, 52 (1947), 91-97.

WATERMAN, John H., "Psychogenic Factors in Parental Acceptance of Feebleminded Children," *Diseases of the Nervous System*, 9 (1948), 184-187.

WEISS, Deso A., "Speech in Retarded Children," *The Nervous Child*, 9, No. 1 (January, 1951), pp. 21-30.

WESTWELL, Arthur E., "The Defective Delinquent," *American Journal of Mental Deficiency*, 56 (1951), 283-289.

The Education and Training of Subnormal Children 16

HABIT TRAINING IN THE HOME

INCULCATION OF good fundamental habits of eating, sleeping, and cleanliness is attempted early by most parents regardless of the child's level of intelligence and, indeed, before that level can be ascertained with any degree of assurance. Even with normal children this apparently simple task affords many difficulties, for the infant is still a savage at heart to whom the ways of civilization are alien. But if he is of normal mind, the example of others proves an impelling stimulus. He struggles to master the use of his spoon, not so much because of urging as because he sees grownups using table implements. He tries to wash himself, chiefly because it is fun to splash in the water but also because father and mother do so. Almost before he is out of the cradle, he begins to enjoy clean fresh clothing and to take an amusing pride in being dressed up. He begins to take some small part in the process of dressing and undressing and objects vigorously when a hurried mother insists upon doing things for him that with slow but persistent effort he has learned to accomplish for himself.

But even in infancy the feeble-minded child is slow to acquire these simple habits and skills. As a rule, he is later than the average child in displaying a desire to acquire them, although, in most cases, such a desire will appear in time. Meanwhile, his mother will have been making fruitless attempts to teach him that which he has no wish to learn. Over and over again, she places the spoon in his unreceptive hand and by word and example urges him to use it. Patiently, and still more patiently, she labors to teach him habits of bladder and bowel control. And if his defect is not too grave, she slowly achieves some measure of success.

But infinite patience is required. Furthermore, care must be taken to see that a uniform procedure is taught. The normal child early learns to modify his techniques as circumstances change. Reason and judgment influence his behavior; he sees that it is more efficient to do things in different ways as circumstances require. But the mentally defective child learns by rote and behaves as he has learned. Much misunderstanding of the feeble-minded child's behavior will be avoided if this simple principle is kept in mind. Often such a child is thought to have acted in a wanton or malicious fashion when he was merely doing what he believed to be right. There is an old story of a feeble-minded woman in an institution who had learned to help in the laundry. One day, as they chanced to be shorthanded in the nursery, she was given a baby to wash. She did so in boiling water, with disastrous consequences.

Because he does not see relationships easily, the subnormal child does not learn readily if the conditions of learning change from time to time or if the instructions given him vary in what, to him, is a puzzling and even conflicting manner. If he is to form the kind of habits and acquire the basic skills that will make his deficiencies less apparent to outsiders and enable him to participate more fully in the life of those about him than he could otherwise do, he must accomplish his learning by uniform methods and must not be expected to vary his habits merely because such variation would lead to greater efficiency.

Confusion and perplexity also arise if an attempt is made to teach too many things at one time or to give too many instructions without waiting for each to be carried out. One of the most striking differences between the mental processes of normal and subnormal children is seen in the relative inability of the latter to keep a number of things in mind at once and respond to each in turn. Experiments on the delayed reaction have shown mentally retarded children to be notably inferior to those of average intelligence with respect to the length of time a response may be delayed, as well as the complexity of the response, that is, the number and meaningfulness of its parts or elements. "One thing at a time" is the safe rule to follow in the training of backward children.

If the training is sufficiently patient and consistent, with each new step carefully outlined and mastered before the next is attempted, mentally deficient children of moron and even imbecile grade can learn to perform many useful tasks about the home and premises. In such work, their very want of adaptiveness can be a virtue, for if a piece of work is begun, it will be done in the same manner each time since the typical feeble-minded child is unable to slight his work. He may refuse to do it at all or he may stop half-way and refuse to go on. But what he does, if he has been properly taught, will be done as he was trained to do it. It is true, of course, that some feeble-minded children never learn good habits of work, and for them the foregoing statement does not hold. But the well-trained mentally defective person can be an amazingly dependable and useful worker so long as changing conditions do not require a change in procedure. It is then that disasters occur.

Habit training in the home thus involves a number of features. There is first the learning of the simple personal habits that all children in our society must acquire. These, like other habits and skills, are usually harder for the subnormal than for the normal child to acquire, and in many cases there are special tendencies— such as drooling, picking the nose, or protuding the tongue—that must, as far as possible, be overcome. There are habits of self-help that also involve skills which the mentally backward child finds hard to master and which therefore must be taught slowly and little by little. And as the child grows older, there are habits of household service which are of great value in the difficult task of integrating his limited life with the fuller and richer lives of the other members of the family. So long as he remains in the home he should be, as far as possible, a part of the home. Even though the time required for training seems greater than the child's service can repay, it is still worth while if it succeeds in its main object, which is to make the child a happy and well-adjusted member of the group in which he is placed.

EDUCATING THE SUBNORMAL CHILD
IN THE PUBLIC SCHOOL

In small communities, the number of children whose mental retardation is serious enough to make a special type of educational program necessary or desirable is usually not large enough to constitute a class of reasonable size, or at least to satisfy the taxpayers that such a class is needed. Various surveys have shown that in a typical population from 2 to 4 per cent of the children of school age earn IQ's below 80 on the Stanford Binet. Of these, not all will require special class instruction, since good work habits and freedom from behavior difficulties will, in many cases, enable them to meet the minimum requirements of the regular curriculum without more help than the ordinary classroom teacher can provide. Thus, unless the school enrollment [1] is at least as large as 300-400, it is unlikely that the retarded children will be withdrawn for placement in a special school or class. They will remain in the regular classrooms.

The old practice of retaining subnormal children in the early primary grades on the grounds that they, like others, must master the work of each grade before being promoted to the next is no longer followed in most modern school systems. Generally, the mentally deficient child is moved through the grades at a pace that is little, if at all, slower than that of the other children, even though the academic work at each level is increasingly beyond his grasp. His inability to participate in much of the work done by the other children creates a problem for the teacher, who must find some other way to keep him occupied and happy. There are many chores about the schoolroom that such a child can learn

---

[1] This, of course, refers to the entire enrollment of the school system, not to that of one particular school. It is usual for a special class to be made up of the retarded children from several adjacent schools within the same city.

to do, and if given some important-sounding name, such as Teacher's helper, the feeling of self-confidence which is likely to suffer from recognition of his inability to do the regular classwork may be largely restored. If the school janitor is kindly and good-natured, he may occasionally find tasks in which the older children can assist him. The girls may be allowed to spend a larger than usual amount of their time in the domestic-science rooms, the boys in the shops and manual-training departments. '

The minimum essentials of academic work should not be neglected for these children. Most school systems nowdays refuse to admit children whose mentality is so low that they cannot learn at least the elements of reading and writing, counting, and easy change making, either in the regular classes or in the special rooms and schools set apart for the mentally retarded. At an earlier date, when special classes were a new and untried educational departure, imbeciles and even idiots were admitted to them. But it was soon found that these low-grade cases profited little by what the public schools were able to offer them and that their presence even in the special classes imposed so much additional work upon the teachers as to interfere seriously with the progress of the other children. At present, most public schools confine the enrollment of the special classes to children of moron and border-line intelligence, that is, to those whose IQ's fall, roughly, between 50 and 80. Most of these children are able to learn something of the three R's; they can learn to read street signs and easy books and even some portions of the newspaper. They learn to compose and write simple letters, to make change and count money, if the amounts are not too large. They learn to make easy measurements and to perform the calculations needed for the construction of simple articles. Through stories and pictures, they learn something of history and geography; field trips and visits to museums provide the minimum elements of information along the lines of science and industry.

A large share of the work of the special classes is devoted to prevocational training. The boys learn shopwork, carpentry, and the like; the girls sewing, cooking, and other household arts. Many of these children will never enter an institution; the aim, therefore, is to fit them as far as possible for life in the outside world.

Character training, however, is perhaps the most important objective of the special class. Many children do not enter these classes until their educational difficulties and the personal maladjustment resulting from unwise treatment of long standing can no longer be overlooked. They come to the special class resentful and suspicious, feeling, like Ishmael, that their hands are against every man and every man's hand against them. To overcome this feeling is the teacher's first and most important task, and it is often not an easy one.

Character training for the mentally deficient child has many points in common with that appropriate for children in general. But the objectives sought for these children have certain points of difference from those usually considered desirable for children of a higher level of mentality. Because they are less able to manage their own lives and conduct their own affairs with the prudence and forethought requisite for successful living under the complexities of modern society, they must be willing to depend more than do their fellows upon the guidance of others if they are to avoid disastrous mistakes. Because their lack of intelligence is likely to cause them to be ridiculed if their behavior or conversation are such as to attract too much attention to them, quietness and inconspicuousness rather than any form of exhibitionism are virtues to be cultivated. The modern stress upon "self-expression" must be exercised with caution in the case of the mentally deficient child. He may express much that would better have been concealed.

Speech training is important. Few feeble-minded children articulate well, and other speech defects are common. The defective child whose speech habits are poor is doubly disadvantaged, for his defective speech tends to call attention to his intellectual deficiencies at times when they might otherwise pass unnoticed.

Many books and articles on the education of defective children in the special class or school have been written since the publication in 1912 of Lightner Witmer's *The Special Class for Back-*

ward Children, which, for a number of years, was the standard reference book for teachers in that field. One of the most recent of these publications is *Educating the Retarded Child* by Samuel A. Kirk and G. Orville Johnson of the University of Illinois. The voluminousness of the literature that has appeared since Witmer's classic publication is suggested by the briefly annotated bibliography of 56 pages and the lists of selected references at the end of each chapter in the book by Kirk and Johnson.

INSTITUTIONAL TRAINING OF THE DEFECTIVE CHILD

States with sufficiently large populations to justify the establishment of more than one institution for the mentally subnormal simplify their training programs by placing the low-grade cases, who can profit little, if any, from training, in a separate institution, thus making it possible to arrange for more highly trained teachers and more adequate training facilities for those of higher grade. When possible, age is also taken into account. Children and adolescents are separated from those who have arrived at physical maturity.

Training for a life to be spent within the institution will obviously differ in some respects from that given in the special classes in the public schools, where many, if not most, of the children will later try to make their way in the world of normal people. The modern institution, however, does attempt to prepare some of its least deficient inmates for a supervised life outside its walls. This means that special diagnostic procedures are called for to determine, as far as possible, which of these higher grade cases are most likely to succeed if paroled or discharged. Such diagnosis is not easy, for character traits and emotional stability are likely to be the main deciding factors, provided, of course, that a certain minimum level of intelligence has been reached. Health and physique must also be taken into account, for, at best, these cases must depend upon brawn rather than brain for gaining a livelihood, though it is true that many find their way into factory jobs that demand manual dexterity and endurance rather than great muscular strength.

As yet, long observation of behavior within the institution appears to be a better criterion of probable success outside the institution than any tests that have been devised. Many variables are involved, and the proper weight to be assigned to each in a test designed to predict success is as yet unknown. In her study of the work records of subnormal adolescent girls, Abel [2] found that those girls were most likely to continue to lead a happy successful life within the framework of normal society who were able, in a sense, to identify themselves with their jobs so completely that they had no wish for any other type of work. They felt no jealousy of those with better paying positions, and did not struggle vainly for advancement that they could not maintain if won. Within the institution, differences from one inmate to another of similar intelligence are likewise seen. Some become faithful, steady workers, carrying out the same routine tasks year after year with no desire to change. Others are restless, wanting to try this and that but never sticking voluntarily to one task long enough to become really attached to it. Sometimes, after many trials, a niche is found into which they fit. Other cases must continually be urged and encouraged.

A striking example of identification with a job is told in one of the Vineland traditions. A boy of about eighteen, a strapping youth of large frame and bulging muscles, was consigned to the school. [3] On several occasions, this lad had been found guilty of arson, and his reception at the school was an occasion for consideration and terror. Fire is the great bugbear of any institution in which many people are housed; if the inmates are of subnormal mind, the dread is even greater. What, then, was to be done with this dangerous new arrival?

Attendants were warned that extraordinary care must be taken

[2] *The Subnormal Adolescent Girl*, ch. 4.

[3] Though Vineland was never a state institution, the state of New Jersey, for a number of years, paid for the maintenance of a certain number of children and adults at the school. These cases were sent by the state at its discretion.

with respect to fire and matches. The boy must at all times be watched; he must never be left alone. But in spite of all these precautions, the boy somehow succeeded in starting a fire which would undoubtedly have had serious consequences had it not been discovered before it had gained much headway. Fearful attendants and teachers now urged that some form of physical restraint must be employed. The boy must be shut up or other means employed that would prevent him from continuing to be a peril to the whole institution.

But the school's kindly superintendent, E. R. Johnstone—"Professor Johnstone" as he was affectionately called—looked at the boy's splendid physique and shook his head. "No," he said, "it would be cruel to confine so strong and active a boy as that. We must find some other plan." During a long and sleepless night, he revolved the question in his mind and, by morning, he had found an answer. "Berto loves to make fires," he announced to his staff at the morning conference. "Very well. We shall let him make them." That very day Berto was transferred to the somewhat alarmed supervision of the man who had charge of the school's heating plant. Under his watchful eye, Berto was allowed to shovel coal into the furnaces.

The plan succeeded. Berto's love for his fires grew as the days passed. His desire for making fires was satisfied in a legitimate way; he no longer felt the urge to start fires elsewhere. The furnaces were his pride and joy. Each received a name of its own; each, to Berto, had a personality of its own, and he loved them as a father loves his children. If Berto received a treat, such as a bag of candy, his first thought was of his beloved fires. Down to the heating plant he sped, and each of the furnaces received its share before Berto allowed himself so much as a taste.

Berto was an imbecile of fairly high grade. Not even a moron is likely to confer such reality of animism to inanimate objects, though as Piaget has shown, normal young children are likely to do so. But the story is a beautiful example of the way in which a sympathetic imagination can transform the uncomprehending and often dangerous impulses of the subnormal mind into useful ones.

Unfortunately, not all such cases find so favorable an outcome. In his *Of Mice and Men,* Steinbeck has given a remarkably well-drawn portrait of an imbecile, who, in many respects, was similar to Berto, but whose life ended in tragedy.

For those who are likely to spend the remainder of their lives within the institution, training will be directed toward making such a future as happy and useful as possible. Practically all, with the exception of the idiots and low-grade imbeciles, learn to perform certain tasks for which they grow to feel responsible. This not only gives them a feeling of personal worth that contributes greatly to their satisfaction with the life that they must lead, but in many cases helps to defray the expenses of the institution. Inasmuch as practically no state institution has a budget that would meet its needs if all work were done by paid help, the training given to the inmates has an economic as well as a personal-social value.

Whether in home, school, or institution, the Vineland slogan—"Happiness first; all else follows," should be the guiding principle of all educational programs for those whose minds have not developed normally. Education comes from within; all that the parent or teacher can do is to provide the conditions under which optimal growth and development will take place. He can provide the materials and conditions for learning, but the learning must be done by the child himself. If this learning is to be accomplished efficiently and well, the process of learning must be pleasant and the child must be strongly motivated to learn. For the normal child there are many incentives by which motivation may be aroused or increased, but for the defective child such incentives are fewer in number and more limited in kind. For both, success is of paramount importance; but whereas for the normal child the successful accomplishment of one task is but a steppingstone that leads to further advancement along the same line, for the subnormal child such advance, if it takes place at all, is accomplished slowly and with much difficulty. For both, success is a spur to continued activity, but the mentally defective child frequently finds his greatest joy in simple repetition of a task of which the normal child would soon tire. The delight that a deficient child takes in the continued performance of a monotonous task and the extent to which he identifies himself with it is a measure of his adjustment to life and to his own limitations. The wise educator realizes this and does not attempt to introduce too much variety into the child's daily routine of activities. A few things well done bring greater satisfaction than many that are attempted but imperfectly mastered.

REFERENCES

ABEL, Theodora M., and HUMPHREYS, Edward I., "Institutional Biographies of Unstable Subnormal Girls," *American Journal of Mental Deficiency*, 46 (1941), 514-518.

———, and KINDER, Elaine F., *The Subnormal Adolescent Girl* (New York, Columbia University Press, 1942).

BAKER, Harry J., "Administration of Special Education," *Review of Educational Research*, 14 (1944), 209-216.

BEAMAN, Florence N., "The Intangibles of Special Education," *Journal of Exceptional Children*, 9 (1943), 35-46.

BERNSTEIN, Charles, "Colony and Extra-institutional Care for the Feebleminded," *Mental Hygiene*, 4 (1920), 1-28.

BERRY, Charles Scott, "Public School Education of Mentally Retarded Children," *Proceedings and Addresses: Annual Session of the American Association on Mental Deficiency*, 41 (1936), 111-120.

BYRNE, May E., "Curriculum Planning for Exceptional Children," *Journal of Exceptional Children*, 12 (1946), 231-234.

———, *Program of Education for the Mentally Retarded Children in a Public School System*, State Department of Education Bulletin (Trenton, N. J., 1947), No. 12.

California State Department of Education, *Questions on the Education of Mentally Retarded Minors in California*, State Department of Education Bulletin (Sacramento, 1950), Vol. 10, No. 1.

CIANCI, Vincentz, "Home Training for Retarded Children in New Jersey," *Training School Bulletin*, 48 (1951), 131-139.

CRUICKSHANK, William M., "Research in the Education of Children with Retarded Mental Development," *American Journal of Mental Deficiency*, 56 (1951), 308-312.

CUTTS, Norma E., "The Mentally Handicapped," *Review of Educational Research*, 11 (1941), 261-276.

DEACON, Kathryn Fitch, "An Experiment in the Cottage Training of Low Grade Defectives," *American Journal of Mental Deficiency*, 47 (1942), 195-202.

DEAKINS, Edna, "Music for the Mentally Handicapped," *Illinois Education*, 36 (1950), 256-257; 267-269.

DELF, Harold A., "Goals for the Mentally Retarded," *American Journal of Mental Deficiency*, 55 (1951), 472-478.

DE PROSPO, Chris J., and HUNGERFORD, Richard, "A Complete Social Program for the Mentally Retarded," *American Journal of Mental Deficiency*, 51 (1946), 115-122.

FEATHERSTONE, W. B., *Teaching the Slow Learner*, rev. ed. (New York, Teachers College Bureau of Publications, 1951).

————, "Realistic Education of the Mentally Retarded," *Teachers College Record*, 52 (1951), 471-480.

FIELDS, Harold, "Good Teachers of the Mentally Retarded," *American Journal of Mental Deficiency*, 56 (1951), 86-112.

FOURACRE, Maurice H., "Improving the Relationship Between the Community and the Class for the Mentally Retarded," *Journal of Exceptional Children*, 12 (1946), 108-112, 121.

GATES, Louise, *Teach Me: A Guide for Parents and Others Who Have the Care of Subnormal Children* (St. Paul, Minn., Division of Public Institutions, Department of Social Security, 1943).

GENS, George W., "The Speech Pathologist Looks at the Mentally-deficient Child," *Training School Bulletin*, 48 (1951), 19-27.

GEER, William C., "Education of Mentally Retarded Children Fourteen Years of Age and Beyond," *American Journal of Mental Deficiency*, 56 (1952), 560-569.

GLANVILLE, A. D., "Psychometric Patterns in Industrial School Boys," *Delaware State Medical Journal*, 9 (1937), 91-94.

HACKBUSH, Florence, "Responsibility of the American Association on Mental Deficiency for Developing Uniform Psychological Practices in Schools for Mental Defectives," *American Journal of Mental Deficiency*, 45 (1940), 235-237.

HAFEMEISTER, Norman R., "Development of a Curriculum for the Trainable Child," *American Journal of Mental Deficiency*, 55 (1951), 495-501.

HARRIS, Leroy A., and KINNEY, Carolyn, "A Program for Reducing Maladjustment in an Institution for the Mentally Deficient," *American Journal of Mental Deficiency*, 52 (1947), 78-84.

HECK, Arch O., "General Problems of Philosophy and Administration in the Education of Exceptional Children," *Review of Educational Research*, 14 (1944), 201-208.

HUNGERFORD, Richard H., "The Detroit Plan for the Occupational Education of the Mentally Retarded," *American Journal of Mental Deficiency*, 46 (1941), 102-108.

————, "A Practical Program of Training and Service for the High Grade Defective and Borderline Group," *American Journal of Mental Deficiency*, 48 (1944), 414-418.

————, *et al.*, "The Mansfield Training Program," *American Journal of Mental Deficiency*, 56 (1952), 493-509.

INGRAM, Christine P., *Education of the Slow-learning Child* (Yonkers, N. Y., World Book Company, 1935).

JACOB, Walter, "Helping Teachers Recognize Some Mentally Retarded Types," *Training School Bulletin*, 48 (1951), 160-165.

JOHNSON, G. Orville, and KIRK, Samuel A., "Are Mentally Handicapped Children Segregated in the Regular Grades?" *Journal of Exceptional Children*, 17 (1950), 65-67, 87-88.

KELLY, Elizabeth M., "Organization of Special Classes to Fit the Needs of Different Ability Groupings," *American Journal of Mental Deficiency*, 48 (1943), 80-86.

————, and STEVENS, Harvey A., "Special Education for the Mentally Handicapped," *Forty-ninth Yearbook of the National Society for the Study of Education* (Chicago, University of Chicago Press, 1950), Pt. 2, pp. 237-263.

KIRK, Samuel A., "A Project for Preschool Mentally Handicapped Children," *American Journal of Mental Deficiency*, 54 (1950), 305-310.

————, "Experiments in the Early Training of the Mentally Retarded," *American Journal of Mental Deficiency*, 56 (1952), 692-700.

————, and JOHNSON, G. Orville, *Educating the Retarded Child* (Boston, Houghton Mifflin Company, 1951).

KLAUMINGER, Frederick A., and KILLE, Eleanor G., "Training Programs for Middle-grade Defective Children at the Southbury Training School," *American Journal of Mental Deficiency*, 51 (1946), 255-263.

MALZBERG, Benjamin, "A World Survey of Facilities for the Institutional Care of Mental Defectives," *American Journal of Mental Deficiency*, 53 (1948), 119-127.

MARTENS, Elise H., *Group Activities for Mentally Retarded Children: A Symposium* (Washington, D.C., U.S. Department of the Interior, Office of Education, 1933), Bulletin No. 71.

————, "Preparation of Teachers for Mentally Deficient Children," *American Journal of Mental Deficiency*, 54 (1950), 449-465.

————, *Curriculum Planning for the Mentally Retarded* (Washington, D.C., U.S. Department of the Interior, Office of Education, 1950), Bulletin No. 21.

MARTINSON, Betty, and STRAUSS, Alfred A., "Education and Treatment of an Imbecile Boy of the Exogenous Type," *American Journal of Mental Deficiency,* 45 (1940), 274-289.

MYER, Lester N., "Educational Therapy and Mental Deficiency," *American Journal of Mental Deficiency,* 54 (1950), 442-448.

O'CONNOR, N., and TIZARD, J., "Predicting the Occupational Adequacy of Certified Mental Defectives," *Occupational Psychology,* 25 (1951), 205-211.

OSTERHOUT, Edna Davison, *Teaching the Retarded Child at Home* (Durham, N.C., Seeman Printery, 1950).

PATTERSON, R. Melcher, "Organization of a Residence Unit for the Preacademic Training of Mentally Defective Children," *American Journal of Mental Deficiency,* 48 (1943), 174-178.

POLLOCK, Morris P., and POLLOCK, Miriam, *New Hope for the Retarded: Enriching the Lives of Exceptional Children* (Boston, Porter Sargent, Publisher, 1953).

ROEWER, William E., "A Program for the Trainable Mentally Defective Child," *American Journal of Mental Deficiency,* 56 (1952), 551-559.

ROSELLE, Ernest N., "Some Thoughts on the Administrative Organization of a Training School for Mental Defectives," *American Journal of Mental Deficiency,* 56 (1952), 524-536.

SCHIECK, R. R., "The Use of Experience Units in Teaching Mentally Deficient Boys," *American Journal of Mental Deficiency,* 46 (1940), 97-103.

"Segregation Versus Nonsegregation of Exceptional Children," *Journal of Exceptional Children,* 12 (1946), 235-240, a symposium.

SHANMAN, Leo, "Vocational Training for the Mentally Retarded in the Schools," *American Journal of Mental Deficiency,* 56 (1951), 113-119.

SHOTWELL, Anna M., "Effectiveness of Institutional Training of Highgrade Mentally Defective Girls," *American Journal of Mental Deficiency,* 53 (1949), 432-437.

STRAUSS, Alfred A., and LEHTINEN, Laura E., *Psychopathology and Education of the Brain-injured Child* (New York, Grune and Stratton, Inc., 1947).

TUDYMAN, Al, "The Financial Aspects of Teaching the Mentally Retarded in California," *American Journal of Mental Deficiency,* 55 (1951), 506-508.

WALLIN, J. E. Wallace, *Children with Mental and Physical Handicaps* (New York, Prentice-Hall, Inc., 1949).

WIENER, Bluma B., *A Preacademic Program for Slow-learning Children*, Supplementary Educational Monographs (Chicago, University of Chicago Press, 1949), No. 69.

WIGHT, M. A., "Teaching the Older Slow Learner," *Journal of Exceptional Children*, 12 (1946), 42-46, 56.

WILLIAMS, Harold A., and STEVENS, Harvey A., *A Public School Program for Retarded Children* (Madison, Wis., Wisconsin Department of Public Instruction, 1947).

WITMER, Lightner, *The Special Class for Backward Children* (Philadelphia, The Psychological Clinic Press, 1911).

The Mentally Deficient
Child Grows Up

AGE CHANGES IN THE APPARENT INCIDENCE OF THE
MENTALLY SUBNORMAL

FEW INFANTS OR very young children are considered seriously retarded. "He's only a baby yet; he'll be all right later on" is the comforting verdict of friends and relatives, even of the family doctor. The mongoloid child, it is true, can often be recognized as such at birth, and some of the other organic types, particularly cretinism, permit early diagnosis if they are examined by an expert. Although children may be known to be backward, the extent of their deficiency is not realized in the majority of cases before school entrance, particularly in those of moron grade. But the demands of abstract learning quickly show the mentally defective child for what he is, and modern methods of mental testing are likely to confirm the opinion of the experienced teacher or school principal. Thus it happens that although not more than one half of 1 per cent of infants and preschool children are likely to be diagnosed as feeble-minded,[1] approximately 2 per cent of school children have generally been found so wanting in ability to do the work of even the primary grades and of such low standing on tests of intelligence usually given them that the designation of mentally deficient, or, in Kanner's words, "intellectually inadequate," is applied to them. The proportions vary

[1] This figure, of course, does not include those in nursery schools or kindergartens where the same or similar criteria can be employed as those used for older children.

in different localities. In some schools, as many as 5 or 6 per cent will be found; in others, few or no cases. But when large and representative populations are considered, 2 per cent or slightly more is the usual figure.

What happens when school days are ended and the child who there was considered mentally deficient leaves his records behind him and moves out into the world of normal people, perhaps into a locality where he is not known? There are a number of possibilities here. If he is stable, good-natured, willing to work, and has a strong body or dexterous and nimble fingers, many occupations are open to him even though his mental age is no more than six to eight years, or even somewhat lower. Well do I remember one of my own early teaching experiences when I was urging a little Italian boy to make a greater effort to learn to read. "Rocco," I said, "if you can't read when you grow up, you won't be able to get a very good job."

Rocco looked at me with a gently patronizing expression. "My brudder," he informed me, "he no read."

"Yes," said I unwisely, "but your brother just works along the railroad tracks, doesn't he? If he could read, perhaps he could get a better job."

Rocco's patronizing look deepened. "My brudder," he announced with finality, "my brudder, he *boss*."

I know little of the mentality of Rocco's brother, but if it resembled that of Rocco it was not high. I do know that there are a fair number of men and women who today hold steady jobs, some of which even involve minor positions of authority, although when they were in school they were considered mentally deficient and were never able to progress byond the level of the lower primary grades.[2]

Despite the number of available jobs that make little demand upon abstract intelligence, and regardless of the good employment records of some whose mental abilities are unquestionably much below the minimum usually considered essential for normality,

[2] The modern custom of promoting by age rather than by accomplishment would, of course, change this situation as far as grade placement is concerned.

the typical feeble-minded child becomes an adult whose intellectual lacks, though judged by a different standard, are equally apparent. Nevertheless, in any formal survey, a smaller proportion of adults than of school children will usually be classified as mentally deficient. Penrose, basing his figures upon the report of Lewis to the Wood committee gives the following table:

INCIDENCE OF DEFECTIVES BY AGE GROUPS
(Figures derived from Tables 2 and 17 of the Wood Report, 1929)

AGE GROUP (years)	POPULATION SAMPLED (in thousands)	DEFECTIVES ASCERTAINED	INCIDENCE (per thousand in population)
0– 4	57	69	1.2
5– 9	57	882	15.5
10–14	58	1486	25.6
15–19	57	617	10.8
20–29	102	860	8.4
30–39	91	515	5.7
40–49	82	441	5.4
50–59	60	294	4.9
60+	59	170	2.9
Total	623	5334	8.6

At least three factors are responsible for the difference in the proportions commonly reported: (1) the use of different criteria with advancing age for classifying an individual as mentally defective; (2) the fact that some who were unable to get on in school and who, as children, stood so low on tests of intelligence that they were placed in classes for the mentally subnormal, nevertheless contrive to lead useful and respectable adult lives;[3] and (3) the somewhat shorter than normal life expectancy of the feeble-minded.

[3] Once more we see the importance of the factor of extensity of a given defect in the life of an individual. For the majority of the feeble-minded the defectiveness extends into many aspects of the personality. Their behavior is childish and unstable; if they secure a job, they soon tire of it and quit, or they make so many mistakes that they are dismissed. There are some, however, whose defect is largely confined to the area of abstract thinking and learning; in other respects, they do not greatly differ from the normal. As children in school, they are properly considered subnormal, but if, as adults, they succeed in finding a place in which their deficiencies are of little moment, whereas their good qualities count for much, they are almost certain to be looked upon as normal, if rather stupid, members of society. It follows that fewer adults than school children are likely to be considered mentally subnormal.

The last factor leads to an actual change in the distribution of persons of low intelligence with advancing age. All of the rare cases of amaurotic family idiocy die in infancy or very early childhood, usually before the age of three years. Benda has estimated that about 50 per cent of all mongoloid infants die before they have reached an age at which their condition is recognized as such. Among the *diagnosed* cases, the median age at death has been variously reported as twelve to fourteen years. Only a few live to reach maturity, though an occasional case survives to the age of fifty or beyond. Since about one pregnancy in 600 results in a mongoloid child, and since mongolians account for about 5 per cent of all recognized cases of mental defect, the early death rate of this group is in itself an important factor in lowering the life expectancy of the mentally defective as a group. This is not all. Most of the organic cases are inferior in physical as well as in mental status, and their average span of life is consequently shorter. Even the so-called exogenous cases, who bear no physical signs of their mental state, have somewhat shorter lives, on the whole, than the normal population. Those in institutions are likely to live somewhat longer than other defective cases, since they are protected from industrial and traffic accidents and from exposure to infectious diseases against which those outside the institution seldom guard themselves. Also, they receive more intelligent care with respect to diet and other matters having to do with their health.

For all these reasons, the distribution of the diagnosed feebleminded in any population differs from that of their normal contemporaries with respect to the proportions found at the various ages. Much of this difference is spurious, due to differing criteria or, as in the case with infants, to the lack of adequate criteria for making the classification. To some extent it is real, the result of the lower viability of the mentally defective, particularly those of certain types. If all were correctly diagnosed, the highest proportion of the mentally defective would be found in infancy; but because of the want of suitable measuring instruments for the younger ages, the highest recorded proportions are found for children of school age. Among adults the proportions again decrease, chiefly because of the use of differing methods of classification but also because of the differential death rate.

THE FEEBLE-MINDED INDUSTRIAL WORKER

In spite of the occasional stable and industrious worker who, having once mastered some particular skill, sticks faithfully to the same job for years, the typical mentally defective person is more of a clog than a cog in the industrial machine. He misunderstands or forgets the simplest instructions, damages apparatus and materials, and soon wearies of his job. He annoys other workmen by asking foolish or unnecessary questions or by constantly requiring help. As a rule, his employment is short-lived, but he often drifts about from one job to another for several years or even, at intervals, throughout his lifetime unless, as many do, he passes over into a life of vagrancy or becomes the tool of a group of criminals.

THE FEEBLE-MINDED DOMESTIC WORKER

With proper training, the moron girl learns to perform many domestic tasks. She may become an expert laundress or be able to dust and clean a room and arrange the furniture exactly as she has been taught it should be placed. She prepares vegetables and even learns to do simple cooking and baking. The fact that she rarely tries to improvise but works as she has been taught makes her a particularly valuable household servant, once she has been trained.

But there remains always the problem of her sex. In some cases, the difficulties are surmounted without much trouble, provided that the nature of the problem is understood and that the home in which the girl is placed is able to provide for her natural cravings for social pleasures and at the same time exercise a careful guardianship over her activities and friendships. But a child's mind does not afford sufficient protection for a woman's body.

Even if her own sexual impulses are not very strong, the unsupervised mentally defective girl is likely to become the victim of the unscrupulous. Sterilization does away with one of the unfortunate results of unlegitimatized intimacy, but it does not prevent prostitution or the spread of venereal disease.

Particularly if the girl is physically attractive, marriage is also a possibility to be considered. Sometimes such marriages work out well. If there are no children and the girl has been trained to be a good housekeeper and the husband is thrifty and industrious, there is no reason why a marriage of this kind may not prove as satisfactory as most. But children constitute a responsibility that few mentally deficient women can assume without disaster.

THE MENTALLY DEFICIENT PARENT

Every social worker knows the family for whom all efforts at help seem unavailing. Emergencies succeed each other in an apparently endless series. As more children are born, conditions become worse. The family is ill fed and poorly clad, the house may present a surface appearance of tidyness, but underneath, grime and vermin abound. Advice and material help alike are wasted; for the advice is rarely followed, and gifts of money or goods are soon squandered with little thought for the future.

Often the number of children in such a family is large, in spite of the high death rate resulting from poor care. Contraceptive advice or devices are unlikely to be used consistently and are therefore ineffective. More stringent methods for controlling the birth rate are needed.

The limitations of the defective mind are not adequately understood by the majority of people. If a man is steady and industrious and his wife well trained in domestic affairs, they see no reason why marriage and the successful rearing of a family are not reasonable and even likely expectations. But self-support is one thing; the support of a family another. Domestic work, when the tasks are laid out by someone else, is by no means the same as the independent planning and carrying out of the duties of a household. And when, to these duties, the care and management of small children are added, the responsibility is likely to be more than the feeble-minded girl, however neat and skillful she may have seemed when her tasks were laid out and her decisions made for her, will be able to handle unaided.

The financial problems of maintaining a home and providing for the care and upbringing of children are infinitely more complex and difficult than those of the unmarried man, who has only himself to consider. They increase greatly as the number of individuals to be provided for increases without proportional increase in the family income. Accustomed before marriage to having, as a rule, enough money for his simple needs, he now finds that his earnings are spent long before they are due, that he is saddled with a burden of debts that he sees no way of repaying. Yet he lacks most, if not all, of the comforts to which he has been accustomed. His home is dirty and cold, his food of poor quality and often insufficient to satisfy his appetite. The place seems full of squalling children. Under these unhappy conditions, some men merely subside into a state of hopeless misery, some take to drink as a temporary solace or turn to petty thievery by way of increasing the family budget. Others desert their families and so escape, at least until they unwisely take up with some other woman and start the whole miserable business over again.

For the wife, the situation is even more difficult. Often she makes a good start. For a time she may retain her former job and with the combined income thus afforded makes out very well. But the discomforts of pregnancy lessen her efforts at homemaking and later force her to stop outside work. This is a contingency but dimly foreseen and in no way planned for. It means a substantial lowering of the family income; added medical expenses; [4] some provision, at least, for the infant's outfit; and so on. The dismayed couple struggle with the problem as best they can, but further worries accumulate faster than they can cope with them. Other

[4] In many places, the major costs of the birth of a child are borne by certain social agencies in the case of families whose income is less than a certain specified amount. Some charges, however, must usually be taken care of by the individual family.

children follow the first; there is sickness and want. Small wonder if they become discouraged and cease to make even as much effort as they are capable of. Small wonder, too, if in helpless desperation one or both sometimes gives up the struggle and leaves home and family to shift for themselves.

What of the children in such a family? If both the parents can fairly be considered mentally defective, geneticists formerly believed that all the children would also be feeble-minded, upon the assumption that mental defect is a unitary trait inherited according to the simplest of the Mendelian principles. More recent work indicates that although there is little doubt that biological heredity plays a part in the determination of many types of mental defect, the principles involved are less simple than was once supposed. There can be no doubt whatever that no matter what their inherent intellectual endowment may be, the children who are born and reared in such an environment as we have described are given a poor start in life.

What is the solution? Sterilization of all clearly diagnosed cases of mental defect would undoubtedly help. It is a specious argument to point out that not all poorly managed homes are attributable to mental deficiency of the parents. It is equally specious to cite the occasional rare case in which exceptionably favorable circumstances have combined to enable two parents of subnormal mentality to create a home in which the children are apparently as well cared for as those whose parents are of average intelligence. A recent newspaper item told of a baby that was accidentally dropped from a fourth-floor window to a brick courtyard below and escaped with no injuries beyond a few minor bruises. But no one, on such evidence, would advocate throwing babies out of fourth-floor windows as a harmless diversion.

Opposition to the sterilization of the mentally unfit has been based for the most part upon emotion rather than judgment. The arguments commonly put forth are these: that procreation is a natural right with which no one should interfere; that any type of unnecessary mutilation of the body is morally unjustified; and, finally, that inasmuch as it is difficult, if not impossible, to be certain that any individual case is due to biologically heritable factors, the selection of those who should be sterilized for genetic reasons is so difficult a matter as to render it both undesirable and, in all probability, ineffective.

None of these reasons can be considered sound. The first disregards the equally great, if not greater, right of children to be born into an environment that will give them at least a reasonable chance of happy and healthy development. The second loses sight of the great benefits that surgery has given to the human race and in all probability involves an erroneous and much exaggerated view of the extent and danger of the operation, which, actually, is a minor affair for either sex and does not affect sexual intercourse. The third objection is based upon the mistaken idea that the only reason for preventing the birth of children in such a situation is the possibility that these children may be the victims of inherited mental defect. Actually, as has been pointed out in preceding sections, this is but one, and perhaps one of the less important, of the reasons for preventing procreation among the mentally unfit. Whether the children born of such parents are normal or feeble-minded, the likelihood of their having the kind of upbringing that should be the right of every child is small. The responsibility of children is too much for those of subnormal mentality to bear. There are a fair number of morons who, if properly trained and freed from all risk of having others than themselves to care for, will become useful though humble citizens; but more than this should not be expected from them.

The consistent use of contraceptive measures is too much to expect from those of subnormal mind. This has been amply demonstrated. Responsibility for preventing the birth of children in such cases must be taken by others who are better equipped to see the need for it.

There is increasing recognition of the fact that sterilization makes it possible to release from state institutions many cases who would otherwise continue to require public support. More than half of the states have passed laws to facilitate such measures.

Aside from the undoubted savings to the state and its taxpayers through reduction of the dependent population, it seems beyond doubt that the individuals thus released are benefited by the chance to lead substantially normal and self-sufficient lives.

With the rights of children in mind, and at the risk of criticism, I therefore propose the following program for all clearly diagnosed mental defectives who are not to be permanently institutionalized.

1. Careful training during childhood and adolescence with respect to attitudes, habits, and some form of useful work. If such training cannot be provided in the home and the public school, institutionalization and, later, release on parole may be the best solution.

2. Sterilization of all cases not to be permanently institutionalized before childbearing becomes possible.

3. Supervision by properly qualified workers. These workers should not be merely political appointees but should receive special training for their jobs. It should be their duty to help the subnormal to find and maintain employment and to see to it that they have suitable recreation for their leisure hours.

4. Marriage at an early age between the sterilized subnormal cases is desirable and should be encouraged. In this way they are permitted many of the satisfactions of normal life without assuming more of its responsibilities than they are able to handle. Often it may be desirable for both to remain employed, at least for a time, in order to keep up payments on home furnishings and possibly even to purchase a small home. Some continued supervision by the social worker is desirable.

REFERENCES

BALLER, Warren R., "A Study of the Present Social Status of a Group of Adults Who, When They Were in Elementary School, Were Classified as Mentally Deficient," *Genetic Psychology Monographs,* 18 (1936), 165-244.

BUTLER, Fred O., "Sterilization in the United States," *American Journal of Mental Deficiency,* 56 (1951), 260-268.

———, and GAMBLE, Clarence J., "Sterilization in a California School for the Mentally Deficient," *American Journal of Mental Deficiency,* 51 (1947), 745-747.

DAYTON, N. A., *et al.*, "Mortality and Expectation of Life in Mental Deficiency in Massachusetts: Analysis of a 14-Year Period from 1917 to 1930," *New England Medical Journal*, 206 (1932), 616-631.

DiMICHAEL, Salvatore G., ed., *Vocational Rehabilitation of the Mentally Retarded*, Rehabilitation Service Series (Washington, D.C., Office of Vocational Rehabilitation, 1950), No. 123.

GAMBLE, Clarence J., "Sterilization of Mentally Deficient under State Laws," *American Journal of Mental Deficiency*, 51 (1946), 164-169.

———, "Sterilization of the Mentally Deficient in 1946," *American Journal of Mental Deficiency*, 52 (1948), 376-378.

———, "The Prevention of Mental Deficiency by Sterilization, 1949," *American Journal of Mental Deficiency*, 56 (1951), 192-197.

HALPERIN, Sidney L., "Human Heredity and Mental Deficiency," *American Journal of Mental Deficiency*, 51 (1946), 153-163.

HILL, Irvin B., "Sterilization in Oregon," *American Journal of Mental Deficiency*, 54 (1950), 399-403.

JOHNSON, Betsy Scott, "A Study of Sterilized Persons from the Laconia State School," *American Journal of Mental Deficiency*, 54 (1950), 404-408.

LEWIS, E. O., "Report on an Investigation into the Incidence of Mental Defect in Six Areas: 1925-1927," *Report of the Mental Deficiency Committee* (London, His Majesty's Stationery Office, 1929), Pt. 4.

MICKELSON, Phyllis, "The Feebleminded Parent: A Study of 90 Family Cases. An Attempt to Isolate Those Factors Associated with Their Successful or Unsuccessful Parenthood," *American Journal of Mental Deficiency*, 51 (1947), 644-653.

O'BRIEN, Margaret, "The Occupational Adjustment of Persons Who Have Been Institutionalized," in *Improving Guidance and Personnel Services Through Research*, ed. S. A. Mamrin (Evanston, Ill., Northwestern University Press, 1946).

PENROSE, Lionel S., *The Biology of Mental Defect* (New York, Grune and Stratton, Inc., 1949).

———, "Propagation of the Unfit," *Lancet*, 259 (1950), 425-427.

STOWELL, Geraldine, "Mental Defectives and the Courts," *American Journal of Mental Deficiency*, 52 (1948), 256-269.

TIZARD, J., and O'CONNOR, N., "The Employability of High-grade Mental Defectives: I," *American Journal of Mental Deficiency*, 54 (1950), 563-576.

WEINTRAUB, Philipp, "Sterilization in Sweden: Its Law and Practice," *American Journal of Mental Deficiency*, 56 (1951), 364-374.

WELLMAN, Beth L., and STODDARD, George D., "The IQ's: A Problem in Social Construction," *Social Frontier*, 5 (1939), 151-152.

PART IV

Marked Inconsistencies
of Development

The Patterning of   18
Aptitudes and Achievements

IN CHAPTER 6 we saw that persons who show greater than average ability along one line are likely to display more than average talent in other lines. A corresponding relationship has been found to exist at the opposite end of the scale. The child who is backward in one respect is likely to show other deficiencies as well. There is positive correlation among inabilities as well as among abilities. In neither case, however, is the correlation so high as to permit no exceptions. Children differ in the pattern as well as in the level of their abilities. Some show special aptitude along one line; others along another. In the majority of cases, these differences are not so great as to interfere noticeably with the child's progress in a school system where all are expected to master a basic curriculum at the same rate of speed. Emily may find arithmetic especially difficult, George may be very weak in spelling; but most of the Emilys and most of the Georges will manage somehow to meet the minimum requirements in all subjects.

Aptitudes, however, cannot be measured directly. We measure the ability to perform certain tasks of known difficulty or the extent of knowledge about a given subject. Only the level of achievement is apparent to us; the extent to which differences in achievement depend upon differences in aptitude as such, and the extent to which they have been determined by differences in opportunity and in the particular experiences giving direction to interest, remains unknown. Of this we may be reasonably sure: early tendencies, regardless of their cause, are likely to become more apparent with the passage of time. They are like snowballs rolled in moist snow. The child who, either because of original aptitude or fortunate experience, does well in his early work in arithmetic usually receives praise for it; his work may be held up for the admiration of others. His pride is aroused, and he resolves to do even better work in the future. In like manner, the one who, for any reason, gets a bad start is likely to accumulate greater and greater distaste for this particular subject as time passes.

It is true that current educational practice, which aims at bringing all children to a common level of achievement in the basic subjects of the curriculum, tends to level out these differences in pattern to some extent. The laggards are urged, punished, given special tutoring to enable them to make up, at least in part, for their deficiencies; and the more able students are left for the most part to go their own way. Years ago, T. L. Kelley found that, on the average, children in the upper grades of the elementary school showed greater uniformity in their mastery of the various subjects of the school curriculum than did those in the primary grades. Whether this would remain true under the common practice of promoting children each year regardless of achievement, is questionable; whether it would have been true in Kelley's time had his comparisons been made by age levels rather than by grade levels is also questionable.

THE FACTOR OF INTELLIGENCE

As was stated in the preceding section, intelligence underlies other abilities to such an extent that the mentally superior are likely to be many-talented as well, and the mentally backward also appear to display many forms of inability. They are likely to be defective in speech, with poor articulation and small vocabularies. Their hands are clumsy, their gait awkward and heavy-footed. They have difficulty with most of the school subjects especially with those requiring abstract thought and reasoning or logical associations. Because of this general weakness along all lines, it has seemed best to exclude the mentally deficient from our consideration of children showing specialized handicaps, even though the backward, as well as the superior, do better along some lines and are more handicapped along others than would be expected on the basis of their average level of ability.

In this and succeeding chapters, children with specialized deficiencies are considered to be those who, in spite of approximately average or superior intelligence and freedom from physical defects of a kind that may reasonably be expected to have a bearing upon the condition in question, nevertheless exhibit some weakness that is quite out of line with their general level of achievement. Among these are the bright children who appear unable to learn to read or who lack the most rudimentary sense of numerical relationships and many speech defectives.

Specialized perceptual defects, such as color blindness and tone deafness, have been studied more from their theoretical interest than from the practical aspect of their effect upon the well-being or happiness of the affected persons. But there is also a group of nondisabling physical blemishes that may have as disturbing an effect upon the development of the child's emotional and social life as many of the overtly more extreme physical defects described in Part V of this book. A disfiguring birthmark or clothes markedly different from those worn by his mates may set a child apart from others almost as completely as if he were blind or deaf. The sense of being different, particularly when it takes the form of feeling inferior to others, is especially dangerous when this feeling is based upon some fact that is constantly being brought home to the child. The school child who cannot read the material that his classmates handle easily is embarrassed and discouraged by his ineptness. The child who cannot look in a mirror without seeing a disfigured face feels that others must hate the sight as much as he himself does; he avoids social contacts as he avoids mirrors.

Each of us has his own pattern of achievements and personal characteristics. These patterns differ for each, but in the majority of cases, the range of difference from one characteristic to another is of moderate length. For some, however, special deficiencies so marked that they are highly disturbing can be noted. In addition, there are rare cases who exhibit fairly marked special talents in spite of extreme general mental backwardness. Some of the more important of these specialized inconsistencies will be discussed in the chapters that follow.

REFERENCES

Committee on Social Adjustment, *The Prediction of Personal Adjustment* (New York, Social Science Research Council, 1941).

GOODENOUGH, Florence L., *Mental Testing: Its History, Principles, and Applications* (New York, Rinehart and Company, Inc., 1949).

HOLLINGWORTH, Leta S., *Special Talents and Defects: Their Significance for Education* (New York, The Macmillan Company, 1923).

KELLEY, Truman Lee, *The Influence of Nurture upon Native Differences* (New York, The Macmillan Company, 1926).

LEWIN, Kurt, *Principles of Topological Psychology* (New York, McGraw-Hill Book Company, 1936).

———, *et al.*, *A Dynamic Theory of Personality* (New York, McGraw-Hill Book Company, 1935).

WITMER, Helen, *Psychiatric Clinics for Children* (New York, The Commonwealth Fund, 1940).

Specialized Educational Inconsistencies 19

WHO IS TO BE CONSIDERED?

THAT INTELLECTUALLY backward children are almost invariably retarded in school is a well-known fact. Under the modern system of promotion by age instead of by achievement, they may not be retarded from the standpoint of grade location, but their educational achievements are almost certain to be far below that which is to be expected for children of their age. This retardation is usually general, embracing all the usual school subjects, though it is likely to be greatest in those demanding abstract thought and reasoning or the logical organization of material. It is least in those subjects depending largely upon rote memory or motor skill, such as spelling, penmanship, and manual arts.

We shall here make only brief mention of the child whose special educational difficulties arise from such obvious physical causes as blindness or deafness. Cases such as these will be considered in detail in Part V. Here we shall be particularly concerned with those children who, in spite of good health and at least average intelligence and generally good school work, find some one subject of the curriculum so difficult that they are wholly or nearly unable to master it. These are the nonreaders and the extremely poor readers, those who seem to be wanting in any real understanding of the relationships of numbers, those who seem unable to learn to write or to spell. There are also those who have great difficulty with some one of the informational subjects, such as geography, history, or science. The last-named difficulties usually arise from some emotional trouble or from poor study habits and are easily corrected once the basis of them has been uncovered.

THE NONREADER

For more than half a century psychologists and educators have been interested in the occasional child for whom all efforts at teaching reading seem fruitless, yet who, in other respects, seems bright and whose standing on intelligence tests not requiring reading may even be higher than the average for children of corresponding age. To this condition, in which the subject seems to be entirely incapable of organizing abstract visual symbols into meaningful terms, the name *alexia* was formerly assigned. Many of the earlier educators believed alexia to be congenital in origin and not susceptible to treatment or to training.

But others were doubtful. They observed that these children could recognize pictures. Why, then, could they not learn to recognize words? These workers were not wholly convinced by the theory suggested by the work of Broca.[1] This theory was that a word-perception center, analogous to the center for speech, exists in the brain, and that some children, otherwise bright, show defective function of this center. The theory was a comforting one, since it exonerated the schools from all blame for the failure of these children to learn to read. They could not learn, it was said, because their brains were crippled. "Too bad," said the relieved educators, "but we are not responsible."

Closely allied to the foregoing theory is that for which Orton and his colleagues are mainly responsible. Their theory assumed that all motor activities, including speech and reading, are primarily directed by one side of the brain. This lateral dominance is manifested in the preferential use of one hand and of one eye, usually the right, and in the less noticeable but observable tendency to lead with one foot rather than the other in walking or

[1] Broca found that there is a definite region in the brain that controls the ability to carry on verbal speech, an injury to which causes the condition known as *aphasia*, or loss of memory for words, with consequent inability to speak.

running. The exponents of this theory believe that when, for any reason, there is interference with the native tendency, as when a child is required to use the right for most or all of the functions for which he would normally use the left, serious interference with all language performance may result.[2] This theory has been much stressed in connection with stuttering and will be considered in more detail in the chapter dealing with speech defects. However, the idea that many cases of marked reading difficulties arise from a change in lateral dominance has also been advanced. The supporting evidence is even more shaky in the case of reading deficiency than it is in respect to stuttering.

Unrecognized visual defects are responsible for a good many failures to learn to read. In this connection, it must be remembered that better vision is required in order to learn to read than to continue reading after the skill has been acquired. The experienced reader makes use of many cues that enable him to respond to that which is not clearly seen; to recognize a total from which many of the details are missing. The beginner cannot do this. For him, all the *i*'s must be dotted and all the *t*'s crossed. An uncorrected visual defect, even a comparatively mild one, may become a serious obstacle to the learner.

A seven-year-old child was brought by her parents to a psychological clinic in the hope of ascertaining the reason for her lack of school progress. She was repeating the first grade, and now, as promotion time again approached and she was still completely unable to read, another failure seemed imminent and the sensitive little girl was, as her mother expressed it, "worrying herself sick over it." She had little appetite, and if breakfast was insisted upon as the family doctor said it should be, vomiting was likely to follow. Sleep was disturbed, and she sometimes cried out loudly at night. The family physician prescribed vitamins. At the advice of the school, the child had been taken to an oculist, who found nothing wrong. That *something* certainly was wrong, however, was attested by the child's pallor and deeply shadowed

<hr />

[2] The theory, of course, is based upon Broca's discovery that the brain center by which speech is governed is located on the left side of the brain in right-handed persons and on the right side in those who are left-handed.

eyes, the tense expression of her small face, and her nervous start
at any unexpected sound.

An intelligence test revealed an IQ of approximately 125. It
was noted at the time that this was probably too low since the
little girl's anxiety and intense desire to do well sometimes interfered with her performance.[3] Evidently the child had no lack of
mental ability; the reason for her inability to read lay elsewhere.

A very easy reading test was then offered. A look almost of
terror overspread the child's face, she flushed deeply and shook
her head. "I can't read it," she whispered.

"Try," the psychologist urged. "Just take it in your own hand
and look to see if there are any words you know."

Hesitantly the little girl took the paper in her right hand, then
shifted it to her left, later replacing it in the right. She peered at
the paper with an anxious expression, bending her head to one
side or the other and moving the paper slightly from side to side
or holding it closer to her eyes. Shyly she pointed out some half
dozen words that she thought she knew. Not all were correctly
named, but in each case there was a surface resemblance between
the printed word and that for which it was mistaken.

The parents were questioned about the oculist's examination.
The mother had been present and was quite certain that only the
Snellen chart had been used. The oculist, it developed, was an
elderly man, the only one available in the small town in which
they resided. "He was in a hurry," the mother added, "he was
going out to play golf. I didn't think he took very much pains
with Jean, but he said she was all right—her eyes were, that is."

At the advice of the clinic, the child was taken to a famous
oculist in a nearby city. His findings were wholly different from
those of the first. He discovered a rare form of retinitis, together
with astigmatism and slight myopia. Treatment was prescribed,
together with corrective lenses. The results were amazingly successful. Before the end of the school year, the child had made
enough progress in reading to justify promotion; and within the
next two years, she had made up for the year originally lost and

[3] A retest a year later yielded an IQ of 138.

was classed with others of her own age. Color returned to her cheeks, the shadows disappeared from her eyes, and she became once more the healthy, happy child she should have been.

Every child who cannot learn to read in spite of good intelligence and effort should have a thorough-going examination by a competent oculist. Not all cases of nonreading arise from poor vision, but the case just reported is by no means an isolated instance. Teachers, particularly those in the primary grades, should be on the alert to note indications of eye trouble in their pupils, especially among those who have difficulty in reading. The usual examinations by the school physician cannot be depended upon to catch all cases of eye defect, although they will identify many of the usual types. The teacher is in a good position to notice such things as the continual shifting of the material the child is trying to read in an apparent attempt to find a more favorable position. The book will be moved forward and backward, from side to side. Similar movements of the child's head can also be seen. Such movements often indicate imperfect vision.

Fernald, in common with others of her time, believed that each person has a certain sensory avenue through which perception is clearest and learning consequently easiest. Some people are "eye-minded"; others are "ear-minded"; still others are "touch-minded" or "motor-minded." The usual methods of teaching reading in the schools are well suited to the eye-minded and reasonably so for the ear-minded. Since these two groups comprise most of the school population, the great majority of children have relatively little difficulty in learning to read. But, said Fernald, there is an occasional child of good general intelligence who learns kinesthetically rather than visually. For him, the usual methods of teaching reading are likely to be ineffective. He needs to become conscious of the form of words through muscular movement.[4] So

---

[4] It may be of interest to note that before 1840 Bronson Alcott had actually employed a kinesthetic technique in teaching his children. When they were only two or three years old, he dramatized the alphabet, forming the letters with his body. The method is described in "Little Women" and appears to have been highly successful, since the Alcott children were keeping journals when they were only four or five years old.

Fernald had a group of children who had been unsuccessful in learning to read experiment with embossed letters and words or those cut out of sandpaper. They made big *A*'s and *O*'s in the air with their arms and traced words on the palms of each other's hands as a guessing game. Soon they began to master the idea of word forms and to learn to recognize a number of them. It was then not difficult to make the transfer from that which their muscles had learned to that which their eyes could see, and from then on, they were able to proceed in a normal fashion.

Although the basic concept upon which Fernald's method of teaching the nonreader is based has never been widely accepted, there is no question that her methods often succeed when others have been fruitless. However, the possible effect of interest and improved motivation must not be overlooked. The child who for months, and perhaps years, has struggled with what to him seem insoluble puzzles that he finds boring and completely un-interesting is suddenly given something that he can *do*. Failure is turned into success, and the self-confidence thus engendered is a tremendous aid to further learning.

Thus, although a generation ago alexia was believed to be incurable, the modern educator has learned that the nonreader of normal intelligence, whose brain is undamaged and whose vision and hearing are normal, presents a challenge. No longer can he be dismissed by means of a learned cognomen. Such children can learn and should be taught, though the method of teaching may require considerable ingenuity on the part of the teacher.

THE POOR READER

In spite of the large sums spent on education at the present time, in spite of better trained teachers, more attractive text-books and children's libraries, the number of students who pass through our public schools today and still read slowly and in-effectively is disturbingly large.

The methods proposed for improving the reading of the child who reads poorly are many and varied. There are mechanical devices designed to speed up the slow reader, photographic methods of analyzing his reading habits with a view to ascertaining where his main faults lie in order to direct corrective training more wisely, and diagnostic tests of reading for the same purpose. There are many ingenious devices for seatwork or for homework that are planned to improve the efficiency of reading.

Consideration of this problem would be beyond the scope of this book. It demands a volume by itself. Moreover, it is primarily a problem of general educational psychology, since the number of poor readers who can nevertheless read after a fashion is so great that such children can hardly be considered exceptional.

EDUCATIONAL DEFICIENCIES OTHER THAN READING

From babyhood the average child is constantly surrounded by number terms. Almost as soon as he can speak, attempts are made to teach him to count. Because adults seem to place so high a premium on his ability to enunciate certain words in sequence, he learns to say his "one, two, three, four," long before the terms have any meaning for him. In like manner, he learns to point to each of a series of objects as he says the words, though his finger often fails to keep pace with his counting. Although most children can count verbally at least to ten when they enter school, for many this has little meaning.

Occasionally a child is found for whom numbers as such never seem to take on real meaning. He learns to perform numerical operations by rule of thumb; he "solves" only problems in which the wording follows a familiar pattern. A student of my acquaintance who, by dint of hard work and a good memory, had maintained a position close to the top of her high school class was greatly distressed when her examination paper in plane geometry was marked zero by the instructor. She had set down the theorems and their demonstrations as given in the book, but, unfortunately, on the examination form the lettering of the diagrams had been changed. Of this she was quite unconscious, for she had never grasped the reasoning involved but had learned the material by rote.

The difficulties experienced by some persons in the comprehension of numerical and spatial relationships may, in the opinion of the present writer, be traced to one or more of the following reasons:

1. Getting a bad start. The child learns to memorize rather than understand and has little, if any, comprehension of the distinction between the two.

2. Promotion without learning. The child finds himself beyond his depth, and difficulty too great to be surmounted engenders dislike. Dislike leads to avoidance. As far as he is able to, the child dismisses the whole subject from his mind. In mathematics classes he is inattentive; his work is slovenly or is neglected in favor of other interests. This leads to punishment that deepens his distaste, and so his troubles increase.

3. In some cases there may have been specific experiences that conditioned the child against this or other subjects of the school curriculum. Unjust or unreasonable punishments, ridicule, or fright sometimes leave lasting results in their wake. Children have their bogies as well as their heroes. They avoid the one and emulate the other.

Not only reading and arithmetic but any one of the other school subjects occasionally seems to offer such insurmountable difficulty to a particular child that he makes little or no progress with it. There are children whose handwriting remains illegible in spite of all efforts to improve it; there are others who appear unable to learn to spell.[5] Lack of interest and lack of practice are apt to be mainly responsible here, although the child whose manual dexterity is markedly below average is obviously likely to have difficulty with handwriting. Poor handwriting and poor spelling frequently go together, since children quickly learn to cause the former to conceal the latter. Informational subjects, such as geography, history, or general science, are unlikely to show such marked cases of specialized deficiency as the four just mentioned since they are overlapped so extensively by everyday experience,

[5] As might be expected, the latter usually have more or less difficulty in reading also.

including the movies and television and conversation with adults. Children differ greatly in their liking for these subjects and in the extent of their proficiency in learning them; but among children whose lives and experiences have not departed too radically from those of the generality, some progress along each of these lines is almost certain to be made.

SPECIALIZED SENSORY DEFECTS

Some forms of color blindness have been recognized for almost a century, though many of its gradations and variations are matters of comparatively recent discovery. Most cases of color blindness date from birth, though the color sense may be damaged by ocular disease and is usually somewhat weakened in old age.

The completely color-blind person sees the world only in varying tones of gray. Actually, he is not likely to see it clearly, even without its glowing colors, for the totally color-blind rarely have normal visual acuity. The majority of color-blind persons lack the sensitivity for certain colors only. Many such persons cannot distinguish red from green. At first thought, it would seem that such persons could never be trusted to operate an automobile along crowded city streets. This, however, is not the case, if the individual is aware of his deficiency and willing to take special care to compensate for it by giving close attention to the lights, for the highway commissioners, aware of the number of persons with deficient color vision who may attempt to drive, have selected certain tones of red and green that to the color blind person appear to differ appreciably in brightness and have also standardized the arrangement so that the red light is usually above the green.

The color-blind person is barred from certain occupations in which a sense of color is needed, and he misses many of the esthetic pleasures that those with normal color vision enjoy. Apart from these matters, he is not seriously handicapped. Beauties of form are still his to enjoy, and if he knows what his condition is and recognizes the limitations it imposes, he need not be seriously inconvenienced by it.

Tone deafness, as the name indicates, is the inability to distinguish differences in the pitch or quality of tones. Like color blindness, it exists in varying degrees and may also differ in intensity for different pitches. Some partially tone-deaf persons can distinguish the low notes fairly well but have difficulty with the higher ones; with others, the reverse condition exists. The tone-deaf person is deprived of the joys of music, except for that which he may derive from its rhythm. His range of possible vocations, however, is but slightly curtailed.

Both color blindness and tone deafness presumably have their roots in some defect of the sensory organization. At present, there is no known method of correcting either.[6]

IDIOTS SAVANTS

For more than half a century psychologists have been interested in the fact that in spite of the usual correlation between general intelligence and special talent, which is high enough to render it extremely unlikely that marked disparity between general and specialized forms of ability will be found, rare instances of such disparity are known to exist. Many years ago Tredgold gave a fairly detailed description of such a case. The "Genius of Earlswood Asylum," as he was called, was an imbecile man, an inmate of an institution for the feeble-minded. This man had a marked talent for fine craftsmanship and spent his time making a wide variety of small objects out of wood, paper, and canvas. His models of sailing ships were beautifully executed, following in every detail the patterns with which he was supplied. Tiny houses, small objects of furniture, and many other things were carefully and lovingly constructed.

---

[6] This statement should not be taken to deny that both color sensitivity and perception of tonal differences can, to a certain limited extent, be improved by the kind of training that teaches the subject how to look and how to listen. But actual color blindness or tone deafness persists in spite of training.

In his *Psychologie des grands calculateurs et joueurs d'échecs*, Binet has described a number of individual cases who, in spite of mediocre or inferior general ability, showed remarkable talent along such lines as mental computation of difficult numerical problems or chess playing. Binet considered that the most important factor in these cases lay in the occurrence of some external circumstance that forced the child's attention and interest to take a single direction almost exclusively, and this at a relatively early age. He reported, for example, the case of a boy who, while still a child, was obliged to work long days in a coal mine. His task was to open a door for the loaded cars as they approached and to close it again after they had passed. All day he sat by the door in complete darkness, for he was allowed no lamp. In an attempt to find some form of amusement, he began to play with numbers, combining them in various ways. As the long years passed, he became more and more adept. Soon he began to display his accomplishments to the wonder and admiration of both children and adults. He discovered various ways of simplifying number combinations with the aid of which he was able to add mentally long columns of three- and four-place numbers as rapidly as they could be dictated to him. In other respects, however, he was ignorant and rather stupid. Binet pointed out that those who possess but a single ability have only one means of winning the admiration that all of us covet. Consequently, the ability, no matter whether its original appearance was due to an innate tendency or talent or, as in the case of the boy in the coal mine, was largely or wholly due to circumstances which made other occupation difficult or impossible, is likely to be increased through intensive practice. Most children have a reasonably wide number of avenues in which they can win at least occasional success; but for the idiots savants [7] as they have been called, the field of possible exploration is hemmed in, either by external conditions that are beyond their control or by their own inability to achieve success and win praise from those about them in any but the one way. Thus, although the average child scatters his interests and

[7] That is, "wise idiots."

activities over a number of fields, the idiot savant centralizes his activities and efforts along a single line which receives excessive amounts of intensive practice. So, in the course of time, a more or less spectacular ability may be achieved.

From time to time, other striking cases of remarkable performance along some one special line have been reported. Early in the present century a Negro known as Blind Tom attracted considerable attention by his musical ability. According to popular report, his talent was first discovered by the white woman for whom his mother worked. She found Tom, then a small boy, seated at her piano, picking out melodies with which he was familiar. Surprised at the accuracy of his performance, the woman began to give him some more or less systematic instruction, under which, in spite of the fact that he had been blind from birth, he made rapid advancement. After a few years, he began to give public recitals, and this he continued to do to the time of his death. His repertoire included both popular and classical numbers, many of them very difficult. He also possessed a remarkable musical memory. A customary feature of his recitals consisted in asking some member of the audience to play anything he wished Tom to reproduce. It is said that he would usually do this without error, even to the repetition of any error made in the original playing.

Blind Tom was an imbecile of low grade. He never learned to dress himself without help; his speech was indistinct and his vocabulary very small. In his case a single marked talent, rather than limitation of circumstances, seems to be the most plausible explanation for his spectacular achievements.

In the institution for the feeble-minded at Faribault, Minn., there is a young woman of imbecile level who possesses a talent similar to that of Blind Tom, though of a less pronounced degree. Like him, she will reproduce any simple musical selection after only a single hearing. Her repertoire of memorized musical selections includes most of the songs, marches, and dances popular with the other inmates. She spends much of her time at the piano, where her performances provide much entertainment for the other members of her group.

One of the most recently reported cases, together with a theoretical explanation as to the underlying etiology, has been given by Scheerer and Goldstein. They suggest that the idiot savant develops on a basis of a subnormal ability to deal with abstracts, combined with a definite gift (although perhaps only relative to his general level) in some performance field. These result in a subnormal intelligence and a narrowing of his interest in his environment to those concrete aspects which can be brought within the field of his talent. The concentration of interest leads to excessive practice, and this, in turn, to the astonishing performances of which he becomes capable.

Cases such as these, in which a special talent of at least a comparatively high order appears in an individual whose general level of mental growth is retarded, present a number of psychological problems that, if answered, would throw much light upon the entire field of mental abilities. What, for example, do we mean by the term *general intelligence* which we use so glibly? Is it a basic quality, essentially indivisible but manifesting itself in varying ways and to differing degrees; or is it a complex of simpler elements related in differing ways? Is the idiot savant merely a chance departure from the line of relationship indicated on the usual type of scatter diagram of a correlation chart? Can such cases be adequately explained on the basis of a simple chance accumulation of the factors making for lack of correlation between abilities whose relationship is less than perfect?

Examination of the available data for the cases thus far reported leads to one clear conclusion. Idiots savants differ, not only with respect to the character of the talent they display but also with respect to the major etiological factors which appear to have given rise to it. Here, as elsewhere, the search for a single and uniform cause that can account for all cases of this type can only be misleading.

SUMMARY

By the time of school entrance, children differ markedly, not only with respect to their general level of ability but also in the specific patterns of their abilities and in the likes and dislikes that underlie and overlay these patterns. Margaret is quick to learn to read but is slow in arithmetic; Jerry is talented in music; but Philip, who sits beside him, is unable to distinguish one note from another.

Exactly how these differences in educational talents have arisen is, in large part, a matter of conjecture, though their existence is a fact with which all educators are familiar. Kelley, among others, does not question the assumption that the pattern, as well as the level of ability, is the result of inherited tendencies or potentialities present from birth. Others take the position that early stimulation along specific lines, which unquestionably occurs in most homes, the special attention and praise that children receive when they do particularly well along some line in which their parents chance to be especially interested, may be enough to weight the balance of interest and effort in favor of these forms of activity while others, in which no encouragement has been given, are neglected. Thus, each child enters school with a fairly well-established pattern of interests and potential abilities, and this pattern is likely to become more clearly marked, for a time, through continuation of the same kind of specialized interest on the part of the parents. Later on, when poor reports in certain subjects begin to arrive, the parents may become concerned over the special subjects in which the child is weak; but as this concern is likely to be shown in the form of scoldings, punishment, or special coaching that encroaches upon the youngster's playtime, not much is likely to be accomplished. To the extent that differences in the readiness with which children master the various subjects of the elementary school curriculum are determined by differences in native talent, correction of the marked special deficiencies shown by some children becomes difficult. Even when persistent home conditioning is the primary factor involved, the negative attitudes thus established may not be easy to eradicate. Nevertheless, granted reasonable normality of mind and body, every child should be able to become sufficiently competent in the basic academic skills to meet his ordinary needs. The child who is markedly deficient along some special branch of learning needs most of all to have his interest aroused and his self-confidence in his ability to master the subject firmly established. He needs also to be given help in mastering the elements of the subject, to be given a good start. Often this can best be done by utilizing some new and different method of teaching. It is quite possible that the success which Fernald's method often appears to have with the nonreader derives mainly from the newness of the materials and procedures, which have the triple advantage of arousing the child's interest, stimulating his self-confidence by giving him things to do that he knows he can do well, and avoiding those materials and procedures against which he has already become strongly conditioned by previous failures. The printed page is withheld from the child who has learned only to hate and to fear it until, by dint of various novel and interesting exercises, he has become master of it.

The time is past when, if a normal child continued to show marked inability to learn some particular subject of the school curriculum, his deficiency could be conveniently ascribed to a special defect of the germ plasm. Now we ask not *whether* such a deficiency can be corrected, but *how* it can be corrected. The modern attitude, although it accepts inequalities in the readiness with which the various subject fields can be mastered by a given child, nevertheless holds that all subjects are sufficiently related to general intelligence to justify the belief that if intelligence is normal and the child is free from hampering physical defects, any of the elementary school subjects can be acquired, provided that the child is sufficiently motivated to do so.

REFERENCES

BARGER, William Calvin, "An Experimental Approach to Aphasic and to Nonreading Children," *American Journal of Orthopsychiatry*, 23 (1953), 158-170.
BENDER, Lauretta, and SCHILDER, Paul, "Graphic Art As a Special Ability in Children with a Reading Disability," *Journal of Clinical and Experimental Psychopathology*, 12 (1951), 147-156.

BETTS, Emmett A., *The Prevention and Correction of Reading Difficulties* (Evanston, Ill., Row, Peterson and Company, 1936).

——, "Reading Problems at the Intermediate Grade Level," *Elementary School Journal*, 40 (1940), 727-746.

——, *Foundations of Reading Instruction: With Emphasis upon Differentiated Guidance* (New York, American Book Company, 1946).

BRONNER, Augusta, *Psychology of Special Abilities and Disabilities* (Boston, Little, Brown and Company, 1917).

EAMES, Thomas H., "The Relation of Reading and Speech Defects," *Journal of Educational Psychology*, 41 (1950), 50-55.

FERNALD, Grace M., *On Certain Language Disabilities: Their Nature and Treatment* (Baltimore, The Williams and Wilkins Company, 1936).

GATES, A. I., *The Psychology of Reading and Spelling, with Special Reference to Disability, Contributions to Education Series* (New York, Teachers College Bureau of Publications, 1922), No. 129.

GILLETT, Myrtle Mann, "Seeing Defects in Non-readers," *American Journal of Ophthalmology*, 27 (1944), 1007-1010.

HALLGREN, Bertil, "Specific Dyslexia (Congenital Word-blindness): A Clinical and Genetic Study," *Acta Psychiatrica et Neurologica, Kjøbenhavn* (1950), Suppl. No. 65.

HARRIS, Albert J., and ROSWELL, Florence G., "Clinical Diagnosis of Reading Disability," *Journal of Psychology*, 36 (1953), 323-340.

HINSHELWOOD, James, *Congenital Word-blindness* (London, Lewis and Company, 1917).

ORTON, S. T., *Reading, Writing and Speech Problems in Children* (New York, W. W. Norton and Company, Inc., 1937).

PHILLIPS, Arthur, "Talented Imbeciles," *Psychological Clinic*, 18 (1930), 246-255.

REID, Gladys, "The Etiology and Nature of Functional Articulatory Defects in Elementary School Children," *Journal of Speech Disorders*, 12 (1947), 143-151.

SCHEERER, Martin, ROTHMAN, Eva, and GOLDSTEIN, Kurt, "A Case of 'Idiot Savant,'" *Psychological Monographs*, 58 (1945), 1-61.

SCHILDER, Paul, "Congenital Alexia and Its Relation to Optic Perception," *Journal of Genetic Psychology*, 65 (1944), 67-68.

SMITH, Linda C., "A Study of Laterality Characteristics of Retarded Readers and Reading Achievers," *Journal of Experimental Education*, 18 (1950), 321-329.

SOLMS, Hugo, "Contributions to the Theory of So-called Congenital Word-blindness," *Monatschrift für Psychiatrie und Neurologie*, 115 (1948), 1-54.

TURVEY, S. E. C., "Dyslexia," *Bulletin of the Vancouver Medical Association*, 26, No. 1 (1949), 15-18.

WELLS, Charlotte G., *A Teacher-parent Guide to Speech Training for Cleft Palate Children* (Madison, Wisconsin Bureau for Handicapped Children, 1944).

YEDINACK, Jeannette G., "A Study of the Linguistic Functioning of Children with Articulation and Reading Difficulties," *Journal of Genetic Psychology*, 74 (1949), 23-59.

Stuttering or Stammering 20

DEFINITIONS

WARREN, IN HIS *Dictionary of Psychology,* defines stuttering as "A disturbance in the rhythm of speech, either an intermittent blocking or the convulsive repetition of a sound." He does not differentiate between stuttering and stammering. The *Webster's New International Dictionary* definition of stuttering is "To speak in a hasty and stumbling way, with spasmodic repetition of syllables and consonants; to hesitate or stumble in uttering words; to utter with spasmodic repetitions or pauses." Stammering is "To make involuntary stops in uttering syllables or words; to hesitate, falter, or block oneself in speaking." It is further noted that the terms are in general used interchangeably, except that stuttering usually refers to a more marked degree of speech disorder than stammering. In this chapter we shall use the words in the sense just mentioned.

FREQUENCY

Almost everyone stammers at times. Excitement, embarrassment, or other emotional conditions may interfere with the speech mechanisms of those who usually speak normally. The effect of alcohol upon speech is well known. Lasting disturbances of speech which are sufficiently serious to constitute real problems of adjustment occur at some time in the lives of at least 1 per cent of the population and are from two to three times as frequent among boys as among girls. Practically every elementary school contains one or more children who stutter so badly that it is a constant source of embarrassment to them and interferes seriously with their personal and social adjustment. They try to avoid speaking whenever possible and shrink from meeting strangers.

An additional 2 or 3 per cent stammer at times, particularly if excited or disturbed. They have difficulty in finding the words they wish to use and frequently repeat the same word or short phrase and, at times, exhibit the same type of reduplication of initial sounds or complete blocking of speech that characterizes the true stutterer. Actually, there is no sharp line of demarcation between the stammerer and the stutterer. The difference is one of degree, not of kind, for the marked stammerer is also the mild stutterer.

AGE OF INCIDENCE

More than half of all cases of lasting stuttering date from the age at which speech is first established as a useful tool; that is, early in the third year. Of the remaining cases, the majority take their origin from around the age of six years; in other words, at the time of school entrance. A smaller peak in the age curve comes at the time of puberty. There are, of course, scattered cases beginning at other ages, but the vast majority of stutterers date their trouble from one or another of these three periods.

THEORIES OF CAUSATION

The three major peaks in the curve of age at incidence obviously represent three periods of unusual strain and stress upon the speech mechanisms. The first is a time when the child first becomes keenly aware of the potentialities of an instrument which he has not yet thoroughly mastered. His desire to speak, to convey his ideas to others, runs far ahead of his ability to do so. As yet, his articulation is likely to be imperfect; he struggles vainly to make people understand what he is trying to say. Often, too, at this time, he is urged to talk by overambitious parents who insist on parading his small accomplishments for the admiration of friends. The second major peak, coinciding with school entrance, is the time when many children first become members of large groups in whose presence they are expected to talk in more or less specified ways; they must answer the teacher's questions, repeat certain words and sentences. Faulty articulation may be publicly corrected, sometimes in a way that is acutely embarrassing to a sensitive child. This makes him keenly aware of the mechanical aspects of his speech; his attention is focussed upon *how he speaks,* rather than upon *what he says.* This division of attention is confusing. His thoughts shift back and forth from the idea he is trying to express to the external mechanisms by which he is to express it. He tries to place lips and tongue as he has been told, but the sound that he makes does not satisfy him. He tries again, and then again. And he stutters.

The third major peak in the onset of stuttering occurs in the early teens. Despite the fact that this is the age of puberty, it seems improbable that physiological maturation has much to do with the matter, although it is true that many children exhibit some indication of nervous strain at this time. The primary factor, however, appears to be social rather than physiological. This is the time when boy-and-girl parties first become really popular. To the majority of children this change from the gatherings of one sex, to which they have largely been accustomed, to those in which the sexes mingle and begin to experiment with love making comes easily and naturally. To a few it at once assumes undue importance and undue strain. They become self-conscious, fearful lest they do or say the wrong thing. They start to speak, hesitate, fumbling for just the right word. And they stutter.

It seems unlikely that age as such has any bearing whatever upon the onset of stuttering, in spite of the marked relationship to the age factor that practically all investigators have found to exist. Rather, it appears that there are certain personal and social factors that tend, at certain ages, to cause many children to become unduly conscious of the speech mechanisms. This leads to hesitation and sometimes to stammering and stuttering. No matter what other theories may be offered as explanations for stuttering, undue attention to the mechanics of speech, accompanied by uncertainty as to one's ability to operate them successfully, is one of the major difficulties with all who stutter.

The theory that an enforced change in cerebral dominance may cause disturbances of many aspects of language, including speech and reading, was mentioned in the preceding chapter. It rests primarily upon Broca's discovery that the control of speech resides principally in a certain small region on that side of the brain opposite to the preferred hand—the left side in right-handed persons and the right side in those who are left-handed. An injury to this center may destroy the power of speech in a previously normal person.[1] A number of investigators, notably Orton and his colleagues, have reported many more left-handed children among those who stutter than among normal speakers. Among right-handed stutterers, according to the claims of some of these workers, both case-history data and various instrumental devices designed to reveal natural hand preference indicate that at least a large proportion of these cases are really left-handed people who, by means of insistent early training, have been forced to use the right hand for most activities.

Not all investigators have accepted this theory. It has been pointed out that many of the reported figures fail to differentiate between the sexes and that, inasmuch as males greatly exceed females with respect to both the number who are left-handed and the number of stutterers, an excess in the former will necessarily mean an excess in the latter if the sexes are combined into a single table. Much of this apparent excess disappears when sex is held constant. In many persons, hand preference is not strongly marked, and the methods of distinguishing between sinistrals and dextrals among these cases are not very reliable. Thus, it may easily come about that those who favor the cerebral-dominance

[1] The loss of speech is rarely permanent. Apparently the speech center on the opposite side of the brain may take over the control formerly exercised by the destroyed center. Although the development of a clear-cut stutter is rare, speech is ordinarily much less fluent than it was before the injury.

theory tend to classify the doubtful cases in the way that is in agreement with their previously formed belief, and that those who disagree with it make the opposite classification.

All that we can say at present is that although the theory of cerebral dominance is no longer so widely accepted as a cause of stuttering as it was a few years ago, the possibility that it may be correct either in many or in a few cases has not been disproved. Since this is true, it would seem the part of wisdom to make no drastic attempts to change the direction of a child's natural tendency to prefer the use of one hand rather than the other. Inasmuch as the world contains a considerable majority of right-handed persons who have adapted its furniture, tools, and social customs for their convenience, it seems desirable to stimulate children to use the right rather than the left hand as far as this can be done casually and without insistence. The practice occasionally followed by parents of punishing or reproving children for the use of the left hand can hardly be too strongly condemned.

Some hold with Knight Dunlap that stuttering is just a bad habit, formed as other habits are and subject to like methods of correction. Still others consider it to be the result of attempts to speak too rapidly and urge the stutterer to speak more slowly. Case-history data indicate that stuttering may sometimes be precipitated by a severe shock, particularly great fright. One such instance known to me was that of a boy whom I first knew at the age of eleven, at which time his stuttering was as severe as any case I have known. According to his parents, this child's early speech was entirely normal up to the age of four years, when he had been knocked down and severely bitten by a large dog. His fright was so severe that he was unable to speak intelligibly for some time, and from then on, so said his mother, he stuttered. I have no way of checking the accuracy of this report, but it is in line with others cited in the literature.[2]

[2] This child was an Italian immigrant whose first acquaintance with the English language began several years after the fright and the onset of stuttering. It is noteworthy that throughout the acquisition of a moderate fluency in English, no stuttering occurred except when he spoke in Italian, when it was as severe as ever. No particular speech therapy was given him.

Daily association with others who stutter, especially at the critical age periods, may sometimes give rise to mild cases of stuttering or stammering. That really serious cases can be induced by this cause alone is questionable. Whether or not the tendency to stutter is a familial trait is also uncertain, although it is known that the number of blood relatives who stutter is somewhat in excess of that to be expected by chance. The possibility of unconscious imitation through close association must be excluded before a hereditary factor can be postulated.

Taking all the reported facts into account, it appears that stuttering may arise from any one or from a combination of many factors. As has so often been the case, the search for causes has been hampered by an attempt to find *the* cause, to make overly simple that which in its nature is complex. That undue parental concern with, and obvious attention to, the mechanical aspects of a child's speech during the formative period may lead to stuttering has been suggested by many. Wendell Johnson is a prominent exponent of this idea, considering that most, if not all, stuttering has parental influence as its major cause. The theory is given some support from the findings of Bloodstein and his colleagues that parents who consider their own children to be stutterers diagnose stuttering in children not their own substantially more often than do parents who do not consider their own children to be stutterers, even when the children being rated are considered by speech therapists to have entirely normal speech.

THE TREATMENT OF STUTTERING

Methods proposed for the treatment of stuttering are as numerous as the theories concerning causation upon which they are based. The explosive repetition of initial sounds often makes it appear that the child is trying to speak too rapidly and that what he needs is to be taught to speak more slowly and deliberately with closer attention to his enunciation. "Don't try to talk so fast; stop and think what you are going to say," urges the parent or teacher when the eager child is stumbling in his speech. Sometimes these admonitions, if given in a casual, good-natured manner that holds no hint of reproof, may be effective when the stammer has not become too pronounced or habitual. The important thing, however, is not the advice to speak slowly but to know in advance what one is going to say. As was mentioned before, the attention of the stutterer is constantly shifting from the content of his speech to the mechanics of speaking. The normal speaker, on the other hand, centers his attention on what he is going to say. He lets the mechanical aspects of speech take care of themselves.

The child who stutters habitually and to a marked degree is but little helped by such admonitions. His difficulties lie deeper. His stuttering has become inextricably bound up with his personality. He cannot think of himself in other terms. All his social relations are colored by the one inevitable fact. He stutters, and this makes people look at him and often laugh at him. If he tries to speak in a crowd of strangers, many of them turn to see who it is that talks in such a fashion and smile with amusement or joke with one another about it. He learns to keep silent.

No matter what other forms of treatment are employed, the restoration of self-confidence and emotional poise is essential if the stutterer is to regain normal speech. The importance of this factor has been particularly stressed by Blanton, who, in common with many other authorities, makes extensive use of relaxation exercises, singing, and reciting memorized selections of poetry. It is noteworthy that many stutterers, even severe cases, can sing or recite poetry without difficulty, although the same words, when occurring in ordinary speech, will all but throw the speaker into convulsions in his efforts to pronounce them. The combined effect of rhythm and complete certainty as to the exact sequence of words to be used appears to be the secret. The apparent effectiveness of rhythm suggested to some persons that accompanying speech with a rhythmic movement might help the stutterer. Accordingly, he was taught to move his arms up and down in a rhythmic fashion as if he were beating time to music, keeping the same rhythm in his speech. As speech improved, the movements would be gradually reduced in force and scope until, eventually, they could be discontinued completely. As is true of most methods designed to help the stutterer, some were helped by it, others were not.

Application of the theory of cerebral dominance, with its correlated assumption that stuttering results from an early enforced change in dominance as indicated by the preferred hand, has led to some curious practices. Right-handed stutterers were trained to use the left hand (assumed to be the naturally dominant one) for such sports as table tennis, handball, or tennis. They were instructed to write and eat with the left hand, to button and unbutton their clothing, and to handle objects of all kinds in this manner. They were assured that if they persisted in this practice until it became the easy and natural way of doing things, their stuttering would disappear. And oddly enough, in some cases it did.

Working upon the double principle that stuttering is nothing more than a thoroughly ingrained bad habit about which the individual has become unduly sensitive and self-conscious, Knight Dunlap proposed a method of treatment that at first thought seems to run counter to most of our current theories of teaching and learning. We say that "practice makes perfect," and we think of repetition as something that strengthens a bad habit as well as a good one. Dunlap did not deny this when the practice is carried on under ordinary conditions of motivation, but he came to believe that practice of a bad habit *when the attention is focussed upon a desire to correct it* is an extremely effective means of accomplishing such a correction. He first demonstrated this with respect to a typewriting habit he had formed. The word *the* was habitually written *het*. Over and over again he corrected the mistake, but the habit persisted. One day in exasperation he put a fresh sheet of paper into his machine and wrote an entire page of *het, het, het,* saying to himself each time, "This is wrong; I will *not* do this again." Nor did he. By the time the sheet was filled the habit had disappeared, never to return.

Dunlap was surprised and fascinated. He began trying out the method with other forms of conduct; he tried it with various small mannerisms in himself and others. Then, somewhat cautiously at first, he applied it to stuttering.

The stutterer was first assured that if he could learn to stutter intentionally he need not do so unintentionally. He was urged to examine his own speech and note the sounds on which he was most likely to have difficulty. He was to spend regular practice periods stuttering on these sounds and also stuttering over common words beginning with them. The more effectively he was able to stutter voluntarily, he was told, the sooner he would be able to avoid doing so involuntarily. At first, the subjects practiced their stuttering in private; but later, as they became more proficient and somewhat less sensitive, small groups were formed who stuttered for each other's admiration and criticism. Of those who honestly tried the method, a large proportion were benefited, and some were completely cured. Some, however, refused to try it, and a good many became discouraged and gave it up. Some failed to comply with instructions. An important feature of this method is the rule that while the experiment is in progress, no attempt to avoid stuttering is to be made at any time. If the subject finds himself stuttering, he should at once direct his attention to the task of stuttering longer and more violently than he would ordinarily do. This is a hard rule to follow, for it often leads to embarrassing situations. The embarrassment will lessen if the procedure is kept up, and the time may come when the subject is even able to laugh with the others at his own ridiculous performance.

Perhaps the most striking thing about all these and other methods that have been used for the correction of stuttering is that all of them have been highly successful in some cases, helpful in others, and useless in some. There is, as yet, no sure evidence as to which of the various methods proposed for the correction of stuttering is the most effective. The data are confused by a number of factors, chief among which is the conviction of each therapist that the etiological theory to which he subscribes and upon which his particular plan of treatment is based is the only sound one. The result is not wholly undesirable, for it unquestionably means that his conviction will be transmitted to at least some of the cases with whom he is working, and their resultant gain in self-confidence, with the corresponding loss of nervous and emotional tension, will almost certainly lead to an improvement in speech. As far as I am aware, there have been no well-controlled studies in which different groups of subjects of similar age, sex, and severity of stuttering have been treated by the same therapist in an unbiased attempt to compare the efficacy of the various methods that have been proposed. Until this has been done, judgment must be suspended. It is true that improvement and, in some cases, complete recovery sometimes take place spontaneously, that is, as a result of unknown factors. If this happens at a time when the child is undergoing some type of special treatment for his defective speech, this treatment receives unwarranted credit. However, the number of cases showing definite improvement after treatment is usually greater than can fairly be attributed to chance.

Two rules have emerged from the welter of theories, facts, and figures. The first is this: the child who stutters should never have his attention called to his stuttering. Above all, he should never be told to try not to stutter. He does try. With all his baffled heart and soul, with all his contorted body he does try. This very intensity of effort is one of the main factors that causes his stuttering. The normal speaker pays little attention to the mechanism of speech. The stutterer is preoccupied with it. The second rule is the converse of the first. Whatever special methods may be adopted for correcting the speech of the child who stutters, an essential feature of the retraining procedure must be the restoration of his self-confidence, with the effective assurance that he *can* learn to speak normally. At the same time, he must be brought to feel that, after all, his stuttering is not the tremendous handicap he has thought it to be, that other people pay little heed to it, that it is not so much how one says a thing as what one says that matters. Some teachers have found that during the retraining period older children may be helped by writing down what they are going to say and either reading it directly or reciting it from memory. But any device of this sort is a crutch which must be discontinued as soon as possible.

Improvement in stuttering means an improvement in personality, especially in that aspect of personality that has to do with the way in which the subject regards himself. Uncertainty, a sense of insecurity, especially in social relationships, anxiety and worry —any or all of these may become attached to the field of speech and give rise to stuttering. No method of re-education is likely to be successful unless it takes account of the stutterer as well as his stuttering.

REFERENCES

BLOODSTEIN, Oliver, JAEGER, William, and TUREEN, Jack, "A Study of the Diagnosis of Stuttering by Parents of Stutterers and Non-stutterers," *Journal of Speech and Hearing Disorders*, 17 (1952), 308-315.

DUNLAP, Knight, *Habits: Their Making and Unmaking* (New York, Horace Liveright, 1932).

ELLIOTT, Charles S., *Bibliography of Stuttering: Tentative Edition* (Evanston, Ill., The Book Box, 1951).

GLAUBER, Helen M., "The Impact of a Shift in the Psychological Constellation of the Family on the Treatment of a Stuttering Boy," *American Journal of Orthopsychiatry*, 23 (1953), 755-774.

GLAUBER, I. Peter, "The Nature of Stuttering," *Social Casework*, 34 (1953), 95-103.

———, "The Treatment of Stuttering," *Social Casework*, 34 (1953), 162-167.

GOTTLOBER, A. B., *Understanding Stuttering* (New York, Grune and Stratton, Inc., 1953).

HALE, Lester L., "A Consideration of Thiamin Supplement in Prevention of Stuttering in Pre-school Children," *Journal of Speech and Hearing Disorders*, 16 (1951), 327-333.

JOHNSON, Wendell, ed., *Speech Problems of Children* (New York, Grune and Stratton, Inc., 1950).

———, ed., *Stuttering in Children and Adults: Thirty Years of Research at the University of Iowa* (Minneapolis, University of Minnesota Press, 1955).

SHAMES, George H., "A Utilization of Adaptation Phenomena in Therapy for Stuttering," *Journal of Speech and Hearing Disorders,* 18 (1953), 256-257.

SHEEHAN, Joseph G., "Theory and Treatment of Stuttering As an Approach-avoidance Conflict," *Journal of Psychology,* 36 (1953), 27-49.

Speech Defects Other Than Stuttering

21

DEFECTIVE ARTICULATION

To a sensitive ear, the number of persons whose articulation is more or less imperfect is very great. For the most part, however, these small imperfections, although they interfere to some extent with the clearness and beauty of speech are not so marked that they are likely to cause misunderstanding. Most foreign and local accents are of this order. Mistakes sometimes occur, however, as in the case of the young woman from the Midwest who, at the close of a long day's motoring in New England stopped at a restaurant for refreshment. When the waiter brought the desserts, he paused at her place and said, rather hesitatingly, "Let's see, now, yours was apple pie, wa'nt it?"

Uncertain whether the waiter was trying to be funny or was merely stupid and too weary for politeness in either case, the woman snapped back, "Want it? Of course I want it. I ordered it didn't I?" The New England habit of eliding the s in "wasn't" was unfamiliar to her, hence the mistake was natural enough.

The number and range of specific articulatory defects is very great. There is *lisping*, in which the sibilant consonants are replaced by some other sound, usually *th*. There is *lalling* in which various consonants, particularly the *r* sound, are replaced by *l*. Other consonants that often give trouble are *f, g, j, th*.

A particular type of slovenly speech to which Blanton has given the name *oral inactivity* is characteristic of the mentally defective but by no means confined to them. As the name implies, speech of this kind results from insufficient movement of one or more of the organs of speech. Thus the vowel sounds are insufficiently interrupted for words to be distinctly pronounced. In pronounced cases of oral inactivity only a few of the "easier" consonant sounds are made. It is sometimes said that the child talks as if he had mush in his mouth. Thus, "I won't do that," becomes "I oh oo a."

Suppression of certain consonants is common in the speech of many persons. How many there are who omit the *t*, and often the first *n* as well, from the word *mountain*, or who substitute the sound of an extra *e* for the *a* in really.[1]

When one considers the complexity of the speech process, the surprising thing is not that so many people have difficulty with it but that any at all succeed in mastering it. The speech organs include the larynx or voice box, at the top of which are two parallel membranes, the vocal cords, tightly stretched to form a narrow slit through which the air passes in breathing. Sound is produced when these membranes are tensed, so that the passage of the air acts in much the same way as the wind in an aeolian harp. Variations in pitch result chiefly from changes in the tenseness of the membranes and the consequent change in the size of the opening between them. When the flow of air passes directly through the throat and mouth the sound *ah* is produced. Other vowel sounds are made by comparatively small changes in the tension of the throat and nasal passages (back vowels) or by slight rounding of the lips and tongue (front vowels).

Consonant sounds are made by interrupting the sound through some highly specific action of the tongue, teeth, lips, or soft palate, together with such movements of the cheeks and jaw as are required.

The larynx in the throat and sinuses (small cavities) in the

[1] It is not always easy to draw the line between mispronunciation of words merely from ignorance and the habitual mispronunciations that are considered poor articulation. In practice, the distinction is usually made on the basis of the readiness with which the error can be corrected when the subject's attention is drawn to it. The person with normal articulation will repeat the correct sound of a word that he has mispronounced after only a single hearing, but the one whose articulation is genuinely defective requires careful training and many trials before he can do this.

bones of the face also act as resonators that affect voice quality. The extraordinarily complicated nature of the actions involved in speech is apparent at once if one stops to examine the number of different sounds involved in a sentence that can be spoken in not over two or three seconds of time. Each of these sounds requires the co-ordinated action of two or more of the organs of speech and the organization of these sounds into a smooth running order in which some overlap but others remain distinct. The muscular adjustments required are delicate in the extreme; the difference in lip movement, for example, between *b* and *p* is almost imperceptible; yet it must be maintained if speech is to be clear. Timing must be equally as exact as the character of the movements of the speech organs. Small wonder that faulty articulation is so common.

Like stuttering, defective articulation is much more common among boys than among girls. With both sexes, the age of the child must be taken into account, for the normal child learns to articulate his words more clearly as he grows older. This, however, is a factor that cuts both ways, for too often poor speech is overlooked in the young child with the expectation that time alone will correct it, until long-continued habit has made the correction doubly hard to bring about. Children of normal intelligence should be pretty well free from habitual faults of articulation by the time they enter school. One of the most important tasks of the primary-grade teacher is to observe and correct the speech habits of the children under her care. Later on, such correction becomes more difficult.

FACTORS ASSOCIATED WITH POOR ARTICULATION

The greater incidence of faulty articulation among boys has already been mentioned. Why this sex difference exists is unknown. It may be just one more example of the generally superior ability of girls in fine-muscle activities. Boys do better in those requiring strength in the use of the larger muscles.

Negative home training—the encouragement of "baby talk"

even to the extent of its use by the parents themselves—is a handicap to which many children are unfortunately subjected. Although in the majority of cases the infantile speech is corrected when the child leaves the limited environment of the home for the wider social life of playground and schoolroom, not all free themselves of the early habits so easily.

That twins, particularly those of like sex, are likely to be somewhat retarded in all forms of language development has been observed by a number of investigators. Using the method developed by McCarthy, Day found a considerable retardation in respect to the mean length of the sentences used by twins of preschool age, as well as a far greater percentage of incomprehensible responses than in the conversation of children of similar age and social status who were born singly. Employing the same method with children of school age, and extending the study to include "only" children, Davis found a marked superiority in all aspects of language development among the "only" children as compared either to the singly born in larger families, or to the twins, who, in conformity to the findings of other investigators, ranked lower than either of the other two groups studied, particularly with respect to articulation. Speech is learned by imitation. The totally deaf child does not learn to speak by means of the ordinary channels, because the models that the hearing child imitates are not perceptible to him. The child whose mother sees a "itty bitty moo-moo" by the roadside, who is put to "beddy-bye" at night and given "beddy-buttah" to eat the next morning, can scarcely be blamed for his incorrect speech.

Children imitate the speech of their associates as well as that of their elders. Those who spend much of their time in the company of other children whose speech is less well developed than their own are likely to be less advanced in linguistic development and to speak less distinctly than those who associate chiefly with those whose speech is superior. Of this, twins provide a striking example. Twins play together, as a rule, for a far greater proportion of their waking hours than do other children. They talk together, and they imitate each other's speech. Occasional cases have been reported of twins who developed a language of their own, comprehensible to each other but to no one else. These "languages," however, are usually less original than they seem. They consist, as a rule, of a series of letter substitutions common to the language of both twins. Because language retardation and, particularly, poor articulation are so frequently found among twins, parents should observe the speech of their twin children with unusual care and should make special effort to see that a reasonable amount of the children's time is spent in the company of persons whose speech habits are, if not completely mature, at least well in advance of those of the twins. Not all twins are retarded in language. None need be merely because he chances to be a twin.

That defects in the organs of speech may give rise to defective articulation is obvious. Such defects include hare lip, with the cleft palate that usually accompanies this condition; misshapen jaws or seriously malformed teeth; occluded nasal passages; and so on through a long list of malformations. Most of these can be corrected or at least greatly ameliorated by the proper orthodontal work or by surgery.

A generation ago, it was commonly believed that many, if not most, cases of defective articulation were caused by too short a *frenum* (the membrane by which the tongue is attached to the lower jaw). Such cases were said to be "tongue-tied," and the usual remedy was to clip the membrane so that the tongue could have freer play. But the results of this operation were rarely as good as was hoped. Now it is recognized that although occasional cases of speech deficiency do result from too short a frenum, these instances are rare.

Minor defects of hearing account wholly or in part for many cases of defective articulation. The child does not hear distinctly and so he speaks indistinctly. To the partially deaf certain sounds often present special difficulties of hearing. Some have particular difficulty with the sibilants; they are likely to lisp. The hearing of all children should be checked as a matter of routine; but those whose speech is defective require much more than a routine examination in order to make sure that a hearing loss is not at least a partial cause of the speech deficiency.

Although physical causes in the form of defective hearing, in some deficiency or malformation of the organs of speech, or as a result of brain damage unquestionably play a part in many cases of defective articulation, examination of the data for large numbers of such cases leads to the conclusion that the early formation of faulty speech habits far outweighs all other factors in the etiology of defective speech.

CORRECTIVE TRAINING

The child whose articulation is poor requires, first of all, a thorough examination by properly qualified experts in order to make sure that his hearing and speech organs are normal. Hasty examination by busy school physicians is not enough.

Home conditions should be ascertained. Is the speech of the parents clear and distinct? Do they employ normal speech when addressing the child?

The correction of faulty articulation in the child who is physically normal is usually a much easier task than is the correction of stuttering. One problem that must always be faced by the therapist is that of making the child so conscious of his speech that he may begin to stutter. As was pointed out in the preceding chapter, undue self-consciousness that is specifically directed toward the area of speech is one of the main causes of stuttering, and this must be avoided at all costs. The interest and efforts of the child must be directed toward the improvement of his speech without causing him to worry about it. Many successful therapists succeed in turning speech correction into a game. By the use of mirrors, the child is able to see the position of his tongue and lips. Successful repetitions of difficult words count toward his score. Errors are overlooked but receive no credit. As skill improves, the "hard" words are incorporated into sentences; the child has to watch out for them.

Here, as in the correction of stuttering, the personality of the therapist presumably counts for more than the particular method of correction or the theory upon which the method is based. In both cases the most important element in bringing about improvement is the development of a proper attitude toward his speech in the child himself. The stutterer directs too much, the child with defective articulation too little attention toward the form of his speech. A change in this attitude is the first and most important aspect of corrective speech therapy.

OTHER FORMS OF LANGUAGE DYSFUNCTION

Mutism in children whose hearing and intelligence are normal is a rare manifestation of extreme emotional disturbance. As a rule, it is one of the manifestations of juvenile schizophrenia.

Motor aphasia, if genuine, is the result of an injury to the speech center in the brain, known as the region of Broca. In motor aphasia, the patient, although he maintains normal or near normal comprehension of speech, loses his ability to speak. He no longer knows how words are formed. For the same reason, he is no longer able to write, for he does not know how to spell the words. He may be able to communicate to a limited extent by means of signs; he nods or shakes his head in reply to a question and indicates his needs by means of other simple signs. But he cannot speak. Recovery from the injury is marked by the gradual return of speech. At first, the patient is able only to repeat words or short phrases that are said to him; or perhaps he becomes able to sing some of the songs that he knew before the accident occurred. Very slowly he regains the ability to use speech as a means of communication, but his articulation is likely to be imperfect, and there will be frequent blocking when the particular words that he wishes to use cannot be brought back to memory. If the original injury was severe, it is unlikely that complete recovery will occur, although the speech may become so nearly normal that the defect is no longer a serious handicap.

Sensory aphasia, like motor aphasia results from an injury to the speech center, but in this case, although the power to speak is little, if at all, impaired and the patient retains his ability to hear sounds, he is no longer able to understand words, either in spoken or in written form. Sensory aphasia, however, does not often occur in this isolated or pure form. It is more likely to be an accompaniment of motor aphasia, in which case neither the understanding nor the use of speech is retained.

These and other rare forms of language disturbance are problems for the neurologist, the psychiatrist, and the clinical psychologist to work out in collaboration through careful study of each individual case. Fortunately, their number is small, and because of the severity of the symptoms it is unlikely that the classroom teacher or the school psychologist will ever encounter them.

REFERENCES

ALLEN, I. M., "The History of Congenital Auditory Imperception," *New Zealand Medical Journal,* 51 (1952), 239-247.

American Speech and Hearing Association, *Speech Problems of Children,* ed. Wendell Johnson (New York, Grune and Stratton, Inc., 1950).

American Speech and Hearing Association Committee on the Midcentury White House Conference, "Speech Disorders and Speech Correction," *Journal of Speech and Hearing Disorders,* 17 (1952), 129-137.

ANASTASI, Anne, and CORDOVA, Fernando A., "Some Effects of Bilingualism upon the Intelligence Test Performance of Puerto Rican Children in New York City," *Journal of Educational Psychology,* 44 (1953), 1-19.

ANDERSON, Virgil A., *Improving the Child's Speech* (New York, Oxford University Press, 1953).

BACKUS, Allie, and BEASLEY, Jane, *Speech Therapy with Children* (Boston, Houghton Mifflin Company, 1951).

BERKO, Martin J., "Mental Evaluation of the Aphasic Child," *American Journal of Occupational Therapy,* 5 (1951), 241-266.

CARRELL, James A., and BANGS, Jack L., "Disorders of Speech Comprehension Associated with Idiopathic Language Retardation," *The Nervous Child,* 9, No. 1 (January, 1951), 64-75.

DARCY, Natalie T., "A Review of the Literature on the Effects of Bilingualism upon the Measurement of the Intelligence," *Journal of Genetic Psychology,* 82 (1953), 21-57.

EVERHART, Rodney W., "The Relationship Between Articulation and Other Developmental Factors in Children," *Journal of Speech and Hearing Disorders,* 18 (1953), 332-338.

GOLDENBERG, Samuel, "An Exploratory Study of Some Aspects of Idiopathic Language Retardation," *Journal of Speech and Hearing Disorders,* 15 (1950), 221-233.

HAWK, Sara Stinchfield, "Helping the Child with Delayed Speech," *American Academy of General Practice,* 3 (1951), 43-49.

HOFFMAN, Jeanette Anderson, "Training of Children with Aphasic Understanding," *The Nervous Child,* 9, No. 1 (January, 1951), 85-88.

JELLINEK, Augusta, "Understanding of Speech," *The Nervous Child,* 9, No. 1 (January, 1951), 15-20.

JOHNSON, Wendell, "To Help the Child with a Speech Handicap," *Child,* 15 (1950), 12-14.

MEYERS, Russell, and MEYERS, Mary E., "Adjustment Problems of the Aphasic Child," *Crippled Child,* 28, No. 6 (1951), 10-11, 28.

MYKLEBUST, Helmer R., "Aphasia in Children," *Journal of Exceptional Children,* 19 (1952), 9-14.

NELSON, Oliver W., "An Investigation of Certain Factors Relating to the Nature of Children with Functional Defects of Articulation," *Journal of Educational Research,* 47 (1953), 211-216.

PALMER, Martin F., and BERKO, Francis, "The Education of the Aphasic Child," *American Journal of Occupational Therapy,* 6 (1952), 241-246.

PEACHER, William G., "Neurological Factors in the Etiology of Delayed Speech," *Journal of Speech and Hearing Disorders,* 14 (1949), 147-161.

———, "The Neurological Evaluation of Delayed Speech," *Journal of Speech and Hearing Disorders,* 14 (1949), 344-352.

RAUBICHECK, Letitia, *Speech Improvement* (New York, Prentice-Hall, Inc., 1952).

SLAUGHTER, Wayne B., and PHAIR, Gretchen Mueller, "A Complete Cleft Palate Program," *Journal of Speech and Hearing Disorders,* 17 (1952), 123-128.

SUGAR, Oscar, "Congenital Aphasia: An Anatomical and Physiological Approach," *Journal of Speech and Hearing Disorders,* 17 (1952), 301-304.

TEMPLIN, Mildred C., "Norms on a Screening Test of Articulation for Ages Three Through Eight," *Journal of Speech and Hearing Disorders,* 18 (1953), 323-330.

VAN GELDER, D. W., KENNEDY, L., and LAGUAITE, J., "Congenital and Infantile Aphasia," *Pediatrics*, 9 (1952), 48-54.

WEISS, Deso A., "Organic Lesions Leading to Speech Disorders," *The Nervous Child*, 7, No. 1 (January, 1948), 29-37.

———, "Speech in Retarded Children," *The Nervous Child*, 9, No. 1 (January, 1951), 21-30.

PART V

The Physically Handicapped Child

Children with Sensory Handicaps: The Blind

22

A DIFFERENCE IN MODE OR A DIFFERENCE IN INTENSITY?

As WAS EARLIER pointed out, some individuals are exceptional principally in the *degree* of their difference from the average, whereas others possess some significant peculiarity which, in general, is not shared at all by the majority. This latter group of exceptional children is largely composed of those who are physically handicapped. At first glance, it might seem that blind or deaf children, for example, belong to the former group; those who are merely "poor-sighted" or "hard of hearing" certainly belong to it. However, those individuals who, from birth or from a very early age, lack vision or hearing to such an extent that these senses cannot play any significant part in the development of their subjective worlds, to whom visual concepts are not matters of direct experience, or to whom sound, at best, is a tactile sensation, surely differ qualitatively rather than quantitatively from the normal child. Even though it is possible to consider them as standing at the extremes of continuous distributions of sensory acuteness, our present knowledge of the course and nature of the normal development of the mind leads to the belief that sight and hearing are each so deeply involved in this development that in the absence of either sense mental development does not proceed along precisely the same lines as it does in the normal child. Even with the best training now available—and, it may fairly be suggested, even with training as ideal as we can now visualize—the world of the congenitally blind or deaf must remain, in many aspects, a world

qualitatively different from that of the child who can see and
hear. This is not so in the case of a child whose hearing or vision,
although deficient, still functions usably. Such a child can have
direct visual and aural experience; his perceptions are limited, as
compared to the normal, but remain similar in nature. Because
of this difference, the blind and deaf will be discussed separately
from, and at greater length than, those who possess defective but
functioning vision and hearing.

THE DEVELOPMENT OF AID TO THE BLIND

In a primitive society the blinded adult may be able to adjust
for survival; it is doubtful whether a child, congenitally blind or
blinded in infancy, would be able to do so except under unusual
circumstances. Occasional references to blind individuals occur
in very early records. More recently, there has developed an increasing concern over the blind, manifesting itself, first, in chari-
table provisions for their care and, later, in attempts to help them
become self-supporting. The first efforts to provide vocational
training or general education were, of course, on an individual
basis, and there was little carry-over of information on subjects
or methods from one case to another. However, in 1785, in Paris,
Valentin Hauy opened the National Institution for the Young
Blind. This first attempt at organized education for the blind
attracted much attention, and its example was soon followed elsewhere. In 1791, Edward Rushton, himself blinded in adulthood,
founded the first school for the blind in Great Britain in Liverpool.
In 1826, Dr. John D. Fisher, returning to the United States after
medical work in France, began the efforts which led to the establishment in 1829 of the New England Asylum for the Blind, which
is now known as the Perkins Institute and Massachusetts School
for the Blind. Dr. Samuel Gridley Howe was its first head, and
after a trip to Europe to acquaint himself with the latest methods
and to find the nucleus of a trained staff, he began active work in
1832. A few months earlier, Dr. John D. Russ had begun work in
New York City under the auspices of the New York Institute for

the Education of the Blind, and, in the following year, what is now the Overbrook School for the Blind was founded in Philadelphia by the Society of Friends. These three schools were, and have continued to be, private institutions; state-supported schools were soon founded in a number of states.

In addition to the schools, which center their attention on the education of blind individuals, a number of organizations have concentrated on helping the blind, once trained, to find places in the outside world and on providing such help as may be needed in carrying on a reasonably normal life. In this group might be mentioned such organizations as the Industrial Home for the Blind in Brooklyn, N.Y., the New York Association for the Blind, the American Foundation for the Blind, various groups providing guide dogs, and the publishing organizations which produce and distribute special books and magazines.

Both state and federal governments provide further aid for the blind, particularly for those who remain at home, through help in learning to read and write Braille; in obtaining reading material and special equipment, such as Braille watches; in social-security and tax-law provisions; and in a number of other ways. The Library of Congress is responsible for the preparation and distribution of much Braille material and of the Talking Book machines and records.

WHO IS BLIND?

A complete lack of vision is easy enough to define. However, the lower limit of useful vision is a relatively variable matter, depending to a great extent on the nature of the use involved. At present, those individuals whose visual acuity is less than 20/200 in the better eye, after correction, or those whose visual field is limited to a maximum angular diameter of 20 degrees are classed as legally blind. Zahl gives the following as the best available values for the number and age distribution of blind persons in the United States in 1940:

AGE DISTRIBUTION OF THE BLIND *

Age	Number of Cases	Per cent of total
under 5 years	1,094	0.5
5—19 years	8,390	3.7
20—59 years	76,205	33.1
60 years and over	144,311	62.7
	230,000	

* From Paul A. Zahl, *Blindness* (Princeton, Princeton University Press, 1950). The total given here represents an over-all incidence of blindness of slightly less than 0.2 per cent.

CAUSES OF BLINDNESS

In any given case, it may be very simple to determine the cause of blindness; when the whole group of blind is under consideration, no over-all description of causes is of any great value, because in the rapidly changing state of medical knowledge and practice over the last few decades, several causes of blindness which were formerly very important have been largely eliminated, and at least one substantially new one—*retrolental fibroplasia* [1]— has developed. For example, 50 years ago, *ophthalmia neonatorum* [2] was responsible for as much as 25 per cent of the cases of blindness in children; today it is a rare occurrence in infants.[3] On the other hand, as mentioned above, retrolental fibroplasia was not recognized at all until very recently. It is now stated to affect something like 10 per cent or more of the survivors among extremely premature births (weight under 1500 grams at birth), or a total of between 400 and 500 children each year. The incidence, however, is extremely variable from one hospital to another. There is some evidence that the use of oxygen in incubators for the prematures is at least an important contributing cause of this condition. Much research on the subject is currently going on, and we may hope that within not too many years a method of handling

[1] Retrolental fibroplasia is an abnormal growth of fibrous tissue behind the crystalline lens of the eye.

[2] Ophthalmia neonatorum is an acute inflammation of the conjunctiva in the newborn caused by a gonorrheal infection acquired from the mother during the birth process.

[3] See p. 321.

these tiny infants will be found which will largely avoid the danger of blindness from this cause without impairing their chances of survival.

These and other very striking changes in the known causes of juvenile blindness mean that any listing of causes in the order of importance is true only for the particular age group under consideration and may probably not hold true for even the same age groups a few years hence. This is strikingly evident if we compare the distribution of four types of causes (as given by Zahl) for two sets of ages:

PERCENTAGE DISTRIBUTION OF CASES OF BLINDNESS
BY CAUSE

	Disease	Injury	Congenital or Prenatal	Uncertain
Social Security Board, 1940-1941 (cases mostly over 20 years old)	30	10	10	50
Schools for the Blind, 1942-1943 (cases 5-25 years old)	27	7	54.5	11.4

If we eliminate the cases of uncertain etiology, the differences in importance of the other three types of causes become even more striking:

PERCENTAGE DISTRIBUTION OF BLINDNESS BY CAUSE

	Disease	Injury	Congenital or Prenatal
Social Security Board	60	20	20
Schools for the Blind	30.5	8	61.5

For children in this country today, then, injury, accounting for less than 10 per cent of the cases, is a comparatively unimportant cause of blindness. Disease accounts for about one third of the cases. The diseases most commonly causing blindness in the past were trachoma, ophthalmia neonatorum, maternal gonorrheal infection, and syphilis. Less important were measles, scarlet fever, meningitis, diphtheria, and a number of other infections. Most of these are currently preventable; their importance as causes of blindness in children should continue to decrease with more wide-spread medical care and, in the case of syphilis and gonorrhea, a stricter adherence to the practice of careful examination of all pregnant women and adequate treatment of both mother and child whenever infection is found. The use of silver nitrate solution in the eyes of all newborns, as is legally required by many states, has virtually eliminated blindness caused by gonorrheal infections.

A number of noninfectious diseases may also cause blindness. Most of these are found much more frequently in the older age groups than in children. Juvenile diabetes and neoplastic growths are two noninfectious causes of blindness which tend to be more common in the years beyond early childhood but may nevertheless be found in some very young children.

Congenital and hereditary conditions are by far the most important causes of blindness among children. Developmental failure of the eyes or the optic nerve, anomaly of the skull (oxycephaly), *congenital glaucoma* (buphthalmia),[4] and congenital cataracts may all result in blindness from birth. Several conditions are known in which a congenital condition causes loss of sight later in life (Leber's hereditary optic atrophy, *macular dystrophies*,[5] *retinitis pigmentosa*.)[6] Albinism is usually associated with markedly deficient vision. Retrolental fibroplasia, as previously stated, is now generally believed to be caused by one or more factors in the treatment of the premature infant, although it also seems clear that the stage of development of the infant's eyes is such as to make them, by comparison with those of the child born at term, abnormally susceptible to this particular type of injury. Congenital cataract is thought, in many cases, to be the result of maternal disease, usually rubella, during the early months of pregnancy. These last two conditions, then, are practically unique among the congenital and hereditary group in that it appears

---

[4] Glaucoma is a disease caused by an increase of the amount of fluid in the eyeball; the raised intraocular pressure causes opacity of the crystalline lens.

[5] Macular dystrophy is a disease in which part of the cornea degenerates.

[6] Retinitis pigmentosa is a chronic, progressive inflammation of the retina, accompanied by atrophy and pigmentary infiltration of its inner layer.

possible that we may soon be in a position to reduce their importance sharply, if not to eliminate them. Success along these lines
would result in a significant reduction in the incidence of blind
babies and is therefore of great practical as well as theoretical
importance.

CHARACTERISTICS OF THE BLIND CHILD

As might be expected, the intelligence distribution among blind
children in residential schools does not appear to differ markedly
from that of seeing individuals. However, in the distribution of
cases registered with the New Jersey State Commission for the
Blind in 1947 (for the whole distribution see table on p. 327)
nearly 11 per cent of the whole group was described as mentally
deficient. Over half of these had been placed in institutions for
the mentally deficient. This is a distinctly higher incidence of
mental deficiency than is found among the sighted population.
Probably much of the increase stems from the tendency of marked
developmental anomalies to be associated with each other. Defective hearing, for example, is also more common among blind
children than among sighted ones, and defective vision is found
in an abnormally large proportion of deaf children. Some of the
causes of blindness, like maternal rubella, are believed to cause
other anomalies, so that for such cases especially, more than one
defect would tend to occur. To some extent, also, the increase may
be a result of the generally observed higher incidence of all physical and mental defects among children at the lower socioeconomic
levels. This particular factor would obviously operate to lower the
average IQ level found for any group of physically defective
children. Nevertheless, most blind infants presumably have the
same mental and physical potentialities as sighted ones, and any
differences appearing as they develop are directly or indirectly
attributable to the lack of vision rather than to inherent differences of ability along nonvisual lines.

It seems to most people self-evident that a blind child should
be slow in walking and, particularly, in the free exploration of his

surroundings by this means; and, in general, this is found to be the case. It may seem surprising at first that the blind child is also frequently retarded in speech development. This, however, on further examination, is seen to be a natural consequence of the extreme limitation of experience which is so often the result of well-meant efforts to preserve him from harm. Because he cannot see approaching danger or hold his own on a visual level in association with other children, he is withdrawn from situations of even slight potential risk and prevented from trying to adjust to sighted age-mates without the constant protection of an adult guardian. He is not, like other children, able to tag along with an older brother or sister from an early age or extend his solo wanderings from his own yard into a gradually enlarging neighborhood as he grows older. All of this ends in his having, by contrast to the seeing child, less to do, less to think about, less to talk about. Only a constant effort on the part of his parents can give him sufficient sensory experience along nonvisual lines to begin to make up for the lack of visual experience. Without such effort he lacks concepts on which to base a spontaneous, healthy verbal development. His difficulty, in fact, is complementary to that of the deaf child. Although the latter can readily form a large number of concepts of his surroundings, the manipulation of sound to describe and discuss them is not natural to him. The blind child, on the other hand, is in constant danger of failing to gain any sense of the reality behind the words. Even when his use of them appears entirely normal, his speech may not be based on the world of his own experience, which alone can be truly real for him. A striking example of this is cited by Cutsforth. He quotes a passage from Helen Keller's autobiography, describing an evening by the sea. It is beautifully phrased, beautifully expressed, and not until it is called to his attention does the sighted, hearing reader become aware of the fact that the experiences described are almost wholly based on the two senses which Miss Keller lacks—sight and hearing. She speaks of the colors of the flowers, the sound of the sea, the rising of the moon and its reflection in the sea. This can only have stemmed from the reports of others.

Cutsforth contrasts this with another description, in which a blind girl, describing an early morning walk, tells of sounds, scents, the varying feel of the path underfoot and of the tree trunks, grasses, and mosses touched by her exploring fingers. The images here are just as vivid as in the other passage, and they are what we may call "real" ones for the author herself.

If the world of the blind child is to provide as rich and varied a field for his thought and experience as that of the seeing child, he must be given the opportunity to examine it as thoroughly and extensively as possible in terms of odor, sound, and touch. If this were to be done, it seems likely that much of the observed developmental lag would fail to appear.

It was long assumed that nature somehow compensated for the lack of vision by providing the blind person with a special sense or senses by which he could perceive obstacles or, at least, by improving his memory so that he could retain much more material than the sighted. Recent investigations seem to prove that this is not so. In the absence of sight, much more use must be made of other abilities; but these abilities seem to be possessed by both the sighted and the blind to the same degree. The subjectively apparent differences are merely differences in conscious utilization of the nonvisual sensations. In fact, Worchel found that sighted individuals, working blindfolded, were actually superior to the blind in space orientation, in tactual perception of form, and in the imaginal manipulation of forms in space. Among blind subjects, the age at which blindness developed was highly correlated with these abilities, particularly the last. It seems that the ability to form some sort of visual image—an ability which is denied to the congenitally blind—is extremely useful even when sight is no longer present.

To sum up, then, the child blind from birth or from an early age is irrevocably handicapped. He has no physical or mental compensatory abilities which will come into play automatically; he has merely the same general equipment as is possessed by the sighted. If he is to develop as freely, to be as independent, to lead as full a life as his seeing brothers and sisters, it will only be because from babyhood special efforts are made to encourage him in the fullest possible development of the abilities he still possesses. As do other handicapped children, he needs certain special protections. However, these must not be allowed to deny him a normal degree of personal independence, even of personal risk. Without these, he can never lead a normal life in a world of sighted people.

The effects of blindness upon the personality have been more frequently discussed than carefully studied; even some of the more painstaking workers in the field have unfortunately limited themselves to the establishment and measurement of a particular characteristic, without determining the extent, if any, of its variation from the normal for sighted individuals. It seems fairly certain that the person congenitally blind or blind from early childhood tends to be somewhat more introverted and less well adjusted than the seeing. The former trait may be, as Cutsforth has suggested, an almost inevitable result of blindness. The latter, however, might readily be merely a reflection of inadequate educational methods. As with personality in general, much more study is needed.

EDUCATION

The education of the blind child presents special problems. Shall he be sent to a residential school; or can he be kept at home? There is an increasing belief that, wherever possible, a day school —perhaps best of all, a special class in the public school—is preferable to the residential school. After all, the more closely he is kept in contact with the world he is to live in, the better adjusted to it he is likely to be. The very fact that the residential school provides an environment largely shaped to his special needs may, in the long run, handicap him for life in an environment not so shaped.

The system followed by the state of New Jersey is an example of a minimal use of the residential school and maximal use of the public schools. Here, any blind child who is otherwise normal is, if possible, placed in a Braille class in the nearest school system which is large enough to have one. In some cases, where the distance is unusually great, he may be placed in a boarding home. By the time he reaches the high school level, he is usually able to dispense with the special class; the State Commission for the Blind sees to it that he is provided with a Talking Book machine, typewriter, and other special equipment, and with the services of a tutor-reader, who gives additional help where Braille material is not available and where difficulties may arise through the student's inability to follow the visual portions of the classroom work. He is also given special educational and vocational guidance and, where necessary, financial aid to complete his vocational training. The child who is mentally, physically, or otherwise handicapped in addition to the visual deficiency, may be provided with home instruction or placed in any one of several in- or out-of-state residential institutions, according to his needs.

The range and flexibility made possible by this sort of program are best shown by the distribution of cases in a fairly recent year, 1947. In this year, 841 blind or partially sighted children registered with the commission were classified as follows:

BLIND CHILDREN IN NEW JERSEY, 1947

	Per cent of cases
Preschool	14.2
Braille classes (public school)	4.0
Sight-saving classes (public school)	20.9
Local public elementary school	17.4
Public high school	11.9
Bedside instruction	1.2
Advanced training	2.5
Mentally deficient	10.9
In state institutions	6.4
At home	4.5
Residential schools for the blind	7.5
Awaiting further analysis before classification or in process of changing classification	9.5

It can be seen that a large number of the school-age children have been successfully handled without residential placement. Indeed, if the preschool, the mentally deficient, the "advanced training," and the unclassified groups are omitted, fewer than 12 per cent of the remaining cases are in residential schools; the rest are either in special or regular classes of the public schools or are physically handicapped and receiving instruction at home. Even when we remember that most of the children are not completely blind but have some useful vision, this is a striking figure.

The specific nature of education for the blind has undergone many changes since the days when it was largely restricted to a few handicrafts and music through an increasing use of Braille and special devices to make the standard academic subjects more readily available; and now it appears to be moving in the direction of the supplementation of Braille with an even greater use of the Talking Books and, in the not too distant future, the use of portable recorders, so that the blind student can take notes more easily than is possible even for one highly skilled in Braille. For the purpose of unspoken communication with the sighted, the typewriter has long been standard equipment. It has, however, its drawbacks. The most important of these is that the blind writer cannot read back what he has written.

So far, there seems to be no one device which a blind student can use to take notes and write reports or letters which both he himself and a sighted person can readily read—whether the "reading" is done visually or by means of hearing. Perhaps some version of the dictating machine will ultimately be so widely used as to be practical for the purpose.

One area in which independence is both difficult and important for the blind child is that of physical action. It is in this field that overprotection is least obvious to his parents and probably most undesirable for himself. If the parents force themselves to encourage the child to try out whatever is not seriously dangerous, he can achieve a high degree of competence, not merely in the details of personal care but in getting around both in and out of doors. The following case is a striking example of the level of action that can be reached and is therefore presented, even though the subject is not a child.

When G. M. was in her middle thirties her vision suddenly began to fail. The trouble progressed rapidly, and within a few weeks she became totally blind. Examination by several of the best oculists in the state indicated that her condition was permanent.

G. M. had been a meticulously neat housekeeper. Now it was thought necessary for her to engage a maid, though the family's limited means rendered it impossible for them to employ really competent help. There followed a succession of ignorant, slovenly girls whose carelessness and untidy ways drove G. M. almost to distraction. She could not see the dirt, it is true; but she could feel the sticky plates, hastily rinsed in tepid water, and her sensitive nostrils were continually offended by the odors of unwashed linen and decaying garbage. At last, she could bear it no longer. "I'll do the work myself," she declared. Painstakingly, slowly, she undertook the tasks of cleaning, laundering, even, although in their rural district it was necessary to use a wood stove, cooking and baking.

She and her husband had long wanted to have children, but it was with decidedly mixed feelings that they learned that G. M. had now become pregnant. She, however, was confident. She had learned to keep a house neat and clean without the aid of sight; she could manage this new problem, too. And manage it she did. When, at the age of two months, the infant was taken to a pediatrician for a check-up, the amazed physician was unwilling to believe that a blind woman could, without help, maintain a baby in such perfect condition, both as to general health and as to the state of his hair and skin. Neighbors were equally astonished to find that regardless of the day or hour at which they might drop in to see her, the house was always tidy and the child's face and clothing clean.

Before the first child was two years old, a second was born. Again G. M. rose to the occasion, and the new baby was as well cared for as the first.

At present, both boys are in the run-about stage; neither has arrived at school age. G. M. is now faced with the problems arising from her inability to see what they are doing since, like most children, they are prone to get into mischief. However, she is fortunate in having acute hearing, which enables her to keep track of them fairly well, and although some of their escapades have been trying, none has had serious consequences.

G. M. is blessed with an exceptional memory and an orderly mind. She has only a grade school education but could probably have progressed much further along academic lines had she been interested in doing so. As it is, her knowledge is sufficient for the life she leads.

The keynote of G. M.'s success appears to lie in these two factors: her tremendous drive to achieve and her supreme confidence that she can do so. By faith ye can move mountains, we are told. G. M. is moving them.

REFERENCES

BAKWIN, Ruth M., "The Blind Child," *Journal of Pediatrics*, 35 (1949), 120-129.

BRIELAND, Donald M., "A Comparative Study of the Speech of Blind and Sighted Children," *Speech Monographs*, 17 (1950), 98-103.

CUTSFORTH, Thomas D., *The Blind in School and Society: A Psychological Study* (New York, American Foundation for the Blind, 1951).

HAWK, Sarah Stinchfield, "The Blind Child of Preschool Age and His Speech," *The Nervous Child*, 9, No. 1 (January, 1951), 28-56.

LENDE, Helga, *Books about the Blind: A Bibliographical Guide to Literature Relating to the Blind*, 2d ed. (New York, American Foundation for the Blind, 1953).

LOWENFELD, Berthold, "Effects of Blindness on the Cognitive Functions of Children," *The Nervous Child*, 7, No. 1 (January, 1948), 45-54.

————, "The Preschool Blind Child and His Needs," *Exceptional Children*, 20 (1953), 50-55.

MIKELL, R. F., "Normal Growth and Development of Children with Visual Handicaps," *New Outlook for the Blind*, 47 (1953), 91-96.

PLATA, José, "Expresión de las imágenes tactiles de los ciegos por medio del modelado," *Revista de Psicología general y aplicada*, 5 (1950), 517-538.

ROSS, Ishbel, *Journey into Light: The Story of the Education of the Blind* (New York, Appleton-Century-Crofts, Inc., 1951).

SHOEMAKER, W. T., *Retinitis Pigmentosa* (New York, J. B. Lippincott Company, 1909).

SOMMERS, Vita Stein, *The Influence of Parental Attitudes and Social Environment on the Personality Development of the Adolescent Blind* (New York, American Foundation for the Blind, 1944).

SPENCER, Steven M., "Mystery of the Blinded Babies," *Saturday Evening Post*, 227 (1955), 19-21, 97.

WORCHEL, Philip, "Space Perception and Orientation in the Blind," *Psychological Monographs*, 65, No. 15 (1951).

ZAHL, P. A., *Blindness* (Princeton, Princeton University Press, 1950).

Children with Sensory Handicaps: The Partially Sighted

23

WHAT IS MEANT BY PARTIAL SIGHT?

THE PARTIALLY sighted are those whose vision is functionally intermediate between blindness and the levels at which—with corrective glasses, if needed—it is adequate for all the needs of normal living. The child with a corrected visual acuity of below 20/70 in the better eye is considered to fall in this class. However, there are children whose visual acuity is above this figure, who are nonetheless classified for educational purposes as partially sighted. These children may have progressive myopia,[1] which frequently can be checked if visual strain is reduced to a minimum, as it should be in a properly conducted sight-saving class; or they may be afflicted with ocular disease or some nonocular condition which has affected the vision in such a way that excessive use of the eyes seems likely to be damaging.

INCIDENCE

It is estimated that approximately 0.2 per cent of all children fall into this group. This figure corresponds to a total of approximately 50,000 children in the United States.

CHARACTERISTICS

There is relatively little material on the characteristics of the partially sighted. One probable reason for this is the wide range

[1] That is, nearsightedness.

of actual visual condition included within the group. It seems *a priori* unlikely that the child who has congenitally poor vision would properly be grouped, for the study of personality, with the one whose vision has been mechanically damaged at a comparatively late age; and even more divergence of any characteristics related to their visual condition would be expected between the child whose vision is just this side of blindness and the one whose visual acuity is rather high, who is only classed as partially sighted because he must avoid eyestrain but who sees well enough to be on fairly equal terms with normally sighted children except in activities where good vision is specifically needed.

The intelligence of the partially sighted has received more attention than the personality, though even here no very specific conclusions can be drawn. Most investigators have reported median IQ's from 90 to 95 for groups of partially sighted children. Although this is at the lower end of the normal range, it must be remembered that the children, in most cases, were being given the standard tests devised for and standardized on normally sighted individuals. The visual handicap could readily interfere with the testing sufficiently to produce the observed results. In any case, it appears that the partially sighted have a substantially normal intelligence range; any inferiority in this respect is slight.

EDUCATION AND TRAINING

For some time after the foundation of the early schools for the blind, partially sighted children were admitted to them for training. However, the obvious unsuitability of failing to take advantage of what vision is present and the impossibility of teaching the blind by methods designed for those who have some useful vision raised grave doubts from the start as to the desirability of training members of the two groups together. Experience soon fully justified these doubts and showed that the ultimate results were bad both for the blind—who tended to use their partially sighted companions as assistants and therefore failed to gain self-reliance—and for the partially sighted—who felt unduly superior and became unfitted for adjustment to the sighted world. In the first years of this century, special classes for the partially sighted were established, first in England and soon thereafter in the United States. Since then they have grown in number, until now most school systems large enough to have an appreciable number of partially sighted pupils provide special teachers and equipment.

In general, the partially sighted child in a sight-saving class follows the same curriculum as do his normally sighted companions. Special attention is paid to the provision of excellent lighting in the classroom, and, wherever possible, the amount of visual work is decreased by using such devices as typewriters, recording machines, and radios. Reading materials are prepared with specially large type; maps and diagrams are large and colored in such a way as to minimize the visual effort involved in studying them. In some schools, the partially sighted child does not spend his entire time in the sight-saving class. Rather, he attends it only for those parts of his work in which vision is principally involved and remains with his normally sighted classmates for the rest of the time. This latter system recommends itself as being less likely to isolate the visually handicapped from the normal child than one in which he is completely segregated so far as his schoolwork is concerned.

REFERENCES

BERTRAM, Fredericka M., "What is Special about Special Education? The Partially Seeing Child," *Exceptional Children,* 20 (1953), 11-15, 27.

GALISDORFER, Lorraine, comp., *A New Selected Bibliography of Literature on the Partially Seeing* (Kenmore, N.Y., privately printed, 1951).

HATHAWAY, Winifred, and LOWENFELD, Berthold, "Teaching the Visually Handicapped," *Forty-ninth Yearbook of the National Society for the Study of Education: The Education of Exceptional Children* (Chicago, Chicago University Press, 1950), Pt. 2.

Children with Sensory Handicaps: The Deaf

24

WHAT IS DEAFNESS?

ALTHOUGH THERE ARE no legal standards for defining deafness, probably because the deaf and hard-of-hearing are not eligible for the type of state and federal financial aid that is provided for the blind, it seems to be generally agreed that a 30 per cent hearing loss in the range of speech sounds constitutes a severe handicap on verbal communication, and a loss of 40 to 50 per cent makes it extremely difficult for the child to establish speech habits at all. Children whose loss is 70 per cent or greater have so little useful hearing, even when wearing a hearing aid, that they may properly be classed as deaf, along with those who have no demonstrable ability to perceive sound aurally.

HOW IS DEAFNESS DETECTED?

In general, the detection of deafness, as distinct from hearing deficiency, should not be unduly difficult even in an infant. The normal child, when only a few weeks old, is likely to jump at the nearby slam of a door or the sudden shout of an older brother. He may pause in any mild fussing for attention at the sound of his mother's voice or approaching footsteps; he begins to respond rather selectively to different sounds. For example, both W. R., a boy, and his younger sister A. R., appeared to be particularly pleased by singing when each was only two months old. At this time, and until they began to acquire verbal comprehension, they

334

would frequently stop fussing and begin to smile and gurgle if their mother sang to them anything with a marked, rather rapid rhythm. That they were genuinely responding to the singing seemed almost certain, since experimental alternations of song and speech, both under otherwise identical conditions, were consistently paralleled by alternations of apparent pleasure and complaint on the part of the infants.

The deaf infant is, of course, not startled by sudden noise alone; nor will he, in general, show any selective response to the sounds made by someone handling him. However, an unusually placid baby may fail to be startled or frightened by noises which he is actually hearing perfectly well. A mentally retarded, physically handicapped, or weak one may be too lethargic to respond. A child of superior intelligence and alertness may respond so eagerly to the sight and touch of his mother that she never suspects that he does not hear. Some years ago, a three-year-old girl was brought to the office of a psychologist by her worried parents. "She *seems* bright enough, but she does not talk," explained the young mother. "Can she be mentally abnormal? If not, what is wrong with her?"

The psychologist, observing the beautiful, well-co-ordinated, healthy, and happy-looking child, who seemed to be keenly alert to all that went on, felt that mental deficiency could scarcely be the answer. In any case, however, a psychometric examination might reveal some clue to the difficulty. The little girl appeared to enjoy the testing procedures greatly and responded rapidly and correctly to the various directions until the examiner, in reaching for additional materials, chanced to give a direction with her face turned away from the child. This time there was no response at all—not even an effort to follow instructions. The examiner repeated the directions, and the child promptly obeyed them. Here, indeed, was a clue! To test her suspicions, the examiner stepped behind the child into a large storage closet and deliberately clapped two books together as loudly as she could. No response. She spoke more and more loudly, finally shouted the little girl's name. Still no response. Careful examination revealed that the child had virtually no hearing. In this case, superior intelligence had actually acted, for a time, to handicap its possessor, concealing her physical defect and thus preventing her need of special training from being recognized. Young as she was, she had acquired enough facility in lip reading to obey commands or requests, particularly as they were likely to be accompanied by significant gestures. She was entered in a special class for training in lip reading and oral speech. Although no other child in the class was younger than five years, her intelligence enabled her not merely to keep up but to excel most of them.

In view of such factors, it might be well if all parents, even in the absence of any particular reason for doubt as to an infant's hearing, were to employ simple tests, ranging from sounds designed to elicit a startle type of response to speech in normal tones behind the infant's back, as soon as his general level of development indicates that he may be expected to show some awareness of it. Cattell considers that at a mental age of four months a child may be expected to turn toward a voice whose source is not seen by him. Failure to give this response by six months of age in an otherwise apparently normal child may then reasonably lead to some question as to the adequacy of his hearing. Whenever there *is* any question on the subject in the minds of his parents—or, indeed, of anyone who has much to do with him—it would seem wise to consult the family physician and, if he advises it, a hearing specialist. The earlier a hearing deficiency is discovered, the better, since it is of great importance to begin remedial work at the earliest possible age.

The hearing of older children can be tested in much the same way as can that of adults, using an audiometer. In dealing with infants, special techniques are necessary. Many of these depend on the establishment of some sort of conditioned reflex to a sound loud enough to be audible to the child. Then the volume and pitch are varied, and the levels at which the reflex does not appear are taken as indicating the range of hearing. Marcus suggests a rather different method, which may be useful with very young infants. Electroencephalograph records are obtained of the normal sleep waves of the subject; then he is allowed to fall asleep or, if necessary, sedated just to the appearance of the sleep waves. At this point, a sound stimulus will provoke a sharp change in the form of the waves if, and only if, it is audible to the subject.

CAUSES OF DEAFNESS

Deafness appears to be congenital in almost 40 per cent of the cases; it is estimated that over 10 per cent are hereditary in nature. The hereditary cases do not, in general, seem to involve any large number of well-known specific syndromes but are inferred from the frequency with which congenitally deaf individuals report that they have one or several deaf relatives. Other conditions believed to cause congenital deafness are maternal rubella, mother-child Rh factor incompatibility, prematurity, and birth injury. Deafness is unquestionably associated with defective vision; Stockwell reports that in the course of ten years, 46 per cent of 960 children seen at the Pennsylvania School for the Deaf needed glasses. This is a substantially higher figure than that found for hearing children. Deafness also appears to be associated with other defects or abnormalities, probably on the same basis as that indicated for congenital blindness.

The causes of acquired deafness are many. Physical damage to the ear, whether by direct injury or by exposure to very loud noise, accounts for many adult and some child cases. Among children, infections of various sorts are important causes of deafness. Meningitis is the commonest cause of acquired deafness; measles, scarlet fever, whooping cough, and local infections also cause many cases.

Some types of deafness, originating in mechanical defect or malfunctioning of the ear, can be cured or improved by medical or surgical means, such as the removal of wax or other obstructive material and drainage by puncture of the eardrum in acute infections. The development and use of powerful antibiotics in recent years should reduce the incidence of deafness due to infection although at present, it seems that undue reliance on them to the neglect of surgical technique may possibly cause some trouble.

CHARACTERISTICS OF THE DEAF

As is the case with other groups that include a number of cases caused by congenital anomaly, the incidence of mental deficiency is somewhat higher than normal among the deaf. It is frequently hard to distinguish between inherent deficiency and the retardation caused by the physical handicap. For this reason, a deaf child should not be dismissed as inherently retarded until every effort has been made to establish communication with him.

Even when it is possible to communicate with a deaf child fairly readily and fluently, the estimation of his mental standing and, more importantly, his mental capacity remains extremely difficult. The Stanford Binet test seems to be too dependent on language experience to be applicable; when the deaf subject does answer a question, his response is often peculiar in a way that leads to doubt as to whether he really comprehended it and, further, as to the basic cause of his incomprehension. Performance tests like the ones devised by Pintner, Arthur and others are substantially better adapted to use in testing the deaf. However, all test results agree in indicating, just as with the blind child, that there is a developmental lag due to the effects of the physical handicap in reducing the amount and narrowing the range of early experience. Again, as with the blind, it seems possible to compensate for much of this handicap by a consistent effort to enrich the child's experience along those sensory channels available to him.

Deafness has not been proven to produce any marked specific effects on personality. As with blindness, it seems probable and reasonable that the lessened area of contact and communication with the outside world leads to a greater concentration upon self and also reduces the ease of social adjustment. Particularly when suitable training is scanty or lacking, so that real communication with others is both delayed and permanently handicapped, a pronounced maladjustment and withdrawal from normal life seem to result.

EDUCATION AND TRAINING OF THE DEAF

Deafness is not an obvious defect, yet it has profound and far-reaching effects. A congenitally deaf child typically fails to learn to speak and will almost always fail to comprehend speech. Unless, like the child described previously, he is above average mentally, the barriers to communication may be so complete that he gives the impression of being mentally deficient. Indeed, the untreated deaf child, though potentially of normal mentality, is quite likely to be severely deficient in terms of mental functioning. This is the natural consequence of the extreme limitation of his effective environment and of his interaction with the environment, which is imposed by his lack of words. Breaking through the communication barrier is more obviously difficult than the comparable task with a blind child—that of making the *content* of communication truly meaningful. It is presumably for these reasons that organized attempts at educating the deaf child came much later than did the beginnings of such work for the blind. During the latter years of the eighteenth century, the Braidwoods in England, Samuel Heinicke in Germany, and two Frenchmen, Abbé de l'Epée and Abbé Sicard, were active in teaching the deaf. In 1817, the American founder of work with the deaf, Thomas Hopkins Gallaudet, opened the first school for the deaf in this country in Hartford, Conn.; schools were soon founded in a number of other states. There are, at present, about one hundred public and private residential schools for the deaf, scattered throughout the country, with an enrollment in 1949 of about 13,000 children. In that year, about 5,000 children were enrolled in over one hundred public day schools and special class units of the regular public schools. Virtually all of these, both residential and day, offer some sort of vocational training. As an increasing number of deaf children complete the elementary schoolwork at earlier ages, more of the residential schools are establishing programs of work at the high school level. The federal government supports Gallaudet College, in Washington, D. C., which is designed exclusively for the deaf, and a number of deaf have successfully attended colleges for the normally hearing.

Much of the early training was based on the use of manual signs for communication; this, of course, requires the hearing individual to learn a special technique, if he is to communicate with the deaf person so trained. From the very beginning, however, some of the workers in the field refused to agree that the admittedly much greater difficulty found in teaching the deaf child to communicate by means of speech and lip reading justified the restriction of social environment that inevitably resulted from the use of the manual method. Their viewpoint has gradually gained ground, until today it seems to be generally accepted that the deaf should be taught to speak and lip-read if they are able to learn these skills. The major disagreements center on the question of how determined and prolonged the effort to teach them should be in individual cases. Those children who appear to be unable to learn them can often be taught to communicate manually and to read and write; and, accordingly, failure along verbal lines is not to be accepted as an indication that communication by more than crude signs is impossible.

As with other congenital abnormalities, the incidence of mental deficiency is somewhat higher than normal among the deaf. It is not easy to distinguish between inherent deficiency and the retardation primarily due to deafness alone. For this reason, a deaf child should not be dismissed as inherently retarded until every effort has been made to establish communication with him. Under the best conditions, the use of words, either manually or orally, is much more difficult for the deaf child than for the hearing. All too often the difficulty is tremendously increased by the failure to recognize the defect or to begin training until the child is well past the age at which speech normally develops. In addition to the handicap thus imposed by the lack of co-ordination between the natural developmental schedule and the educational program, such a child may have developed more or less severe emotional problems stemming from the failure of communication. It is for these reasons that early diagnosis and training are tremendously important. Some schools for the deaf are admitting pupils as young as three years, in order to lessen the time lag. This, however, does not seem to be the best solution conceivable; on one hand, so young a child may readily be profoundly disturbed by the separation from his family, and, on the other, delay in beginning training until the age of three has already permitted a lag of approximately two years behind the normal to develop. A more satisfactory solution, if admittedly more difficult to put into practice, would perhaps be the provision of visiting teachers who could both provide training in the home and show the parents how to extend and supplement the training, both along specific verbal lines and by means of a generally enriched environment. Under such a program, it should be possible to begin training as soon as the hearing defect is discovered, thus reducing the developmental lag to a minimum.

Although a hearing aid is obviously most useful to the child who is merely hard of hearing, Hudgins presents data indicating that even where the hearing loss is so severe that no comprehension of words based on hearing alone can be obtained, nevertheless the use of a hearing aid seems to help in lip reading. If his observations hold true for the deaf in general, perhaps the use of an aid would make the difference, for many children, between success and failure in learning verbal communication.

Ever since the beginning of organized work in training the deaf there have been attempts at developing a method of mechanically reducing speech to easily understood visual terms. Necessarily crude at first, devices for this purpose have been continually improved, until, today, it is possible for a deaf person to do such things as carry on a telephone conversation with the aid of a machine developed by the Bell Telephone Laboratories. This machine, though not yet widely used, seems to have much potential value in training the deaf to speak, but it is not yet certain how old a child must be before he can take advantage of it. In such training, the deaf child is shown the visual pattern of a sound. He then speaks into the machine, attempting to produce a duplicate pattern on its screen. Practice of this sort is extremely useful in teaching him to speak, not merely intelligibly but with normal pitch, inflection, and intonation, so that his speech is not markedly odd or unpleasant to the hearing person.

REFERENCES

BEEBE, Helen Hulick, "Testing the Hearing of Young Children," *The Nervous Child,* 9, No. 1 (January, 1951), 8-14.

BERLINSKY, Stanley, "Measurement of the Intelligence and Personality of the Deaf: A Review of the Literature," *Journal of Speech and Hearing Disorders,* 17 (1952), 39-54.

BIRCH, Jane R., and BIRCH, Jack W., "The Leiter International Performance Scale As an Aid in the Psychological Study of Deaf Children," *American Annals of the Deaf,* 96 (1951), 502-511.

CHRISTENSEN, Aage V., "Studies on the Psychology of Hearing," *Acta Oto-Laryngologica,* 39 (1951), 95-101.

Cleveland Hearing and Speech Center, *A Child Doesn't Hear* (Cleveland, Ohio, Cleveland Junior Chamber of Commerce, 1949).

FIEDLER, Miriam Forster, *Deaf Children in a Hearing World* (New York, The Ronald Press Company, 1952).

HARDY, William G., "Children with Impaired Hearing: An Audiologic Perspective," *United States Children's Bureau Publication,* No. 326 (1952).

———, and BORDLEY, John E., "Special Techniques in Testing the Hearing of Children," *Journal of Speech and Hearing Disorders,* 16 (1951), 122-131.

———, and PAULS, Miriam D., "So That Children May Hear Better," *Child,* 15 (1950), 18-22.

HEDGECOCK, Leroy D., "Counseling the Parents of Acoustically Handicapped Children," *American Annals of the Deaf,* 97 (1952), 329-339.

HEIDER, Grace M., "Adjustment Problems of the Deaf Child," *The Nervous Child,* 7, No. 1 (January, 1948), 38-44.

HILLER, B., "Rubella Congenital Inner Ear Deafness in Tasmania," *Medical Journal of Australia,* 2 (1949), 277-283.

HUDGINS, Clarence V., "Problems of Speech Comprehension in Deaf Children," *The Nervous Child,* 9, No. 1 (January, 1951), 57-63.

———, "The Response of Profoundly Deaf Children to Auditory Training," *Journal of Speech and Hearing Disorders,* 18 (1953), 273-288.

INGVARSSON, Ivar M., "Language Teaching in Schools for the Deaf: Psychological Aspects," *American Annals of the Deaf,* 97 (1952), 267-271.

KLEINFELD, Louis, "Otologic Aspects of Speech Comprehension," *The Nervous Child*, 9, No. 1 (January, 1951), 43-47.

LASSMAN, Grace Harris, "Parent Participation in Teaching Speech to the Deaf Child," *Journal of Speech and Hearing Disorders*, 13 (1948), 366-368.

———, *Language for the Preschool Deaf Child* (New York, Grune and Stratton, Inc., 1950).

LEESON, Lavell H., "Hearing Defects in Children," *Canadian Medical Association Journal*, 62 (1950), 167-169.

MACPHERSON, J. R., "The Status of the Deaf and/or Hard of Hearing Mentally Deficient in the United States," *American Annals of the Deaf*, 97 (1952), 375-386.

MARCUS, Richard E., "Hearing and Speech Problems in Children," *Archives of Otolaryngology*, 53 (1951), 134-146.

MYKLEBUST, Helmer R., *Your Deaf Child* (Springfield, Ill., Charles C Thomas, Publisher, 1950).

———, and BRUTTEN, Milton, "A Study of the Visual Perception of Deaf Children," *Acta Oto-Laryngologica*, Suppl. No. 105 (1953).

OLERON, Pierre, *Les Sourds-muets* (Paris, Presses Universitaires de France, 1950).

———, "Le Role du langage dans le développement mental; contribution tirée de la psychologie de l'enfant sourd-muet," *Enfance*, 5 (1952), 120-137.

PINTNER, Rudolf, EISENSON, Jon, and STANTON, Mildred, *The Psychology of the Physically Handicapped* (New York, Appleton-Century-Crofts, Inc., 1941).

PRONOVOST, Wilbert, "A Survey of Services for the Speech and Hearing Handicapped in New England," *Journal of Speech and Hearing Disorders*, 16 (1951), 148-156.

ROACH, Robert E., "The Meaning of Severe Deafness in the Life of the Young Child," *Cerebral Palsy Review*, 14, No. 9 (1953), 8, 12-14.

STOCKWELL, Eunice, "Visual Defects in the Deaf Child," *American Medical Association Archives of Ophthalmology*, 48 (1952), 428-432.

TEMPLIN, Mildred C., *Development of Reasoning in Children with Normal and Defective Hearing*, University of Minnesota Institute of Child Welfare Monograph Series (Minneapolis, University of Minnesota Press, 1950), No. 24.

———, "Personal References and Illustrations Used in Explanation of Physical Causality," *American Annals of the Deaf*, 96 (1951), 482-493.

WATSON, Leland A., and TOLAN, Thomas, *Hearing Tests and Hearing Instruments* (Baltimore, The Williams and Wilkins Company, 1949).

WISHIK, Samuel M., and KRAMM, Elizabeth R., "Audiometric Testing of Hearing of School Children," *Journal of Speech and Hearing Disorders,* 18 (1953), 360-365.

Children with Sensory Handicaps: The Hard-of-hearing 25

DEFINITION

THE HARD-OF-HEARING are those whose hearing ability is significantly less acute than that of the normal child but still great enough to be used for the understanding of verbal communication. The upper limit of the range is fairly definite, usually being specified as an average loss of about 30 decibels in the speech range in the better ear. The lower limit, however, is necessarily indeterminate. Individuals with a loss of 70 to 75 decibels or more cannot use hearing alone to understand speech, even with the assistance of a hearing aid. Those with losses above 55 to 60 decibels cannot *learn* speech by means of their unaided hearing; but, once it is learned—through training or because their hearing was more nearly adequate until after the acquisition of speech—they can, with the aid of sound amplification, *comprehend* speech. Those with losses of between 30 and 55 decibels can usually learn and use verbal speech unaided, but their hearing defect is sufficient to handicap them in this field of communication. It has been proven repeatedly that the correlation between organic hearing ability, as measured on instruments like the audiometer, and functional hearing ability—the synthesis of ear and brain to perceive and interpret sound stimuli—is far from perfect. In some extreme cases, a child of apparently normal mentality and hearing ability fails completely to utilize his hearing. It has repeatedly been demonstrated that a large proportion of untrained individuals with moderate or severe hearing losses show much poorer speech comprehension than would be expected on the basis of the instrumentally measured loss. That this is not primarily an indication of inadequacy of the instruments to give a correct indication of usable hearing ability is proven by the fact that, in most cases, suitable auditory training reduces or eliminates the discrepancy by raising the level of speech comprehension. From the standpoint of the effect on the child and of the type of training which he needs, it is necessary to place more initial weight on the level of adequacy at which his hearing actually functions than on the level organically possible, if the two are found to differ significantly. For such a child, the hearing ability as measured by instruments is chiefly valuable as indicating the goal to be aimed at. Cases like this cannot be classified on a permanent basis, until the degree to which they can profit by training has been experimentally determined.

For educational purposes, the child who becomes deaf well after the use of language has become established should usually be treated as though he were only hard-of-hearing.

DETECTION AND INCIDENCE

It is relatively simple to identify the deaf infant; the hard-of-hearing infant, however, can easily remain unsuspected. Because he does use and respond to speech, any failure of communication due to the hearing defect may be ascribed to inattention, laziness, stubbornness, or stupidity. The young child who must constantly ask to have things repeated, who rarely responds when called from the next room, who cups his hand to his ear and tilts his head at odd angles in conversation, should be given a hearing test. In school, the hard-of-hearing child shows any or all of the previously mentioned signs; he is also likely to make poor grades and to be described by the teacher as "just not paying enough attention," since he will be particularly deficient on all work that is dictated or given orally and will frequently show by his answers that he did not correctly understand the questions asked. Defective speech is also rather characteristic of the hard-of-hearing child.

When actual testing is employed, the methods that are used with the deaf are generally applicable to the hard-of-hearing. In addition, by a number of simple tests, the classroom teacher can eliminate at least the normally hearing children from a group, leaving only the obviously and possibly hard-of-hearing for more detailed examination. Of these, the watch-tick test and the whisper test are the most widely used. In the first, a watch with a fairly loud tick is moved away from, and then towards, each ear in turn, with the subject's other ear covered. A normally hearing person should hear the tick as long as the watch is less than 48 inches from his ear. In the second, the child is placed 20 feet away from the examiner, with one ear covered and the other turned toward him. The examiner speaks in a conversational tone; if the child does not respond, the distance is lessened until he can hear the examiner. In both of these tests a rough measure of hearing loss is provided by the ratio of the distance at which the stimulus is perceived to that at which it is perceived by the normally hearing. Such tests must, of course, be carried out in a quiet room. Obviously they are more reliable in indicating which children have normal hearing than which have not and, hence, should be used mainly to eliminate those for whom more intensive examination does not seem necessary. Any child for whom the results are doubtful should be tested further.

As with poor sight, the estimates of the number of cases of defective hearing vary widely. A fairly generally accepted figure is about 5 per cent, which corresponds to about 1,500,000 children of school age in the United States.

CAUSES

The same causes that lead to deafness may produce defective hearing. In addition, adenoid growths and accumulation of wax may result in temporary hearing loss, which is relieved by removal of the mechanical impediment.

CHARACTERISTICS OF THE HARD-OF-HEARING

It appears that the hard-of-hearing, as a group, differ only slightly, if at all, from the normal with respect to personal-social adjustment. They may be slightly less stable emotionally, slightly more shy, slightly more introverted. Educationally, they tend to be somewhat retarded, particularly if special training facilities are lacking. There appears to be no significant difference in intelligence between the hard-of-hearing and the normal child.

The hard-of-hearing show a marked tendency toward defective speech. This is to be expected, since they cannot perceive all the nuances in the speech of others, hence are forced to copy an imperfect model, and also cannot accurately perceive their own speech to compare with the model. Obviously the frequency and severity of speech defects increases with the degree of hearing loss.

EDUCATION AND TRAINING

Efforts directed specifically at the hard-of-hearing as distinct from the deaf child began to be made in the first year of this century. In 1920, the first lip-reading classes for children in the regular grades were begun in Lynn, Mass., and in Rochester, N.Y. Since then, more and more communities have made arrangements for special training for the hard-of-hearing within the framework of the regular schools.

There is rarely any justification for more than temporary placement of a hard-of-hearing child in a school designed for the deaf. Such temporary placement may be desirable for the child who is functionally deaf; but as soon as some degree of communication has been established, all efforts should be directed toward increasing his use of hearing so that he may continue his training in a class for the hard-of-hearing. Most hard-of-hearing children should be trained, depending on the degree of their disability, either in the regular classes or in the special class of the public schools. Children with slight to moderate losses can usually get along in the regular classes without special instruction beyond speech therapy when needed, if they are given favorable seating and if the teacher makes certain that they do hear what is going on. If the loss is as high as 25 decibels in the speech range in the better ear, they will usually profit by the addition of special classes in lip reading. As the loss increases, the use of a hearing aid becomes more desirable and may make the difference between success and failure of adjustment. When the hearing loss approaches 50-55 decibels some children may need placement in a special class. This is particularly likely if the loss is of long duration, if the child has not had auditory training, if he is a slow learner, has trouble reading lips, or is not well adjusted. Losses above this level usually handicap the child sufficiently to necessitate special class placement, although adequate auditory training and training in lip reading at an early age may make regular class attendance possible.

Within the special class, the usual classroom work is given for those students who are not attending regular classes; this work need not differ from the regular classes, except in the use of amplified sound and in the provision of a greater amount of individual attention than is possible in the regular class. In addition, training in the use of a hearing aid and in lip reading is given and, if the child needs it, speech therapy.

The special class should be as little separated from the regular classes as possible. It should be physically located in the regular school; its pupils should share in the activities of the normal group to as great a degree as is possible for each. The aim should be to use the special class as a rehabilitation center which retains each child only so long and to that degree as may be necessary for him. As his skill in lip reading and in the use of the hearing aid increases, the amount of time spent in the special class should be diminished and that in the regular class increased until complete return, except perhaps for continuing speech corrective work and lip-reading training, has been effected.

REFERENCES

ALBRIGHT, M. Arline, "Mental Health of Children with Hearing Impairments," *Exceptional Children*, 19 (1952), 107, 110-113, 124.

CURRY, E. Thayer, "The Efficiency of Teacher Referrals in a School Hearing Testing Program," *Journal of Speech and Hearing Disorders*, 15 (1950), 211-214.

JELLINEK, Augusta, "Education of Hard of Hearing Children," *The Nervous Child*, 9, No. 1 (January, 1951), 77-84.

LESSER, Arthur J., "Some Principles in the Development of Services for Children with Hearing Impairment," *Journal of Speech and Hearing Disorders*, 15 (1950), 101-105.

———, "Services for the Child Who Is Hard of Hearing—A Guide for the Development of Programs," *United States Children's Bureau Publication*, No. 334 (1950).

SHERIDAN, Mary D., "Speech Defects and Deafness in Childhood," *Medical Press*, 221 (1949), 411-414.

The Child with Cerebral   26
Palsy: The Brain-damaged Child

BRAIN DAMAGE, particularly that arising in fetal life, at birth, or shortly thereafter, is a major factor in the production of many different abnormalities. Among these, cerebral palsy is one that is particularly important in terms of both the number of children affected and the severity of the handicap that may be imposed. It is defined by Crothers as a condition in which a child has suffered injury to the brain, during the period from conception to three years of age, which distorts orderly development and leads to abnormality in motor control.

CLASSIFICATION OF CASES

Cerebral palsy may be divided into a number of types, depending on the nature of the motor-control abnormality. The broadest distinction is that between the cases exhibiting *hypertonicity* [1]—the spastics—and those exhibiting *hypotonicity*.[2] An older and more frequently used classification is that based on the predominant motor handicap exhibited. According to Phelps, the approximate proportion of cases falling into each group is as follows:

1. *Cerebral spastic paralysis*—20 per cent. These cases are characteristically hypertonic. Their muscles contract involuntarily and to such an extent that orthopedic deformities may result.

2. *Athetosis*—40 per cent. Athetoids are afflicted with involuntary movements; although they differ from the spastics in being able to

---

[1] That is, more than normal excitability of the muscles.
[2] That is, less than normal excitability of the muscles.

relax, any attempt at voluntary motion is apt to set off a wave of involuntary movements which frequently completely block the desired action.

3. *Rigidity*—20 per cent.

4. *Ataxia*—10 per cent. Here the chief handicap is in the co-ordination of muscular motion to perform physically complex actions like walking, writing, and speaking.

5. *Tremor*—5 per cent.

Yannet reports on a group whom he designates *atonic*. They all showed hyperflexibility of the joints; most could not even sit without support. All exhibited gravely defective mentality—the average IQ of his 15 cases was 15—and he suggests that brain damage sufficient to cause such complete lack of muscular tone and control is incompatible with a normal mentality.

CHARACTERISTICS

By definition, the child with cerebral palsy is physically handicapped to greater or less degree. The disorganization of muscular control may be relatively slight, or it may be so great as to result in complete helplessness of part or all of the body. Since the brain damage always occurs in infancy, usually at or before birth, it naturally results in deviations from the normal course of motor development. It is not merely large-muscle activities that are affected. There may be difficulty with the swallowing mechanism, so that drooling persists long after it would normally have disappeared, or with the breathing apparatus. Retarded speech and persistently defective speech are very often found. Dolphin and Cruickshank have reported disturbances of visuomotor perception that make it difficult for cerebral palsied children to distinguish figures from the background. Poor-sightedness and hearing defects are also rather common.

Brain damage sufficient to impair motor control is likely to produce effects not limited to this area. As with any child who is markedly handicapped in both range of experience and ease of communication, mental testing of the cerebral palsied is difficult, and its results must be cautiously evaluated. In general, any effect of the handicap on the test results will be to lower the apparent level of intelligence. However, a skilled examiner, with time and patience, and often by modification of the tests to facilitate response—for example, a severe spastic can scarcely be asked to string beads or draw pictures unless one is testing his motor rather than his mental abilities—can usually arrive at such conclusions as the following:

1. This child's physical handicap prevents reliable testing; he gives the impression of having potentially normal or near-normal intelligence;
2. Test results on this child indicate an IQ of 55. His true intelligence is probably markedly higher than this figure;
3. This child attains a rating of IQ 80. The physical handicap does not appear to have interfered seriously with the tests, and this value is probably a reasonably good indication of his true level.

Conclusions like the first two are most likely to be reached in dealing with a child who has received little or no rehabilitative training; his response to such training is, in itself, often a good way of evaluating his potentialities. Miller and Rosenfeld have reported a series of over 300 cases seen at Buffalo Children's Hospital between 1947 and 1951. 20 per cent of them could not be tested and were subjectively evaluated; it was found possible to rate the remaining 80 per cent by means of the Cattell Infant Intelligence Scale or the Stanford Binet. Some of those who were not testable when first seen became so later. The results of formal testing on this group indicated that the subjective evaluation had a reasonably good degree of reliability.

There is general agreement that the incidence of mental defectives among the cerebral palsied is substantially higher than that found among normal children; several large series have been reported, in which approximately half of the cases were estimated to rank below IQ 70. However, many cerebral palsied individuals have apparently suffered little, if any, mental damage and obtain superior ratings. Professor E. C. Carlsen of the University of Chicago is a striking example of this fact. Phelps suggests that the observed distribution is approximately what would result if about 70 per cent of all cases were mentally unaffected by the brain damage, thus falling into a normal spread of IQ from the lowest to the highest levels, and about 30 per cent sustained damage of such nature as to cause mental deficiency. It is obvious in any case that although any individual may be, and many are, mentally normal or superior, the numbers of intellectually inadequate among the cerebral palsied constitute a serious problem of institutional care.

It appears that the cerebral palsied share with other severely handicapped groups a tendency to emotional instability, introversion, and social maladjustment; but, as with others, this tendency is not very striking and could probably be prevented to a large degree by adequate early training. It seems that the greatest source of difficulty for these children comes not from within but from without them, in the damaging amount of overprotection likely to be forced on them by their parents.

ETIOLOGY AND DETECTION

It has long been established that the form of brain damage usually occurring at or before birth which results in cerebral palsy is not directly due to disease in the fetus. For many years, the chief factor was believed to be mechanical injury caused during the process of birth, either by the muscular forces of the mother or by the use of instruments to facilitate a difficult delivery. More recently, it has been suggested that *fetal anoxia*,[3] which may result from maternal anoxia or hemorrhage, premature detachment of the placenta, mechanical compression of the umbilical cord, erythroblastosis fetalis, or other causes, is even more likely to produce cerebral palsy than simple mechanical damage. Other maternal factors thought possibly to be involved are certain specific diseases, such as rubella and *toxoplasmosis*.[4] It also seems likely that the prematurely born infant may be inherently

[3] That is, insufficient oxygen supply to the fetus.
[4] A rare infection caused by a protozoan.

more susceptible to brain damage—as it is known to be more susceptible to anoxia—than the normal and that among term infants there may be a varying degree of susceptibility, so that brain injury which produces permanent damage in one infant is sustained without harm by another.

In the older child, the motor effects of cerebral palsy are sufficiently obvious to make it clear to the layman that something is wrong, and to the experienced physician what that something is. In the neonate and the young infant, motor development is at too low a level for ready detection of any but the severe cases. However, even the newborn is likely to show certain signs which, although they do not indicate that cerebral palsy is present, do mean that the infant exhibiting them is far more likely to develop it than is the normal infant. Wilson examined birth records of a group of cerebral palsy cases, then compared the frequency of appearance of certain abnormal conditions with the frequency of the subsequent development of cerebral palsy. She divided the symptoms into two groups: (1) delayed breathing, *cyanosis*,[5] etc.; (2) nursing difficulties, convulsions, paralysis, rigidities, fever not due to disease.

An infant who showed one or more of the signs in only one of the groups did not appear particularly likely to develop cerebral palsy; but only 1 in 170 of those exhibiting some sign from both groups, and less than 1 in 1,000 of those who showed signs in both groups and additionally had jaundice or similar symptoms, developed normally. This would seem to indicate the necessity for keeping a careful watch on the development of such infants, so that therapy, if needed, can be begun as early as possible.

TREATMENT

In general, little can be done through medical or surgical means —other than the orthopedic amelioration of deformities due to muscular contractures of long standing—for the cerebral palsied. Occasional cases, however, may benefit from surgical removal of

[5] That is, blue discoloration of skin from nonoxidation of blood.

the abnormal brain areas. As is the case with epileptics, the success of this treatment is dependent on the degree of localization of the brain abnormality, the amount of tissue involved, and the actual location of the abnormality. If it is too close to the areas governing important functions, it may not be safe to attempt the removal of even a small area of abnormal tissue.

With the majority of cerebral palsied children, treatment consists of the long-continued use of exercises designed to re-establish motor control so as to permit more or less normal functioning and to prevent the development of muscle contractures and permanent deformities. Cases showing speech defects should also receive therapy specifically directed to this handicap. Since for best results this treatment must be started as soon as the abnormality is detected and be carried on for long periods, it is usually advisable to train the parents to administer it under expert supervision. Aside from its economic advantages, this permits much more intensive therapy without the use of any individual exercise periods so long as to be unduly tiring for the child.

In addition to the obvious physiological value of early therapy, the psychological effects are extremely important. The normal child shows such an intense and persistent interest in learning to crawl, to sit up, to walk, and to talk, such a strong desire to acquire these skills, that it is natural to assume the presence of the same interest and desire in the handicapped child. Perhaps fortunately, in the absence of therapy, but surely unfortunately when therapy is given, the cerebral palsied child may seem to have no such feelings. It may be that failure in the very earliest efforts has caused him to lose interest even before his efforts have gone far enough to be noticeable to the adult observer. In any case, it is often found that one of the major obstacles to successful therapy is the child's lack of adequate motivation toward the goals set for him. The earlier therapy is begun, the less likely is such an obstacle to arise. Although much can be done for the older child, six months of age is considered none too early to start rehabilitation for the infant who is in need of it.

EDUCATION

The nature of the formal education of the cerebral palsied child must be governed by his intellectual capacity and the manner in which it is carried out by his motor handicap. The child of normal or superior intelligence can profit from academic work to the same extent as the normal, although it should perhaps be taken into account that his physical handicap may frequently prevent him from being employed at a level fully commensurate with his training and abilities. When the motor difficulties are substantial, education in the special schools and classes for crippled children —with speech therapy as it may be indicated—or home tutoring may be required. The personal adjustment of the child to his handicap must also be considered in determining whether attendance in the regular classes is desirable for him. It is to be hoped that the recent widespread growth of public interest in, and knowledge concerning, cerebral palsy will substantially lessen the external difficulties with which these children have thus far had to cope.

BRAIN-INJURED CHILDREN

In recent years, a good deal of material has appeared dealing with a group usually designated the "brain-injured." Strauss and Lehtinen, who are among the most prominent workers in the field, describe the typical brain-injured child as being physically normal so far as the usual examinations reveal; they state that many such children may present no physical abnormalities, even on searching investigation. Their difference from the normal child is most prominent with respect to behavior; they are likely to be difficult to manage, emotionally unstable, and to resemble the postencephalitic in many overt characteristics. Like many post-encephalitics, the brain-injured child may achieve a normal or superior rating on carefully given intelligence tests but be unable to govern his behavior and the use of his intelligence in such a way as to lead a normal, noninstitutionalized life. These children have a short attention span and are extremely distractible. Specially designed tests reveal that they have disturbances in perception (as indicated by difficulty in distinguishing figures from a patterned background) and in concept formation.

By definition, these children have suffered brain injury of the same sort as that leading to cerebral palsy. The fundamental etiology of the two groups should therefore be substantially the same.

The distractibility, impulsiveness, and emotional instability of the brain-injured child usually make him unable to profit by regular academic training, even in special classes. Strauss and Lehtinen report that special techniques, involving for the most part the removal of distracting influences from the schoolroom and the simplification of the material to be studied so as to present as unitary a stimulus as possible—for example, the masking of reading material so that only one line at a time is seen against a uniform neutral background—result in moderate improvement of academic performance and such marked improvement in social adjustment that it is frequently possible to return the child to his normal environment.

REFERENCES

American Psychological Association, Division of School Psychologists, and the National Society for Crippled Children and Adults, Inc., *Psychological Problems of Cerebral Palsy*, a symposium (Chicago, National Society for Crippled Children and Adults, Inc., 1952).

BAKWIN, Ruth M., and BAKWIN, Harry, "Cerebral Palsy in Children," *Journal of Pediatrics*, 38 (1951), 113-122.

BENDA, Clemens E., *Developmental Disorders of Mentation and Cerebral Palsies* (New York, Grune and Stratton, Inc., 1952).

BURTON, Mary Louisa Hart, and JENNINGS, Sage Holter, *Your Child or Mine* (New York, Coward-McCann, Inc., 1949).

CASS, Marion T., *Speech Habilitation in Cerebral Palsy* (New York, Columbia University Press, 1951).

COLLIS, Eirene, "Infantile Cerebral Palsy," *Lancet*, 265, No. 6789 (1953), 757-758.

COLLIS, W. R. F., and O'DONNELL, Mary, "Cerebral Palsy," *Archives of Diseases of Childhood*, 26 (1951), 387-398.

CROTHERS, Bronson, "Clinical Aspects of Cerebral Palsy," *International Records of Medicine*, 164 (1951), 300-306.

CRUIKSHANK, William M., "The Multiply Handicapped Cerebral Palsied Child," *Exceptional Children*, 20 (1953), 16-22.

———, and DOLPHIN, Jane E., "The Educational Implications of Psychological Studies of Cerebral Palsied Children," *Journal of Exceptional Children*, 18 (1951), 52-58.

DENHOFF, Eric, "Needs in the Field of Psychologic Appraisal of Children with Cerebral Palsy," *New England Journal of Medicine*, 243 (1950), 524-527.

———, and HOLDEN, R. H., "The Significance of Delayed Development in the Diagnosis of Cerebral Palsy," *Journal of Pediatrics*, 38 (1951), 452-546.

DERSE, Peggy, "The Emotional Problems of Behavior in the Spastic, Athetoid and Ataxic Type of Cerebral Palsy Child," *American Journal of Occupational Therapy*, 4 (1950), 252-260.

DOLL, Edgar A., "Mental Evaluation of Children with Cerebral Palsy," *Crippled Child*, 30, No. 1 (1952), 6-7, 28.

DOLPHIN, Jane E., and CRUICKSHANK, William M., "The Figure-background Relationship in Children with Cerebral Palsy," *Journal of Clinical Psychology*, 7 (1951), 228-231.

———, and CRUICKSHANK, William M., "Visuo-motor Perception in Children with Cerebral Palsy," *Quarterly Journal of Child Behavior*, 3 (1951), 198-209.

———, and CRUICKSHANK, William M., "Pathology of Concept Formation in Children with Cerebral Palsy," *American Journal of Mental Deficiency*, 56 (1951), 386-392.

———, and CRUICKSHANK, William M., "Tactual Motor Perception of Children with Cerebral Palsy," *Journal of Personality*, 20 (1952), 466-471.

FLEISCHER, Ernest, "Higher Education for the Cerebral Palsied," *American Journal of Occupational Therapy*, 7 (1953), 254-267.

FOURACRE, Maurice H., and THIEL, Ellen A., "Education of Children with Mental Retardation Accompanying Cerebral Palsy," *American Journal of Mental Deficiency*, 57 (1953), 401-414.

FULDNER, Russell V., "Physical Examination of the Cerebral Palsied Child," *Journal of the American Medical Association*, 148 (1952), 34-41.

GAUGER, Adeline B., "Statistical Survey of a Group of Institutionalized Cerebral Palsy Patients," *American Journal of Mental Deficiency*, 55 (1950), 90-98.

GRAYSON, Elizabeth, "Occupational Therapy for the Cerebral Palsied Baby," *American Journal of Occupational Therapy*, 4 (1950), 64-65.

HADRA, Ruth, "Developmental Factors in the Cerebral Palsied Child: I," *Crippled Child*, 28, No. 2 (1950), 18-19, 29-30.

———, "Developmental Factors in the Cerebral Palsied Child: II," *Crippled Child*, 30, No. 3 (1950), 22-23, 30.

HAEUSSERMANN, Else, "Evaluating the Developmental Level of Cerebral Palsy Preschool Children," *Journal of Genetic Psychology*, 80 (1952), 3-23.

HARDY, William G., "Hearing Impairment in Cerebral Palsied Children," *Cerebral Palsy Review*, 14, No. 9 (1953), 3-7.

HOLDEN, Raymond H., "Improved Methods in Testing Cerebral Palsied Children," *American Journal of Mental Deficiency*, 56 (1951), 349-353.

———, "A Review of Psychological Studies in Cerebral Palsy: 1947-1952," *American Journal of Mental Deficiency*, 56 (1952), 92-98.

JEWELL, Bruce T., and WURSTEN, Helmut, "Observations on the Psychological Testing of Cerebral Palsied Children," *American Journal of Mental Deficiency*, 56 (1952), 630-637.

KEATS, Sydney, "Rehabilitation of the Child with Cerebral Palsy," *Journal of the International College of Surgeons*, 18 (1952), 935-939.

KLAPPER, Zelda S., and WERNER, Heinz, "Developmental Deviations in Brain-injured (Cerebral-palsied) Members of Pairs of Identical Twins," *Quarterly Journal of Child Behavior*, 2 (1950), 288-313.

LEWIS, Richard S., STRAUSS, Alfred A., and LEHTINEN, Laura E., *The Other Child: The Brain-injured Child* (New York, Grune and Stratton, Inc., 1951).

LINCK, Lawrence J., "The Care of the Cerebral Palsied Child in the U.S.A.," *The Nervous Child*, 8, No. 4 (October, 1950), 519-523.

LONG, Elinor H., *The Challenge of the Cerebral Palsied Blind Child* (New York, American Foundation for the Blind, 1952).

MALZBERG, Benjamin, "Statistical Aspects of Mental Deficiency with Congenital Cerebral Spastic Infantile Paralyses," *American Journal of Mental Deficiency*, 55 (1950), 99-104.

McINTIRE, J. T., "A Study of the Distribution of Physical Handicap and Mental Diagnosis in Cerebral Palsied Children," *American Journal of Mental Deficiency*, 51 (1947), 624-626.

MILLER, Elsa, and ROSENFELD, George B., "The Psychologic Evaluation of Children with Cerebral Palsy and Its Implications in Treatment: Preliminary Report," *Journal of Pediatrics*, 41 (1952), 613-621.

PALMER, Martin F., "Speech Therapy in Cerebral Palsy," *Journal of Pediatrics*, 40 (1952), 514-521.

PEINS, Maryann, "You Can Help at Home," *Crippled Child*, 27, No. 2 (1949), 20-23.

PENFIELD, Wilder, "Ablation of Abnormal Cortex in Cerebral Palsy," *Journal of Neurology, Neurosurgery, and Psychiatry*, 15 (1952), 73-78.

PHELPS, Winthrop M., "The Differential Characteristics of Spasticity and Athetosis in Relation to Therapeutic Measures," *New York State Journal of Medicine*, 41 (1941), 1287-1288.

———, "Characteristic Psychological Variations in Cerebral Palsy," *The Nervous Child*, 7, No. 1 (January, 1948), 10-13.

———, "General Management of the Cerebral Palsy Problem," *Cerebral Palsy Review*, 13, No. 11 (1952), 3-4, 9.

POHL, John F., *Cerebral Palsy* (St. Paul, Minn., Bruce Publishing Company, 1950).

SCHERER, Isidor W., "Vocational Planning for the Cerebral Palsied," *Cerebral Palsy Review*, 13, No. 8 (1952), 3-6, 16-17, 19.

SCHWARTZ, Ralph, "To You . . . the Parent," *Cerebral Palsy Review*, 14, No. 9 (1953), 9-10, 15.

SIEVERS, Dorothy J., and NORMAN, Ralph D., "Some Suggestive Results in Psychometric Testing of the Cerebral Palsied with Gesell, Binet and Wechsler Scales," *Journal of Genetic Psychology*, 82 (1953), 69-90.

STRAUSS, Alfred A., "The Education of the Brain-injured Child," *American Journal of Mental Deficiency*, 56 (1952), 712-718.

———, and LEHTINEN, Laura E., *Psychopathology and Education of the Brain-injured Child* (New York, Grune and Stratton, Inc., 1947).

THIEL, Ellen Akins, "Employment of the Cerebral Palsied: Begin with the Beginners," *Crippled Child*, 29, No. 1 (1951), 14-15, 29.

United States Children's Bureau, and United States Office of Education, *The Child with Cerebral Palsy* (Washington, D.C., Government Printing Office, 1950).

WALLACE, Helen M., BAUMGARTNER, Leona, and COOPER, William, "Cerebral-palsied Children Attend Special Classes in Public Schools," *Child*, 18, No. 1 (1953), 2-5.

WESTLAKE, Harold, "Muscle Training for Cerebral Palsied Speech Cases," *Journal of Speech and Hearing Disorders*, 16 (1951), 103-109.

WILSON, Ruby K., "An Investigation of the Birth Records of Children with Cerebral Palsy as Given by the Attending Physicians," Unpublished master's thesis (Wichita, Municipal University of Wichita, 1951).

WOLFE, William G., "A Comprehensive Evaluation of Fifty Cases of Cerebral Palsy," *Journal of Speech and Hearing Disorders*, 15 (1950), 234-251.

YANNET, H., "The Etiology of Congenital Cerebral Palsy," *Journal of Pediatrics*, 24 (1944), 38-45.

———, and HORTON, Frank, "Hypotonic Cerebral Palsy in Mental Defectives," *Pediatrics*, 9 (1952), 204-211.

The Postencephalitic Child 27

NOT LONG AGO, the newspapers told the story of a twelve-year-old boy who has become a difficult problem for the authorities in one of the western states. His police record includes armed robbery, arson, burglary, auto theft, and two occasions on which he got hold of firearms and "shot it out" with the police, who managed to draw his fire by shooting into the air until, having run out of ammunition, he could be approached with relative safety. It was the latter of these battles which earned him nationwide attention. What can be done with him? He cannot be committed to the state mental hospital, because he is not insane within the legal meaning of the term. He himself rather expects to be sent to the penitentiary; to adult minds, however, such a course seems certain to do no good and likely to do great harm, even if our present mores were not so strongly opposed in principle to penitentiary terms for twelve-year-olds. Although this child is unusual in that he has repeatedly been able to get hold of a gun and thus present a very difficult problem to the adults who were trying to bring him under control, the behavior patterns involved and lack of adequate means to deal with him are rather typical of the post-encephalitic.

WHAT IS ENCEPHALITIS?

Encephalitis is not a single disease, but a group of diseases presenting similar clinical features both during the acute phases and in the residual effects on the victims. Some are known to be caused by a virus; the others are believed to be. Epidemic encephalitis is the term often used for the most important one of this group; however, many authorities feel that it is too general a term and, even as used in the past, has been applied to epidemics which were probably not all caused by the same virus. They would prefer to speak of the individual epidemic in unequivocally specific terms—such as "von Economo's encephalitis," "Japanese encephalitis type B," "St. Louis encephalitis," and so forth. If this is done, epidemic encephalitis would refer to any and all of these and would also include any other epidemic types of encephalitis; but any individual outbreak would be designated either by its place (and, if necessary, time) of occurrence when the virus is unidentified or be grouped appropriately if the virus is identified as being identical with that which caused some previous epidemic.

Four types of epidemic encephalitis have been associated with specific viruses. These are St. Louis encephalitis, Japanese B encephalitis, equine encephalomyelitis, and Russian encephalitis. Although von Economo's encephalitis is the longest known of the epidemic encephalitis group, having been described by von Economo in 1917, and has since then been studied both intensively and extensively, its etiology is not yet clear.

In addition to the diseases grouped under epidemic encephalitis, a large number of virus infections which do not usually attack the nervous system may, on occasion, be followed by encephalitis. The mechanism of this action is not clear. Perhaps in certain cases the original, *non-neurotropic* [1] virus is somehow modified in the body of the patient so that it becomes neurotropic. Perhaps a neurotropic virus is already present, but latent, in the patient, and is stimulated to attack by the presence of the infection or enabled to overcome the body's defenses because they have become weakened in combating the other virus. Perhaps it is a matter of synergistic action, through which a combination of two viruses produces results that differ from those which would be produced by either one acting in the absence of the other. Whatever the operating mechanism, the results are usually extremely serious.

[1] That is, having no tendency to attack the nervous system preferentially.

Measles is more often associated with central nervous system complications than any other acute infection. The incidence of complications is extremely low—series of as many as 12,000 cases of measles with as few as one occurrence of encephalitis have been reported—but because measles is so nearly universal a childhood disease in this country, it is probable that most adults have heard, at first or second hand, of such cases. Sometimes a whole group of them will occur in one small measles epidemic; in a city of about 26,000 population, during the course of an otherwise mild epidemic of measles, I heard of six cases of encephalitis, at least two of which were fatal, within a two-week period. The children involved came from different parts of the city.

German measles, chicken pox, mumps, scarlet fever, and smallpox may all, though rarely, be followed by encephalitis. Even the mild virus infection involved in a successful vaccination appears sufficient, in some cases, to lead to central nervous system complications.

Although the incidence of encephalitis as a complication of other infections is not known with any certainty, there is general agreement that it has risen appreciably in the last 20 or 30 years. Better diagnosis, of course, can be invoked to account for some of the increase in the number of cases reported; but that so severe a complication, with such marked symptoms, could have been overlooked to the point of not being considered worth mention by highly competent clinicians of long experience seems most unlikely. There has, then, been a change in incidence; its time, extent, and cause are equally unknown.

ACUTE ENCEPHALITIS

Like poliomyelitis, encephalitis varies in the severity of the acute attack from a mild, unimpressive, and transient illness that may not even seem worth mentioning to a physician to an obviously severe, violent, and frightening condition. Except during an epidemic, the milder cases are likely to escape diagnosis unless and until the sequelae call attention, retrospectively, to the probable true nature of the initial attack. Although estimates vary widely, it seems probable that something like half of all cases in which there are definite long-range sequelae fail to be recognized as encephalitis during the acute stage. In one series of more than 500 cases, over one fourth of the cases gave a history in which no illness suggestive of acute encephalitis was described. When to these are added the numbers of cases without marked sequelae, it becomes obvious that there must be many cases of encephalitis which go entirely unsuspected; perhaps as many as four or five for every one that is recognized.

The onset of a severe attack may be gradual, consisting of hours or days of general malaise, headache, irritability, fatigue, and other vague symptoms; or it may be strikingly abrupt, consisting of convulsions, paralysis, severe pain, vomiting, or, in rare cases, acute psychosis. Headache is one of the most common of the early symptoms. Vomiting, dizziness, fever, and signs of *meningeal irritation* [2] occur with reasonable frequency. The prominence of sleep disturbances is indicated by the term *encephalitis lethargica,* which has been used as an alternative for epidemic encephalitis. These disturbances usually involve more or less lethargy; but they may consist of insomnia or of an inversion of the sleep patterns. Important though they are, however, sleep disturbances are entirely absent in perhaps one third of the recognized cases. Many cases show oculomotor disturbances of varying type and degree of severity; the optic nerve itself is sometimes, although much less often, involved. With involvement of other nerves or brain areas facial paralyses, difficulty in speech, swallowing and respiration, Parkinsonian symptoms, and decerebrate reactions may occur. A general motor excitability may be present, as indicated by insomnia, muscular twitches, delirium, and even mania. Epileptiform seizures may occur but are not common. Aphasia, indicating cortical involvement, seems to be more common among young individuals.

It is obvious from the extreme variety of the symptoms that an isolated case of acute encephalitis, even if severe, may be dif-

[2] That is, irritation of the membranes of the brain and cord.

ficult to identify unequivocally. Cases occurring during an epidemic, of course, are more likely to be recognized; however, certain identification depends on the isolation of the virus from the blood or spinal fluid of the patient or through neutralization or complement fixation studies of the convalescent serum. The appearance of typical sequelae, particularly if there is a history of an illness suggestive of encephalitis, is also considered fairly good evidence that an acute attack, even though unrecognized, has occurred.

CHRONIC ENCEPHALITIS

The chronic stage of encephalitis presents a rather different picture from the acute one. The symptoms may be as widely varying as are those of the acute stage, but by far the greatest number of cases fall into the two categories of Parkinsonism and mental and behavior disorders. Parkinsonism tends to occur when the acute episode has taken place in or after late adolescence, though it may also be found in children. Tremor, rigidity, facial immobility, and a loss of associated movements are its outstanding characteristics. The condition usually develops gradually and is progressive. Even when recovery from an acute attack appears complete, it is not safe to assume that the chronic phase will not appear later. Substantial numbers of cases have been reported in which the symptom-free interval was five or ten years or even longer. Although the mortality is known to be high in encephalitis, the known existence of many cases that are not diagnosed in the acute stage makes it difficult to present any reasonably reliable estimates; the incidence of development of the chronic stage in adults is also uncertain.

In children, the case seems to be rather different; the incidence of mental or behavior disorders following encephalitis seems almost certainly to be extremely high, even after taking into consideration cases undiagnosed until the appearance of the chronic phase. In a group reported by Gibbs only 8 per cent of the children, who were all under the age of fourteen at the time of the acute infection, apparently recovered completely; 10 per cent died; and 84 per cent of those surviving developed a chronic phase. After a little less than ten years, about half of the chronic cases, all of whom had initially shown behavior disorders, had also developed progressive Parkinsonism. The others had not shown this physical deterioration, but their behavior disorders had progressed or remained substantially unimproved; there was every indication that they would remain permanently institutionalized. In infants, encephalitis may cause such widespread damage as to arrest mental development; in children over three years of age, a very common result is the occurrence of extensive and typical personality changes, but intelligence, as measured by standard tests, has not been markedly affected, and physical signs are minimal or entirely lacking. Such cases are particularly distressing because the affected child may exhibit high ability in remembering, reasoning, and other mental functions, but his lack of inhibitions and of fear of consequences, combined with destructiveness and impulsiveness, virtually eliminate any chance that he may lead a normal, happy, constructive life.

TYPICAL CHARACTERISTICS OF THE
POSTENCEPHALITIC CHILD

These characteristics will vary somewhat according to the age of the child at the time of the acute attack, its severity, and the length of the time since its occurrence. Two forms of sequelae may be noted. The first is by comparison rare; it seems to be more common among those in whom the original attack was so severe that few cases survive. These children appear almost catatonic; they make few voluntary movements and do not speak, except in response to insistent demands. Then their speech is slow, monotonous, and, in many cases, consists only of a repetition of the last words spoken to them. If given a book or toy, they do not examine it but hold it patiently until it slips from their nerveless grasp.

Much more frequent than these are the cases in which the

brain damage resulting from the disease reveals itself in greatly increased excitability and unresponsiveness to ordinary means of control. The child who has hitherto been reasonable and at least ordinarily docile now becomes restless, highly excitable, and pays little heed to warnings or to reproof. His behavior takes on a peculiarly compulsive appearance: he *must* do this thing that is in his mind; he *must* respond to each fleeting perception. So he dashes from one thing to another, giving only brief attention to each. Often he becomes destructive; some become surprisingly adept at a particular method of dismembering furniture or other objects, removing screws with their fingers or teeth, or ripping the seams of their own garments or those of others. Punishment is rarely a deterrent, for their behavior is dictated by the interests of the moment, by that which they perceive at the time.

Their emotions are shallow. They show little affection for others, and though some of them seem to like fondling, they are usually indifferent to the fondler.

Intellectually, many appear normal, some even superior. An alert examiner finds it possible to give such a child a mental test, though at the cost of nearly complete exhaustion for himself. The effect of the disease upon mental ability is not, as a rule, to destroy or even seriously damage it but rather, as it were, to divorce it from the child's life and behavior. He knows, but the knowledge is not related to his actions. He may, as some do, acquire a surprising store of information on some particular subject. He may have an excellent memory for facts. He may learn to read and write and show a good understanding of numerical relationships. But he still cannot be trusted to control himself. He still has tantrums without apparent cause; he still destroys property or his own clothing; he still kicks and strikes without provocation. Not that these things are done constantly. Such a child, if not irritated, may go for weeks without causing difficulty. But he remains unpredictable. With no more warning than a slight increase in restlessness and excitability, or even no warning at all, the postencephalitic child may suddenly display behavior that may have serious consequences for himself or for others as he grows older.

The behavior effects do not always appear in full force at once. In some cases, the parent will observe that one or both of the child's eyes are becoming inturned but is unlikely to relate this condition [3] to the illness. Only the experienced clinician is likely to observe the masklike facial expression, one of the most conspicuous features of the Parkinsonian syndrome [4] that usually follows an attack and may persist for some time afterward. Before many weeks have passed, the changes in the child's behavior become so marked that they can no longer be overlooked. "I don't know what has come over him; he was never like this before," exclaims the distracted mother. Rewards for good behavior or punishment for misbehavior are alike ineffective. She becomes desperate.

SOME TYPICAL CASES

R. D. is the idolized only child of wealthy Jewish parents. He had always been healthy until, one day, when he was about four and a half years old, his mother noticed his flushed face and found that he was running a slight fever. Alarmed, she called the family physician. The busy doctor made only a cursory examination. "Just a little cold," he pronounced easily. "Lots of them around. Keep him in bed for a day or so if you can and call me again if he doesn't get all right. Good morning."

The child was put to bed. He made surprisingly little protest and soon slept. His temperature continued to be slightly above normal for the next two days, and he seemed rather drowsy and content to stay in bed. By the third day, however, the fever had subsided, and he demanded to get up. Now his mother noticed for the first time a slight strabismus in the left eye. She took the child to an oculist, who outlined a series of corrective exercises.

It soon became apparent, however, that more serious difficulties were at hand. The child had always been an active rather inquisitive youngster, but now he seemed always in motion and no prohibitions

---

[3] Strabismus is a frequent but not invariable aftereffect of this disease.

[4] This results from a partial paralysis of the facial muscles of expression. The child laughs or cries audibly but his facial expression does not undergo the usual change or changes but little. Even in repose, his face presents a peculiar fixed expression that the expert is likely to notice.

were effective in keeping him out of mischief. He destroyed a number of valuable articles that he had been forbidden to touch, broke his toys, and seemed impervious to reproof. Only active physical punishment seemed to affect him, and that did not serve as a deterrent.

Now began the long and fruitless round of visits to doctors and to behavior clinics. Most of the authorities consulted shrugged the matter off. "Just another spoiled child," they thought, and gave the mother advice regarding child management. This she followed but without noticeable effect. Finally she chanced upon a physician who had had experience with such cases. He learned of the "slight cold," which the mother had not previously thought worth mentioning, and at once sent the child to a hospital for a series of tests, including a spinal puncture which demonstrated beyond reasonable doubt that the boy was suffering from the aftereffects of a very mild case of encephalitis. He advised institutional placement, but to this the parents were unwilling to agree. He was their only child; they wanted to keep him at home. They were then advised to try to enter him in a local nursery school, where he could have the advantage of more consistent and impersonal discipline than the parents were likely to give him. This was tried, but after two or three days, the parents were asked to withdraw him. The teacher stated that he demanded an impracticable amount of her care and attention, that he had struck some of the smaller children and destroyed school equipment.

The parents, however, were reluctant to withdraw him. The school seemed their last hope. In this dilemma, the father inquired whether the teacher would be willing to retain him in school if he were willing to pay for a special teacher who would devote all her time to looking after the boy so as to forestall his damaging either children or property.

With some hesitation the teacher assented. A teacher was found, and the boy remained in school for almost a month. But in spite of her vigilance, occasional accidents occurred. A five-year-old moves so quickly and unexpectedly that even the most watchful adult will sometimes be caught napping. And when these movements take on the compulsive character that is so typical of the postencephalitic, it becomes almost impossible to control them.

In spite of the parents' great desire to keep their only child at home, as age advanced and his strength increased it became evident that this was no longer possible. Eventually a small private school was found willing to undertake his care. "It was the most expensive one we looked up," reported the father with a mixture of pride and ruefulness.

At last hearing, R. D. was still in this school. To some extent, he had learned to conform to the school's usual routine, but he still required much supervision. He still appeared nervous and was readily excited. That he will ever be able to live in a normal community seems improbable.

Unlike many others, the case of B. W. was diagnosed as encephalitis at the time of the acute attack. It was a moderately severe case, but the boy recovered. However, as his strength returned, he became increasingly unmanageable. His restless activity can best be described in the notes taken by the psychologist at a behavior clinic to which he had been sent for advice. Wishing to get a picture of the boy's usual behavior, the psychologist decided to leave him entirely to himself for a period of fifteen minutes.

A small waiting room for children, equipped with a sand box, toys, and picture books, was vacant at the time. The psychologist took him there, directing him to sit down and wait, stating that he would soon be sent for. B. W. agreed very cheerfully, and the psychologist left but remained within visual range.

The boy's eyes fell on the sand table. Instantly he sprang up, seized a small shovel, and began to dig, scattering the sand in all directions. He then noticed an unframed picture thumbtacked to the wall above the table. He jumped onto the table, gazed at the picture for a few seconds, then tore it down, crumpling it into a ball which he tossed away. He then jumped to the floor again and for a moment continued to dig in the sand until his attention was diverted by the sight of a drinking fountain in the hall. He spent a moment or two in turning the water on as far as he could and making it squirt all about by putting his thumb over the stream. He then ran back to the sand table returning with a handful of sand which he proceeded to pack into the fountain. At this point, the psychologist stepped forward to intervene, but B. W. did not wait for her expostulations. He ran at full speed down the hall to a door at the end through which he escaped, followed by the psychologist. Outside was a playground with swings, in one of which a small girl was slowly swinging back and forth. With no apparent ill-will but treating her exactly as he might have treated any other obstacle, B. W. pushed her out of the swing and jumped into it himself, "pumping" vigorously for a moment and then trying to climb up the rope. He paid not the slightest attention to the crying child on the ground who, more frightened than hurt, picked herself up and ran off. However, he may have anticipated punishment, for when he caught sight of the psychologist, he ran back at once into the building. An open door attracted him, and in he went. A clerk was sitting at a desk, behind her on the wall was a calendar. Onto the desk he leaped, scratching its polished surface with his heavy shoes. He shoved the clerk aside, snatched the calendar, and tore off the leaves one after another.

Although only eight of the fifteen-minute observation period had expired, the psychologist decided to terminate the experiment at this point. It is noteworthy that like many such children, this lad would yield cheerfully and at once to verbal commands or requests. These constituted a new stimulus, to which he responded as readily as he did to those suggested by other sounds or sights. But his obedience lasted only until something else claimed his attention, when he would be off like a flash.

TRAINING

A great deal of time and energy has been spent in attempting to devise some method of training or rehabilitating the post-encephalitic child so as to enable him to lead a normal life. So far, no adequate solution to the problem has been found. A very few cases improve, in time, so that they no longer need to be institutionalized; some appear to recover completely. But, for the majority, the prognosis is not good. For them, it appears that the personality disorders which make them dangerous to themselves and to those around them, far from improving with the passage of time, tend to become worse. In addition, the progressive neurological symptoms so typically found in adults frequently appear, even though this appearance may be delayed for years after the initial attack.

REFERENCES

APPEL, K. E., "Encephalitis in Children," *Journal of Pediatrics,* 7 (1935), 478-487.

BROWN, A. W., JANKINS, R. F., and CISLER, L. E., "Influence of Lethargic Encephalitis on Intelligence of Children," *American Journal of Diseases of Childhood,* 105 (1938), 304-321.

GIBBS, C. E., "Behavior Disorders in Chronic Epidemic Encephalitis," *American Journal of Psychiatry,* 9 (1930), 619-636.

HEERSEMA, P., "Prognosis in Post-encephalitic Disorders," *American Journal of Diseases of Childhood,* 60 (1940), 783-788.

KASTEIN, Shulamith, "Speech and Language Habilitation in a Post-encephalitic Child," *American Journal of Mental Deficiency,* 56 (1952), 570-577.

NEAL, Josephine B., *Encephalitis: A Clinical Study* (New York, Grune and Stratton, Inc., 1942).

TIMME, Arthur R., "What Has Neurology to Offer Child Guidance?" *Neurology,* 2 (1952), 424-440.

VON ECONOMO, C., *Encephalitis Lethargica: Its Sequelae and Treatment,* trans. K. O. Newman (London, Oxford University Press, 1931).

The Child with Epilepsy 28

THE NATURE OF EPILEPSY

EVEN A LAYMAN who has no previous acquaintance with epilepsy is likely to suspect the correct explanation if a child has repeated, violent, generalized convulsions. A major convulsion is a very frightening thing for the unsophisticated bystander. Probably for this reason, epilepsy has been both recognized and, usually, assigned a somewhat special character since very early times. Although the major convulsion is probably responsible for a large proportion of the emotional distress and certainly constitutes much of the handicap of epilepsy, it is by no means the only, or even a universal, sign of the disease. It is also not confined to epilepsy; under a sufficiently powerful and suitable stimulus, such as the hypoglycemia caused by excess insulin, a major convulsion can be induced in anyone.

A reasonably complete definition of epilepsy is that it consists of repeated attacks of loss of consciousness, with physical manifestations which may range from what, to the casual observer, appears to be no more than a moment's pause, usually accompanied by staring, through a variety of localized or mild general movement patterns to the severe generalized convulsions of *grand mal*.

In general, the minor seizures—which limit themselves to a few seconds of staring, usually without loss of balance (some children may even continue walking during such an episode) and with no motor involvement or with minimal involvement, such as slight flickering movements of the eyelids and face—constitute the classic type of simple *petit mal*.

Minor motor seizures are sometimes classed with *petit mal*, but seem to represent a distinctly different phenomenon; although they do resemble *petit mal* in the brevity of the seizure and the fact that frequently the loss of motor control is so slight that the child, if standing, does not fall, they show all the characteristics of the early stages of a convulsion. They also merge into the full-blown convulsion, both in duration and in extent and degree of motor involvement.

The akinetic seizure is a minor seizure in which there is a sudden inhibition of postural tone, so that the child slumps to the floor as he would if suddenly knocked out by a blow. The drop is so abrupt that in spite of the quick recovery of control, serious injury may result. In young children the loss of tone may be limited to the head and arms, so that instead of general collapse, there is merely a sudden falling forward of the head, often with simultaneous raising of the arms. This latter pattern has been described as the "salaam" seizure. The akinetic seizure, although it is a minor seizure involving motor groups, is distinguished from the minor motor seizure in that it does not have any particular resemblance to a convulsion; nor, if it were to be prolonged, would it become one.

There are several other forms of minor seizures, but they are not often seen in children. The psychic equivalent, in which complex automatic acts are carried out in a state of clouded consciousness, is extremely rare, and the fugue apparently does not occur before adolescence.

The typical major seizure is in the form of the generalized convulsion. This is often, but not always, preceded by an aura. It may consist of a vague feeling of impending disaster, of fear, of what may be described as faintness, or of general or specific physical sensations. Although the aura is thus seen to have no generally consistent characteristics for all epileptics, it may be quite invariable in form and duration for a given case. When this is so, it may indicate that the convulsion involves a specific local area of activity in the brain.

From the observer's viewpoint, the aura is not particularly conspicuous. The child may change color, either growing pale or flushing, or may appear frightened. As the convulsion approaches and consciousness recedes, a glassy stare may appear. The convulsion itself starts with a contraction of all voluntary muscles (*tonic phase*), and loss of consciousness; in a minority of cases the child may scream involuntarily. With the loss of motor control, the child falls. The initial rigidity is soon replaced by rapid twitching movements (the *clonic phase*), which gradually diminish, ending in a state of general relaxation and exhaustion. During the clonic phase the tongue or cheek may be caught between the clenched jaws and cause bleeding from the mouth. The combination of increased salivation and inhibition of swallowing produces what is usually described as "foaming at the mouth." If the visceral muscles are involved, involuntary urination and defecation may occur. At the end of the clonic phase, the exhaustion and relaxation may be so profound that the child sinks into a state of coma and cannot be roused for some time. After he begins to rouse, confusion and lethargy are likely to persist, gradually giving way to a normal state of consciousness.

The cycle, from the initial tension to relaxation, usually lasts only one or two minutes. In a severe attack, the clonic phase may be somewhat prolonged. More importantly, however, as soon as the recovery from fatigue permits, a second convulsion takes place. It is rare for a series of epileptic convulsions to continue for longer than 20 or 30 minutes. However, on occasion, the condition known as *status epilepticus* may develop. In this condition, the sequence of tonic, clonic, and relaxation phases persists, lasting for hours or even days. It is extremely serious, since the prolonged and repeated convulsions and coma readily lead to severe brain damage and even death.

The focal type of major seizure differs from classic *grand mal* in that it particularly involves only certain areas, differing from case to case but consistent for a given child. Such seizures arise on the basis of localized brain damage, and, in them, the abnormal brain activity does not spread to involve the whole body in the seizure. In many cases this localization of the area of abnormal brain function permits surgical treatment; in many others, however, the area involved is too large, too inaccessible, or too near areas controlling vitally important functions, such as speech, to permit surgery.

There is general agreement that epilepsy is a manifestation of abnormal brain function. Since typical convulsive attacks may appear in a previously normal individual after traumatic brain damage, and since the surgical removal of areas showing demonstrable pathology will frequently eliminate attacks, it appears certain that such abnormal function can be caused by physical damage to a normal brain. Also, as was mentioned above, convulsions can be induced in any individual by means of suitable stimuli. In view of this, it would seem to be equally certain that brain damage is not a prerequisite for convulsions. In the course of work with therapeutic shock treatments, it has been observed that, just as is found for most biological characteristics, the ease with which a convulsion can be produced varies markedly from person to person. Obviously, the lower the convulsive threshold of the intact brain, the more likely it becomes that stimuli arising in the ordinary course of life may be strong enough to produce a seizure. Furthermore, once convulsions have occurred, it is possible for a vicious circle to be established. Brain damage predisposes to convulsions; but convulsions, particularly if severe and prolonged, are likely to produce brain damage, which, in its turn, increases the convulsive tendency. This is what makes it so dangerous for the epileptic to refuse or discontinue medication or to be careless about the regularity with which it is taken.

These facts make the role of heredity in the etiology of epilepsy very difficult to pin down. It has been repeatedly proven that the families of epileptics have an abnormally high proportion of epileptics. This is generally accepted as indicating the presence of a genetic factor or factors. Its precise nature, however, is not clear. Indeed, in the presence of so undifferentiated a form of response as epilepsy, different genetic factors may be operative in different cases. An inherently low convulsive threshold may provide the major foundation for epilepsy in one child, but in another the important factor may be an unusual susceptibility to brain injury with perhaps only a slightly greater than normal predisposition for convulsive reactions. Further difficulty in evaluating the importance of heredity is caused by the uncertain significance of the presence of abnormal brain waves. These last are found in as much as 15 per cent of the population. Some investigators accept their presence as indicating "latent epilepsy"; others do not.

INCIDENCE

Surveys of the general population here and in Europe indicate that there are between three and five epileptics per 1000 people. As many as one in 20 may have some sort of convulsive episode at some time, most frequently as an isolated occurrence. Data on the occurrence of epilepsy among relatives of epileptics clearly indicate that nonhereditary factors are important; they also make it clear that heredity plays an important role in the causation of epilepsy.

If all forms of pre-, para-, and postnatal brain injury could be avoided, the incidence of epilepsy would quite possibly be more greatly reduced than by the elimination of any other factor, even the hereditary one. Among Bridge's cases, 70 per cent had definite indications of brain injury to some degree, as shown either in their history or by clinical investigation. Of this group, 43 per cent gave a family history of convulsive seizures. The observation that a family history of epilepsy is less often found for cases with a history of brain damage than for cases without it indicates that either of these factors can produce the syndrome without the aid of the other. When the two are present, they reinforce one another, so that epilepsy may appear when neither factor would have been strong enough, acting by itself, to produce seizures.

Within the field of brain damage, a number of different causes of markedly varying importance are seen. For Bridge's group, injuries occurring at birth or in the neonatal period appeared to be most important in causing brain damage. Vascular occlusions are next, followed by head injuries. Encephalitis, lead poisoning, degenerative disease, abscesses and tumors, tuberous sclerosis, and syphilis are recognized causes but of minor importance. In 30 per cent of the cases, no definite conclusion as to the cause was reached. Some investigators have suggested that birth injury, both in the form of mechanical damage and as asphyxia, is an even more important cause of epilepsy than is indicated by the above. They have usually based this on the higher proportion of first-born as compared to later-born children among epileptics. It is not yet clear whether there are reliably more first-born among epileptics than among the general population.

PHYSIOLOGICAL FACTORS IN EPILEPSY

In addition to the relatively permanent factors of heredity and brain damage, a number of known physiological conditions can contribute to precipitate individual seizures. They may even make the difference between a normal child, whose predisposition to epilepsy never reveals itself in a seizure, and one who is a clinical epileptic. Infection, with or without fever; disturbances of fluid balance, whether spontaneous or induced by abnormal fluid intake; the changes incident to the sleep cycle; the changes involved in puberty and recurring at the menstrual period; chronic fatigue; and emotional disturbance all appear to have much to do with the occurrence of seizures. The first of these, infection with or without fever, is particularly associated with infantile convulsions. Indeed, some investigators have concluded that fever is so powerful a stimulus to convulsive reactions that simple febrile convulsions should be considered to be virtually unrelated to epilepsy. It is certainly true that many children who in infancy have one or two seizures associated with a rapidly rising temperature remain perfectly well thereafter. It appears likely that when convulsions occur in infancy, being seen only when the child has a rapid rise of temperature, and are not repeated after three or four years of age, the child should not be considered epileptic. However, there can be no doubt that any child who has a seizure should be carefully examined at the time, in order to rule out such causes as brain tumor or lead poisoning, and he should be followed for a considerable period of time before it is definitely assumed that the tendency to recurrence is absent.

EMOTIONAL INFLUENCES

It is not uncommon for the frequency of seizures to diminish greatly or for them to disappear entirely when succesful efforts are made to improve the emotional situation of a child, even though medication is discontinued or remains unchanged. Sometimes the difficulties have arisen largely as the result of the seizures. In other cases, severe emotional disturbances may appear to be an important cause rather than the result of the epilepsy. The question of such disturbances should always be investigated, and efforts made to ameliorate them when found.

EFFECTS OF EPILEPSY

As has been previously mentioned, epilepsy, particularly if seizures are severe and prolonged, can produce widespread and increasing brain damage. Status epilepticus, if not adequately treated, would often end in death. Even under the best conditions, it is occasionally fatal. However, many children who have not in fact suffered permanent damage may appear to have done so. If seizures are frequent, the state of lethargy and dullness which characteristically follows a convulsion may persist from one seizure to the next. Such a child is never in a fully recovered condition. The absence of permanent damage is indicated if, with better medical control and a consequent increase in the length of the seizure-free periods, the appearance of retardation disappears. If large doses of sedative drugs are given, they in themselves can produce a false appearance of dullness. It appears most probable that epilepsy, considered as a *tendency to seizures*, has no effect upon mental level; but the seizures themselves, particularly as their severity, frequency, and total number increase, are capable of causing widespread severe brain damage with consequent impairment of physical function, mental function, or both.

THE PERSONALITY OF THE EPILEPTIC

Although the importance of physical damage is great, the amount of emotional and social difficulty caused by seizures which have no lasting physical effect probably far outweighs any other handicapping effect. The question of whether there is such a thing as an "epileptic personality" has received a good deal of attention. Epileptics have been typified as self-centered, emotionally unstable, prone to fits of temper, stubborn, defective in the ability to make moral judgments, slow of mind and body. A number of these descriptive terms have been applied on the basis of comparisons between institutionalized epileptics and normal or even superior nonepileptics. For example, in one investigation of moral insight, the test group consisted of individuals in a state colony, all of whom were subject to *grand-mal* seizures; the control group was drawn from a small college community. The institutionalized epileptic presumably has suffered more brain damage than the one who remains in the community; it would seem that a more justifiable comparison would include noninstitutionalized cases and probably would have to take the intellectual level into consideration. Bridge states that in the typical child suffering from major seizures, epilepsy has neither arisen on the basis of a characteristic personality nor does it necessarily produce any consistent personality changes. However, most epileptic children do show evidence of more or less severe personality difficulties. In many, they appear to be a reaction, not to the disease itself but to the circumstances surrounding it and conditioned by it. If an entirely normal, emotionally stable child were suddenly to find himself sharply limited in his activities and his freedom from supervision, visibly the cause of profound emotional disturbance in his parents and immediate family; if his playmates avoided him or became nervous in his presence, and his teacher watched him in mingled expectation and fear; if from time to time he lost consciousness of his surroundings and, on awakening, found himself exhausted, dull, perhaps bruised or cut, perhaps with a sore tongue where he had bitten it—could he reasonably be expected to remain serene, happy, and well adjusted in the usual meaning of the term? And yet, the typical epileptic must endure many, if not all, of these experiences. The most damaging of these experiences are, in large part, the unnecessary and inappropriate reactions of normal people to the epileptic. It may be questioned whether this obvious fact is a greater cause for shame on the part of society or for rejoicing that so great an improvement in the circumstances of living of the victims of this disease could result from adequate education of the public, even in the absence of any change in the status of medical treatment.

THE TREATMENT OF EPILEPSY

A moderate number of epileptics exhibit symptoms of such nature as to lead to the conclusion that a single, possibly small area of brain damage is intimately involved in the initiation of seizures. If, on exploration, this is found to be the case, and if the damaged area can safely be removed, appropriate surgery is often followed by prompt and permanent disappearance of the seizures. Epilepsy following head injuries or resulting from brain tumor or abscess is more likely than epilepsy of other etiology to be amenable to surgical treatment.

In the majority of cases, however, no such simple solution is possible. From the standpoint of cure, epilepsy is often comparable to diabetes, in that suitable, continued medical supervision and treatment will suppress virtually all manifestations of the disease; but the underlying condition is not much changed, and any discontinuance of treatment is promptly followed by a return of the symptoms. The variety and range of etiological factors in epilepsy make it necessary for treatment, if it is to be really adequate, to extend over most aspects of the child's life. Immediate symptomatic relief without unduly pronounced sedative effects can often be obtained by the use of anticonvulsant drugs. *Grand mal* is most likely to respond to the bromides, phenobarbital, or drugs of the hydantoin series, like dilantin and mesantoin. The last are usually much less effective in young children than in adolescents and adults; this appears to be a true age effect rather than a matter of individual variation. *Petit mal* is usually not improved by drugs and may even be made worse. The selection and dosage of medication must be found by experiment for each case.

Regardless of other treatment, it is essential to establish and maintain a regime designed to keep the epileptic child in good general health, with a well-balanced diet, adequate exercise and rest, and avoidance of situations likely to produce undue emotional disturbances, as well as specific measures to eliminate any conditions which have been observed to lead to seizures in the individual case. Formal or informal psychotherapy should be used as indicated by circumstances.

Young children, in particular, may be greatly benefited by the *ketogenic diet*. This is a special diet containing large proportions of fat, smaller amounts of protein, and minimal amounts of carbohydrate. Although it is equally effective in both *grand* and *petit mal* and tends to produce more lasting improvement than the anticonvulsants, it has a number of practical disadvantages. Like the diabetic diet before the introduction of saccharine, it is both monotonous and not very appetizing for most persons; to be effective, it must be rigidly followed over a period of months or years. These characteristics obviously make it difficult of application in the home.

From the aspect of the personal-social adjustment of the child, one of the most important factors in treatment is the resolve on the part of his parents that he shall be both permitted and encouraged to lead as normal a life as possible. It must be remembered that all life entails risk. In regulating any child's activities, a common-sense balance must be maintained between the hazards of over- and underprotection. This is just as true for the epileptic as for the normal; after all, even the act of standing up entails *some* danger in the case of an unexpected seizure. The unavoidable restrictions laid upon the epileptic child are sufficiently hampering that the addition of unnecessary ones is almost certain to lead to psychic handicaps more undesirable in their effects and more difficult to remove than the physical ones due to the epilepsy.

EDUCATION

For the mentally normal epileptic child whose seizures are not frequent, attendance in the regular classes is desirable unless the attitude of the school authorities or of the teacher prevents it. The teacher should be informed of the child's condition, and, if possible, provision should be made for segregation of the child during any seizure that may occur. It has been demonstrated that even an occasional major seizure occurring in the classroom need not be unduly disturbing to the other children if the teacher handles the situation in a calm way.

Mentally retarded epileptics should be handled in accordance with their intellectual status. A child with marked behavior problems, emotional difficulties, or frequent seizures may have to be withdrawn from school or placed in a special class.[1] This, however, should be done on a temporary basis; as soon as his condition warrants, he should be returned. If only *petit-mal* seizures occur, regular school attendance should be a matter of course.

PROGNOSIS

As has been pointed out, in most cases to speak of a *cure* for epilepsy in the fundamental sense of the word is not justifiable. Individuals whose seizures occur on a basis of head injury, however, may show a spontaneous, complete recovery as the injury heals. Although a patient may have been able to discontinue all medication and has been symptom free for years, the brain lesion or its constitutional susceptibility to convulsive phenomena

[1] Some of the larger school systems maintain special classes or even special schools for epileptics who are not able to attend regular classes.

has, in all likelihood, remained unchanged. Nonetheless, such a patient is, in fact, substantially free of handicap, and, in this sense, he may be said to be cured. Indeed, for most purposes, he may be considered cured even if medication continues, providing that the amount needed is not so great as to produce hampering side effects, and if seizures, though still occurring, are not more frequent than once a year. On this basis, nearly half of all epileptic children in Bridge's group of almost 700 were rated as cured. The proportion so rated was not affected by the duration of the condition before treatment or by the presumed etiology, except in the case of brain injury, where the presence of signs of actual brain damage was associated with a markedly lower rate of cure. Children with akinetic attacks were more difficult to control and had a lower cure rate than children showing other types of seizure.

It is impossible to estimate the over-all effect of epilepsy on the life span. Where severe brain damage or progressive tumors are involved, the life of the afflicted individual is obviously likely to be shortened. On the other hand, mortality statistics published by New York state indicate that the incidence of deaths ascribed to epilepsy is only about one fifth as high as the estimated proportion of the population affected by the condition.

Marriage is not always contraindicated for the epileptic. In view of the multiplicity of the etiologic factors involved, the probability of occurrence of socioeconomic difficulties may often be a more important factor in deciding on the desirability of marriage than the risks of transmitting epilepsy or a predisposition for it to any children resulting.

BEHAVIOR DISORDERS AND ABNORMAL ELECTROENCEPHALOGRAMS

A number of investigators have reported a high incidence of abnormal electroencephalographic patterns among children who showed no signs of epilepsy but had marked behavior disorders. In some of these cases, treatment with anticonvulsant drugs reportedly improved the behavior. It is possible that such cases may represent a group holding the same relationship to epilepsy as the brain-injured group appears to hold to cerebral palsy. Further investigation of this question seems needed.

REFERENCES

ALPERS, Bernard J., "The Diagnosis and Treatment of Epilepsy," *Delaware State Medical Journal*, 22 (1950), 178-187.

ALSTROM, Carl Henry, "A Study of Epilepsy in Its Clinical, Social, and Genetic Aspects," *Acta Psychiatrica et Neurologica, Kjøbenhavn* (1953), Suppl. 63.

BAKER, Harry, FOWLER, W. L., ACKLAND, N. L., KENNARD, Margaret A., and RICHARDSON, N. L., "Symposium on Epilepsy," *Bulletin of the Vancouver Medical Association*, 28 (1952), 119-137.

BAKWIN, Ruth M., and BAKWIN, Harry, "Epilepsy," *Journal of Pediatrics*, 39 (1951), 776-784.

BRIDGE, E. M., *Epilepsy and Convulsive Disorders* (New York, McGraw-Hill Book Company, 1949).

COLLINS, A. Louise, "Epileptic Intelligence," *Journal of Consulting Psychology*, 15 (1951), 392-399.

DAVIES-EYSENCK, Margaret, "Cognitive Factors in Epilepsy," *Journal of Neurology, Neurosurgery, and Psychiatry*, 15 (1952), 39-46.

FORD, F. R., *Diseases of the Nervous System in Infancy, Childhood, and Adolescence*, 3d ed. (Springfield, Ill., Charles C Thomas, Publisher, 1952).

FORSSMAN, Hans, and FREY, Torsten, "Electroencephalograms of Boys with Behavior Disorders," *Acta Psychiatrica et Neurologica, Kjøbenhavn*, 28 (1953), 61-73.

HARRIMAN, P. L., "The Ethical Discrimination of the Epileptic," *Journal of Abnormal and Social Psychology*, 30 (1935), 411-418.

JONES, H. Gwynne, "Experimental Studies in the Psychology of Epilepsy," *Revue de psychologie appliquée*, 3 (1953), 209-227.

KAYE, Irving, "What Are the Evidences of Social and Psychological Maladjustment Revealed in a Study of Seventeen Children Who Have Idiopathic Petit Mal Epilepsy?" *Journal of Child Psychiatry*, 2 (1951), 115-160.

LENNOX, William G., "Saving Epileptic Children," *Child*, 14 (1950), 187-190.

———, "The Heredity of Epilepsy As Told by Relatives and Twins," *Journal of the American Medical Association*, 146 (1951), 529-536.

LEVY, Sol, "Supervision and Activity of Epileptics As Related to Their Behavior and Frequency of Convulsive Seizures," *American Journal of Mental Deficiency*, 55 (1951), 316-319.

LILIENFELD, A. M., and PASAMANICK, Benjamin, "Association of Maternal and Fetal Factors with the Development of Epilepsy," *Journal of the American Medical Association*, 155 (1954), 719-724.

McCOOL, Dick C., and ROARK, Marion E., "Cerebral Dysrhythmia Associated with Childhood Behavior—A Clinical Report," *Mississippi Doctor*, 29 (1951), 8-11.

NIELSEN, J. M., and COURVILLE, C. B., "Role of Birth Injury and Asphyxia in Idiopathic Epilepsy," *Neurology*, 1 (1951), 48-52.

PASAMANICK, Benjamin, "Anticonvulsant Drug Therapy of Behavior Problem Children with Abnormal Electroencephalograms," *American Medical Association Archives of Neurology and Psychiatry*, 65 (1951), 752-766.

REED, Homer R., "The Intelligence of Epileptics," *Journal of Genetic Psychology*, 78 (1951), 145-152.

SHANKS, Robert A., "Convulsions in Childhood and Their Relation to Epilepsy," *Glasgow Medical Journal*, 32 (1951), 257-267.

WINFIELD, Don L., "Intellectual Performance of Cryptogenic Epileptics, Symptomatic Epileptics, and Posttraumatic Encephalopaths," *Journal of Abnormal and Social Psychology*, 46 (1951), 336-343.

ZIMMERMAN, Frederick T., BURGEMEISTER, Bessie B., and PUTNAM, Tracy J., "Intellectual and Emotional Makeup of the Epileptic," *American Medical Association Archives of Neurology and Psychiatry*, 65 (1951), 545-556.

The Child with Other   29
Physical Handicaps

THE ORTHOPEDICALLY HANDICAPPED CHILD

THE TERM *orthopedic handicap* covers a wide range of conditions, from the child with widespread severe arthritis to the one who has lost a hand or foot in an automobile accident. For our purposes, it will be limited to the child who is mentally normal and whose defect does not involve abnormalities of perception or cerebral abnormalities of motor control.[1] There is a voluminous literature dealing with orthopedically handicapped groups of differing specific etiologies; at present, there appears to be no good evidence that the cause of the crippling is of any great significance in determining the effects on the crippled child. The major factors in this respect seem to be:

1. The degree to which the crippling, after maximal correction by medical, surgical, and prosthetic means, interferes with any particular pre-existing vocational aims.
2. The attitude to the crippling prevalent among the child's immediate family and close associates.
3. The attitude and overt reactions of the general public.
4. The age at crippling.
5. The personality of the crippled child.

The actual degree of crippling often seems less important than the other factors. Perhaps this is inherent; perhaps it is because the limitations imposed by a severe handicap are more obvious to

[1] The cerebral palsied child is a typical example of abnormal motor control on the basis of cerebral abnormality; the postpoliomyelitic one, of abnormal motor control on the basis of peripheral nerve damage.

others, so that the victim has no feeling that his failure to compete on equal terms with the normals may be ascribed by them to fear, laziness, or some other undesirable characteristic. Or it may be that the less definite boundaries of the limitations imposed by a mild handicap foster a constant effort to ignore them, with its results of repeated failures and, sometimes, a temporary or permanent increase in the degree of the handicap. The importance of parental and social attitude toward the handicapped child has been repeatedly discussed and is substantially the same, regardless of the cause or nature of the handicap. The young child, lacking extensive experience of normal life, is often less rebellious and unhappy over his limitations than the older child, who cannot evade a keener realization of his loss. A well-adjusted, emotionally stable personality, or one predisposed to be so, will obviously tend to react better to adverse conditions than a maladjusted, unstable one.

In common with other inferior deviates, these children are usually found to be somewhat less well adjusted and emotionally stable than the normal. The indications are that much of the observed difference is due to unfavorable environmental factors.

EDUCATION AND TRAINING OF THE
ORTHOPEDICALLY HANDICAPPED

Whenever the degree of crippling and the personal-social adjustment of the individual child do not preclude it, these children should receive their education in the regular classes. Placement in special classes or schools may, however, need to be made either on a temporary or on a permanent basis. The nature of the special techniques and equipment employed will vary in accordance with the nature and degree of the individual handicap, as will the nature of the vocational goals toward which the child may be encouraged to direct his aims. In general, he should be given every encouragement to share the work and play of normal children whenever it is not clearly impossible for him to do so.

THE CHILD WITH HANDICAP DUE TO
CARDIAC CONDITION OR CHRONIC DISEASE

These include the children with diabetes, tuberculosis, disorders of glandular function and growth when these do not involve abnormalities of mental development, severe allergies, and other similar conditions. Most of the statements made with respect to the orthopedically handicapped group are equally applicable to them, with the exception that special school placement should not ordinarily be necessary except as a result of maladjustment or in the case of cardiacs with extreme limitation of activity. Generally, if the physical condition makes attendance in the regular classes undesirable, it is likely to be such as to require that the child remain at home or even be hospitalized. In the schools, these children need to be carefully supervised to avoid undue fatigue or specifically undesirable activities—such as the consumption of large amounts of sweets by a diabetic child—and to make sure that any physiological danger signs that may appear are promptly reported to each child's parents or doctor. To a far greater degree than is the case with the orthopedically handicapped child, whose condition is likely to be relatively static and also not subject to changes of a nature threatening his health and even his life, the school authorities must be kept informed of each child's medical status, the nature and degree of limitations placed upon his activities.

REFERENCES

BARKER, Roger G., WRIGHT, Beatrice A., and GONICK, Mollie R., *Adjustment to Physical Handicap and Disease: A Survey of the Social Psychology of Physique and Disability* (New York, Social Sciences Research Council, 1946), Bulletin No. 55.

BAUER, Irving L., "Attitudes of Children with Rheumatic Fever," *Journal of Pediatrics*, 40 (1952), 796-798.

BILLIG, Albert L., "A Psychological Appraisal of Cleft Palate Patients," *Proceedings of the Pennsylvania Academy of Sciences*, 25 (1951), 29-32.

CALDWELL, Bettye McDonald, "Factors Influencing Reactions to Crippling Disorders," *Journal of the Missouri Medical Association*, 49 (1952), 219-222.

CARTER, Victor E., and CHESS, Stella, "Factors Influencing the Adaptations of Organically Handicapped Children," *American Journal of Orthopsychiatry,* 21 (1951), 827-837.

COBB, Katharine, "Special Disabilities," *Annual Reviews of Psychology,* 4 (1953), 361-386.

Committee for the Study of the Care and Education of Physically Handicapped Children in the Public Schools of the City of New York, *Physically Handicapped Children in New York City* (New York, Board of Education of the City of New York, 1941).

CRUICKSHANK, William M., "The Relation of Physical Disability to Fear and Guilt Feelings," *Child Development,* 22 (1951), 291-298.

DE RIDDER, Lawrence M., "Education for Teachers of Handicapped Children," *Elementary School Journal,* 50 (1950), 521-529.

FOURACRE, Maurice, "Educational Opportunities for the Handicapped Child," *Cerebral Palsy Review,* 14, No. 12 (1953), 7-10.

FREED, E. X., and CRUICKSHANK, William M., "Cardiac Children's Adjustment to Parents and Family," *Quarterly Journal of Child Behavior,* 4 (1952), 299-310.

GARRETT, James F., ed., *Psychological Aspects of Physical Disability* (Washington, D.C., U. S. Government Printing Office, 1952).

HARRIS, Dale B., "Behavior Ratings of Post-polio Cases," *Journal of Consulting Psychology,* 14 (1950), 381-385.

HOHMAN, Leslie B., "The Emotional Aspects of Crippling in Childhood," in *Alfred I. DuPont Institute of the Nemours Foundation: Tenth Anniversary Celebration* (Wilmington, Del., 1951), pp. 60-68.

LEVI, Joseph, and MICHELSON, Barbara, "Emotional Problems of Physically Handicapped Adolescents—A Study of Ten Adolescent Boys," *Exceptional Children,* 18 (1952), 200-206.

LOWMAN, Charles LeRoy, and SEIDENFELD, Morton, "A Preliminary Report of the Psychosocial Effects of Poliomyelitis," *Journal of Consulting Psychology,* 11 (1947), 30-37.

MENNINGER, William C., "Emotional Adjustments for the Handicapped," *Crippled Child,* 27, No. 4 (1949), 4-7.

PHILBROOK, Anna L., "Emotional Problems and the Crippled Child," *Child,* 18 (1953), 22-24.

SEIDENFELD, Morton A., "Psychological Sequelae of Poliomyelitis in Children," *The Nervous Child,* 7, No. 1 (January, 1948), 14-27.

STERN, Edith M., and CASTENDYCK, Elsa, *The Handicapped Child* (New York, A. A. Wyn, Inc., 1950).

ZINTZ, Miles V., "Academic Achievement and Social and Emotional Adjustment of Handicapped Children," *Elementary School Journal,* 51 (1951), 502-507.

Multiple Handicaps 30

CLASSIFICATION

EVEN MORE THAN do those with a single type of handicap, children who suffer from more than one form of physical or mental incapacity require thoroughgoing diagnosis and classification along all lines. Each of their handicaps should be carefully considered with reference to the four aspects of behavior described in Chapter 2. At first sight, the *kind* of handicaps involved may seem to be self-evident, but this is not always the case, especially when the child in question is the victim of more than one. Mental deficiency may conceal or be concealed by the presence of deafness; the mental level of the child with cerebral palsy is not easy to determine. Educational backwardness may be the result of mental backwardness, of poor vision or hearing, of emotional disturbance, or of all three, along with many other possible factors. Too often clinicians are satisfied when a single source of difficulty has been uncovered. "The fallacy of the single cause" is a popular phrase in clinical psychology, but all too often it is only a phrase. Diagnoses continue to be one-sided and incomplete; diagnosticians continue to be satisfied with finding the *kind* rather than the *kinds* of difficulty from which the child suffers.

Each of the ascertained types of handicap should be examined with much care. Its intensity should be classified with respect to both the standards for normal children and, as far as possible, the relative importance of the various handicaps in the life of the child. If adequate standards of variability are available, a quan-

titative statement of this comparison will be possible; one may
say that a child's hearing is at the 1 percentile level of acuity,
that is, that only 1 per cent of children of his age have suffered
hearing losses equally severe but that his mental level, though
retarded, is at the 10th percentile. Intellectually, then, he would
be classed with those who, with some difficulty, are able to get
along in the regular classes in school, and this fact has a highly
important bearing upon his subsequent treatment. As a rule, a
deaf child whose mental retardation is no greater than this will
be placed in a school or class for the deaf in the expectation that
he will be able to profit, at least to some extent, by the training he
will receive there. But a feeble-minded child learns little in a
school for the deaf and interferes with the progress of others. Such
a child is properly placed in a school for the feeble-minded.

Although, as has been mentioned in preceding chapters, the
extensity of a given defect may often be reduced by improvement
in the child's attitudes or by the kind of training that helps him
to compensate for his loss through more effective use of the abilities he possesses, nevertheless, there are inescapable bounds beyond which neither attitude nor training can be effective. The
clinician and the teacher should realize, first, that such bounds
exist, and, second, that they do not fall at the same level for all
children. The extraordinary intelligence of Helen Keller, together
with the careful training she received from Miss Sullivan and the
further advantages made possible by a home of moderate wealth,
have enabled her to reduce the extensity of her double deprivation to an almost unbelievable degree as far as her general personality and participation in the social life of the world at large
are concerned.

Finally, the *time factor*—the age at which each of the several
defects originated, the length of time they have persisted and are
likely to persist [1]—is of major importance. The blind-deaf child
in whom one or the other defect appeared at an appreciably
later age than the other is in a very different case from one in

[1] Assuming, of course, that every known method of improvement is
employed.

whom both date from birth or early infancy. If deafness did not begin until after speech had been well established, the problem of training the child is greatly simplified. If he has been sent to a school for the deaf, he should, if his intelligence is normal, have learned something of lip-reading and, perhaps, of the manual alphabet. Now both these abilities, so painfully acquired, must be translated into a new sensory area—that of touch. This is a confusing and often discouragingly difficult task for the child. Moreover, for the child who has once known the joys of vision, its loss may have a more disrupting effect upon the personality than is true for the one who has never experienced it. In spite of the advantage given by his previous experience of communication, the isolation caused by the loss of the chief means of distance perception is so serious a blow to the child's entire personality that great efforts are required to help him overcome it.

THE ABILITIES OF THE MULTIPLE HANDICAPPED

As the number and kind of defects increase, the importance of an intensive examination of those things which a child *can* do increases in geometric ratio; of paramount importance in these cases is the level and pattern of mental ability. It is not enough to determine the IQ. The normal child has many gifts, of which his intelligence is but one. The handicapped child, whose resources are few, cannot afford to ignore any, however small they may be. Although as both Goodenough and McNemar have pointed out, the particular pattern of success and failure on the Stanford Binet is not sufficiently reliable to justify the conclusions regarding special aptitudes that many unwise enthusiasts have drawn from it, nevertheless, this pattern may provide clues that suggest the directions that further examination can most profitably take.

The child's general health and physique are also of outstanding importance. Robust health is an asset for all; when multiple handicaps are present in other areas, the physical condition is of crucial significance. Helen Keller's remarkable accomplishments would have been difficult, perhaps impossible, had she not possessed the two great advantages: high intelligence and a strong healthy body. A searching physical examination should always be made in these cases, and all possible measures to improve the physical status should be employed.

Last but by no means least, the child's temperament must be considered. This includes his typical emotional response, his attitudes and urges, the uniformity of his behavior under similar external conditions. Unquestionably, many aspects of a child's temperament are subject to modification by training; undoubtedly, too, they have been affected by the child's state of health and by the many frustrations arising from his handicaps. Nevertheless, when all these factors are equalized, there appears to be a residuum that is either inborn or is the result of some factor or factors of which we have no knowledge. The child's temperament may be an asset or an additional handicap. Cheerfulness, an even disposition, an urge for independence and self-help, coupled with frank acceptance of the bounds necessarily set by infirmities,[2] count for much in life. As the number of defects increases, the number of abilities necessarily decreases. The correlation between abilities, so often demonstrated, implies a corresponding correlation between disabilities, and this, also, has been found to exist. The child having one outstanding defect is more likely to have others than is the child who has none. Multiple handicaps are by no means rare, and experience has shown that many such cases may be helped to become partially or wholly self-supporting, provided always that the intelligence is normal or nearly so. Even when complete self-support is out of the question, a program of training, in which the child's abilities rather than his disabilities are emphasized, can do much to increase his happiness and to enable him to care for himself to a much greater extent than would otherwise be possible.

---

[2] These bounds, however, are more flexible than either the handicapped child or those responsible for his care and training often realize. See, for example, a number of the case histories presented in previous chapters of this book, among which that of G. M. (p. 329) is a notable example. The will to achieve can accomplish more than most of us realize.

THE CARE AND TRAINING OF CHILDREN
WITH MULTIPLE HANDICAPS

Few homes have the financial resources needed to provide the doubly handicapped child with so well-trained and capable a teacher as Helen Keller had in Miss Sullivan, even if such teachers could readily be found. In most cases, it is impossible for the parents to give such teaching themselves. The special classes in the public schools are designed, as a rule, for children with a single major handicap. Their methods assume the existence of abilities that the child with multiple handicaps usually lacks. Institutional placement, at least for a time, seems to provide the best solution. The question then arises, what institution shall be chosen? The answer will depend chiefly upon three conditions: the kinds and relative intensity of the child's handicaps and the existing conditions in the various institutions or schools that may be available. The child of profoundly defective mentality, regardless of his other handicaps, is best placed in an institution for the feeble-minded at as early an age as the nature and gravity of his mental condition can be reliably established. His presence in a school for handicapped children of normal mind interferes with the progress of those who properly belong there, although he himself derives no benefit from it. Much care must be exercised, however, in determining the mental level of the child with two or more major physical defects, except in the case of vegetative idiots. A superficial appearance of mental backwardness is not uncommon in the doubly or triply handicapped, who lack both the means of acquainting themselves with the outside world that their better endowed mates possess and the means of expressing such information as they may have gained. Here the extent of the child's apparent interest in the world about him and his attempts to come into contact with it in such ways as are at his command are of paramount importance in indicating the degree of intelligence when the ordinary methods of testing are inappropriate.

If careful observation, together with the results of such tests as appear suitable, justifies the opinion that the child in question is mentally normal or approximately so, he should be given the advantage of expert training [3] at a relatively early age, if possible by the age of five years. In all questionable cases, the child should be given the benefit of the doubt. The selection of the proper school will depend upon the child's most apparent needs and upon local facilities. As was said earlier, the feeble-minded child, regardless of his other handicaps, should usually be placed in an institution for the mentally deficient. The deaf child of normal mentality, even though additionally handicapped, is ordinarily placed in a school for the deaf where training in communication can best be given. In like manner, blindness normally takes precedence over other physical handicaps—except deafness—in determining school placement. Institutionalization for such conditions as cerebral palsy or postpoliomyelitic paralysis is less uniformly desirable and usually of briefer duration. It depends largely on the possibility of amelioration of the child's condition. It should be unnecessary to say that no matter where a child is placed, he must be looked upon as an individual, not as an abstract condition. Treatment must take all his needs into consideration.

However, as was previously stated, local conditions may also affect the question of placement. Overcrowding in one institution may warrant the choice of a second, in which the child's other major defect will be given attention. This is particularly true when the blind-deaf child is to be considered. A few institutions take particular interest in training children with double sensory defects such as this. If such an institution is available, obviously it should be selected.

Even with the best of training, only a few of the children who suffer from more than one major defect can become capable of *complete* self-support in a world of normal people. But many can later be returned to their homes, where they will lead lives of moderate usefulness and quiet happiness. They will have acquired some means of communicating with others; they can care for most of their own personal needs and have acquired at least the rudi-

[3] There are a number of different sources from which victims of disability can obtain financial aid, if needed.

ments of formal school education. They will have learned to read either ordinary printed material or Braille, in the case of the blind. Usually they will have learned to perform knitting, sewing, or basket making, and they can assist in many household tasks.

In the absence of training, the child with more than one major defect is rarely either useful or happy. He is likely to require constant supervision lest he injure himself or destroy property. The happiness of more than one home has been sacrificed to a mistaken notion that to "send the poor helpless child away" is to fail in parental responsibility. The fallaciousness of such an idea can hardly be too strongly emphasized. Parents should be brought to see that their real responsibility lies in the opposite direction. The child whom neither they nor the public schools can train or educate must be placed in the hands of those who are equipped to do so. On this future happiness depends.

REFERENCES

CRUICKSHANK, William M., "The Multiply Handicapped Cerebral Palsied Child," *Journal of Exceptional Children,* 20 (1953), 16-22.

FOURACRE, Maurice H., and THIEL, Ellen A., "Education of Children with Mental Retardation Accompanying Cerebral Palsy," *American Journal of Mental Deficiency,* 57 (1953), 401-414.

GOODENOUGH, Florence L., *Mental Testing: Its History, Principles, and Applications* (New York, Rinehart and Company, Inc., 1949).

McNEMAR, Quinn, *The Revision of the Stanford Binet Scale* (Boston, Houghton-Mifflin Company, 1942).

MACPHERSON, J. R., "The Status of the Deaf and/or Hard of Hearing Mentally Deficient in the United States," *American Annals of the Deaf,* 97 (1952), 375-386.

MALZBERG, Benjamin, "Statistical Aspects of Mental Deficiency with Congenital Cerebral Spastic Infantile Paralyses," *American Journal of Mental Deficiency,* 55 (1950), 99-104.

SCHUNHOFF, Hugo F., and MACPHERSON, J. R., "What About the Deaf or Hard-of-hearing Mentally Deficient?" *Training School Bulletin,* 48 (1951), 71-75.

PART VI

The Deviate and
Social Progress

OBSERVATION OF PHENOMENA

THE EFFECT OF contrast upon perception is well known to everyone. A black figure against a dark gray background is easily overlooked, but it stands out clearly when placed upon a white ground. In a quiet room, the proverbial pindrop may be heard, but far louder sounds are needed to pass the threshold of perception in a noisy street. That small differences are harder to distinguish than large ones is a fact well known to laymen and psychologists alike.

Contrast is important in the observation of relationships as well as in that of stimuli. As Lewin has so ably pointed out, no matter how slight a difference may be, it will invariably appear if all disturbing conditions are removed. In many cases, however, such a situation can be obtained only in the laboratory. Truth is absolute without degrees or gradations; but the manifestations of a scientific truth as seen in an uncontrolled state of nature vary greatly in their universality and apparent degree, according to the number and intensity of the disturbing factors. The rather apocryphal story of Newton and the apple is a case in point. Gravitational forces were exerted in equal degree upon the apple that fell and upon those that remained on the tree. In the case of the latter, however, the opposing forces were so strong that for the time the gravitational pull had no visible effect. In the case of the falling apple, the deviate, the antigravitational forces had become weakened and the apple fell, not because of a stronger gravitational force than that exerted upon the other apples but because enough of the opposing forces had been removed to bring the true nature of the law of falling bodies into view, though not, of course, in full degree, since this can be observed only in a vacuum. It is because they owe their position to the partial or complete removal of some of the factors that obscure relationships actually existent that the deviates who stand at the extremes of a distribution provide such excellent material for scientific observation and study. Differences that are so slight as to be overlooked in the generality, or that may even appear to be completely reversed in the welter of confusing and often opposing factors, appear with all the advantages of contrast in such deviates.

THE FORMULATION OF HYPOTHESES

The observation of phenomena is ordinarily the first step in the establishment of a scientific principle or law. But it is only the first step, beyond which the vast majority of people never go. Millions of people before Newton must have witnessed the fall of apples and other unsupported objects toward the earth without giving the matter any special thought. Newton himself must have witnessed similar manifestations of gravitational force many thousands of times preceding the one which gave rise to his great discovery. But on this occasion, so runs the legend, he was lying idly under the tree, his thoughts free of conscious aim or direction. His attention was thus caught by a phenomenon that under other circumstances he would, in all probability, have ignored.

The contrast between the deviate and the generality of his age and sex arrests the attention and sharpens observation. Questions arise, to which tentative answers are given. The more precisely these hypotheses are phrased, the more readily can they be subjected to experimental or statistical testing; and the more clearly and universally a phenomenon is noted, the more readily, as a rule, can it be formulated in clear and objective terms. Compare the following examples:

1. Intelligence and personality tend to go together.
2. More than 75 per cent of children whose IQ's exceed 125

(Stanford Binet) are more dependable, more truthful, more attentive and interested in class, more popular with their classmates, and more often chosen as leaders than the average child of corresponding age and sex.

Statements of the first kind are likely to be made on the basis of observation of unclassified groups, where contrasts are not sufficiently marked to clarify what is seen. Those of the second type are more likely to emerge when those who deviate from the generality in a known direction and degree are compared with the generality. Preliminary observation will usually suggest fruitful areas of modes of behavior for more intensive study, on the basis of which more precise hypotheses, frequently involving some degree of quantitative statement, such as those in the example given, can be postulated.

TESTING A HYPOTHESIS

Unverified hypotheses are fruitful sources of error. Superstitions, unverified beliefs, and popular opinions, as well as scientific principles, originate in much the same way; that is, from the observation of phenomena and the formulation of hypotheses with respect to their etiology, their relationships with each other, and their prognostic significance. The difference between science and superstition lies just here: the former has been verified, at least within stated degrees of probability; the latter has not. We have seen how greatly the observation of phenomena and the formulation of hypotheses are facilitated by the study of deviate groups. But hypotheses are of little worth and may actually lead to much erroneous thinking unless they have been subjected to rigid examination and testing either by laboratory experiment or by statistical analysis.

Here, once more, the deviate comes into his own. There are few conditions in which a principle that is true for the generality will not appear more nearly universally as the extremes of a distribution are approached, for even in the laboratory, it is not easy to exclude all the extraneous conditions that affect the behavior of human beings. And there are many aspects of behavior that do not respond to laboratory conditions, but must be observed as they naturally occur. In such cases, only statistical tests of the hypotheses that may be formulated can be had. Such tests are usually easier to apply, and clear-cut results can be obtained from smaller samples, at the extremes.

Thus the use of extreme deviates for at least the preliminary formulation and testing of hypotheses is a time-saving device that merits more attention than it has often received. True, in the final analysis, a larger group of subjects so chosen as to constitute a representative sample of the population for whom the hypothesis in question is presumed to hold good is always desirable and frequently essential. If, however, the postulated rule or principle does not hold good at the extremes of the distribution, the likelihood that it will apply at other points is small. The use of deviate groups for the preliminary testing of postulated rules and principles thus constitutes an important screening device.[1]

OBSERVATION OF DEVELOPMENTAL PROCESSES

One of the most striking characteristics of the normal child is the rapidity of his growth and development; changes occur so frequently that observation is difficult. The retarded child develops more slowly. One can follow his progress in more detail and with greater exactness. The difference between the development of normal and that of the retarded child is largely, though not entirely, one of rate. One sees in the retardate something like a slow-motion picture of the normal child; one can study this picture in greater detail because it changes less rapidly. Thus from the subnormal, one gains a better understanding of the normal, of his phases of growth, and of the factors by which this growth is affected. The intelligence quotient of a retarded child is a more

---

[1] It must be remembered that deviates vary in mode as well as in degree or intensity. The deviation may be one of intelligence, of height, of popularity, of visual acuity, or any one of a host of others. Selection is obviously of paramount importance when deviates are to be used in the testing of postulates.

stable measure than is that of one of average of superior mentality,[2] and this enables one to select one's subjects for study with somewhat greater assurance than would otherwise be possible.

Both bright and dull must learn, and although the superficial characteristics of the process may differ somewhat for the two groups, its basic features are much the same for both. The learning of subnormal children is slow, in accordance with their slow rate of development. This renders it possible to observe the learning process, to see what difficulties beset the learner, and to experiment with different methods of teaching him. The slower acquisition of knowledge and skills by retarded children thus provides a valuable opportunity for educational experiments, the results of which are of value in teaching all children.

Science thus owes much to the study of those who differ in some way from what is usually seen. Because they are different they attract attention and pose questions. Attempts to answer these questions give rise to hypotheses, which, if found valid, are likely to have far wider applicability than merely among the deviate cases by which the principles were suggested. In the case of the retarded, for whom growth and learning are slow, but otherwise in many important respects comparable to those of the average child, this very slowness makes possible a more precise and detailed knowledge and understanding of the factors involved than could easily be had from other sources.

REFERENCES

GOODENOUGH, Florence L., *Mental Testing: Its History, Principles, and Applications* (New York, Rinehart and Company, Inc., 1949).

LEWIN, Kurt, *Principles of Topological Psychology* (New York, McGraw-Hill Book Company, 1936).

———, *A Dynamic Theory of Personality* (New York, McGraw-Hill Book Company, 1935).

TERMAN, Lewis M., and MERRILL, Maud, *Measuring Intelligence: A Guide to the Administration of the New Revised Stanford Binet Tests of Intelligence* (Boston, Houghton Mifflin Company, 1937).

[2] See the discussions of this point in Terman and Merrill, *Measuring Intelligence,* and Goodenough, *Mental Testing.*

The Deviate and
Social Welfare

32

SYMPATHY VS. SENTIMENTALITY

EVEN THOUGH they sometimes repel, inferior deviates such as those described in Parts II and V of this book are likely to arouse our pity. "How dreadful," we exclaim, on visiting an institution for one or another of the various classes of physically handicapped children. Although the first reaction of the novice when visiting the wards for idiots and low-grade imbeciles in any large institution for the feeble-minded may be mainly one of disgust, nevertheless, when viewed retrospectively, pity for these unfortunates will be found a major component in his emotional response, however overlaid with repulsion it may be.

This is as it should be. But pity is a cup filled to the brim which must be carried with a steady hand if it is not to overflow before reaching its destination. Words are dangerous; they are likely to fix the attention of the afflicted person upon his infirmities rather than upon outside matters. This, of course, need not be true, for words are weapons that may be used either to break down a defense or to maintain it. Every nurse has observed the differences in the emotional, and even in the physical, well-being of their patients that follow upon the visits of equally loving and well-meaning friends and relatives. "Oh you poor little fellow; I'm so sorry for you," exclaims sympathetic Aunt Martha, as she stares tearfully at the brace on Johnnie's leg. And Johnnie, who had not previously worried much about the matter, begins to feel very sorry for himself. He goes to his room and frets instead of

408

watching the baseball game on television as he had intended to do.

James, another polio victim is more fortunate. His cousin Walter calls up and the following conversation takes place.

"Say, Jim, you going to be home this afternoon? Well say, did you know the Giants are going to play off the last game of the world series? Can I come over and watch it on TV with you? Your set's better than ours. O.K., boy, I'll be there. Bye." And James, who, from the window seat, had been enviously watching the tough and tumble play of a group of boys in an adjoining vacant lot, turns from the telephone with a shining face to tell his mother of the expected visit. His self-esteem is heightened by two of the other boy's remarks. First, he has been asked whether he would be at home; the implication being that his movements are as free and unhampered as those of anyone else. Second there was the comment about the superiority of his TV set. He, therefore, cripple though he may be, has something to offer that the normal boy lacks. Of such small things is happiness made.

COMMUNITY RESPONSIBILITY FOR THE DEVIATE

The special needs of the deviate as regards physical care and education have been discussed in previous chapters. Every state makes some special provision for these needs, but in few, if any, are they adequate. Now, as in the past, the public needs to be awakened to the continuing need for more dollars, more workers, and more knowledge.

No matter whether he be bright or dull, crippled in body or deficient in sensory acuity, the child who is made aware that he differs from his mates has a double handicap to bear. Physical defects impose certain limitations upon activity, but these are less disturbing than the social isolation brought about by the careless remarks or thoughtless solicitude of adults which call attention to the handicap and increase a child's sense of being different. Children tend to imitate their elders in these matters; they sympathize verbally with the deviate but are too conscious of his defect to make him one of themselves. Or, if it chances that the deviation is in the direction of intellectual superiority, covert jealousy of parents is also likely to be sensed and shared by the children. The child of extraordinary gifts, who is already isolated to some extent by the wide variance in his interests and abilities from those of his mates, finds himself set still further apart by reason of being pointed out as a prodigy by thoughtless adults who fail to consider the effect of these comments upon other children who overhear them or upon the child himself.

Thus community education with respect to the needs of the extreme deviate is urgently needed. Of his differences he and those about him are, in all probability, too keenly aware; his similarities, however, though equally marked, are likely to be overlooked.

Every normal person who examines his own impulses becomes conscious of two competing urges. On the one hand, he desires to be and do as others of his group are doing; to dress according to the prevailing mode, to know the popular songs and games, the current books and plays. This urge for "belongingness" is one of the strongest of all human desires; it is no less strong in the deviate, who often finds it difficult of fulfillment, than it is in the rest of us. On the other hand, each of us, within limits, wishes to be considered an individual. The woman who would feel acutely embarrassed at finding herself in street clothes at a formal dinner party is equally annoyed when she discovers that the woman next to her is wearing a replica of her own dress. The balance between individuality and oddity is a delicate one that can easily be disturbed by such small happenings as a chance remark, an ill-timed laugh, or a meaningful glance.

The deviate child should be made to feel that his specialized difference does not set him apart from others of his age and sex but gives him his own particular place within the group. A crippled boy of my acquaintance acted as referee at all the baseball games of his set. His thorough knowledge of the rules and his impartial judgment made him a real participant in a game for which the brace on his leg would otherwise have unfitted him. It should be noted that his position was not specially created because of sympathy but was a standard and important feature of the game. The creation of a position not truly functional simply in order to permit the deviate's formal inclusion in the group does not fulfill his need; for an ordinarily bright child will usually see through the stratagem, and, in any case, the normals, naturally lacking respect for a useless participant, are apt to make the true position only too clear. Fortunately, there are few handicaps of such nature as both to permit their victim to live among normals and, at the same time, deny him all share in their activities.

THE DEVIATE'S CONTRIBUTION TO SOCIETY

The actual and potential value to society of the deviate whose mental or physical characteristics are above the average have been discussed in the sections dealing with such cases; in the preceding chapter, we have indicated some of the ways in which deviates as such contribute to scientific progress. The physically handicapped are often thought of as being, because of their handicap, necessarily a burden on the community to greater or less degree. However, in recent years, more and more handicapped individuals have proven that almost no condition need keep them from leading useful lives. Many industrial firms have found that if some thought is given to matching job requirements to the nature of the individual handicap, such workers can equal or surpass the normal in the rate of production. Accident rates are frequently lower than normal. In some types of work—for example, with deaf workers where the surroundings are noisy—the handicap is actually an advantage.

One aspect of the relationship between the physically or mentally handicapped individual and society is perhaps rarely considered but seems important. A consideration of the characteristics usually rated as desirable in a fully mature personality in our civilization reveals that the capacity to respect and make due allowance for the needs, desires, and feelings of others is essential. Such a capacity has, as a prerequisite, the awareness that people differ in these respects; and for a child, this awareness is more readily evoked by the visible differences between himself and a deviate than by the more intangible ones between himself and other normals. It is, then, in his dealings with the handicapped that the normal child may take his first steps toward maturity of interpersonal relationships. The adult, too, and his society reveal the level of their ethical values by their attitude and behavior toward the inferior deviate. To some extent, these values may even be formed and raised or lowered in accordance with the treatment of such individuals.

NAME INDEX

SUBJECT INDEX

THE CENTURY PSYCHOLOGY SERIES

Richard M. Elliott, *Editor*

Kenneth MacCorquodale, *Assistant Editor*

427

PRINCIPLES OF PSYCHOLOGY, by Fred S. Keller and William N. Schoenfeld

PSYCHOLOGICAL STUDIES OF HUMAN DEVELOPMENT, by Raymond G. Kuhlen and George G. Thompson

THE ACHIEVEMENT MOTIVE, by David C. McClelland, John W. Atkinson, Russell A. Clark, and Edgar L. Lowell

STUDIES IN MOTIVATION, edited by David C. McClelland

THE CULTURAL BACKGROUND OF PERSONALITY, by Ralph Linton

PRINCIPLES OF APPLIED PSYCHOLOGY, by A. T. Poffenberger

THE BEHAVIOR OF ORGANISMS: AN EXPERIMENTAL ANALYSIS, by B. F. Skinner

THE DYNAMICS OF HUMAN ADJUSTMENT, by Percival M. Symonds

DYNAMIC PSYCHOLOGY, by Percival M. Symonds

DIAGNOSING PERSONALITY AND CONDUCT, by Percival M. Symonds

THE EGO AND THE SELF, by Percival M. Symonds

THE PSYCHOLOGY OF PARENT-CHILD RELATIONSHIPS, by Percival M. Symonds

SELECTED WRITING FROM A CONNECTIONIST'S PSYCHOLOGY, by Edward L. Thorndike

INTRODUCTION TO METHODS IN EXPERIMENTAL PSYCHOLOGY, 2d ed., by Miles A. Tinker

THE PSYCHOLOGY OF HUMAN DIFFERENCES, 2d ed., by Leona E. Tyler

THE WORK OF THE COUNSELOR, by Leona E. Tyler

EXPERIMENTAL PSYCHOLOGY: AN INTRODUCTION, by Benton J. Underwood

ELEMENTARY STATISTICS, by Benton J. Underwood, Carl P. Duncan, Janet A. Taylor, and John W. Cotton. Also accompanying WORKBOOK by the same authors.

PERSONS AND PERSONALITY, by Sister Annette Walters and Sister Kevin O'Hara